Disability Hate Speech

This book, the first to specifically focus on disability hate speech, explains what disability hate speech is, why it is important, what laws regulate it (both online and in person) and how it is different from other forms of hate. Unfortunately, disability is often ignored or overlooked in academic, legal, political, and cultural analyses of the broader problem of hate speech. Its unique personal, ideological, economic, political and legal dimensions have not been recognized – until now.

Disability hate speech is an everyday experience for many people, leaving terrible psycho-emotional scars. This book includes personal testimonies from victims discussing the personal impact of disability hate speech, explaining in detail how such hatred affects them. It also presents legal, historical, psychological, and cultural analyses, including the results of the first surveys and in-depth interviews ever conducted on this topic in some countries.

This book makes a vital contribution to understanding disability hatred and prejudice and will be of particular interest to those studying issues associated with hate speech, disability, psychology, law, and prejudice.

Mark Sherry is Professor of Sociology at The University of Toledo in Ohio, USA. He is Editor of the Routledge Interdisciplinary Disability Studies Series. His books include *If I Only Had a Brain: Deconstructing Brain Injury* (Routledge, 2006) and *Disability Hate Crime: Does Anyone* Really *Hate Disabled People?* (Routledge, 2010).

Terje Olsen, PhD in Sociology, is Research Director at Fafo Institute for Labour and Social Research in Oslo, Norway. His research interests include welfare state issues, disability studies, youth research, marginalization, labour market participation, legal rights and access to justice for persons with disabilities. He is Editor-in-chief of the journal *Nordic Welfare Research.*

Janikke Solstad Vedeler, PhD in Sociology, is a Senior Researcher at Norwegian Social Research at OsloMet – Oslo Metropolitan University and at the Nordland Research Institute. Her research interest includes disability and topics like hate speech and inclusive working life practices.

John Eriksen holds a BA in Economics and Business Administration and a Master's degree in Sociology. He is an Emeritus Researcher and formerly a Research Director at NOVA – Norwegian Social Research Institute, Oslo, Norway, and Editor-in-chief of the *Scandinavian Journal of Disability Research.* His former research interests include welfare policies, quality of life, disability studies, and family organization.

Interdisciplinary Disability Studies

Series editor: Mark Sherry, The University of Toledo, USA

Disability Studies has made great strides in exploring power and the body. This series extends the interdisciplinary dialogue between disability studies and other fields by asking how disability studies can influence a particular field. It will show how a deep engagement with disability studies changes our understanding of the following fields: sociology, literary studies, gender studies, bioethics, social work, law, education, or history. This ground-breaking series identifies both the practical and theoretical implications of such an interdisciplinary dialogue and challenges people in disability studies as well as other disciplinary fields to critically reflect on their professional praxis in terms of theory, practice, and methods.

Manifestos for the Future of Critical Disability Studies
Volume 1
Edited by Katie Ellis, Rosemarie Garland-Thomson, Mike Kent and Rachel Robertson

Interdisciplinary Approaches to Disability
Volume 2
Edited by Katie Ellis, Rosemarie Garland-Thomson, Mike Kent and Rachel Robertson

Disability and Social Representations Theory
The Case of Hearing Loss
Vinaya Manchaiah, Berth Danermark, Per Germundsson and Pierre Ratiaud

Identity (Re)constructions After Brain Injury
Personal and Family Identity
Chalotte Glintborg

Global Perspectives on Disability Activism and Advocacy
Our Way
Edited by Karen Soldatic and Kelley Johnson

Disability Hate Speech
Social, Cultural and Political Contexts
Edited by Mark Sherry, Terje Olsen, Janikke Solstad Vedeler and John Eriksen

For a full list of titles in this series, please visit www.routledge.com/series/ASHSER1401

Disability Hate Speech

Social, Cultural and Political Contexts

Edited by Mark Sherry, Terje Olsen, Janikke Solstad Vedeler, and John Eriksen

Routledge
Taylor & Francis Group
LONDON AND NEW YORK

First published 2020
by Routledge
2 Park Square, Milton Park, Abingdon, Oxon OX14 4RN

and by Routledge
52 Vanderbilt Avenue, New York, NY 10017

Routledge is an imprint of the Taylor & Francis Group, an informa business

First issued in paperback 2021

British Library Cataloguing-in-Publication Data
A catalogue record for this book is available from the British Library

Library of Congress Cataloging-in-Publication Data
A catalog record has been requested for this book

ISBN: 978-0-367-19342-3 (hbk)
ISBN: 978-1-03-208605-7 (pbk)
ISBN: 978-0-429-20181-3 (ebk)

Typeset in Times New Roman
by Deanta Global Publishing Services, Chennai, India

Contents

Contributors

Solomon Amoatey is a graduate student at The University of Toledo in the USA. His research explores the experiences of people with disabilities in the Global South and he has conducted fieldwork in his homeland of Ghana. Solomon is deeply committed to improving the rights, freedoms and opportunities experienced by people with disabilities and by people in the Global South more broadly.

Beata Borowska-Beszta, Habilitation degree in Social Sciences, PhD in Education, specialty: Special education, is Head of Chair of Disability Studies at Nicolaus Copernicus University in Torun, Poland. Her research focus is on disability studies, including intercultural aspects, culture and disability research, transmission of cultural knowledge about disability, empowerment, re-education, and qualitative methodology.

Leah Burch is a PhD student at the University of Leeds, UK. Her PhD project is researching disabled people's experiences and understandings of "everyday hate" and disablist hate crime. Her research interests include disablist hate crime, intersectionality, the welfare system and austerity measures, and the use of arts-based methods within disability research.

Lisa Davies is a UK-based PhD student in the School of Social Work, Care and Community at the University of Central Lancashire, UK. Her PhD is entitled Writing the Disabled Self. She identifies as disabled and her research utilises her personal experience. Her current research interests include the impact of austerity on disabled people, psycho-emotional disablism, and aut-ethnography.

John Eriksen holds a BA in Economics and Business Administration and a Master's degree in Sociology. He is an Emeritus researcher and formerly a research director at NOVA – Norwegian Social Research Institute, Oslo, Norway, and Editor-in-chief of the *Scandinavian Journal of Disability Research*. His research interests include welfare policies, quality of life, disability studies, and family organization.

Hege Gjertsen, PhD in Sociology, is Associate Professor at Department of Social Education at UiT, the Arctic University of Norway. Her research interests are disability studies, work inclusion, and welfare state issues.

Damian Milton, PhD, is a Lecturer in Intellectual and Developmental Disabilities at the Tizard Centre, University of Kent, UK. He also works as a consultant for a number of autism-related organisations. His primary research interests are in regard to the meaningful participation of autistic people in research processes from design to interpretation.

Line Melbøe, PhD in Health Science, is Associate Professor at the Institute for Social Education at UiT, the Arctic University of Norway. Her research interests are disability studies, citizenship, participation in school and in democratic processes, and the situation of indigenous people with disabilities.

Mark P. Mostert, PhD, is Professor of Special Education and Director of the Doctoral Cognate in Special Education at Regent University in Virginia Beach, Virginia, USA, where he is also the Director of the Institute for the Study of Disability and Bioethics. His research interests include bioethical aspects of disability, issues related to Africans with disabilities, and empirical interventions for students with disabilities.

Terje Olsen, PhD in Sociology, is Research Director at Fafo Institute for Labour and Social Research in Oslo, Norway. His research interests include welfare state issues, disability studies, youth research, marginalization, labour market participation, legal rights, and access to justice for persons with disabilities. He is Editor-in-chief of the journal *Nordic Welfare Research.*

Erin Pritchard, PhD in Human Geography, is a lecturer in disability studies at Liverpool Hope University in the UK. She is a core member of the Centre for Cultural Disability Studies. Her research interests include cultural representations of disability, geographies of disability, and geographies of body size, with a particular focus on dwarfism.

Stephen A. Rosenbaum, MPP, JD, is Visiting Researcher Scholar at Haas Institute for a Fair and Inclusive Society (Disability Studies Cluster) at the University of California, Berkeley, USA, and Frank C. Newman Lecturer at Berkeley's School of Law. He is a former Senior Litigation Attorney with Disability Rights Education & Defense Fund and Associate Managing Attorney with Disability Rights California. His research and advocacy interests include disability discrimination, dignity and self-determination, 'special' education, mental health treatment, and international human rights.

Mark Sherry is Professor of Sociology at The University of Toledo in Ohio, USA. He is Editor of the Routledge Interdisciplinary Disability Studies Series. His books include *If I only had a brain: Deconstructing brain injury* (Routledge, 2006) and *Disability hate crime: Does anyone really hate disabled people?* (Routledge, 2010).

Armineh Soorenian PhD in Disability Studies is an independent researcher. Her research interests include inclusive education, disability arts and representations, disability and gender, and disability hate crime. Soorenian has published articles in international journals such as *Scandinavian Journal of Disability Research* and *Mediterranean Review of Educational Research.* She has contributed to several collected edition books as well as various UN initiatives. In May 2018, Soorenian was recruited by the Alliance for Inclusive Education (ALLFIE) to lead a project on the effectiveness of schools' Accessibility Plans funded by the Disability Research on Independent Living and Learning (DRILL) grants programme.

Janikke Solstad Vedeler, PhD in Sociology, is a researcher at Norwegian Social Research at OsloMet – Oslo Metropolitan University and at the Nordland Research Institute. Her research interest includes disability and topics like hate speech and inclusive working life practices.

Louise Walker is an independent researcher from Melbourne, Australia. She has worked in Australian Universities for over 20 years and has also been deeply involved in community organizing. Her broad interests include labour history, social justice, and social inequality.

Claire Wells-Jensen is an artist, musician and actor, currently working toward her undergraduate degree at Bowling Green State University, Ohio, USA.

Sheri Wells-Jensen is an Associate Professor specializing in linguistics, disability studies, and astrobiology at Bowling Green State University, Ohio, USA.

Introduction

Mark Sherry, Terje Olsen, Janikke Solstad Vedeler, and John Eriksen

Disability Studies has been engaged with the topic of disability hate crime for some time, and it is clear that disabled people are more likely than their nondisabled peers to be the victims of hate crimes (Macdonald, Donovan, & Clayton, 2017; McCarthy, Hunt, & Milne-Skillman, 2017; Roulstone & Mason-Bish, 2013; Shah & Giannasi, 2015; Sherry, 2010; Pam Thomas, 2011). However, disability hate speech (which is often a precursor to more serious attacks on disabled people) is an area that is still largely neglected, even though low-level hate speech is far more common than the often-violent hate crimes which have captured the imagination of the public. Until now, however, there has never been a book dedicated specifically to exploring the problem of disability hate speech. This book highlights the multitude of forms and expressions of disability hate speech and the ways they are embedded in social, cultural, political, and economic settings, as well as identifying some ways of countering it. It will help inform the debates within Disability Studies on the nature of disability oppression and the multiple forms of harm and victimization which disabled people experience. And by directly engaging with disabled people in the community, both as targets of hate speech and as people who challenge it, the book highlights both the harms caused by such speech acts and also disabled people's resistance to them.

Disability is missing in the general literature on hate speech. This literature has addressed the consequences of hate speech for ethnic minorities (Baez, 2013; Lasson, 1985; Shiffrin, 1994; Turner, 2007) religious groups (Delgato, 1993; Lidsky, 2008; Modood, Hansen, Bleich, O'Leary, & Carens, 2006), sexual minorities (Davies & McInnes, 2012; Goodall, 2009; Reddy, 2002) and others, but has largely ignored disabled people. Thus, this book is a groundbreaking foray into this important and previously under-researched topic. It highlights the ways that disability hate speech can be understood both within the context of previous studies of "words that wound" (Delgato, 1993), but also the unique dynamics of disability hate speech which have previously been unrecognized. These dynamics will become evident throughout this book.

The Equality and Anti-Discrimination Ombud of Norway (2015) defines hate speech as "degrading, threatening, harassing, or stigmatising speech which affects an individual's or a group's dignity, reputation, and status in society by means of linguistic and visual effects that promote negative feelings, attitudes, and perceptions based on characteristics such as ethnicity, religion, gender, disability, sexual orientation, gender expression, gender identity, and age." This broad definition of hate speech is useful because it includes both lawful and unlawful speech and focuses on the harms that particularly result from degrading, harassing, or stigmatizing speech. It is also associated with wider government policies on nondiscrimination, equality, and community safety.

Laws around disability hate speech (and even definitions of hate speech) seem to be constantly in flux because of the changing nature of online harassment, the transnational nature of the internet, and the links between actual violence and hate speech. The rise of live-streamed hate, for instance, is a relatively new issue which has captured public attention (particularly after the Islamophobic hate-inspired massacre in New Zealand in 2019), so governments and internet providers are currently grappling with the issues of how to prevent and punish such online activity. But pressure to address online hate against disabled people has been growing for many years. For instance, after disabled victims and their family members spoke publicly about the abuse they had received online, over 220,000 people signed a petition to the UK Government and Parliament in 2017 to make online abuse a specific criminal offence and create a register of offenders (UK Parliament, 2017).

Hate speech may or may not be a criminal act, depending on the laws governing a country. In the United States, all forms of hate speech (including disablist hate speech) are lawful and unregulated; the expansive free speech protections offered by the First Amendment protect the right to commit hate speech. In some other countries, only the most severe forms of hate speech may be forbidden by law and recognized as crimes. There are two apparently conflicting values at stake when we address hate speech: freedom of expression and freedom from discrimination, both closely linked to central values in liberal, democratic societies in the Global North. Some regard restricting free speech as a threat to an open exchange of opinions and views in democracies. Less attention is given to the fact that hate speech makes many disabled people withdraw from public debate and thus deprive disabled people of *their* democratic rights.

Brown (2015) has identified ten main aims of hate speech laws:

1. Proscribe group defamation.
2. Prevent negative stereotyping or stigmatization.
3. Disallow the public expression of hatred.
4. Ban speech which will stir up, incite, or promote hatred.
5. Prohibit threats to public order.
6. Prevent people from denying, justifying, or glorifying acts of mass cruelty, violence, or genocide.
7. Preventing speech which itself would be a dignitary crime or tort.
8. Prevent harm to the civil or human rights of others.
9. Prevent expression-oriented hate crime.
10. Providing indirect restraints on speech acts.

One issue that arises when discussing the nature of hate speech is the intention of the person who made the hateful utterance. The chapters in this book suggest that hate speech is socially constructed and culturally specific – in some countries, for instance, the term "hate" is almost never used, but the same dynamics are framed in terms of disability and bullying. Studies of abuse, bullying, and disability can therefore help us understand the motivations of those who engage in such acts. These are complex, multi-dimensional and heterogeneous phenomena, but previous studies have identified both personal characteristics of bullies/abusers and contextual factors (such as a social climate that devalues certain groups) as being key issues (Boffey, 2011; Calderbank, 2000; Conway, 1994; Curry, Hassouneh-Phillips, & Johnston-Silverberg, 2001; Hassouneh-Phillips, 2005; Kamavarapu, Ferriter, Morton, & Völlm, 2017; Macdonald et al., 2017; Øksendal, Brandlistuen, Holte, & Wang, 2019; Pinquart, 2016; Sherry, 2010; Zeedyk, Rodriguez, Tipton, Baker, & Blacher, 2014).

Individual factors that may lead some people to engage in abuse include lack of empathy, callousness, failure to appropriately regulate emotions, a need for control, problems with impulse control, jealousy, resentment, and/or anti-social, psychopathic, narcissistic, or sociopathic traits. Social issues that are associated with the abuse/bullying of disabled people include: wider patterns of devaluation, marginalization and Othering of disabled people; social and economic rewards for conformity and 'normality' and prejudices against difference and disability; the social isolation, segregation, and lack of supports and safeguards experienced by many disabled people; social practices that reward bullying; institutional cultures that cover-up abuse; and gendered inequalities which place disabled women and girls at higher risk of certain types of abuse. There are also impairment-related issues which also leave certain groups of disabled people at higher risk (Øksendal et al., 2019; Pinquart, 2016; Zeedyk et al., 2014).

The concept of Othering is useful for understanding prejudice and hatred. The affective dimensions of Othering often involve contempt, disgust, and loathing. Othering invokes a sense of superiority/inferiority, insiderness/outsiderness, respect/contempt, inclusion/exclusion, domination/subordination, and acceptance/rejection. Fear is also an important element of Othering (and hate more broadly) – fear of an imagined outsider who threatens the health, wealth, or security of the imagined insider community. The differences between insiders and outsiders are exaggerated; insiders are framed as homogenous (and safe) whereas outsiders are considered different, incompatible, and threatening. In hate speech, the Other is always the enemy. Prejudice is naturalized and discrimination is normalized, rationalized, and defended in hate speech.

Harmer and Lumsden (2019, p. 2) suggest that the concept of "online Othering" is a useful framework for:

> Making sense of the myriad behaviours, conversations and discourses which seek to (re)draw boundaries in, around, and between virtual spaces, and which shape the rules and norms concerning which individuals and groups are endowed with status and legitimated to participate in these spaces, and those who are not.

New technologies have not simply allowed online prejudice to move into new arenas – the very nature and content of such prejudices have changed. New discourses of hatred and new forms of harassment emerge online (such as cyberbullying, online harassment, doxxing, swatting, cyberstalking, and trolling).

The literature on rhetoric and speech acts can also shed some light on the issue of hate speech. In particular, Austin's (1975) concept of "perlocutionary acts" (where the speaker achieves something simply through an utterance) can be applied to situations involving disablist hate speech. Simply by uttering certain words (such as the statement "you are retarded," "you are bipolar" or "you are crazy"), the speaker assumes both a position of superiority and labels, demeans and devalues the target. In the case of disablist hate speech, either the broad term "disability" or any specific diagnosis can be used to create a devalued subjectivity. The fact that a diagnosis itself may be sufficient to be weaponized in hate speech draws attention to the broader relationship between disability and medical power. There is a connection – albeit indirect – between diagnostic utterances and disablist hate speech; the terms used in medical encounters are often circulated more broadly to convey messages of devaluation. It is incredibly easy to find someone being insulted through the broad use of a diagnostic term such as "schizophrenic," "intellectually disabled," "brain damaged," "bipolar," and so on.

Such hate speech frames the subject as less than, different, and deserving maltreatment. It draws on a long cultural repertoire of disability devaluation associated with eugenics that included the murder, violent castration, sterilization, institutionalization and segregation of thousands of disabled people across the globe (Mitchell & Snyder, 2003; Mostert, 2002). Contemporary disability hate speech often recirculates the messages of eugenics, such as the idea that disabled people are useless, a burden on society, and that their lives are not worth living. These are some of the components of disablism more broadly, but authors in this volume suggest that they have a specific hateful intent in many contexts. For them, the matter is not simply prejudiced, ill-informed, or antiquated opinions, but the active circulation of ideas that devalue the lives of disabled people, individually and *en masse*.

Eugenic policies and attitudes were accompanied by rhetorics of disgust (Schweik, 2009) – a discourse which still affects perceptions of disability today (Soldatic & Meekosha, 2012; Soldatic & Pini, 2009). Such dehumanizing discourses of disability continue to exert a profound material and cultural influence today in multiple practices that exclude, Other, and disqualify disabled people (Bérubé, 2018; Capozza, Di Bernardo, Falvo, Vianello, & Calò, 2016; Mik-Meyer, 2016). For instance, eugenic themes and rhetorics of disgust were evident in the letter by the perpetrator of the mass killings of disabled people in Sagamihara, Japan, in 2016. That murderer killed 10 women and 9 men and injured 26 more. In a letter to the Lower House Speaker, he stated:

> Thinking about the tired faces of guardians, the dull eyes of caregivers working at the facility, I am not able to contain myself, and so I decided to take action today for the sake of Japan and the world…I envision a world where a

> person with multiple disabilities can be euthanized, with an agreement from the guardians, when it is difficult for the person to carry out household and social activities. I believe there is still no answer about the way of life for individuals with multiple disabilities. The disabled can only create misery.
>
> (Peckitt, 2016)

As this case demonstrates, hate speech and hate crime are interconnected. Exposure to hate speech creates desensitization towards extremism, may encourage radicalization, harms and demoralizes its victims, and the targets of hate speech online are also commonly victims of physical attacks offline (Boeckmann & Liew, 2002; Hawdon, Oksanen, & Räsänen, 2014; Müller & Schwarz, 2018; Oksanen, Hawdon, Holkeri, Näsi, & Räsänen, 2014; Soral, Bilewicz, & Winiewski, 2018). The 2019 Christchurch terrorist attacks demonstrated the link between online hate and offline hatred, violence, and even terrorism; people on the website often frequented by the gunman cheered as he live-streamed his murderous rampage (Quek, 2019). In the words of Cohen-Almagor (2018, p. 38), "speech can and does inspire crime."

Previous studies of other forms of hate confirm the link between online and offline actions. Müller and Schwarz (2018) found that the spread of anti-refugee hatred on the internet in Germany could be used to predict local outbreaks of violence against the targeted groups. Similarly, the Kenyan Human Rights Commission (2008) reported strong links between the incitement to hatred by politicians and violent attacks on target groups in the post-2007 election. Such rhetoric led to very large numbers of crimes including murders, rape and other forms of sexual violence, arson, forced displacement, robbery, and theft. However, the Kenyan case is also illustrative of the effectiveness of countering hate speech. Hate speech laws were introduced in the wake of this violence, to prevent its recurrence. Also, a large-scale campaign was mounted by television stations, newspapers, churches, nonprofits, and others to maintain peace and unity. The result was that even though the results of the 2013 election were contested, there was no outbreak of mass violence (Benesch, 2014).

We must be aware that many acts of hostile and dangerous speech may not be included in the category of "hate speech" per se because of the ways that laws around such utterances are framed in specific national and local jurisdictions. By analyzing disability hate speech in many different countries, the book highlights political and regional variations in the right to express hate speech and the punishment for such speech acts. The book does not suggest that hate speech laws are the complete answer to hate speech. It suggests that seeking recourse through the courts is not always a solution, not only when courts prioritize the right to free speech over the effects of hate on victims, but also when the courts themselves are implicated in hate speech via prejudicial attitudes towards disabled people. As Brown (1995, 2006) argued, a legalistic approach tends to assume the neutrality of the state, thereby depoliticizing the uneven nature of access to (and responses from) state power.

To reduce hate speech to its legal dimensions also fails to fully capture the role of the state in enacting, reproducing, signifying and validating some forms of prejudice and hate speech but not others. Furthermore, positioning the state as an even-handed protector of the rights of all is itself a form of neoliberal governmentality which depoliticizes the uneven nature of power relations in contemporary society (Gedalof, 2018). Another reason to be critical of assumptions that the state is a neutral agent in terms of disability is because the rights and freedoms (and even the lives) of disabled people have been threatened in the past by many state actions. Eugenic policies, mentioned earlier, were enacted through the state; they would have been impossible without it (Kerr & Shakespeare, 2002).

Using evidence from many countries and different contexts, this book demonstrates that disability hate speech is a political, discursive, cultural, and sociolinguistic practice, as much as a legal one. Such speech draws on the unique cultural repertoire and history of particular national contexts. Additionally, criminalizing all utterances that are reasonably termed hate speech is no simple solution. As with many other kinds of harassment or unwanted behaviour, only severe violations of societal norms are subject to legal judgement. Disablist hate speech is an everyday experience, but the likelihood of criminal prosecution largely depends on whether the speech acts are considered threatening and when they are accompanied by other crimes such as property crimes or crimes against the person. When hate speech occurs in the commission of a hate crime, the speech is evidence of hate as a motivation and may be used during prosecution.

Disability hate speech occurs along a continuum of disablist practices, from the micro to the macro level – and for many disabled people, micro level hate speech is so common that it is often not even recognized as hate speech. For instance, Hall (2019) suggests that low-level harassment and disablist hate speech is far more common than the violent disablist hate crimes which get far more attention. And yet such speech acts are an important element of "psychoemotional disablism" (Reeve, 2002; C. Thomas, 1999) which affects the self-image and sense of security of disabled people. Many authors in this volume find the concept of psychoemotional disablism to be particularly helpful in theorizing disablist hate, because disablism creates psychological scars on disabled people individually and collectively, and it also helps to sustain broader cultural patterns of intolerance. Disability hate speech communicates important messages about superiority and inferiority, normality and abnormality, acceptance and exclusion, and lives that do (or do not) deserve respect.

Disability hate speech is also enacted through microaggressions (Keller & Galgay, 2010). While some disablist microaggressions may not escalate beyond the level of unpleasant or unwanted interactions, others may indeed be best understood as hate speech. Certain environments may be conducive to more disability hate speech and microaggressions than others – and these hate speech acts may overlap with other forms of bullying, prejudice, discrimination, and marginalization, as Dávila (2015) has demonstrated in a study of disabled Latino students in special education. A multidisciplinary and multifaceted approach to understanding these phenomena is therefore needed.

Given the role of the state in recognizing, legitimating, and funding welfare services, it has a particularly powerful economic, cultural, and political relationship with disabled people (Stone, 1984). The state may itself be responsible for the production and circulation of various forms of hate speech. For instance, UK policies of austerity have been framed around the notion of disabled people as "scroungers" unworthy of state support – basically treating them as "folk devils" (Briant, Watson, & Philo, 2013). Discursive and sociolinguistic approaches to hate speech are particularly useful in highlighting the connections between the cultural scapegoating of disabled people by the state and wider levels of prejudice, hostility, hate speech, and hate crimes towards disabled people (Ralph, Capewell, & Bonnett, 2016). Such hostility has also been reproduced in the media in 'reality' television shows that demean impoverished disabled people receiving welfare benefits – shows that have been labelled "DisPovertyPorn" (Runswick-Cole & Goodley, 2015).

Existing literature strongly suggests that bias-motivated actions leave much more profound emotional damage on their victims than other types of crimes. One oft-cited study compared bias and non-bias victims of assault and found that those who were the victims of bias crimes "experience more severe psychological sequelae, for a longer period of time… the level of intrusive thoughts, feelings of safety, nervousness, and depression were significantly higher for bias crime victims" (McDevitt, Balboni, Garcia, & Gu, 2001, p. 697). Similarly, Fetzer and Pezzella (2016) measured victim harm through a multi-dimensional analysis, finding more severe violence and greater psychological trauma for bias crime victims. The contributors to this book likewise identify the psychoemotional elements of disablism as a profound effect of disability hate speech.

Gelber and McNamara's (2016) study of Aboriginal and ethnic minority people in Australia demonstrated multiple forms of harm that result from hate speech. Most obviously, hate speech directly harmed the physical and mental health of its intended victims, as well as silencing them in certain situations. Equally importantly, it had snowball effects on the treatment of the target group more generally – hate speech focused and legitimated hostility directed at such groups. Hate speech stigmatizes these groups by attributing negative characteristics to them. It adds to the prejudice that marginalized groups already experience. This book draws similar conclusions regarding disability hate speech.

The book is divided into three parts. Part One explores the nature of disability hate speech, Part Two focuses on its personal impact, and Part Three assesses the dynamics of disablist hate speech within specific economic, geopolitical and cultural contexts.

Part I: The nature of disability hate speech

The authors in this book demonstrate that one definition of disability hate speech may not always be feasible, since hate speech is culturally constructed, politically defined, contextual, and contested. Some adopt a more expansive approach to hate speech than others. These differences are also important in terms of the recommended remedies, responses, and punishments for disability hate speech. It is therefore vital to explore the motivations, effects, governmental responses, community resistance, and power dynamics associated with disability hate speech in multiple regional contexts. As Bleich (2014) has commented in the context of discussing differences between US and European responses to racist hate speech, analyses must recognize cultural variables, reliance on different legal texts, and differences in jurisprudence.

In Chapter 1, "Disablist hate speech laws," Mark Sherry and Louise Walker demonstrate that there is no universally accepted definition of disability hate speech, either in international law or academic literature. They explore the different ways disability hate speech is – or isn't – prohibited in many different countries. Indeed, they stress that disability is excluded from hate speech laws in many countries. Sherry and Walker's argument is that there is a hierarchy of hate, with disability relegated to the bottom, often unacknowledged and ignored within laws and policies designed to combat hate. They also demonstrate the ways in which hate speech is also commonly framed as a conflict between the right to free speech and values such as respect, equality, human dignity, community cohesion, and freedom from harassment and intimidation

Mark Sherry discusses "Disablist hate speech online" in Chapter 2, highlighting its unique content as well as the responses of governments and social media companies to it. There are, he argues, unique features of online disability hatred which are not present for any other group. For instance, websites run by epilepsy organizations have been targeted for hacking by people who insert flashing animations in order to trigger seizures among people with photosensitive seizure disorders. These acts demonstrate that the online word targets disabled people in unique ways, that such acts are often planned and deliberate, and that there are very real links between online hate and offline harm. Sherry's chapter also demonstrates that online hate speech can agitate and motivate those who commit offline hate-inspired criminal acts. For instance, the emotional payoff of online hate has resulted in the live-streaming of both acts of hate speech and hate crime by people who have no interest or intention in disguising their identities. The use of images of real disabled people in memes and other disparaging and hateful posts are further examples of the real effects of online communication. Unfortunately, as Sherry demonstrates, even when disabled people or disability advocates identify material as hateful, they often encounter resistance and refusal to remove it from social media providers.

In Chapter 3, "Towards a conceptual and experiential understanding of disablist hate speech," Leah Burch suggests that a more holistic understanding of hate is necessary in order to understand, theorize and respond to the experience of disablist hate speech. Burch demonstrates that disablist hate speech is an everyday experience for many disabled people. By carefully researching such experiences, Burch offers a sophisticated analysis of disablist hate speech as well as a nuanced understanding of victimization and resistance. Burch's chapter also demonstrates the vital need for close collaboration with disabled people and their organizations in researching such hate. Her study, from England, draws on the accounts of people who have experienced disablist hate speech to emphasize its multiple forms and modes of expression. This experiential knowledge, she suggests, is key to developing a more nuanced understanding of the ways disablist hate speech is expressed, received, and interpreted. Likewise, she demonstrates the various forms of resistance to such speech practices that disabled people employ to challenge both disablism and disablist hate speech.

Burch's chapter raises an important concern regarding the terminology which should be used to describe the type of hate speech that is the focus of this book. Burch uses the term "disablist hate speech," as opposed to "disability hate speech," in order to highlight the broader systemic patterns of disablism and their connection to these forms of speech. Disablism, in this sense, refers to active prejudice against disability, which is manifested both on a micro-level through interpersonal interactions and at a macro-level through broad and systematic discrimination and prejudice, which is present in multiple layers of society including employment, education, transport, criminal justice, community participation, and many other areas. Burch's case for using the term "disablist hate speech" is indeed strong. However, some of the authors in this volume have used "disability hate speech" instead. Choosing this language is not meant to deny the widespread nature of disablism, but instead it may be related to the specific language used in particular national contexts or the closest translation of a term in a language other than English.

Part II: The personal impact of disability hate speech

Chapter 4, "Disability hate speech: 'They think they can call me anything'" by Armineh Soorenian discusses some of the forms that disability hate speech can take (including verbal comments as well as written communication) and discusses the effects that such crimes can have on their victims. Soorenian demonstrates that name-calling and other types of hate speech which are officially designated as criminal offences under the UK Criminal Justice and Public Order Act 1994 are not being enforced. They are also usually unreported and classed as "just what happens" to disabled people. The normalization of crimes against disabled people is reinforced by a legal system which does not recognize, fully investigate, or prosecute them, adding further injury to the victims of such crimes. Soorenian suggests that awareness-raising strategies are necessary to pressure these bodies to change.

Disability hate speech has multiple effects beyond the denial of the dignity of disabled people. It harms disabled people psychologically, damages their sense of rights and freedom, and makes them feel alienated from society. Hate speech affects disabled people's lives because it brings them face to face with disablism, and can leave them shocked, angry, sad and scared about the widespread nature of such prejudice. It can also lead them to feel less connected to the community, lose faith in the world as a safe place, and make them feel suspicious. Additionally, hate speech is often a shaming activity: it can lead people to feel embarrassed, guilty, disgraced and humiliated about identities which are essential to their very being. Shaming associated with hate speech frequently leads people to be ostracized and punished for their very being.

Disability hate speech has some unique dynamics. For instance, this form of hate speech has a particular relationship with medicine. Terms which were once medical diagnoses ("spastic," "retard," "idiot," "moron," "cripple," "insane") go out of style in medical parlance, but then frequently morph into disability hate speech in the community. Moreover, many of these terms become generic terms for abuse, but still retain a (complicated) historical and ongoing connection with disability as a form of abjection (Sherry & Neller, 2016). The relationship between a medical approach and disability hate speech deserves further exploration, as Sheri Wells-Jensen and Claire Wells-Jensen demonstrate in their exploration of medical speech about disability in Chapter 5, "Very bad bedside manner: medical professionals and hate speech." They analyse the way that medical personnel adopt the general theme of "better dead than disabled" and the connections between such assumptions about disability and disability hate speech more broadly. Using the autobiography of British neurosurgeon Henry Marsh as an example, Sheri and Claire Wells-Jensen highlight the authority of doctors in speech utterances that disparage disabled lives. The chapter also draws extensively on Sheri's personal experience of blindness to demonstrate the effects of such attitudes and hate speech in the lives of disabled people.

Damian Milton's aut-ethnographic narrative, "Everyday ableism and hate speech: A tale of three encounters in one day," connects subtle forms of marginalization such as gaslighting with more extreme cases of disability hate speech. Milton is both the parent of an autistic child and an autistic person himself, and he uses his own experiences to demonstrate the ways in which both gaslighting and extreme hate speech fundamentally disrespect autistic people and constitute psychoemotional disablism. The entire personhood of autistic people is often called into question, thereby creating a context that demeans, excludes, and denigrates against autistic people. Like the other authors in this book, Milton demonstrates the continuum of invalidation that disabled people experience, from the everyday to the extreme.

The hate speech directed at disabled people is specific to particular types of embodiment. For instance, the language and discourses associated with one impairment are often quite different from another. As the chapters in this volume demonstrate, various forms of disability hate speech may have commonalities – such as the overall connection to wider forms of power connected to normativity and disablement – but the hate speech directed towards one impairment can be quite different from another. In Chapter 7, "Hate speech and dwarfism: The influence of cultural representations," Erin Pritchard emphasizes that the word "midget" is hate speech – it is not funny, or in poor taste, it is hate speech. She describes the ways in which the term "midget" denigrates people with dwarfism. It needs to be understood against the historical background of freak shows and other demeaning discourses about disability that positioned people with dwarfism as sub-human, a hateful discourse that still directly harms people with dwarfism. Nevertheless, the term remains in widespread usage and continues to harm the rights, freedoms, and opportunities of people with dwarfism. One such effect is that people with dwarfism carefully navigate (or avoid) certain public spaces. Other responses, including resistance by people with dwarfism to this demeaning language, are also discussed.

Pritchard's first-person testimony is crucial, both for the literature on hate speech and on disability more broadly, in part because it reveals the intense harm inflicted by the term "midget" – a point which is missed in some previous studies. For instance, one review of racist, homophobic, and disablist hate speech suggested that disablist slurs (and the term 'midget' was specifically used) involved "less explicit othering terms" and more mockery, rather than hate (Burnap & Williams, 2016). Pritchard's ability to weave together the literature on hate speech and disability within her much broader cultural and personal understanding of dwarfism is a powerful counter to such arguments, as well as a reminder of the need to prioritize the voices of those who experience such hate.

Part III: Disablist hate speech within a geopolitical context

Disability hate speech is both nationally-specific and therefore connected to what Mitchell calls "ablenationalism" (Mitchell, 2015), but it is also transnational, particularly when it is shared on the internet. One of the strengths of this edited collection is the wide range of countries which are included in the discussion, and the focus on internet-based hate. Additionally, regional resistance to such hatred is also highlighted. Specific national characteristics of hate speech emerge in the chapters in this section of the book.

In Chapter 8, "Hate speech targeting Sami people with disabilities" Hege Gjertsen and Line Melbøe discuss the use of disability hate speech against the European indigenous group, Sami people. This hate speech is tied to the broader experience of threatening behaviour and bullying in multiple arenas, including group homes, schools, and sheltered workshops. Gjertsen and Melbøe rely on two sources – a quantitative analysis of the experiences of people with an intellectual disability in Norway in 2017 and a qualitative analysis of Sami people with disabilities from 2016. The links between racism and disablism are also emphasized as intersectional factors in the victimization of Sami people with disabilities. Their chapter also explains that the term "hate speech" is rarely used in their region; the term "bullying" is far more common. They explore the effects of bullying on Sami people, including the ways it damages a person's self-esteem and creates stress associated with identity.

Mark P. Mostert's chapter "Stereotypes fomenting hate: Perceptions, stigma, and real-world consequences for Africans with disabilities" discusses another regional context where disabled people experience stigma, prejudice, hostility and hate speech. Even the vocabulary associated with "disability" is stigmatizing in this context. Mostert highlights disablism and disability hate speech in three African countries: the treatment of people with leprosy in Nigeria, people with albinism in Tanzania, and disabled people more generally in Kenya. He also demonstrates the links between hate speech and hate crime, connecting prejudicial attitudes, stigma and hate speech with crimes such as physical abuse, murder and the trafficking of human body parts. For Mostert, stigma is a key factor in the production and reproduction of disability hate speech.

Beata Borowska-Beszta describes disability hate speech in Poland in Chapter 10, "Amputation of disability as hate speech pattern in Poland." For Borowska-Beszta, it is not possible to understand current hate speech against disabled people without recognizing the effects of Communist ideology (and the glorification of a productive, working, "socialist man"). The political and cultural context of such hate speech – occurring in a post-communist country – is vitally important, since Communist countries often denied the existence of disabled people entirely. Those disabled people who could not work were oppressed, isolated, stigmatized, and regarded as a lower form of humanity; for Borowska-Beszta, these are the foundation stones of contemporary disability hate speech in Poland.

British scholars particularly emphasize the connection between disability hate speech, disability hate crimes, and the politics of austerity (Burch, 2018; Cross, 2013; Philip Thomas, 2016). This is the theme of Chapter 11 by Lisa Davies, "Disability under austerity: Do some forms of political rhetoric constitute disability hate speech?" Davies explores utterances by British politicians that blame and stigmatize disabled people for economic and social problems. She further suggests that the politics of blame conducted under austerity regimes needs to be carefully analysed in terms of its underlying disablist hate speech. Davies' socio-political analysis of disablist hate speech is another important contribution to theorizing this phenomenon. Her focus on hostility towards people on disability assistance is a reminder that disablist hate speech is often directed towards those in lower socio-economic positions. These are often people struggling to make ends meet, in very precarious economic as well as social positions, who are being targeted.

Mark Sherry and Solomon Amoatey's chapter, "Hate speech by carers: Exploring an Australian case" provides another international example. It begins by discussing disability hate speech by two carers in Australia who were secretly recorded using both slurs (and violence) against a disabled person in a nursing home. Their chapter is another important reminder that disability hate speech is unlike many other forms of hate: whereas the perpetrators of racist hate speech or hate crimes, for instance, are usually unknown to victims, those who commit disablist hate speech are often well-known to their victims. Indeed, in this case, the perpetrators were actually paid to care for their victim – an abrogation of their professional duties as well as an act of unrestrained enmity.

Chapter 13, by Stephen Rosenbaum, is entitled "Hammerin' Hank, (dis)ablism, racism, homophobia, and hate speech." It discusses the *Doghouse*, an American radio programme that routinely involves low-level harassment and hate speech against Henry Oaks, an intellectually disabled man referred to as "Hammerin' Hank" who is featured on the show. Rosenbaum's chapter also highlights the significant commercial support for the programme drawn by its ratings, regardless of its hateful content. Hate speech is endemic against many groups on the show, Rosenbaum suggests. His chapter, written in the context of the United States Constitution's free speech protections, also discusses the use of hateful language in the context of humour, resistance, and re-appropriation by marginalized groups. As well, it discusses the issues of freedom of choice and abuse in the context of Hank's participation in this programme.

The question of what happens after hate speech incidents is the subject of Chapter 14 by Terje Olsen, Janikke Solstad Vedeler, and John Eriksen, "Hate speech as an expression of disablism: An examination of reported hate speech experiences and consequences." Their research breaks new ground in exploring the ways follow-up (or non-follow-up) occurs after a hate speech incident. Using a survey of almost a thousand disabled people in Norway, they discuss what happens after hate speech is reported to professional welfare services, caregivers, police, family or friends. The experience of disability hate speech was alarmingly high: 38% reported at least one experience of hate speech during the previous year. Among these people, 74% had told other people, including 32% who had reported the incident to the police. One of their disturbing findings is the inappropriate responses of police: even when people had phoned police, asked them what to do, or filed a formal case, the police did not recognize these crimes in their official files. Indeed, police files did not recognize even one case of discrimination due to disability according to the Norwegian Penal Code. Olsen, Vedeler, and Eriksen's chapter is a fitting end to the book, since it reflects the sad realities of today's political climate. Large numbers of disabled people are experiencing disability hate speech, and while most do not report it to the police, those who do rarely receive the appropriate responses. Their chapter is a wake-up call to those concerned with justice, rights, inclusion, prejudice, and criminal victimization. The practices of disablism and disability hate speech demand much more serious responses than they currently receive.[1]

Note

1 Terje, John and Janikke would like to thank the Norwegian Fritt Ord Foundation for support in the final stages of this book project.

References

Austin, J. L. (1975). *How to do things with words*. Oxford: Oxford University Press.

Baez, B. (2013). *Affirmative action, hate speech, and tenure: Narratives about race, law, and the academy*. London: Routledge.

Benesch, S. (2014, 10 February). Countering dangerous speech to prevent mass violence during Kenya's 2013 elections. Retrieved from https://dangerousspeech.org/countering-dangerous-speech-kenya-2013/

Bérubé, M. (2018). *The secret life of stories: From Don Quixote to Harry Potter, how understanding intellectual disability transforms the way we read*. New York: New York University Press.

Bleich, E. (2014). Freedom of expression versus racist hate speech: Explaining differences between high court regulations in the USA and Europe. *Journal of Ethnic and Migration Studies*, *40*(2), 283–300.

Boeckmann, R. J., & Liew, J. (2002). Hate speech: Asian American students' justice judgments and psychological responses. *Journal of Social Issues*, *58*(2), 363–381. doi:10.1111/1540-4560.00265

Boffey, D. (2011, 15th May). Disabled people face abuse and threats of violence after fraud crackdown. *The Observer*. Retrieved from http://www.guardian.co.uk/society/2011/may/15/disability-living-allowance-scope-cuts

Briant, E., Watson, N., & Philo, G. (2013). Reporting disability in the age of austerity: the changing face of media representation of disability and disabled people in the United Kingdom and the creation of new 'folk devils'. *Disability & Society*, *28*(6), 874–889. doi:10.1080/09687599.2013.813837

Brown, A. (2015). *Hate speech law: A philosophical examination*. New York: Routledge.

Brown, W. (1995). *States of injury: Power and freedom in late modernity*. Princeton, NJ: Princeton University Press.

Brown, W. (2006). *Regulating aversion: Tolerance in the age of identity and empire*. Princeton, NJ: Princeton University Press.

Burch, L. (2018). 'You are a parasite on the productive classes': Online disablist hate speech in austere times. *Disability & Society*, *33*(3), 392–415.

Burnap, P., & Williams, M. L. (2016). Us and them: Identifying cyber hate on Twitter across multiple protected characteristics. *EPJ Data Science*, *5*(1), 11. doi:10.1140/epjds/s13688-016-0072-6

Calderbank, R. (2000). Abuse and Disabled People: Vulnerability or social indifference? *Disability & Society*, *15*(3), 521–534.

Capozza, D., Di Bernardo, G. A., Falvo, R., Vianello, R., & Calò, L. (2016). Individuals with intellectual and developmental disabilities: Do educators assign them a fully human status? *Journal of Applied Social Psychology*, *46*(9), 497–509.

Cohen-Almagor, R. (2018). Taking North American white supremacist groups seriously: The scope and challenge of hate speech on the Internet. *International Journal for Crime, Justice and Social Democracy*, *7*, 38–57.

Conway, R. N. F. (1994). Abuse and intellectual disability: A potential link or an inescapable reality. *Journal of Intellectual and Developmental Disability*, *19*(3), 165–171.

Cross, M. (2013). Demonised, impoverished and now forced into isolation: The fate of disabled people under austerity. *Disability & Society*, *28*(5), 719–723.

Curry, M. A., Hassouneh-Phillips, D., & Johnston-Silverberg, A. (2001). Abuse of women with disabilities: An ecological model and review. *Violence Against Women*, *7*(1), 60–79.

Davies, C., & McInnes, D. (2012). Speaking violence: Homophobia and the production of injurious speech in schooling cultures. In S. Saltmarsh, K. H. Robinson, & C. Davies (Eds.), *Rethinking school violence* (pp. 131–148). London: Palgrave Macmillan.

Dávila, B. (2015). Critical race theory, disability microaggressions and Latina/o student experiences in special education. *Race Ethnicity and Education*, *18*(4), 443–468.

Delgato, R. (1993). Words that wound: A tort action for racial insults, epithets, and name calling. In M. J. Matsuda, C. R. I. Lawrence, R. Delgato, & K. W. Crenshaw (Eds.), *Words that wound: Critical race theory, assaultive speech, And the first amendment* (pp. 89–110). Bouilder, CO: Westview Press.

Fetzer, M. D., & Pezzella, F. S. (2016). The nature of bias crime injuries: A comparative analysis of physical and psychological victimization effects. *Journal of interpersonal violence*, Online ahead of print. Retrieved from http://journals.sagepub.com/doi/full/10.1177/0886260516672940

Gedalof, I. (2018). *Narratives of difference in an age of austerity*. London: Palgrave Macmillan.

Gelber, K., & McNamara, L. (2016). Evidencing the harms of hate speech. *Social Identities*, *22*(3), 324–341.

Goodall, K. (2009). Challenging hate speech: Incitement to hatred on grounds of sexual orientation in England, Wales and Northern Ireland. *The International Journal of Human Rights*, *13*(2–3), 211–232.

Hall, E. (2019). A critical geography of disability hate crime. *Area*, *51*(2), 249–256.

Harmer, E., & Lumsden, K. (2019). Online othering: An introduction. In K. Lumsden & E. Harmer (Eds.), *Online othering: Exploring digital violence and discrimination on the web* (pp. 1–33). Cham, Switzerland: Palgrave Macmillan.

Hassouneh-Phillips, D. (2005). Understanding abuse of women with physical disabilities: An overview of the abuse pathways model. *Advances in Nursing Science*, *28*(1), 70–80.

Hawdon, J., Oksanen, A., & Räsänen, P. (2014). Exposure to online hate among social media users. In M. N. Warehime (Ed.), *Soul of society: A focus on the lives of children and youth* (pp. 253–274). Bingley, UK: Emerald.

Kamavarapu, Y. S., Ferriter, M., Morton, S., & Völlm, B. (2017). Institutional abuse – Characteristics of victims, perpetrators and organsations: A systematic review. *European Psychiatry*, *40*, 45–54.

Keller, R. M., & Galgay, C. E. (2010). Microaggressive experiences of people with disabilities. In D. W. Sue (Ed.), *Microaggressions and marginality: Manifestation, dynamics, and impact* (pp. 241–268). Hoboken, NJ: John Wiley & Sons, Inc,.

Kenya National Commission on Human Rights. (2008). *On the brink of the precipice: A human rights account of Kenya's post-2007 election violence*. Nairobi, Kenya: Kenya National Commission on Human Rights.

Kerr, A., & Shakespeare, T. (2002). *Genetic politics: From eugenics to genome*. Cheltenham: New Clarion Press.

Lasson, K. (1985). Racial defamation as free speech: Abusing the first amendment. *Columbia Human Rights Law Review*, *17*, 11–55.

Lidsky, L. B. (2008). Where's the harm: Free speech and the regulation of lies. *Washington and Lee Law Review*, *65*, 1091–1101.

Macdonald, S. J., Donovan, C., & Clayton, J. (2017). The disability bias: Understanding the context of hate in comparison with other minority populations. *Disability & Society*, *32*(4), 483–499.

McCarthy, M., Hunt, S., & Milne-Skillman, K. (2017). 'I know it was every week, but I can't be sure if it was every day': Domestic violence and women with learning disabilities. *Journal of Applied Research in Intellectual Disabilities*, *30*(2), 269–282.

McDevitt, J., Balboni, J., Garcia, L., & Gu, J. (2001). Consequences for victims: A comparison of bias-and non-bias-motivated assaults. *American Behavioral Scientist*, *45*(4), 697–713.

Mik-Meyer, N. (2016). Othering, ableism and disability: A discursive analysis of co-workers' construction of colleagues with visible impairments. *Human Relations*, *69*(6), 1341–1363.

Mitchell, D. (2015). *The biopolitics of disability: Neoliberalism, ablenationalism, and peripheral embodiment*. Ann Arbor, MI: University of Michigan Press.

Mitchell, D., & Snyder, S. (2003). The Eugenic Atlantic: Race, disability, and the making of an international eugenic science, 1800–1945. *Disability & Society*, *18*(7), 843–864.

Modood, T., Hansen, R., Bleich, E., O'Leary, B., & Carens, J. H. (2006). The Danish cartoon affair: Free speech, racism, Islamism, and integration. *International Migration*, *44*(5), 3–62.

Mostert, M. P. (2002). Useless eaters: Disability as genocidal marker in Nazi Germany. *The Journal of Special Education*, *36*(3), 157–170.

Müller, K., & Schwarz, C. (30 November 2018). Fanning the flames of hate: Social media and hate crime. Retrieved from http://dx.doi.org/10.2139/ssrn.3082972

Norway Equality and Anti-Discrimination Ombud – Likestillings og diskrimineringsombudet. (2015). *Hate speech and hate crime*. Oslo.

Oksanen, A., Hawdon, J., Holkeri, E., Näsi, M., & Räsänen, P. (2014). Exposure to online hate among young social media users. *Sociological Studies of Children & Youth, 18*(1), 253–273.

Øksendal, E., Brandlistuen, R. E., Holte, A., & Wang, M. V. (2019). Peer-victimization of young children with developmental and behavioral difficulties – A population-based study. *Journal of Pediatric Psychology, 44*(5), 589–600.

Peckitt, M. (August 2016). Disability hate crime & the Sagamihara victims. Retrieved from https://www.accessible-japan.com/disability-hate-crime-sagamihara-victims/

Pinquart, M. (2016). Systematic Review: Bullying involvement of children with and without chronic physical illness and/or physical/sensory disability – A meta-analytic comparison with healthy/nondisabled peers. *Journal of Pediatric Psychology, 42*(3), 245–259.

Quek, N. (2019). Bloodbath in Christchurch: The rise of far-right terrorism. RSIS Commentaries, No. 047. Singpore: Nanyang Technological University.

Ralph, S., Capewell, C., & Bonnett, E. (2016). Disability hate crime: Persecuted for difference. *British Journal of Special Education, 43*(3), 215–232.

Reddy, V. (2002). Perverts and sodomites: Homophobia as hate speech in Africa. *Southern African Linguistics and Applied Language Studies, 20*(3), 163–175.

Reeve, D. (2002). Negotiating psycho-emotional dimensions of disability and their influence on identity constructions. *Disability & Society, 17*(5), 493–508.

Roulstone, A., & Mason-Bish, H. (Eds.). (2013). *Disability, hate crime and violence*. London: Routledge.

Runswick-Cole, K., & Goodley, D. (2015). DisPovertyPorn: Benefits Street and the dis/ability paradox. *Disability & Society, 30*(4), 645–649.

Schweik, S. M. (2009). *The ugly laws: Disability in public*. New York: New York University Press.

Shah, R., & Giannasi, P. (Eds.). (2015). *Tackling disability discrimination and disability hate crime: A multidisciplinary guide*. London: Jessica Kingsley Publishers.

Sherry, M. (2010). *Disability hate crimes: Does anyone really hate disabled people?* Surrey: Ashgate.

Sherry, M., & Neller, A. (2016). Intellectual disability, stigma, and hate crimes. In K. Scior & S. Werner (Eds.), *Intellectual disability and stigma: Stepping out from the margins* (pp. 111–126). London: Palgrave Macmillan.

Shiffrin, S. H. (1994). Racist speech outsider jurisprudence and the meaning of America. *Cornell Law Review, 80*, 43–103.

Soldatic, K., & Meekosha, H. (2012). The place of disgust: Disability, class and gender in spaces of workfare. *Societies, 2*(3), 139–156.

Soldatic, K., & Pini, B. (2009). The three Ds of welfare reform: Disability, disgust and deservingness. *Australian Journal of Human Rights, 15*(1), 77–95.

Soral, W., Bilewicz, M., & Winiewski, M. (2018). Exposure to hate speech increases prejudice through desensitization. *Aggressive Behavior, 44*(2), 136–146.

Stone, D. A. (1984). *The disabled state*. Philadelphia, PA: Temple University Press.

Thomas, C. (1999). *Female forms: Experiencing and understanding disability*. Buckingham: Open University Press.

Thomas, P. (2011). 'Mate crime': Ridicule, hostility and targeted attacks against disabled people. *Disability & Society, 26*(1), 107–111.

Thomas, P. (2016). Psycho politics, neoliberal governmentality and austerity. *Self & Society, 44*(4), 382–393.

Turner, R. (2007). Cross burnings and the harm-valuation analytic: A tale of two cases. *Berkeley Journal of African-American Law and Policy*, *7*, 3–31.

UK Parliament. (2017, 3 May). Petition: Make online abuse a specific criminal offence and create a register of offenders. Retrieved from https://petition.parliament.uk/archived/petitions/190627

Zeedyk, S. M., Rodriguez, G., Tipton, L. A., Baker, B. L., & Blacher, J. (2014). Bullying of youth with autism spectrum disorder, intellectual disability, or typical development: Victim and parent perspectives. *Research in Autism Spectrum Disorders*, *8*(9), 1173–1183. doi:10.1016/j.rasd.2014.06.001.

Part I

The nature of disability hate speech

1 Disablist hate speech laws

Mark Sherry and Louise Walker

Political debates about the legal status of hate speech within liberal democracies tend to revolve around two competing values. One side of these debates prioritizes the value of freedom of speech while the other emphasizes the harm that hate speech inflicts in terms of respect, equality, human dignity, community cohesion, and freedom from harassment and intimidation (Bleich, 2011; Cram, 2006; Heinze, 2016; S. Walker, 1994). In most countries, it is recognized that at least some forms of hate speech must be prohibited because such speech harms, degrades, demeans, humiliates, scares, intimidates, hurts, and wounds. However, disability is often excluded from categories in such hate speech laws. This pattern reflects a hierarchy of hate, where other forms of hatred are given more acknowledgement than disability – as a discussion of United Nations human rights treaties will demonstrate. Also, using examples from a number of different countries, this chapter will discuss the ways disability may (or may not) be recognized in hate speech legislation. It will also demonstrate that what is considered disablist hate speech not only differs between countries, but also within them.

Hate speech lacks a universally accepted definition, both in jurisprudence and in academic literature (Calvert, 1997; Davidson, Warmsley, Macy, & Weber, 2017; Heinze, 2009; Klubička & Fernández, 2018; Strossen, 2018). An oft-cited early definition of hate speech was provided by Farrior (1996, p. 3) who defined it as any expression that is "abusive, insulting, intimidating, harassing and/or which incites to violence, hatred or discrimination." Unfortunately, Farrior narrowed this definition to a limited number of target groups – those selected on the basis of race, religion, ethnicity, or national origin. This pattern of excluding disability mirrors the wider historical development of jurisprudence and is also typical of broader academic literature, which may expand the categories included but still omits disability (see for example Rosenfeld, 2002; Warner & Hirschberg, 2012).

Another interesting element of international differences in hate speech legislation is that some countries' legislation places hate speech in the category of hate crimes, and some countries publish reports which do not separate hate speech from hate crimes, whereas others make a strong distinction between the two. From a UK perspective, hate speech is now a hate crime in many cases. There are also prohibitions on hate speech that have been developed by the European Union. But in the US, even if it was recognized as hate speech, it would be legal and constitutionally protected. In India, certain types of hate speech are prohibited, but disablist hate speech is not. Each one of these cases, and more, will be discussed later in the chapter.

Diagnostic terms for an impairment can be used without any hatred implied (such as in a medical context), but they can also be used as terms of derision in disablist hate speech. In such circumstances, simply saying someone has a mental illness (or a particular diagnosis, such as schizophrenia or bipolar disorder) can be used to discredit the person – especially when the person doing the insult has no knowledge as to whether that label is true or not. For instance, calling someone "autistici" (autistic) is a common slur in Italy (Di Merlo, 2018). Long-abandoned medical terms such as "idioti" (idiot) or "cretini" (cretin) and many words deriving from Roman or Vulgar Roman are often used in Italian disablist hate speech. An example is the word "scemi" (which derives from the Latin *exsemāre* and the Vulgar Latin *semis*, meaning half). In Italy, the word "deficienti" (someone with deficiencies) is used in disablist hate speech to suggest that the person is less than fully human. Such an attitude clearly has links to wider eugenic ideologies, which are stubbornly persistent and widespread.

In English-speaking countries, the term "retard" – otherwise referred to as the "r word" by disability advocates is also a widespread term of disablist abuse. An abbreviation, "tard," is also used as a term of abuse. Disablist hate speech abuse is also aimed at those connected to disabled people – for instance, a personal assistant might be called a "tard guard" or a "tard wrangler." Even objects associated with disability can be given disablist names. For instance, an accessible school bus might be called a "tard barge," "tard trolley," "tard truck," or (for those who are still disablist but avoid the r word) a "short bus." Another common disablist slur towards people with intellectual disabilities in English-speaking countries is the term "window-licker" (suggesting that disabled people lick bus windows). Terms associated with antiquated medical classifications of intellect, including "moron," "idiot," and "imbecile" are also widely used both as generic terms of abuse and also as specific hate speech insults towards particular disabled people.

For those with physical impairments, the terms "spastic" and "spaz" are often used in disablist hate speech in English-speaking countries. While the term has also been used in medical settings (for instance, in describing spastic cerebral palsy or spastic paralysis), its more widespread in the language of insult. The terms "cripple" and "lame" are also widely used, but seem to have less stigma attached (and are seen as less hateful), even though they still function in ways that reinforce stereotypes, prejudice, and negative images of disability (Deal, 2007). Of course, language must always be understood in context: in certain situations, terms such as "cripple" can be menacing, harassing, and hate-filled.

Another common practice is to use an abbreviation of a diagnosis as a slur – for instance, a French study of slurs found that a common insult involved calling someone with schizophrenia "schizo" and calling someone with Down Syndrome "triso" – short for Trisonomy 21, the chromosome which is affected in Down Syndrome (Ratouis, 2016). "Schizo" is also used in disablist hate speech in many countries (Findlay, 2017; Pryal, 2017; Reeve, 2012). The term "flid," a crude variation of "Thalidomide," is also used in disability hate speech, in Britain in particular (Conroy, 2013). It Italy, the slur *mongoli* is common – it translates to "Mongoloid," a form of disablist hate speech which is also used in many other countries. This hate speech is noteworthy because it combines both disablism and racism – one might hope that such hate speech was therefore prohibited under racist hate speech laws. But unfortunately, in this case, it seems like the connection to disability trumps the racist connotations of the term, and prosecutions are non-existent. This connection is an example that also demonstrates the importance of intersectionality in discussing hate speech. The links between hate speech based on racism and disability are profound (Benton & Dionne, 2015; Farmer, 2001, 2006; Idoiaga Mondragon, Gil de Montes, & Valencia, 2017; McCauley, Minsky, & Viswanath, 2013; Santiago-Irizarry, 2001; Sherry, 2007; Smedley, Stith, & Nelson, 2002).

Often, courts have made decisions which have greatly disappointed disability activists, seemingly allowing the perpetrators of disability hate speech free reign for their words. A notorious case from Italy involved a person without a disability parking permit being reported for his actions and replying

> To you handiccap (sic) that yesterday you called the brigade I would like to tell you that to me 60 euro do not change anything but you always remain a poor handicapped. I'm glad that this misfortune happened to you.
>
> (De Grillo & Stimolo, 2017)

The basis for this decision was that the comment did not name any individual victim in particular – even though it said it was directed to the person who made the complaint. From the point of view of disability activists, such decisions fail to recognize that hate speech has two victims: the individual person to whom it is aimed, and the broader community who share the same identity (Sherry, 2010).

Interestingly, one court in a particular country may support strongly punishing hate speech while another does not. In Italy, for instance, a contrasting decision was made by the Court of Verbania in 2016, which sentenced two people for hate speech against a woman with achondroplasia. She has been the victim of denigration on Facebook, where hateful, defamatory, and discriminatory comments were made about her dwarfism. The two defendants were sentenced to 12 months imprisonment, even though the prosecutor had recommended a sentence of 8 months. As well, they were ordered to pay compensation for damages to the victim and also to three organizations that had joined the civil action. Including legal fees, they were ordered to pay €50,000 (Lega Per I Diritti Delle Persone Con Disabilità, 2016).

Some jurisdictions within a country adopt much more stringent laws against hate speech than others. For instance, the Australian state of Tasmania has some of the strictest hate speech laws. Section 9 of its Anti-Discrimination Act 1998 prohibits people from inciting "hatred towards, serious contempt for, or severe ridicule of, a person or a group of persons" on the ground of race, disability, sexual orientation, or religion. In contrast, similar wording in Part 4, Section 124A of Queensland's Anti-Discrimination Act 1991 prohibits the incitement of hatred on the grounds of race, religion, sexuality, or gender identity, but omits disability. The New South Wales legislature excluded disability from its 2018 law entitled "Public threats or incitement of violence on grounds of race, religion, sexual orientation, gender identity, or intersex or HIV/AIDS status." The failure to include disability as a protected category demonstrates how obtuse lawmakers can be when it comes to disablist hate speech.

While this chapter provides a broad overview of hate speech legislation, it does not cover laws around the transmission of hate speech online since that is the focus of a specific chapter later in this volume. Additionally, the chapter does not cover the raft of other criminal and civil laws which might be broken concurrently with acts of hate speech. For instance, hate speech can involve threats, including threats of bodily harm and threats of murder. These are obviously serious criminal acts in any country, but they are not within the remit of this chapter. Likewise, criminal behaviours such as stalking or harassment may occur alongside hate speech. Malicious communications (online, through the media, or through other mechanisms) may also break the law in some countries. Certain types of hate speech may also be offences under anti-terrorism laws. These criminal acts are not the subject of this chapter, but they are an important part of the criminal justice landscape that should not be forgotten.

The following discussion of hate speech laws will highlight the ways in which disablist hate speech is covered (or not) under international treaties.

Hate speech and international treaties

There are many international treaties and agreements which are designed to protect and promote human rights, and which could (in theory at least) be used to address hate speech. This section of the chapter will now highlight how such arrangements might be used to deal with disability hate speech, using United Nations treaties and the European Union as examples. It will demonstrate that there has been a hierarchy of hate which largely sidelines disability issues. While issues of racist or religious hate speech have long been recognized as central to international human rights concerns, states have been much slower to recognize the issue of disability hate speech.

United Nations

At the most basic level, it could be argued that hate speech is inconsistent with the Universal Declaration of Human Rights, since hate speech denies the inherent dignity and humanity of its victims. However, this Declaration has tended to prioritize Article 19, which states in part that "Everyone has the right to freedom of opinion and expression" over the competing message in Article 29 (2), which says

> In the exercise of his rights and freedoms, everyone shall be subject only to such limitations as are determined by law solely for the purpose of securing

> due recognition and respect for the rights and freedoms of others and of meeting the just requirements of morality, public order and the general welfare in a democratic society.
>
> (United Nations Human Rights Office of the High Commissioner, 2014)

This question – whether people retain the right to express hatred that demeans and threatens the dignity of others – is one of the core issues which lays at the heart of hate speech laws, an issue which is complicated by online hate speech which crosses multiple jurisdictions. Most countries have decided against free speech absolutism because of the harms created by hate speech – in the words of Tseis (2009, p. 532), they believe respect for human dignity "supersedes bigots' self-determined desire to spread destructive messages." In making these decisions, however, the Universal Declaration of Human Rights has not been the mechanism through which they have fostered such laws.

There are nine other United Nations treaties which (in their most expansive interpretations) could be seen as limiting at least some forms of the human rights abuses involved in hate speech. Some of these treaties also have optional protocols which further expand their scope for parties that are signatories. There are nine human rights treaties adopted by the United Nations (United Nations Human Rights Office of the High Commissioner, 2014):

1. International Convention on the Elimination of All Forms of Racial Discrimination
2. International Covenant on Civil and Political Rights (which also has two Optional Protocols)
3. International Covenant on Economic, Social and Cultural Rights (which has one Optional Protocol)
4. Convention on the Elimination of All Forms of Discrimination against Women (which has one Optional Protocol)
5. Convention against Torture and Other Cruel, Inhuman or Degrading Treatment or Punishment (which has one Optional Protocol)
6. Convention on the Rights of the Child (which also has three Optional Protocols)
7. International Convention on the Protection of the Rights of All Migrant Workers and Members of Their Families
8. International Convention for the Protection of All Persons from Enforced Disappearance
9. Convention on the Rights of Persons with Disabilities (with one Optional Protocol)

Even in international agreements where there are punishments for certain types of hate speech, disability is rarely included. For instance, Part 2 of Article 20 of the United Nations International Covenant on Civil and Political Rights states, "any advocacy of national, racial or religious hatred that constitutes incitement to discrimination, hostility or violence shall be prohibited by law." Disability is not protected under such conventions. This failure to include disability (let alone identify its specific harms and dynamics) is a major failure of both international treaties and national laws.

The Convention on the Rights of Persons with Disabilities is particularly relevant to this discussion, since it specifically promises to protect the rights of the population under discussion in this chapter. The General Principles of this Convention include non-discrimination; full and effective participation and inclusion in society; and respect for difference and acceptance of persons with disabilities as part of human diversity and humanity (United Nations Human Rights Office of the High Commissioner, 2014). The General Obligations set out under Article 4 include "To take all appropriate measures to eliminate discrimination on the basis of disability by any person, organization or private enterprise." For many people concerned with disability rights, the very essence of disablist hate speech is both discrimination in itself and a call for broader discrimination, thereby undermining this Convention. But it needs to be said that when explored critically, the promise of this Convention has not been realized in many areas and not simply the area of hate speech (Sherry, 2014).

European Union

Many of the policies of the European Union provide protections against hate speech toward various minorities, but disability is often not mentioned. Perhaps the hate speech that is directed at disabled people could be included in the generic concept of "other forms of hatred," but there are no guarantees that this will happen. The Council of Europe's Committee of Ministers, Recommendation No. (97) 20 is a good example. It states:

> The term hate speech shall be understood as covering all forms of expression which spread, incite, promote or justify racial hatred, xenophobia, antisemitism or other forms of hatred based on intolerance, including: intolerance expressed by aggressive nationalism and ethnocentrism, discrimination and hostility against minorities, migrants and people of origin.
>
> (Council of Europe Committee of Ministers, 1997)

If one assumes that "other forms of hatred based on intolerance" includes disability, such an approach still positions disability almost as an afterthought. It certainly would not guarantee equal attention in law enforcement training programmes or other publicity compared to the forms of hatred which are specifically mentioned. And yet this problem – positioning disability as "another Other" – has long been criticized by disability studies scholars for its failure to grasp the specifics and nuances of disabled people's experiences of oppression (Kudlick, 2003).

The European Commission's definition of hate speech, based on the Council of the European Union's Framework Decision 2008/913/JHA, has the same limitation. There is an informal hierarchy of hate, where disability is not considered worthy of mention – that is evident in the title, "Framework Decision on combating certain forms and expressions of racism and xenophobia by means of criminal law" (Council of the European Union Framework, 2008). The Decision defines many forms of hate speech as criminal acts, but does not specifically mention disability. For instance, it prohibits "public incitement to violence or hatred directed against a group of persons or a member of such a group defined on the basis of race, colour, descent, religion or belief, or national or ethnic origin" as well as "publicly condoning, denying or grossly trivialising crimes of genocide, crimes against humanity and war crimes."

The most recent report on hate crimes internationally by the Organization for Security and Co-operation in Europe indicates that only 11 governments included disability in their reports. The report does not distinguish between disability hate crimes and disability hate speech, which is an important limitation because only some of the governments prohibit such speech. It states:

> A limited but growing number of governments provide official data on hate crime against people with disabilities… There is a low awareness of disability hate crime, and knowledge about how to monitor incidents motivated by hostility against people with disabilities among civil society organizations and the general public. As a result the data in this section is sparse.
>
> (Organization for Security and Co-operation in Europe, 2019a)

Again, it is noteworthy that the reporting on disablist hate crimes is presented under the heading "bias against other groups – people with disabilities" – literally Othering the entire category.

The governments which reported under the category of disability were Belgium, Finland, Germany, Greece, Italy, Netherlands, Norway, Spain, Ukraine, United Kingdom, and the United States of America. Of these countries, only six reported that disability hate crimes actually occurred. The following governments did not file reports about disability hate crimes, though they did participate in at least some of the other identified categories: Albania, Andorra, Armenia, Austria, Azerbaijan, Belarus, Bosnia and Herzegovina, Bulgaria, Canada, Croatia, Cyprus, Czech Republic, Denmark, Estonia, France, Georgia, Greece, Holy See, Hungary, Iceland, Ireland, Italy, Kazakhstan, Kyrgyzstan, Latvia, Liechtenstein, Lithuania, Luxembourg, The former Yugoslav Republic of Macedonia, Malta, Moldova, Monaco, Mongolia, Montenegro, Poland, Portugal, Romania, Russian Federation, San Marino, Serbia, Slovakia, Slovenia, Sweden, Switzerland, Tajikistan, Turkey, Turkmenistan, and Uzbekistan. It was left to non-governmental agencies to make additional reports – but even then, there were a small number of reports. The context of austerity in many states also means that such organizations often lack the resources to make comprehensive reports.

The next section of this chapter will describe in more detail the legislative approaches adopted at a national level by a number of countries in terms of the regulation of hate speech.

The variety of national responses to hate speech

Specific political cultures are enormously important in terms of framing hate speech. Disablist slurs may be regarded as hate speech in one country, but the entire category of "disability" may not be included in hate speech laws in another country. Some countries include hate speech within the broader category of hate crime, whereas other countries might treat the two as quite distinct. Additionally, some countries may place much more emphasis on acknowledging, reporting, and prosecuting hate speech than others, where such acts may be tacitly normalized and accepted. This section of the chapter will highlight this pattern of inconsistency by discussing the responses to hate speech of seven countries: Poland, United Kingdom, United States, China, India, South Africa, and Canada. Grech (2015) has criticized disability studies for assuming that disability experiences in the Global North apply equally to the Global South. These diverse countries were chosen in response to such criticisms and in order to avoid such limitations.

Poland

Although Poland has been a member of the European Union since 2004, it is worth discussing in particular because the Polish Constitution specifically protects free speech while prohibiting Nazism, Fascism, and Communism. It also prohibits the promotion of racial, national, ethnic, or religious hatred. Additionally, the Broadcasting Act of 1992 requires broadcasts to show respect for the religious beliefs of the public, especially the Christian system of values. Arguably, disablist hate speech contradicts many of these principles. For instance, disablist hate speech could (in theory) be prohibited in Poland on the basis of disrespecting the Christian system of values. Swinton (2012) argues that Christians have a moral obligation to oppose injustice, and that disablism and ableism specifically contradict the Christian system of values. However, this interpretation of Christian ethics has not been used as the basis for responses to disablist hate speech in Poland.

Disablist hate speech could also be prohibited under the Polish Constitution if it was accepted that totalitarian ideologies are underpinned by disablism. In Nazi Germany, for instance, thousands of disabled people were sentenced to death because they were considered "useless eaters" and psychiatric hospitals were turned into killing centres to "eradicate" disabled people en masse (Biesold, 1999; Friedländer, 1998; Mostert, 2002). The disablist eugenic ideology was also practised widely in Eastern European countries under the control of the USSR (Fefelov, 1986; Phillips, 2009; Turda, 2015; Turda & Weindling, 2007). The discipline of "defectology" was further used in Poland to justify state policies of segregated schools and segregated housing (Grigorenko, 1998). But even though disablist beliefs and practices were arguably a key element of such totalitarian regimes, they have not been recognized as therefore being prohibited under the sections of the Polish Constitution.[1]

Disablist hate speech flourishes in Poland (see Borowska-Beszta in this volume). Commitments to report disablist hate crime under European Union agreements are basically ignored in Poland. Poland does not report hate crimes separately from cases of hate speech. But even more importantly as far as this discussion is concerned, in its reports to the Organization for Security and Co-operation in Europe, as recently as 2017, Poland was only reporting hate crimes under the following categories: racism and xenophobia, bias against Roma and Sinti, anti-Semitism, bias against Muslims, and bias against other groups – sexuality and gender (Organization for Security and Co-operation in Europe, 2019b). Disability is noticeably absent.

United Kingdom

The UK is another country where the history of legislation involved a hierarchy of hate, and disability was essentially rendered an afterthought. The UK still has a number of laws regulating hate speech which unfortunately ignore disability, including the Racial and Religious Hatred Act 2006, the Criminal Justice and Immigration Act 2008, and the Football Offences and Disorder Act 1999. The Public Order Act 1986 prohibits racial hatred defined as hatred based on colour, race, nationality (including citizenship), or ethnic or national origins. Section 4, which includes sections "Fear or provocation of violence" and "Intentional harassment, alarm or distress" contains prohibitions against causing alarm or distress via threatening, abusive or insulting words or behaviour, disorderly behaviour, or causing harassment, alarm, or distress via writing, signs, or other visible representations. The Racial and Religious Hatred Act 2006 also prohibits threatening words or behaviour or displaying any written material which is threatening. The Criminal Justice and Immigration Act 2008 prohibits incitement to hatred based on sexual orientation. The Football Offences and Disorder Act 1999 prohibits indecent or racialist chanting at football matches.

Disabled people in the UK can receive protection or remedy under some criminal and civil laws. For instance, the Protection from Harassment Act 1997 allows a victim to seek compensation for harassment. Local laws concerning anti-social behaviour may also provide disabled victims with some rights. Disablist hate speech which does not rise to the level of a hate crime can be responded to by police as a hate incident.

It is important to remember that the use of hate speech may occur simultaneously with other offences. The public policy organization ARTICLE 19 has identified a number of other criminal offences under UK laws that may be indirectly related to hate speech.

> Threats: A threat to kill – however communicated – is an offence contrary to Section 16 of the Offences Against the Person Act 1861.83 Threats short of a threat to kill are more likely to be dealt with as harassment or under the Malicious Communications Act 1988, the Communications Act 2003, or as public order offences… By Section 4 of the 1861 Act, it is also an offence to solicit, encourage, persuade or endeavour to persuade, or propose to any person, to murder another person.
>
> (ARTICLE 19, 2018, p. 20)

ARTICLE 19 also discusses the ways in which laws surrounding harassment can be utilized in response to hate speech incidents.

> Harassment: By Section 1 of the Protection from Harassment Act 1997, a person must not pursue a course of conduct which amounts to harassment of another person and which he knows, or ought to know, amounts to harassment of that person… Harassment is both a crime (by Section 2) and a civil cause of action (by Section 3). Additionally, there is a statutory offence of stalking (Section 2A) which has a more severe sentence (51 weeks) than ordinary harassment.
>
> (ARTICLE 19, 2018, p. 21)

Harassment can occur online or by publication, including in the media. A relevant disability case involved online harassment by Saul Nyland, who had targeted his victim over Facebook (and when blocked, via telephone) over a six-month period. This harassment not only involved disablist hate speech, but also involved death threats towards the disabled victim. The case was successfully prosecuted as a disability hate crime (Crown Prosecution Service, 2016).

Another law which may be violated by hate speech, according to ARTICLE 19, is the Public Order Act 1986 (Sections 4 and 5). That Act prohibits people from using threatening, abusive, or insulting words or behaviour that cause, or are likely to cause, another person harassment, alarm, or distress. Section 5 prohibits displaying any writing, sign, or other visible representation which is threatening, abusive, or insulting within the hearing or sight of a person likely to be caused harassment, alarm, or distress, whether in a public or a private place.

Other laws regulating communication may also include some hate speech. The Malicious Communications Act 1988 makes it an offence to send to another person any message, letter, email, photograph, or recording which is indecent, grossly offensive, false and known or believed to be false, or which conveys a threat. Similarly, under Section 127 of Communications Act 2003, it is an offence to make improper use of a public electronic communications network, such as by sending grossly offensive, indecent obscene, menacing, or annoying phone calls, emails, or other electronic communications.

There are also penalty-enhancement mechanisms for offences motivated by hostility towards the victim based upon disability, sexual orientation, or transgender identity within Section 146 of the Criminal Justice Act 2003. Other UK laws which may also be violated in the context of hate speech include the Crime and Disorder Act 1998 for racially or religiously aggravated offences and the Terrorism Act 2006 which makes it an offence to disseminate terrorist material, either intentionally or recklessly.

Canada

Canada is an example of a country which has both a comprehensive Charter of Rights and Freedoms that expressly protects freedom of speech alongside a criminal justice system which penalizes hate speech. The Canadian Charter of Rights and Freedoms is a part of the Constitution of Canada and it outlines fundamental freedoms, democratic rights, mobility rights, legal rights, equality rights, and language rights. The Charter has been described as a "uniquely Canadian document" (Monahan, 1987, p. 74). It expressly protects "freedom of thought, belief, opinion and expression, including freedom of the press and other media of communication." However, the Canadian legal system interprets these freedoms within a broader context – one which recognizes that some limits can be placed on certain rights and freedoms in the context of a free and democratic society. This practice of situating hate speech in terms of broader cultural and political values associated with the right to human dignity is similar in some respects to the treatment of hate speech in Europe.

> Canadian courts have stated that expression will be protected if it is focused on: (i) seeking and attaining truth; (ii) encouraging participation in social and political decision-making; and (iii) cultivating diversity in forms of individual self-fulfillment and human flourishing.
>
> (Ontario Justice Education Network, 2019)

Canada's hate speech laws began with limited scope – seeking to prohibit the propaganda being distributed in the 1960s racist and white supremacist groups (Walker, 2010). However, the range of areas they cover has greatly expanded over time. The Canadian Criminal Code prohibits advocating genocide against any identifiable group (and the term "identifiable group" includes mental or physical disability, as well as colour, race, religion, ethnic origin, or sexual orientation, gender identity or expression). It also criminalizes publicly inciting hatred likely to lead to a breach of the peace, and wilfully promoting hatred. Spoken, printed, and online material can be prosecutable under Canada's laws. Hate propaganda can also be seized by Canadian authorities.

There are specific defences to promoting hatred which are set out in the Canadian Criminal Code. A person will not be convicted if the statements were true; if they expressed an opinion in good faith about a religious subject or an opinion based on a belief in a religious text; if they concerned a matter of public interest or were for the public benefit, and if the person believed them to be true; or if the person intended to point out matters producing hatred so that they could be removed.

United States

The US Constitution has been interpreted as providing specific protection for hate speech, which is regarded as fundamentally different from hate crime (Gerstenfeld, 2017; Lawrence, 1992; Winer, 1992). Hate speech, US Courts have found, is simply a form of expression. It is not illegal in any context. Even when they involve burning a cross or displaying a Nazi swastika – acts which would undeniably be recognized as being both an example of hate speech and hate crime in other countries – US courts have consistently upheld the legality of such acts by regarding them simply as a form of expression that is protected under the constitutional right to free speech (Winer, 1992). As a result, hate speech against disabled people flourishes in the US.

The law is an incredibly conservative institution in countries such as the US. In terms of this discussion, such conservatism means that judicial decisions often reflect the broader social context of prejudice against disabled people. An infamous American case involving such disablist hate speech at the US Supreme Court demonstrates disablist hate speech that was used by the court. In his decision, US Supreme Court Justice Oliver Wendell Holmes Jr. stated, "three generations of imbeciles are enough" (Supreme Court of the United States, 1927). That case became the legal precedent used for 60,000 additional sterilizations throughout the US (Lombardo, 1985). Such disablist hate speech – and the horrendous human rights implications it can have when utilized as the basis for a decision – demonstrates that the courts can not only accept, but actively adopt and promote disablism. This decision, linked to the widespread acceptance of Social Darwinism in the 20th Century, led to the identification, institutionalization, and sterilization of thousands of people who were deemed "defective," "unfit," and "degenerate." (Not to mention that such eugenic ideas were used to justify the millions of disabled people killed by the Nazis.)

Disablist hate speech is often intersectional – it is commonly combined with racist, sexist, anti-Semitic, and other forms of hatred (Sherry, 2010). For example, throughout US history, immigrants have often been likened to disabled people in order to suggest they are "defective" (Baynton, 2016). Indeed, immigration law in the US historically was specifically designed to prevent disabled people from entering the country, as they were perceived as a drain on the nation's resources. Disability, in this judicial and policy context, was the antithesis of the nation (for more on this discursive construction of disability and the nation, see Sherry, 2007). But the disability movement has challenged such discourses, and markers of its success include the Americans with Disabilities Act and other legislation protecting the rights of disabled people. In terms of the focus of this chapter, disability was included as a protected category in Federal hate crime laws under the Matthew Shepard and James Byrd, Jr. Hate Crimes Prevention Act of 2009. While this law does not (and constitutionally cannot) punish hate speech, such hate speech may be evidence of motivation that can be used in the prosecution of hate crimes.

China

The Chinese Constitution prohibits hate speech on the basis of religion, gender, or ethnicity. Like the previous examples discussed earlier, disability is omitted. The hierarchy of hate is present in China as well, but there are also unique legislative and judicial dynamics which deserve attention. For instance, there is no Chinese statute that defines hate speech and describes punishments that apply to it; there are different regulations and interpretations of laws in different parts of China

(Xu & Cai, 2019). Some of the regulations which could in theory cover disablist hate speech (but do not in practice) include the Regulations on the Administration of Publication, Regulations on the Administration of Radio and Television, and Regulations on the Administration of Movies. These regulations all use the same phrases, and they prohibit the following:

(1) Contents which defy the basic principles determined in the Constitution;
(2) Contents which endanger the unity of the nation, sovereignty, or territorial integrity;
(3) Contents which divulge secrets of the State, endanger national security or damage the honour or benefits of the State;
(4) Contents which incite the nation to hatred or discrimination, undermine the solidarity of the nation, or infringe upon national customs and habits;
(5) Contents which propagate evil cults or superstition;
(6) Contents which disturb the public order or destroy the public stability;
(7) Contents which propagate obscenity, gambling, violence or instigate crimes;
(8) Contents which insult or slander others, or infringe upon the lawful rights and interests of others;
(9) Contents which endanger public ethics or the fine folk cultural traditions;
(10) Other contents prohibited by laws, regulations, or provisions of the State.

In practice, there are three (sometimes competing) approaches applied by various judiciaries and the state in China, according to Fu (2019, p. 1):

> There is first of all a political approach that treats hate speech primarily as a national security issue that may threaten the legitimacy of the Chinese state. Secondly, there is a legal approach that treats hate speech primarily as a violation of law, especially criminal law. Finally, there is a rights-based approach which treats hate speech as a rights issue in the larger context of ethnic relations.

The Chinese political system involves heavy censorship in general, and there are many (formal and informal, legal and extra-legal) repercussions for speech acts deemed intolerable, even if disability is not recognized as one of the areas where hate speech may occur. However, the term 殘廢 (informally understood as useless cripple) is widely used throughout China, both at official and unofficial levels, but it is slowly being replaced in some contexts alongside other disability hate speech (Wang, 2016; 来源： 新华网, 2008).

India

In India, hate speech laws are designed for protecting identities such as religion, nationality, and caste/class; disability is completely omitted. Section 153A of the Indian Penal Code provides for punishment for verbal and written hate speech "on grounds of religion, race, place of birth, residence, language, caste or community." Similarly, Section 295(A) of the Indian Penal Code also punishes deliberate and malicious hate speech with religious motivations. This omission of disability among the protected categories in hate speech legislation mirrors a wider marginalization of disabled people more broadly in India. Prejudice and discrimination against disabled people in India is still widespread (Bhattashali, Ostrosky, & Monda-Amaya, 2018; Kayama, Johnstone, & Limaye, 2019; Loganathan & Murthy, 2011; Mathias et al., 2018; Paul, 2018). Such discriminatory attitudes can have the effect of (at least tacitly) reducing the perceived severity of such crimes.

Even serious crimes such as sexual assault against disabled women are not appropriately prosecuted in India and, in many cases, they are not even recorded in medical records (Chandra, Carey, Carey, Shalinianant, & Thomas, 20w 503; Dawn, 2014). In a cultural context where serious crimes against disabled people are not regarded as equivalent to crimes against nondisabled people, it is little wonder that disabled people are not given appropriate protection when it comes to crimes that may be considered less severe, such as hate speech. However, multiple rapes and violent assaults (particularly against non-speaking deaf women and children) have gained significant media attention in India recently; perhaps the tide towards equality is turning with regard to such crimes (Hearth, 2018; India.com News Desk, 2018; Indian Express News Service, 2018; Storypickers, 2018; United News of India, 2018). Nevertheless, there are no signs that disablist hate speech is even on the political radar in India. This absence of disability within the categories of hate speech is not an anomaly – far from it. As this chapter suggests, the informal hierarchy of hate recognition means that disability is largely ignored.

South Africa

South Africa is another country which does not specifically address disablist hatred in its Constitution, although it does mention other forms of hate. Its Constitution protects freedom of expression with certain exceptions, including advocating hatred based on race, ethnicity, gender, or religion. However, a separate Act has (at the time of writing) been tabled in Parliament for debate which will greatly expand the prohibitions on hate speech. "The Prevention and Combating of Hate Crimes and Hate Speech Bill," introduced in the National Assembly on 29 March 2018, is currently being debated (Northglen News, 2019 "Prevention and Combating of Hate Crimes and Hate Speech Bill, 2018"). It specifically prohibits hate speech on many grounds, including disability, albinism, and HIV status. There are some exceptions to this law, but in general, the Act is expansive and clearly identifies state responsibilities with regard to prosecution, prevention, and administration. To conclude, South African laws regarding disability hate speech are in a state of flux and the outcome of the current debates will determine the degree to which South Africa enacts protections from disablist hate speech – or not.

Conclusion

This chapter has summarized the ways in which disablist hate speech has (or has not) been included in national laws and international treaties. It has suggested that there is an informal hierarchy of recognition in terms of different forms of hate speech, and disability has been relegated to an afterthought in many instances. Many countries still do not include disablist hate speech in laws that prohibit other forms of hate speech. Human rights treaties and international agreements have promised to protect the rights of disabled people, but this promise has largely not been met when it comes to disablist hate speech. As this chapter has demonstrated, disablist hate speech is a widespread global problem, but legislative and judicial responses to it have been largely inadequate. There are some positive developments (for instance, the debates around including disablist hate speech in South African laws), but it is far too early to tell whether these laws will even be enacted, let alone how they will be implemented or monitored.

Note

1 One of the reasons why eugenics may not be seen as a specific component of totalitarian ideologies could be that they were also influential in liberal democracies (Berson & Cruz, 2001; Kerr & Shakespeare, 2002; Lombardo, 1996; Snyder & Mitchell, 2010).

References

ARTICLE 19 (2018). *United Kingdom (England and Wales): Responding to "hate speech"*. London: ARTICLE 19.

Baynton, D. C. (2016). *Defectives in the Land: Disability and Immigration in the Age of Eugenics*. Chicago, IL: University of Chicago Press.

Benton, A., & Dionne, K. Y. (2015). International political economy and the 2014 West African Ebola outbreak. *African Studies Review*, *58*(1), 223–236.

Berson, M. J., & Cruz, B. (2001). Eugenics past and present. *Social Education*, *65*(5), 300-306.

Bhattashali, A., Ostrosky, M. M., & Monda-Amaya, L. (2018). Perceptions of typically developing children in India about their siblings with disabilities. *International Journal of Inclusive Education*, *22*(12), 1257–1271.

Biesold, H. (1999). *Crying Hands: Eugenics and Deaf People in Nazi Germany*. Washington DC: Gallaudet University Press.

Bleich, E. (2011). The rise of hate speech and hate crime laws in liberal democracies. *Journal of Ethnic and Migration Studies*, *37*(6), 917–934.

Calvert, C. (1997). Hate speech and its harms: A communication theory perspective. *Journal of Communication*, *47*(1), 4–19.

Chandra, P. S., Carey, M. P., Carey, K. B., Shalinianant, A., & Thomas, T. (2003). Sexual coercion and abuse among women with a severe mental illness in India: An exploratory investigation. *Comprehensive Psychiatry*, *44*(3), 205–212.

Conroy, C. (2013). Paralympic cultures: Disability as paradigm. *Contemporary Theatre Review*, *23*(4), 519–531.

Council of Europe Committee of Ministers. (1997). Recommendation No. R (97) 20 of the Committee of Ministers to Member States on 'Hate Speech' (Adopted by the

Committee of Ministers on 30 October 1997 at the 607th meeting of the Ministers' Deputies), Council of Europe, Strasbourg.

Council of the European Union Framework. (2008). *Decision 2008/913/JHA of 28 November on Combating Certain Forms and Expressions of Racism and Xenophobia by Means of Criminal Law*.

Cram, I. (2006). *Contested Words: Legal Restrictions on Freedom of Speech in Liberal Democracies*. Aldershot: Ashgate.

Crown Prosecution Service. (2016, 27 January). Man sentenced to six weeks imprisonment for harassing victim because of disability. Retrieved from https://blog.cps.gov.uk/2016/01/man-sentenced-to-six-weeks-imprisonment-for-harassing-victim-because-of-disability.html

Davidson, T., Warmsley, D., Macy, M., & Weber, I. (2017, May 15–May 18). *Automated Hate Speech Detection and the Problem of Offensive Language*. Paper presented at the Eleventh International AAAI Conference on Web and Social Media. Montreal, Quebec.

Dawn, R. (2014). "Our lives, our identity": Women with disabilities in India. *Disability and Rehabilitation, 36*(21), 1768–1773.

De Grillo, F., & Stimolo, S. (2017, 21 August). *Multato per sosta in zona disabili, insulta il portatore di handicap*. Retrieved from https://www.ilgiorno.it/martesana/cronaca/cartello-disabile-parcheggio-1.3344504

Deal, M. (2007). Aversive disablism: Subtle prejudice toward disabled people. *Disability and Society, 22*(1), 93–107.

Di Merlo, G. (2018, 29 October). *L'insulto della disabilità: Uno "spettacolo" che si ripete da secoli*. Retrieved from http://www.superando.it/2018/10/26/linsulto-della-disabilita-uno-spettacolo-che-si-ripete-da-secoli/.

Farmer, P. (2001). *Infections and Inequalities: The Modern Plagues*. Berkeley, CA: University of California Press.

Farmer, P. (2006). *AIDS and Accusation: Haiti and the Geography of Blame, Updated with a New Preface* (2nd ed.). Berkeley, CA: University of California Press.

Farrior, S. (1996). Molding the matrix: The historical and theoretical foundations of international law concerning hate speech. *Berkeley Journal of International Law, 14*(1), 1–98.

Fefelov, V. (1986). *V SSSR Invalidov net!* London: Overseas Publications Interchange.

Findlay, C. (2017, May 1). *Disability Slurs Are as Damaging as Racism and Homophobia*. Retrieved from https://www.smh.com.au/opinion/disability-slurs-are-a-damaging-as-racism-and-homophobia-20170501-gvw8v3.html

Friedländer, S. (1998). *Nazi Germany and the Jews Volume I: The Years of Persecution, 1933-1939*. London: Phoenix.

Fu, H. (2019). *China's Hate Speech Conundrum*. New York and Geneva: United Nations Office of the High Commissioner Retrieved from https://www.ohchr.org/Documents/Issues/Expression/ICCPR/Bangkok/FuHualing.pdf.

Gerstenfeld, P. B. (2017). *Hate Crimes: Causes, Controls, and Controversies* (4th ed.). Los Angeles, CA: Sage Publications.

Grech, S. (2015). Decolonising Eurocentric disability studies: Why colonialism matters in the disability and global South debate. *Social Identities, 21*(1), 6–21.

Grigorenko, E. L. (1998). Russian "Defectology" anticipating perestroika in the field. *Journal of Learning Disabilities, 31*(2), 193–207.

Hearth, K. (2018, 27 July). Deaf children targeted for sexual crimes. Retrieved from https://www.mnnonline.org/news/deaf-children-targeted-for-sexual-crimes/.

Heinze, E. (2009). Cumulative jurisprudence and human rights: The example of sexual minorities and hate speech. *The International Journal of Human Rights*, *13*(2–3), 193–209.

Heinze, E. (2016). *Hate Speech and Democratic Citizenship*. Oxford: Oxford University Press.

Idoiaga Mondragon, N., Gil de Montes, L., & Valencia, J. (2017). Understanding an Ebola outbreak: Social representations of emerging infectious diseases. *Journal of Health Psychology*, *22*(7), 951–960.

India.com News Desk. (2018, 13 April). Several deaf and mute girls sexually assaulted at Karjat School; caretaker arrested. Retrieved from https://www.india.com/news/india/maharashtra-several-deaf-and-mute-girls-sexually-assaulted-by-caretaker-at-boarding-school-in-karjat-2997953/

Indian Express News Service. (2018, 5 November 8:38 AM). Deaf and dumb woman sexually assaulted. Retrieved from http://www.newindianexpress.com/states/odisha/2018/nov/05/deaf-and-dumb-woman-sexually-assaulted-1894468.html

Kayama, M., Johnstone, C., & Limaye, S. (2019). Adjusting the "self" in social interaction: Disability and stigmatization in India. *Children and Youth Services Review*, *96*, 463–474.

Kerr, A., & Shakespeare, T. (2002). *Genetic Politics: From Eugenics to Genome*. Cheltenham: New Clarion Press.

Klubička, F., & Fernández, R. (2018). Examining a hate speech corpus for hate speech detection and popularity prediction. Retrieved from https://arxiv.org/pdf/1805.04661.pdf

Kudlick, C. J. (2003). Disability history: Why we need another "other". *The American Historical Review*, *108*(3), 763–793.

Lawrence, F. M. (1992). Resolving the hate crimes/hate speech paradox: Punishing bias crimes and protecting racist speech. *Notre Dame Law Review*, *68*, 673–721.

Lega Per, I, & Diritti, D. (2016, 24 February). Persone con disabilità *Discriminazione, LEDHA riconosciuta parte civile*. Retrieved from http://ledha.it/page.asp?menu1=12&menu2=29&notizia=5863&page=1

Loganathan, S., & Murthy, R. S. (2011). Living with schizophrenia in India: Gender perspectives. *Transcultural Psychiatry*, *48*(5), 569–584.

Lombardo, P. A. (1985). Three generations, no imbeciles: New light on buck v. bell. *New York University Law Review*, *30*, 30–62.

Lombardo, P. A. (1996). Medicine, eugenics, and the Supreme Court: From coercive sterilization to reproductive freedom. *The Journal of Contemporary Health Law and Policy*, *13*(1), 1–25.

Mathias, K., Kermode, M., Goicolea, I., Seefeldt, L., Shidhaye, R., & San Sebastian, M. (2018). Social distance and community attitudes Towards people with psycho-social disabilities in Uttarakhand, India. *Community Mental Health Journal*, *54*(3), 343–353.

McCauley, M., Minsky, S., & Viswanath, K. (2013). The H1N1 pandemic: Media frames, stigmatization and coping. *BMC Public Health*, *13*(1), 1116.

Monahan, P. J. (1987). *Politics and the Constitution: The Charter, Federalism, and the Supreme Court of Canada*. Toronto: Carswell.

Mostert, M. P. (2002). Useless eaters: Disability as genocidal marker in Nazi Germany. *The Journal of Special Education*, *36*(3), 157–170.

Northglen News. (2019, 13 January). *Have Your Say on Hate Speech Bill*. Retrieved from https://northglennews.co.za/144695/say-hate-speech-bill/

Ontario Justice Education Network. (2019). Freedom of Expression, Wilful Promotion of Hatred and the Charter of Rights and Freedoms: R v. Keegstra. Retrieved from http://ojen.ca/wp-content/uploads/Keegstra-English.pdf

Organization for Security and Co-operation in Europe. (2019a). Bias against other groups – People with disabilities. Retrieved from http://hatecrime.osce.org/what-hate-crime/bias-against-other-groups-%E2%80%93-people-disabilities

Organization for Security and Co-operation in Europe. (2019b). Poland. Retrieved from http://hatecrime.osce.org/poland

Paul, S. (2018). Are we doing enough? Stigma, discrimination and human rights violations of people living with schizophrenia in India: Implications for social work practice. *Social Work in Mental Health, 16*(2), 145–171.

Phillips, S. D. (2009). "There are no invalids in the USSR!" A missing Soviet chapter in the new disability history. *Disability Studies Quarterly, 29*(3). Retrieved from http://www.dsq-sds.org/article/view/936/11

Prevention and Combating of Hate Crimes and Hate Speech Bill. (2018, 29 March) (As introduced in the National Assembly (proposed section 75) – Bill published in *Government Gazette No. 41543*.

Pryal, K. R. G. (2017, 3 August). Still screaming, but not over nothing. Retrieved from https://chroniclevitae.com/news/1871-still-screaming-but-not-over-nothing

Ratouis, A. (2016, 5 December). Choisissez bien vos insultes! Retrieved from https://www.lepoint.fr/choisissez-bien-vos-insultes-12-05-2016-2038728_19.php

Reeve, D. (2012). Psycho-emotional disablism in the lives of people experiencing mental distress. In J. Anderson, B. Sapey, & H. Spandler (Eds.), *Distress or Disability?* Proceedings of a symposium held at Lancaster Disability, 15–16 November 2011 (pp. 24–29). Lancaster: Centre for Disability Research, Lancaster University.

Rosenfeld, M. (2002). Hate speech in constitutional jurisprudence: A comparative analysis. *Cardozo Law Review, 24*, 1523–1567.

Santiago-Irizarry, V. (2001). *Medicalizing Ethnicity: The Construction of Latino Identity in a Psychiatric Setting*. New York, NY: Cornell University Press.

Sherry, M. (2007). (Post) Colonizing disability. *Wagadu: A Journal of Transnational and Women's Studies, 3*, 10–23.

Sherry, M. (2010). *Disability Hate Crimes: Does Anyone Really Hate Disabled People?* Surrey: Ashgate.

Sherry, M. (2014). The promise of human rights for disabled people and the reality of neoliberalism. In M. Gill & C. Schlund-Vials (Eds.), *Disability, Human Rights and Humanitarianism* (pp. 15–26). Surrey, England: Ashgate Publishing.

Smedley, B. D., Stith, A. Y., & Nelson, A. R. (2002). *Unequal Treatment: Confronting Racial and Ethnic Disparities in Healthcare*. Washington, DC: The Institute of Medicine.

Snyder, S. L., & Mitchell, D. T. (2010). *Cultural Locations of Disability*. Chicago, IL: University of Chicago Press.

Storypickers (2018, 13 April). Caretaker of a Mumbai deaf and mute home sexually assaulted all minor students, Arrested. Retrieved from https://www.storypick.com/deaf-mute-girls-molested-mumbai/

Strossen, N. (2018). *Hate: Why We Should Resist It with Free Speech, Not Censorship.* New York, NY: Oxford University Press.

Supreme Court of the United States. (1927). *Buck v. Bell*, 274 U.S. 200. In.

Swinton, J. (2012). Disability, ableism, and disablism. In B. J. Miller-McLemore (Ed.), *The Wiley-Blackwell Companion to Practical Theology* (pp. 443–451). Hoboken, NJ: Wiley Blackwell.

Tseis, A. (2009). Dignity and speech: The regulation of hate speech in a democracy. *Wake Forest Law Review, 44*, 497–532.

Turda, M. (2015). *The History of East-Central European Eugenics, 1900–1945: Sources and Commentaries*. London: Bloomsbury Publishing.

Turda, M., & Weindling, P. (2007). *"Blood and homeland": Eugenics and Racial Nationalism in Central and Southeast Europe, 1900-1940*. Budapest: Central European University Press.

United Nations Human Rights Office of the High Commissioner. (2014). *The Core International Human Rights Treaties*. New York and Geneva: United Nations.

United News of India. (2018, 10 August). MP hostel rape: 2 more girls lodge complaints. Retrieved from http://www.uniindia.com/mp-hostel-rape-2-more-girls-lodge-complaints/states/news/1315629.html

Walker, J. (2010). *Section 13 of the Canadian Human Rights Act, Anti-Hate Laws and Freedom of Expression*. Ottawa: Library of Parliament.

Walker, S. (1994). *Hate Speech: The History of an American Controversy*. Lincoln, NE: University of Nebraska Press.

Wang, Y. (2016, 7 March). A glance at people with disabilities in China. Retrieved from https://www.chinasource.org/resource-library/articles/a-glance-at-people-with-disabilities-in-china

Warner, W., & Hirschberg, J. (2012). Detecting hate speech on the world wide web. Paper presented at the Proceedings of the Second Workshop on Language in Social Media, Montreal, Canada.

Winer, A. S. (1992). R.A.V. v. City of St. Paul, 112 S. Ct. 2538. *William Mitchell Law Review*, *18*, 971–978.

Xu, J., & Cai, S. (2019). Online Intermediary Liability for Hate Speech under Chinese Laws. Retrieved from https://www.law.uw.edu/media/.../china-intermediary-liability-of-isps-hate-speech.pdf

来源：新华网 (2008, 12 September). 从"残废人"到"残疾人"--一字之差 天壤之别. Retrieved from https://www.law.uw.edu/media/140454/china-intermediary-liability-of-isps-hate-speech.pdf

2 Disablist hate speech online

Mark Sherry

This chapter will begin by exploring the nature of disablist hate speech over the internet, using examples of some of the most common words that are used as slurs against disabled people. Then it will discuss the different manifestations of online hate, including cyberbullying, cyberstalking, doxxing, and more. The laws covering such speech acts are often distinct from hate speech laws – indeed, even when hate speech laws do not exist, such acts are often prohibited. Awareness of these laws (as well as those discussed in the previous chapter) can be useful for opponents of disablist hate speech. The chapter will also highlight the case of Sophia Weaver and her mother Natalie, who have been relentlessly trolled by people with online disablist hate. The case is an excellent example both of the viciousness of online hatred, but also the resilience of disabled people and their families, and their determination to make online spaces safer. The chapter then discusses the options open to individuals and groups who wish to respond to hate speech online. These options range from ignoring, blocking, or reporting the posts (or poster) to engaging in counternarratives or alternative narratives. Next, the chapter will outline the policies of social media companies and internet providers to such speech and will also discuss "hate speech havens" where hate speech flourishes in online echo chambers. Finally, some of the emerging challenges in responding to hate speech (such as hate speech generated by bots) are considered.

The nature of disablist hate speech online

At first glance, it might seem easy to spot disablist hate speech on the internet. The most well-known terms expressing disablist hate speech online match those in the offline world. In English, terms such as "retard," "spastic," "cripple," "gimp," and "mongol" are among those words used to wound disabled people. Each of those terms may have variants. Variants of the retard slur include calling people "tards," "retardees," or "ree-rees." An additional slur might be added, alongside the disability hatred, such as the term "Jewtard" which combines both disablist and anti-Semitic hate. The term "retard" might also be written in a language other than English, such as "palerma" (a variant of retard in Portuguese) or "retrasado mental" in Spanish. Other terms which denigrate disabled people on the basis of intelligence may also be used in English or in other languages. Disablist hate speech involving the use of the English terms "imbecile,"` "stupid," and "idiot," have parallels in many other countries (for instance, the parallel Portuguese terms "imbécil," "estúpido," and "idiota," or "idiotismo").

The reason why detecting disablist hate speech online is so important is because, in the words of Citron (2014, p. 16), "hate expresses something uniquely damaging." Avivo, an Australian disability organization which campaigns against "the R word" has stated:

> The word appears on social media approximately every 5 seconds. And few people question the use of it as everyday language. But the R word is incredibly offensive, hurtful and demeaning. Not just to people with intellectual and physical disability, but to the friends, families and carers of these people.
> (Avivo, 2019)

Avivo's website has embedded technology with a rolling count of how many times the word "retard" has been used in the previous 7 days. On the day of writing (21 February 2019), that count was over 120,000. Avivo's approach is similar to one which might be adopted by an inexperienced scholar: simply search for a particularly vile word associated with disability, and when you find it online, notice how it is often used as a weapon against people. The hate soaks through the words spoken or the images displayed. Count the total number of times the word is used, and you get a good overview of the extent of disability hate speech online.

But it is also necessary to consider the context in which words are used. For instance, it is possible to use the word "retard" in a way that has nothing to do with disability (such as in the phrase "to retard the progress" of something). Some of the difficulties associated with identifying hate speech which have been identified in the literature include different dictions, the use of artificially manipulated or merged terms as insults, context-specific meanings, and the use of sarcasm (Köffer, Riehle, Höhenberger, & Becker, 2018, p. 85). An example of manipulating the hate term being identified or censored is the use of euphemisms, variations and derivatives of words instead of using the word itself, specifically to avoid deletion by automatic detection programs on social media (Agbedejobi, 2017; Magu & Luo, 2018). Recently, the author saw an online conversation explicitly aimed at teaching a newcomer how to avoid such detection. The person was instructed to use "retread" instead of "retard" in victimizing a particular disabled person.

One way that opponents of hate speech have been able to flag and record the use of such terms is through online crowdsourcing. Through such crowdsourcing, people have provided a more coherent, context-specific overview of the use of hate speech. An example of a crowdsourced hate speech database is Hatebase, https://hatebase.org. The Hatebase database is timestamped and geotagged so that the use of the term is monitored for frequency, localization, migration, and transformation. Hatebase illustrates one of the unique elements of online hate: while the use of disablist hate speech in the offline world is impossible to quantify, the online world offers much more possibilities for quantifying hate speech, analyzing its components, identifying its origins.

Regional patterns for hate speech emerge from the Hatebase data. In order to identify global patterns in such hate speech, Hatebase is a multi-lingual platform. This is a useful attribute in the study of disability hate speech, because there are many variations of disablist slurs due to language differences. A good example is the word "Mong." It is a disablist slur which is often attributed to people with intellectual disabilities. On Hatebase, it is possible to identify cases where people have used this term in disablist hate speech, alongside other reported variations of the word. There are separate citations and geolocations for the use of the following words in disablist hate speech: "Mong," "Mongs," "Mongol" (in English), "Mongolo" (in Spanish), "Mongool" (in Dutch), and "Mongo" (in Swedish).

Because people identify the specific site and occasion when such hate speech is used, the database avoids the problems with the broader approach adopted by Avivo, where every use of the term is counted. In the case of the word "Mong," the word's meaning in some Asian languages is completely the opposite, conveying love, hope, or good. Such uses of the word would not be reported to (or recorded) on the Hatebase database, since it is crowdsourced, based on the specific use of the term. (A later section of this chapter will include a discussion of the use of automated detection technology to identify online hate speech.)

People who report hate speech on the Hatebase database are asked to consider four questions before adding a term to the database. The questions are quoted directly below:

1. Does it refer to a specific group of people or is it a generalized insult? If the latter, it's probably not hate speech.
2. Can it potentially be used with malicious intent? If not, it's probably not hate speech.
3. Are there objective third-party sources online which can be used as citations? If not, it's probably not hate speech.
4. If you were to write a program which monitors hate speech on Twitter, would finding it in a random tweet be potentially meaningful? If not, it's probably not hate speech (Hatebase, 2013).

Different types of online disablist hate speech

Disability hate speech is manifested in many different types of hateful, harassing, predatory, or otherwise hostile forms of online utterances. This section of the chapter will now outline some of the most common forms of disablist hate speech: trolling, flaming, RIP trolling, cyberbullying, cyberstalking, swatting, online impersonation, doxxing, online sexual solicitation, and the use of graphic images as weapons against people who have photosensitive epilepsy. Each of these forms of online hate (and the ways in which they are used against disabled people) will now be described. It is important to be aware of these different manifestations of hate because some of them are specifically prohibited in laws beyond the realm of hate speech.

Trolling and flaming are perhaps the most common forms of disability hate and harassment. Trolling and flaming are the terms used to describe attempts to provoke or offend participants in discussions, or to divert conversations into pointless arguments; they are particularly common in the forums of groups experiencing social inequality (Herring, Job-Sluder, Scheckler, & Barab, 2002). Neither trolling nor flaming are illegal, and they are more common than other forms of online harassment, but are usually ignored completely by social media companies (Karppi, 2013). Trolling is often done as a source of amusement for the troll (or as they call it, 'for the lulz') (Mantilla, 2015). But even though trolling is legal, it still can be particularly hurtful – especially when people engage in "RIP trolling." RIP trolling involves mocking, disrespectful, or demeaning comments about deceased persons on memorial sites, or making fake profiles of the dead person or their relatives in order to mock or demean them (Karppi, 2013). It is always important to consider the intersection of various identities in assessing internet harassment – Bishop (2014) highlights the fact that most victims of "RIP trolling" are female. Many were also disabled before their deaths.

Sometimes online disablist hate speech is called "cyberbullying." Even though its definition is commonly contested, "cyberbullying" is the most common term used to describe the online harassment of children (Bottino, Bottino, Regina, Correia, & Ribeiro, 2015; Kofoed & Staksrud, 2019; Olweus & Limber, 2018; Ovejero, Yubero, Larrañaga, & Moral, 2016; Selkie, Fales, & Moreno, 2016). One simple and easy to understand definition is that "Cyberbullying is defined as an intentional online act via electronic media, to harm, embarrass and/or humiliate another person" (Heiman, Olenik-Shemesh, & Eden, 2015, p. 15). Cyberbullying is different from offline bullying in a number of ways. Henry (2013) explains that cyberbullying can be encountered whether the victim is at home or not (there is no safe space against victimization if the person is online); it extends to a much wider audience than the usual victim-perpetrator encounter; and the effects of cyberbullying (such as photos, video images, or other content) can go viral and become almost impossible to remove.

Cyberbullying is commonly directed at disabled people (Kowalski & Fedina, 2011; Wells & Mitchell, 2014) and also seems to have more harmful effects on them than their nondisabled peers (Kowalski, Morgan, Drake-Lavelle, & Allison, 2016). People with different impairments may experience different combinations of cyberbullying as well as offline bullying (Wells, Mitchell, Jones, & Turner, 2018). Hall (2019) further argues due to various disabling barriers, disabled people may rely on the online interactions more than nondisabled people and online hatred and harassment therefore harms them far more.

"Cyberstalking" is another term that may be used to describe online disablist hate speech. Cyberstalking it has been defined as:

> a group of behaviours in which an individual, group of individuals or organisation, uses information and communications technology to harass one or more individuals. Such behaviours may include, but are not limited to, the transmission of threats and false accusations, identity theft, data theft,

> damage to data or equipment, computer monitoring, me solicitation of minors for sexual purposes and confrontation.
>
> (Bocij & McFarlane, 2002, p. 38)

A summary of all cyberstalking and cyberbullying laws is beyond the scope of this chapter, but it is worth noting that many countries have laws specifically prohibiting these acts (including Australia, the Philippines, India, New Zealand, South Africa, Singapore, Poland, and the US) and they also are covered under anti-harassment or cybercrime laws in other jurisdictions (such as Canada and the UK). This is an important point because even in the US, where there is a right to hate speech, there are still laws against cyberstalking under broader stalking, violence, harassment, and slander laws.

Swatting – making a false report to the police in order to get them to visit a victim – is another form of cyberbullying (or a manifestation of hate) which contravenes other laws about making a false police report (Jaffe, 2016). Online impersonation, which is another form of online harassment that is illegal, will be discussed later in the chapter with regard to the experiences of Sophia Weaver.

Another form of online harassment which may be covered under other laws is doxxing. "Doxxing" involves publishing private information such as a home address, employer, or phone number. It seems that this is a particular form of misogynist hate aimed almost exclusively at women, which is often accompanied by threats of rape, assault, and even murder (Buni & Chemaly, 2014; Harmer & Lumsden, 2019; Wu, 2015). These types of misogynist online activities have been called "gendertrolling" – something that "happens to women because they are women" (Mantilla, 2015, p. 147). Young girls are commonly victim of such practices – even the teenage daughter of a political opponent has been doxxed by protestors (Colton, Holmes, & Walwema, 2017). This combination of age and gender raises the issue of the use of the internet against children.

Other forms of harmful and hateful speech, such as the sexual solicitation of disabled women and children, also occur. It is important to note that that disabled children in special education seem to be at increased risk of such sexual predation (Wells et al., 2018). After predatory grooming and the solicitation of naked pictures, this material is sometimes shared online accompanied by terms that suggest the victim is repulsive because of their disability status. These hateful acts are usually covered under broader laws concerning internet sexual predation rather than hate speech.

The sharing of such photographs highlights a unique element of online disablist hate speech: the fact that the photo itself is considered proof of a person's lack of dignity and humanity. A common expression of such hate is to turn the photo into a meme (misrepresenting themselves as speaking from the voice of the disabled person) saying "Kill me." Such photos are usually aimed at women with intellectual disabilities, and when posted among a community of like-minded people, they elicit comments condemning the person as unworthy of life and a burden on others. In response to one such photo, posters often reply with additional pictures of other disabled people whose appearance is also seen as enough to warrant derision, mockery, demeaning comments, and hate. In such online disablist hate speech, the victim's image is sometimes accompanied by their name. The long-term harm done by this type of viral hatred towards disabled people and their families is unknown; research simply has not been done with the victims.

Amputees – and women who are amputees in particular - are also commonly subject to significant online (as well as offline) harassment by stalkers (Bruno, 1997; Kafer, 2004; Williams, 2017). Their photos are often shared online without their consent, and many have received unsolicited sexual advances as well as online hatred as a result (DysNet: The Online Dysmelia Community, 2013). Such hatred often uses the language of freakery. Disabled people's embodiment, as represented in such photographs, is seen as enough evidence to deserve condemnation and hate. Unlike other forms of online hatred, in which photos of the victim of hate are almost always surrounded in narratives (such as those that frame the target group as dangerous or immoral), disability photographs are seen as enough evidence in themselves to warrant obscene remarks, derision, and comments suggesting they deserve to die.

Online hate has real effects offline. Another unique element of disablist hate speech online (as opposed to other forms of online hate) is the use of specific information technologies that are designed to trigger those with medical conditions. One way that such harm has been done is through the hacking of the websites of epilepsy organizations. In these hateful attacks, hackers infect the websites of epilepsy organizations with programs that create flashing animations. Such animations trigger seizures among people with photosensitive epilepsy. This type of hacking has been done for many years – it seems to have been first reported during Epilepsy Awareness Month in 2007 (which itself may indicate targeted animosity) but many more people and organizations have been targeted since then (Ehrenfreund & Olivo, 2017; Joh, 2016; Popa, 2008; Ramadge, 2009; Wagenseil, 2008).

In one case of online disablist hate speech, a journalist whose epilepsy was well-known was specifically targeted for such attacks by supporters of US President Donald Trump (Eichenwald, 2016). The offending video, full of flashing lights and images, specifically mentioned his epilepsy. He received more than one email with this directed hate – one stated "You deserve a seizure for that post" (Zilber, 2016). There can be no doubt this was a disability-specific form of hate speech. It was designed to physically harm him – such hate speech is dangerous speech. Online hate has real effects offline.

In order to further illustrate the vicious nature of online disablist hate, the next section of the chapter will discuss the victimization of Sophia Weaver and her mother Natalie.

Sophia Weaver's story

The case of the late Sophia Weaver demonstrates how disablist hate speech is often directed at specific individuals, and (as discussed above) their photos are seen as enough evidence to elicit hate. Sophia Weaver was a 9-year-old girl with a severe facial impairment and neurological and developmental disabilities who died in 2019. She lived in North Carolina, USA. Her mother Natalie has provided me with permission to share this story. Sophia was often pictured on her mother's account on Twitter, @Nataliew1020, under the hashtag #SweetSophia. Her case became well-known after an internet troll stole created a fake ID using her photo to advocate abortion of disabled fetuses. Natalie reported the troll to Twitter, which informed her that the post did not violate their rules against abusive behaviour. It was only after Natalie called on her friends and supporters to report the tweet that Twitter responded by apologizing and banning the account.

Sadly, the Weaver family has been constantly vilified on social media for years. In one YouTube video, Natalie shares some of the comments that have been directed at them. These comments include:

- "Your daughter is a nasty ass piece of shit monster she needs to be removed from this planet."
- "Just put her out of her misery before its too late. also go back into to (sic) hiding no one wants to see your hideous family."
- "Your child is hideous monster" (which was accompanied by a Photoshopped image of Sophia with pig features).

In the YouTube video, Natalie stated that she receives this type of abuse daily.

More online hate directed came after Natalie posted a lovely Christmas photo of Sophia's father cradling her in his arms as he stood by a Christmas tree. Natalie posted:

> We are grateful for another beautiful holiday season with Sophia. She continues to overcome and fight every daily challenge and difficulty she faces. She does it with so much sweetness, laugher and positivity. She is the definition of strength. I'm so proud of my girl. #SweetSophia

In response to this post, another posted calling themselves "winner winner chicken dinner" posted the following tweets:

> You should've ended the pregnancy for sure. You just want attention. This kid is creepy af. No one wants to see that in public… Well she is defective. What is the point of her life? She cannot be a productive, responsible human being and only costs $$$ and extra problems for her caretakers… That thing is fucking terrifying. Put it out of its misery. We are overpopulated, when this happens in nature the mother kills it. Why try to drag that thing around? It's only going to cause problems. Life is hard enough when you're normal.

Of course, Natalie reported these posts to Twitter. But (as in many cases, unfortunately) Twitter did not respond appropriately when they received the report. They replied that "We have reviewed your report carefully and found there was no violation of Twitter Rules against abusive behavior."

Natalie successfully rallied her friends and supporters to complain about Twitter's decision. On 24 December 2018, she discussed the plight of people who cannot organize similar support:

> It took mass reporting for Twitter to find these tweets in violation. What happens to the people who don't have a larger following to help? They continue to get harassed. That is unacceptable. Cyber bullying can cause real harm & is dangerous.

As Sophia was about to undergo her 29th surgery in 2019, another online disablist hate campaign was directed at her and her mother. In the words of Natalie Weaver on Twitter on January 22, 2019:

> Wow. I never imagined that my mission to create a world more accepting of #SweetSophia & other kids w/facial deformities & profound disabilities would be met w/so much anger, resistance and vile hatred. I'm currently being cyber bullied, harassed & getting a restraining order… I'm currently being raided on Instagram by a troll gang (wtf, I didn't know that was a thing). The hate towards my child bc of her differences runs deep. I won't stop fighting for Sophia's basic human rights, I won't stop exposing the hate and I won't stop fighting for change. I'm happy that my child will never know the hate she is receiving. She will never know that people are telling me to murder her in various ways and she will never know they are making fun of her beautiful face. For the people receiving this hate bc of disabilities, I'm so sorry.

Disablist hate continued to be directed at Sophia until her death on 23 May 2019. In January 2019, the following ten comments were made in one Instagram thread. I have included the spelling and grammatical mistakes in the posts by ten people:

- Imagine waking up, turning over and seeing that in ur bed;
- What a mess;
- Hahahaha your ugly face horror hahaha;
- When mothers don't take care of themselves before-during pregnancy;
- OMG, how can you post this picture she is so Flippin gross!
- Jesus christ (sic) who wants to look at that;
- Kill it before it breeds;
- ACTUALLY NAH KILL ME;
- Drown her;
- I can say stuff like that but she can't get it, because she can't speak.

Despite the thread including comments such as "Drown her," Instagram responded to a report by Natalie saying that "It does not violate our Community Guidelines." Again, Natalie decided to publicize this decision and ask for support from her followers to get the posts removed.

Natalie has tirelessly campaigned for social media companies to adopt better policies against disablist hate (Schroeder, 2018; Willingham, 2018). Twitter did adjust its social media rules after Natalie went to the press; without Natalie's commitment, resilience, strength, and courage, these changes would not have happened. But changes in the official rules have not been followed up in practice. When Natalie has reported similar ongoing abuse of her daughter, Twitter has still replied that the posts do not violate their Community Guidelines-until Natalie again organized her supporters to have the posts banned. Her and Sophia's story is such a reminder of the importance of sustained advocacy by disabled people, their families, and their allies in the fight against online disablist hate speech.

The cost of such principled advocacy is high, however:

> I receive verbal abuse, criticism, snarky, passive-aggressive & aggressive comments, judgments, cruelty and death threats towards my child and myself (for fighting for Sophia's basic human rights & to normalize facial deformities & profound disabilities) but that won't stop me.

It is interesting to note that Natalie Weaver's principled advocacy also extends to emphasizing the knowledge and value of disability activists. She routinely comments that if Facebook, Instagram and Twitter are willing to change their platforms to make them safer for people with facial differences and disabled people, she will connect them with disability activists who have those skills – but she also stresses that they must pay for such expertise.

Natalie Weaver's post on 23 December 2018 speaks volumes about her character and values. Under the heading "Goals for 2019" she listed her own objectives, which could almost be a model for others fighting against hate to emulate:

- Make the world better and more accepting place for kids like mine;
- Normalize facial deformities & profound disabilities;
- Build a larger community around us that will fight for equality & basic human rights for kids like mine;
- Share my love & pride for Sophia.

An earlier tweet from Natalie explained her philosophy even more:

> I'm the proud Mom of a profoundly disabled child who also has facial deformities. I hid away from the hate for 7.5 years. I will not hide any longer. I am fighting for very basic things. See my child & treat her as a human being. Give her the dignity and respect that she deserves.

Again, this is a message that could be embraced by all people who have loved ones that are the victims of online abuse, as could another of her Twitter posts:

> I will continue to educate others about our lives. I will continue to expose hate to create change, and I will continue to fight to change the stigma that

surrounds people who are profoundly disabled and in my child's case also facial deformities. Thank you for your support!

The Weaver family are unique in the sense that they have experience sustained online harassment for many years. But disabled people encounter online disablist hate speech on a routine basis. The next section of this chapter will discuss some of the ways other individuals and groups respond to online hate.

Responding to online disablist hate

Disabled people usually encounter disablist hate speech in one-off situations, rather than being targeted individually over a long-term. For instance, a post on Facebook might contain disablist hate speech. There are a number of potential responses to such a post. Jakubowicz et al. (2017, p. 79) have listed the options available to people encountering a post containing hate speech:

- Liked it
- Ignored it
- Made a comment disagreeing with it
- Reported it
- Blocked the poster
- Defriended the poster
- Complained to another body
- Shared it
- Campaigned to remove the content
- Made a comment agreeing with it
- Made an active dissonant response
- Made an active dissonant response within the platform.

These are important tools to remember – given the harm that hate speech can inflict, people can sometimes feel they have no options to get away from the hate. The list helps people to remember that they have multiple choices (including ignoring the person or blocking them) and that they do not simply have to feel that they are powerless victims.

In the process of responding to such material, opponents of hate speech also need to think about a number of questions:

- Should they call out the person, or the post, as hate?
- Should they name the specific type of hate (for instance, disablism)?
- Should they prioritize removing the content over engaging with the conversation?
- Should they try to disprove the argument?
- Should they focus instead on supporting the target of the hate speech?
- Should they focus on building "communities of resistance and solidarity" (Oboler & Connelly, 2018)?

The distinction between generalized hate speech and directed hate speech, emphasized by ElSherief et al. (2018, pp. 42–43) may be a useful guide for some instances of disablist hate. They indicate that (individually) directed hate speech "explicitly uses words to hinder the action of the target (e.g. calling the target a retard)," whereas generalized hate speech aims at entire groups, but is still often accompanied by lethal words "such as murder, beheaded, killed, exterminate." Generalized hate speech tends to regard the target as monolithic, completely separate (as an Other) to the rest of society, inferior, the enemy, as manipulative, and their perspectives are rejected out of hand, so discrimination/prejudice against them is seen as natural (Evolvi, 2018). In cases where individuals are specifically targeted, supporting them is an immediate priority, though both types of hate speech should also be recognized as hateful, should be reported to relevant authorities including internet service providers or social media companies, and should be opposed when encountered (if that is safe).

Safety is an important consideration for opponents of hate speech. Some of the people who express disablist hate do so because they are committed to an extremist ideology. These people can be very dangerous and may be a part of an extremist "criminal microenvironment" (Miró-Llinares, Moneva, & Esteve, 2018, p. 1). This environment helps remind us all that hate speech is dangerous speech. Direct online engagement with extremists is potentially very dangerous; it could even get someone killed. Some counter-extremist programs have engaged in activities that challenge extremists both online and in person – but they have robust screening and assessment mechanisms, strict safety and safeguarding procedures, and many different types of intervention specialists (such as ex-radicals, former victims, and specialist counsellors). They also liaise with both social media companies to ensure that they have more privacy and anonymity than other posters. These types of safeguards are often absent for individuals and private groups.

The importance of online safety in engaging with extremists cannot be emphasized enough. When dealing with extremists, it is important to note that their hatred exists both online and offline. Online hate speech and offline hate speech – as well as actual hate crimes – can reinforce each other (Köffer et al., 2018; Müller & Schwarz, 2018). In conducting research for this chapter, a number of anti-hate activists asked the author not to mention them or their organizations by name. One said that a different branch of their organization had experienced a bomb threat. They specifically requested that the chapter emphasize the importance of safety.

Those who express strong opinions on various forms of social inequality (such as on disability, feminism, and LGBTIQ issues) seem to be particularly targeted for harassment (Greyson, Cooke, Gibson, & Julien, 2018). Extremists do target disabled people: a study of the White Supremacist hate group StormFront found that 2% of their posts directly involved online disablist hate (Gibert, Perez, García-Pablos, & Cuadros, 2018). The Radicalisation Awareness Network (2017) has provided advice for groups who wish to challenge such online extremism. They recommend adopting goals that are clear, realistic and measurable; employing relevant messages that the audience considers credible; using the preferred medium or online platforms of the audience at the same time as the audience is expected to be online; continually monitoring and evaluating every element of the process; and considering all the security risks that might be involved. They also stress the need for opponents of extremism to carefully prepare (lest they inadvertently harm the cause or put themselves in danger). They also suggest that untrained people engage in "alternative narratives" rather than "counter-narratives" when dealing with extremists:

> Alternative narratives promote positive alternative perspectives, courses of action and role models, and foster critical thinking. Counter-narratives, which aim at debunking extremist propaganda, should only be directed at a well-researched and understood audience which is already engaged with extremist content.
>
> (Radicalisation Awareness Network, 2017, p. 2)

Counter and alternative narratives combat hate speech by discrediting and deconstructing the narratives on which they are based. They also emphasize human rights and democratic values such as openness, respect for difference and equality. They may do so by providing alternative and accurate information, by using humour and appealing to emotions on the issues involved, and by accounting for different perspectives and views (De Latour, Perger, Salag, Tocchi, & Otero, 2017, p. 12). Alternative narratives spread messages of tolerance and civility, show affinity for targeted groups, and demonstrate public dissent from hate (Rieger, Schmitt, & Frischlich, 2018). Responding to hate speech in this way will probably not change the views of people deeply committed to such views; its effectiveness largely depends on the ability to convince undecided people (Schieb & Preuss, 2016).

Alongside these options, people who encounter hate-filled messages can report them to third party anti-hate organizations. These are not law enforcement agencies, but they are organizations which are committed to stopping hate. They may be grassroots organizations with deep connections to the relevant community and they often have established relationships with social media companies (as "trusted reporters") so that their reports to the company are processed quicker than many others. But people in these organizations can often suffer burnout and emotional exhaustion. In such situations, it is essential to practice self-protection. At a minimum, everyone who is involved in the activities of a third-party organization should be trained in online safety. This is essential, but often difficult and even dangerous, work.

Online hate speech does not occur in a social vacuum. It is directly linked to offline activities, particularly in the case of extremist groups. Cohen-Almagor has identified some of the ways online activities interact with the offline world:

- Spreading propaganda which is used to foster hate and inspire offline activities;
- Encouraging offline socialization with others committed to hate;

- Linking people with such ideas, both regionally and cross-nationally;
- Providing fundraising opportunities;
- Identifying new targets for recruitment; and
- Promoting offline violence.

Another function of exposure to hate speech is desensitization. Soral, Bilewicz, and Winiewski (2018) suggest that people who are regularly exposed to hate speech are more prejudiced to target groups and less sensitive to such speech.

Given the violent tendencies of some perpetrators of online hate speech, some opponents focus on a more general and less interactive approach, countering hate speech through educational initiatives. One such example is the "digital resilience" project which aims to provide people from the ages of 16 to 19 with the critical thinking skills to be able to identify manipulated images, bias, echo chambers, and disinformation in order to counter hate speech (Reynolds & Parker, 2018). This is an area which needs to be explored in far more detail by opponents of online disablist hate speech.

People who are committed to opposing and removing online hate should also be aware of the policies of social media companies and internet providers. This is the theme of the next section of the chapter.

Social media companies and online hate speech

Social media companies are private companies, so the policies they adopt on hate speech are largely discretionary. Their policies are changing rapidly, as are governmental regulations over their behaviour. Even during the time this chapter was written, there were major changes in the policies of social media companies regarding hateful content. This section of the chapter will therefore summarize the current policies, in broad terms, with a caveat that they may change by the time the chapter is published. It will focus on four major social media companies which have adopted policies against hate speech: Facebook, Twitter, YouTube, and Instagram, and then it will discuss the rise of "hate speech havens" – areas of the internet such as Gab and Reddit where hate speech flows unchecked.

In response to widespread concerns about internet hate speech and its flow-on effects offline, many corporations have agreed to tackle illegal hate speech online. For instance, in May 2016, Facebook, Microsoft, Twitter and YouTube agreed to a European Commission "Code of Conduct on Countering Illegal Hate Speech Online," and by 2019, other companies such as Instagram, Google+, Snapchat, Dailymotion, and Jeuxvideo.com had also said they would join the Code of Conduct. The Code of Conduct involves improved responses to notifying illegal hate speech on social media platforms. It requires the companies to respond to the majority of user notifications of hate speech within 24 hours, respecting European Union and national legislation on hate speech and removing illegal messages, and improving feedback to users (European Commission, 2019). The specific policies of some of these companies will now be outlined.

Facebook

Facebook has a Hate Speech policy which states:

> We do not allow hate speech on Facebook because it creates an environment of intimidation and exclusion and in some cases may promote real-world violence. We define hate speech as a direct attack on people based on what we call protected characteristics – race, ethnicity, national origin, religious affiliation, sexual orientation, caste, sex, gender, gender identity and serious disease or disability. We also provide some protections for immigration status. We define "attack" as violent or dehumanizing speech, statements of inferiority, or calls for exclusion or segregation.
>
> (Facebook, 2019)

Facebook divides attacks into three tiers.

It defines a Tier 1 attack as:

- Any violent speech or support in written or visual form
- Dehumanizing speech such as reference or comparison to:
  - Insects
  - Animals that are culturally perceived as intellectually or physically inferior
  - Filth, bacteria, disease and feces
  - Sexual predator
  - Subhumanity
  - Violent and sexual criminals
  - Other criminals
- Mocking the concept, events or victims of hate crimes even if no real person is depicted in an image
- Designated dehumanizing comparisons in both written and visual form. (Facebook, 2019)

Tier 2 attacks involve:

- Statements of inferiority or an image implying a person's or a group's physical, mental, or moral deficiency
  - Physical (including but not limited to "deformed," "undeveloped," "hideous," "ugly")
  - Mental (including but not limited to "retarded," "cretin," "low IQ," "stupid," "idiot")
  - Moral (including but not limited to "slutty," "fraud," "cheap," "free riders")
- Expressions of contempt or their visual equivalent, including (but not limited to) 'I hate,' "I don't like," "X are the worst"
- Expressions of disgust or their visual equivalent, including (but not limited to) "Gross," "Vile," "Disgusting"
- Cursing at a person or group of people who share protected characteristics. (Facebook, 2019)

Tier 3 attacks call for the exclusion or segregation of a person or group of people based on the above-listed characteristics. They also include content that describes or negatively targets people with slurs (insulting labels attached to the groups listed).

Twitter

Twitter's Hateful Conduct policy states:

> You may not promote violence against or directly attack or threaten other people on the basis of race, ethnicity, national origin, sexual orientation, gender, gender identity, religious affiliation, age, disability, or serious disease. We also do not allow accounts whose primary purpose is inciting harm towards others on the basis of these categories.
>
> Hateful imagery and display names: You may not use hateful images or symbols in your profile image or profile header. You also may not use your username, display name, or profile bio to engage in abusive behavior, such as targeted harassment or expressing hate towards a person, group, or protected category.
>
> (Twitter, 2019)

Twitter also identifies specific forms of hate speech that they prohibit, including violent threats, wishing, hoping or calling for serious harm on a person or group of people, inciting fear about a protected category, and hateful imagery. Twitter's policies indicate that responses to hate speech can include removing the hateful content, preventing people from posting (but allowing them to read Twitter material), and permanent account suspension. Twitter further indicates that it has "a zero tolerance policy" against violent threats, and that "those deemed to be sharing violent threats will face immediate and permanent suspension of their account" (Twitter, 2019). It is not necessary for a victim to be a member of a protect group for Twitter to respond in this way.

YouTube

During the writing of this chapter, YouTube's hate speech policy changed. It now states:

> Hate speech is not allowed on YouTube. We remove content promoting violence or hatred against individuals or groups based on any of the following attributes:
>
> - Age
> - Disability
> - Ethnicity

- Gender
- Nationality
- Race
- Immigration Status
- Religion
- Sex
- Sexual Orientation[1]
- Veteran Status

Prior to this version of the policy, YouTube's hate speech policy was far more ambiguous. It made statements such as "We encourage free speech and try to defend your right to express unpopular points of view, but we don't permit hate speech," "there is a fine line between what is and what is not considered to be hate speech" and "keep in mind that not everything that's mean or insulting is hate speech."

YouTube's policies allow people to flag and report hateful speech in a video, a thumbnail, a link, a comment, a live chat message, and/or a channel. There is also safety reporting tool which enables people to flag a range of issues including: harassment and cyberbullying, impersonation, violent threats, child endangerment, hate speech against a protected group, and other concerns. An immediate notification pops up if someone reports violent threats that if they feel it is an emergency, or an imminent threat of physical violence, they should contact law enforcement.

Instagram

Instagram's policies regarding hateful content have also changed during the writing of this chapter. They have added sections which repeatedly state "follow the law" as well as saying "Instagram is not a place to support or praise terrorism, organized crime, or hate groups" (Instagram, 2019). As part of their requirements for respectful interactions, they state:

> We remove content that contains credible threats or hate speech, content that targets private individuals to degrade or shame them, personal information meant to blackmail or harass someone, and repeated unwanted messages. It's never OK to encourage violence or attack anyone based on their race, ethnicity, national origin, sex, gender, gender identity, sexual orientation, religious affiliation, disabilities, or diseases. When hate speech is being shared to challenge it or to raise awareness, we may allow it. In those instances, we ask that you express your intent clearly.
>
> (Instagram, 2019)

At the bottom of their lengthy community guidelines, Instagram states "We may work with law enforcement, including when we believe that there's risk of physical harm or threat to public safety." This is the only reference to the involvement of law enforcement, and it is not in the context of hate speech.

Hate speech havens: Gab and Reddit

Although social media companies such as Facebook, Twitter and Instagram have developed anti-hate speech policies, others have deliberately refused to adopt such policies and have arguably become "hate speech havens." The websites Gab.com and Reddit.com are perhaps the most well-known of such hate speech havens. A study of the diffusion of hateful versus non-hateful posts on the Gab platform found that hateful comments are "more influential, popular and cohesive" (Mathew, Dutt, Goyal, & Mukherjee, 2018, p. 1).

When users sign up for a Gab account, they see a long list of terms and conditions, including the following statement:

> Gab's mission is to put people and free speech first. We believe that the only valid form of censorship is an individual's own choice to opt-out. Gab empowers users to filter and remove unwanted followers, words, phrases, and topics they do not want to see in their feeds. However, we do take steps to protect ourselves and our users from illegal activity, spam, and abuse…Gab's policy is to follow all applicable laws in The United States of America, the Constitution and the Supreme Court's rulings on the First Amendment. We use the Court's rulings, precedents and judgments as our guiding principles for protecting and empowering free speech and expression. You may not use our service for any unlawful purposes or illegal activities… Users are prohibited from calling for the acts of violence against others, promoting or engaging in self-harm, and/or acts of cruelty, threatening language or behaviour that clearly, directly and incontrovertibly infringes on the safety of another user or individual(s). We may also report the user(s) to local and/or federal law enforcement, as per the advice of our legal counsel.
>
> (Gab, 2017)

Like the other social media companies mentioned above, Gab indicates that people can be suspended on a temporary, intermittent, or permanent basis, or outright expelled from Gab and its services for violating its guidelines (Gab, 2017). But one look at the content in Gab shows how different its community standards are from the other social media companies discussed in this chapter. Hate seems endemic to the site.

Rather than engage on Twitter (where they may be more likely to be blocked for hate speech – though that is far from guaranteed), people often post a screenshot from Twitter onto Gab and then engage in hate speech there. There is a thread on Gab entitled "What did you get banned for?" where people list (and often brag about) their hate speech, and they often disclose the reasons they were banned in general posts. A poster known as Gemstar (@Gemstar2080) posted a screenshot of the post which saw them banned from Twitter. The spelling mistakes are uncorrected here. They wrote "Were you just born retarded or did yours parent just beat you retarded because of its one or the other I'd feel sorry for you and the other is probably a punishment from god." Gemstar's (uncorrected, repetitive, and poorly written) post on Gab discussing this ban was to say, "Yeah to bad if call them call them retarded on twitter they get you ban until you delete it and suck their dicks."

The victims are often unaware and the posters on Gab often post images of the hate messages they posted and the bans they received from other sites for engaging in hate speech. So, for instance, a trans person in a wheelchair posted on Twitter that they should be a runway model. The image was copied and posted on Gab, with the comment, "The only 'runway' these people should be on is one right where a 747 is landing." A large number of posters replied with either comments or images suggesting they needed to pour bleach on their own eyes to remove the sight of this person. One reply by Red Ryder Ralphie (@RalphieBBadd) commented, "Work a bikini? Come back when you can work the stairs." In a longer post (again with spelling and grammatical errors), a self-described White Nationalist, Harley Rose (@HarleyRoseTX) wrote:

> Good lord, this is madness! Whoever thought it a good idea to 'empower' these mental defects with a false sense of inclusiveness is cruel and maliscious! They should be 'equal' among their own kind. Mainstreaming delusion has been an abysmal failure in our society! Mass institutionalization and re-education!

Further (poorly written and misspelt) disablist and sexist comments included, "and people get annoyed when I plead for the restablishment of asylums in the UK!" as well as "The fucks with the wheel chair. This thing a transformer now? I bet that bitch would take the transformer name of BumbleREEEEEE." Another image, a GIF, involved a cartoon character using an automatic machine gun. Someone else posted ""I'm a mentally unstable sideshow freak and shame on you for not hiring me." Lol." Sexist comments included "Nice tits" and "I bet she can suck some dick like no ones business."

The level of hate speech on Gab is not simply because of its lax policies towards such language, but also because it is an "echo chamber" which successfully attracts like-minded people. This is an element of disablist hate speech which is rarely (if ever) acknowledged. "Echo chambers" are sites where like-minded people reinforce each other's prejudices and (multiple forms of) hate (O'Hara & Stevens, 2015). They may also enable or assist other forms of online harassment such as trolling, doxxing, or cyberbullying victims.

Reddit is another platform which is well known for its hateful content – for years, its policy was almost entirely "free speech," including hate speech. After some time, it did institute a policy of labelling some subreddits (threads) "controversial," but for years its policy was essentially to allow almost anything to be said. Reddit's current content policy (at the time of writing, May 2019) indicates that "The nature of this content might be funny, serious, offensive, or anywhere in between." However, Reddit's policy states:

Content is prohibited if it

- Is illegal;
- Is involuntary pornography;

- Is sexual or suggestive content involving minors;
- Encourages or incites violence;
- Threatens, harasses, or bullies or encourages others to do so;
- Is personal and confidential information;
- Impersonates someone in a misleading or deceptive manner;
- Uses Reddit to solicit or facilitate any transaction or gift involving certain goods and services;
- Is spam.

(Reddit, 2019)

Reddit's content policy indicates that its responses to infringements of this policy may range from:

- Asking you nicely to knock it off;
- Asking you less nicely;
- Temporary or permanent suspension of accounts;
- Removal of privileges from, or adding restrictions to, accounts;
- Adding restrictions to Reddit communities, such as adding NSFW tags or Quarantining;
- Removal of content;
- Banning of Reddit communities.

(Reddit, 2019)

But it seems these official policies are rarely enforced strictly. Even when hateful content in social media was under intense scrutiny after the 2019 Christchurch terrorist attack where 50 people were killed and 48 injured, Reddit was full of Islamophobic hate speech (Breland, 2019).

In 2015, five subreddits were banned, but these were for harassment, rather than hate speech per se (Dewey, 2015; National Coalition Against Censorship, 2015). A post on the Announcements section of Reddit stated that they were taking action to stop

> Systematic and/or continued actions to torment or demean someone in a way that would make a reasonable person (1) conclude that reddit is not a safe platform to express their ideas or participate in the conversation, or (2) fear for their safety or the safety of those around them.

An example was given where people's e-mails were flooded with messages telling them to kill themselves. A follow-up post indicated that "Mocking and calling people stupid is not harassment. Doxxing, following users around, flooding their inbox with trash is" (Reddit CEO Steve Huffman, 2015).

The disability-related term "stupid" was specifically identified as acceptable, but this is not an aberration on Reddit regarding disablist abuse. As of the time of writing, a subreddit "OkBuddyRetard" has 291,000 members, "Retards in Action" has 5,000, and "Conspiratard" has 61,800 members. A subreddit entitled "Retard" has many photos of people with intellectual disabilities accompanied by derogatory words, though it also has a lot of other content. Specific (and often popular) posts also commonly use the word "retard." For instance, a post with 10,000 votes and 1,700 comments was called "Saying 'Retard' is not Hate Speech" ("YeezyDiseezy", 2019), a post entitled "Having retards compete as athletes is pointless" had 43,800 votes and 1,000 comments ("Uhgio", 2019). Hate speech against people with mental illness is common – one post entitled "Batshit Crazy People" has 23,500 responses, a reddit with 562 members called "Crazy People" has the subheading "Show/tell us about all the crazy people you encounter," and there are countless posts discussing "nut jobs."

As well as dealing with hate speech havens and the ways in which policies of social media companies are often not enforced, those who oppose online disablist hate speech also face other challenges, including the use of bots to spread hate speech, and the presence of hate on the Deep Web and the Dark Web. The next section of the chapter will discuss these emerging challenges.

Emerging challenges

The rise of automated programs known as "bots" presents an emerging challenge for those seeking to address disablist hate speech. Some bots have been programmed to use hate speech in order to deliberately escalate conflict online (Evolvi, 2018). They may be programmed to take one (or both) sides of an argument – while they usually function as propaganda platforms for a particular political agenda, sometimes they take both sides simply to escalate conflict (Broniatowski et al., 2018; Hegelich & Janetzko, 2016; Keller, Schoch, Stier, & Yang, 2017; Michael, 2017; Schäfer, Evert, & Heinrich, 2017). Bots are a growing online problem, and for opponents to avoid wasting their time engaging with their posts, it is necessary to identify them more effectively. Being able to identify their characteristics may help in this regard.

Costa-Roberts (2018) identifies five characteristics of bots that differentiate them from other internet users:

1. They are hyperactive, averaging over 50 or 60 tweets per day.
2. They are more likely to use suspicious images (such as stolen photos) which can be identified by reverse image searching.
3. They are more likely to use URL shorteners (such as trib.al, bit.ly or tinyurl.com).
4. They may post in five or more languages.
5. They are more likely to have a small number of followers (themselves bots) working in combination to amplify their effect on social media. Such a coordinated network of bots is called a 'botnet.'

Even though they are widely criticized for failing to address the problem of online hate, social media companies are spending hundreds of millions of dollars to develop detection programs that use algorithms to detect bots and address the problem of online hate speech (Davidson, Warmsley, Macy, & Weber, 2017;

Gaydhani, Doma, Kendre, & Bhagwat, 2018; Zhang & Luo, 2018). However, online hate speech can be subtle, indirect, and hard for computerized programs to direct (Alorainy, Burnap, Liu, & Williams, 2018). Researchers suggest that keyword-based automatic detection programs are less effective than might be assumed (Anagnostou, Mollas, & Tsoumakas, 2018) and many other approaches are being developed. Increasingly sophisticated algorithms identifying such hate speech are being developed which can move beyond lexicon and include such factors as the display of emotions and even "weak" or "strong" expressions of hate (Alorainy, Burnap, Liu, Javed, & Williams, 2018; Ben-David & Matamoros-Fernández, 2016; Burnap & Williams, 2015; Gitari, Zuping, Damien, & Long, 2015; Jansen, Zhang, Sobel, & Chowdury, 2009; Kurniasih et al., 2018).

Part of the problem is that even though program developers are constantly working on improving their detection algorithms, separation of hate speech from profane or offensive speech is often difficult. Another problem is that it is not simply individual words which may be hateful, but also the surrounding comments which convey emotion and intent. Moreover, the lexicon used in online hate speech is continually morphing, in part to avoid detection, so automated programs need to be continually updated and improved. As well, the deletion of online hate speech is often not permanent. Material that has been deleted can be reposted; people or bots which have had one account banned for hate speech can create another fairly easily. In this way, banned online hate speech can resurface almost immediately.

Dealing with hate on the Dark Net and the Deep Net is another emerging challenge. Many online hate groups operate as closed groups, where membership is only offered to those who can be verified by other members, usually because they have met in person (Cohen-Almagor, 2018). Such groups operate in what is known as "the Deep Web," since their content is not freely available or searchable, even though it exists on the surface web, which is normally searchable. The Dark Net, on the other hand, is even more secretive and privacy-protected; its content is not only hidden from search engines such as Google, but entirely different browsers are required to access it and posters have much more anonymity than on the surface web:

> Darknet (also known as TOR-network, Dark Web or Dark Net) is located outside what we consider "the normal internet" and requires downloading a specific TORbrowser (also known as The Onion Router). With the TOR-browser a person has access to both the normal internet (also known as Clear Net or Surface Web) and Darknet. The pages in Darknet are not accessible through the normal internet browsers (e.g. Firefox, Chrome) and only exist in Darknet
>
> (Kaján, 2017).

In the Dark Net, hate can flourish in echo chambers that are far away from even the modest standards of accountability that are found in the regular (surface) web.

Conclusion

This chapter has outlined the nature of disablist speech online, discussing some of the most common forms of this hate, the ways in which opponents may respond to it, and some of the policies adopted by social media companies in response to this problem. It has also emphasized that even when the hatred in an online post is obvious, it may be covered by completely different legislation such as cyber-bullying. Victims of online disablist hate may be able to take advantage of these laws, even if online hate speech is not covered in their national or local laws. The chapter has also highlighted some of the ways in which online disablist hate may be different from other forms of hate. The hateful use of animated images to deliberately trigger seizures among people with photosensitive epilepsy was provided as an example. The ways in which disabled women and children in particular are targeted online was another theme of the chapter. This is an important reminder of the need for intersectional awareness in recognizing and responding to online disablist hate. There are many options available to people who are the victims of online disablist hate, as well as the individuals and organizations whose focus is to engage in anti-hate activities. This chapter has outlined many of these options as well.

Note

1 We refer to Gender, Sex, and Sexual Orientation definitions mindful that society's views on these definitions are evolving. (YouTube, 2019)

References

Agbedejobi, P. (10 March 2017). Challenging online radicalisation: A refutation of counter-radicalisation strategies, counter-narratives and a new approach. Retrieved from http://dx.doi.org/10.2139/ssrn.2931179.

Alorainy, W., Burnap, P., Liu, H., Javed, A., & Williams, M. L. (2018). Suspended accounts: A source of tweets with disgust and anger motions for augmenting hate speech data sample. Paper presented at the 2018 International Conference on Machine Learning and Cybernetics (ICMLC). London.

Alorainy, W., Burnap, P., Liu, H., & Williams, M. (January 2018). The enemy among us: Detecting hate speech with threats based "othering" language embeddings. Retrieved from https://arxiv.org/ftp/arxiv/papers/1801/1801.07495.pdf.

Anagnostou, A., Mollas, I., & Tsoumakas, G. (2018). Hatebusters: A web application for actively reporting youTube hate speech. *In Proceedings of the Twenty-Seventh International Joint Conference on Artificial Intelligence* (pp. 5796–5798). Stockholm.

Avivo (2019). The R Word. Retrieved from https://therword.com.au/.

Ben-David, A., & Matamoros-Fernández, A. (2016). Hate speech and covert discrimination on social media: Monitoring the Facebook pages of extreme-right political parties in Spain. *International Journal of Communication, 10*, 1167–1193.

Bishop, J. (2014). Representations of "trolls" in mass media communication: A review of media-texts and moral panics relating to "internet trolling". *International Journal of Web Based Communities, 10*(1), 7–24.

Bocij, P., & McFarlane, L. (2002). Online harassment: Towards a definition of cyberstalking. *Prison Service Journal, 139*, 31–38.

Bottino, S. M. B., Bottino, C., Regina, C. G., Correia, A. V. L., & Ribeiro, W. S. (2015). Cyberbullying and adolescent mental health: Systematic review. *Cadernos de Saude Publica, 31*(3), 463–475.

Breland, A. (2019, 21 March). Anti-Muslim hate has been rampant on Reddit since the New Zealand shooting. Retrieved from https://www.motherjones.com/politics/2019/03/reddit-new-zealand-shooting-islamophobia/.

Broniatowski, D. A., Jamison, A. M., Qi, S., AlKulaib, L., Chen, T., Benton, A., Quinn, S. C., Dredze, M. (2018). Weaponized health communication: Twitter bots and Russian trolls amplify the vaccine debate. *American Journal of Public Health, 108*(10), 1378–1384.

Bruno, R. L. (1997). Devotees, pretenders and wannabes: Two cases of factitious disability disorder. *Sexuality and Disability, 15*(4), 243–260.

Buni, C., & Chemaly, S. (2014, 9 October). The unsafety net: How social media turned against women. *The Atlantic*. Retrieved from https://www.theatlantic.com/technology/archive/2014/10/the-unsafety-net-how-social-media-turned-against-women/381261/.

Burnap, P., & Williams, M. L. (2015). Cyber hate speech on Twitter: An application of machine classification and statistical modeling for policy and decision making. *Policy and Internet, 7*(2), 223–242.

Citron, D. K. (2014). *Hate Crimes in Cyberspace*. Cambridge, MA: Harvard University Press.

Cohen-Almagor, R. (2018). Taking North American white supremacist groups seriously: The scope and challenge of hate speech on the Internet. *International Journal for Crime, Justice and Social Democracy, 7*(2), 38–57.

Colton, J. S., Holmes, S., & Walwema, J. (2017). From NoobGuides to #OpKKK: Ethics of anonymous' tactical technical communication. *Technical Communication Quarterly, 26*(1), 59–75.

Costa-Roberts, D. (2018, 1 August, 6am). "How to spot a Russian bot." https://www.motherjones.com/media/2018/08/how-to-identify-russian-bots-twitter/.

Davidson, T., Warmsley, D., Macy, M., & Weber, I. (2017, May 15 – May 18). *Automated Hate Speech Detection and the Problem of Offensive Language*. Paper presented at the Eleventh International AAAI Conference on Web and Social Media. Montreal, Quebec.

De Latour, A., Perger, N., Salag, R., Tocchi, C., & Otero, P. V. (2017). *We Can! Taking Action against Hate Speech through Counter and Alternative Narratives* (Revised ed.). Strasbourg, France: Council of Europe.

Dewey, C. (2015, 10 June). These are the 5 subreddits Reddit banned under its game-changing anti-harassment policy – And why it banned them. Retrieved from https://www.washingtonpost.com/news/the-intersect/wp/2015/06/10/these-are-the-5-subreddits-reddit-banned-under-its-game-changing-anti-harassment-policy-and-why-it-banned-them/.

DysNet: The Online Dysmelia Community. (2013, 13 February). *Online Safety: Amputee Devotees - Part Two*. Retrieved from https://www.dysnet.org/online_safety__amputee_devotees___part_two.

Ehrenfreund, M., & Olivo, A. (2017, 19 March). Seizure-inducing tweet leads to a new kind of prosecution. Retrieved from https://www.washingtonpost.com/national/seizure-inducing-tweet-leads-to-a-new-kind-of-prosecution-for-a-new-kind-of-crime/2017/03/18/c5915468-0c10-11e7-b77c-0047d15a24e0_story.html?utm_term=.0e503d85190f.

Eichenwald, K. (7 October 2016). How Donald Trump supporters attack journalists. Retrieved from https://www.newsweek.com/epileptogenic-pepe-video-507417.

ElSherief, M., Kulkarni, V., Nguyen, D., Wang, W. Y., & Belding, E. (25–28 June 2018). Hate lingo: A target-based linguistic analysis of hate speech in social media. Paper presented at the Twelfth International AAAI Conference on Web and Social Media. Palo Alto, CA.

European Commission. (18 March 2019). Countering illegal hate speech online #NoPlace4Hate. Retrieved from https://ec.europa.eu/newsroom/just/item-detail.cfm?item_id=54300.

Evolvi, G. (2018). Hate in a tweet: Exploring internet-based islamophobic discourses. *Religions*, *9*(10), 307.

Facebook. (2019). Community standards: Hate speech. Retrieved from https://www.facebook.com/communitystandards/hate_speech.

Gab (2 January 2017). End user license agreement. Retrieved from https://gab.com/about/eula.

Gaydhani, A., Doma, V., Kendre, S., & Bhagwat, L. (September 2018). Detecting hate speech and offensive language on twitter using machine learning: An N-gram and TFIDF based Approach. *IEEE International Advance Computing Conference*. Retrieved from https://arxiv.org/pdf/1809.08651.pdf

Gibert, O. D., Perez, N., García-Pablos, G., & Cuadros, M. (2018). Hate speech dataset from a White Supremacy Forum. Retrieved from https://www.aclweb.org/anthology/W18-5102.

Gitari, N. D., Zuping, Z., Damien, H., & Long, J. (2015). A lexicon-based approach for hate speech detection. *International Journal of Multimedia and Ubiquitous Engineering*, *10*(4), 215–230.

Greyson, D., Cooke, N., Gibson, A., & Julien, H. (2018). Online targeting of researchers/academics: Ethical obligations and best practices. *Proceedings of the Association for Information Science and Technology*, *55*(1), 684–687.

Hall, P. (2019). Disability hate speech: Interrogating the online/offline distinction. In K. Lumsden & E. Harmer (Eds.), *Online Othering: Exploring Digital Violence and Discrimination on the Web* (pp. 309–330). Cham, Switzerland: Palgrave Macmillan.

Harmer, E., & Lumsden, K. (2019). Online othering: An introduction. In K. Lumsden & E. Harmer (Eds.), *Online Othering: Exploring Digital Violence and Discrimination on the Web* (pp. 1–33). Cham, Switzerland: Palgrave Macmillan.

Hatebase. (2013). FAQs. Retrieved from https://hatebase.org/faqs.

Hegelich, S., & Janetzko, D. (2016). Are social bots on Twitter political actors? Empirical evidence from a Ukrainian social botnet. Paper presented at the Tenth International AAAI Conference on Web and Social Media. Cologne, Germany.

Heiman, T., Olenik-Shemesh, D., & Eden, S. (2015). Cyberbullying involvement among students with ADHD: Relation to loneliness, self-efficacy and social support. *European Journal of Special Needs Education*, *30*(1), 15–29.

Henry, J. (2013). Bias-based cyberbullying: The next hate crime frontier? *Criminal Law Bulletin*, *49*(3), 481–503.

Herring, S., Job-Sluder, K., Scheckler, R., & Barab, S. (2002). Searching for safety online: Managing "trolling" in a feminist forum. *The Information Society*, *18*(5), 371–384.

Instagram. (2019). *Community Guidelines*. Retrieved from https://help.instagram.com/477434105621119.

Jaffe, E. M. (2016). Swatting: The new cyberbullying frontier after Elonis v. United States. *Drake Law Review*, *64*, 455–483.

Jakubowicz, A., Dunn, K., Mason, G., Paradies, Y., Bliuc, A.M., Bahfen, N., Oboler, A., Atie, R., Connelly, K. (2017). *Cyber Racism and Community Resilience*. Cham, Switzerland: Palgrave Macmillan.

Jansen, B. J., Zhang, M., Sobel, K., & Chowdury, A. (2009). Twitter power: Tweets as electronic word of mouth. *Journal of the American Society for Information Science and Technology*, *60*(11), 2169–2188.

Joh, E. (2016, 14 October). Does a tweet designed to trigger seizures count as assault? Retrieved from https://www.newscientist.com/article/2109028-does-a-tweet-designed-to-trigger-seizures-count-as-assault/.

Kafer, A. (2004). Inseparable: Gender and disability in the amputee-devotee community. In B. G. Smith & B. Hutchison (Eds.), *Gendering disability* (pp. 107–118). New Brunswick, NJ: Rutgers University Press.

Kaján, E. (2017). Hate online: Anti-immigration rhetoric in Darknet. *Nordia Geographical Publications*, *46*(3), 3–22.

Karppi, T. (2013). Change name to no one. Like people's status: Facebook trolling and managing online personas. *The Fibreculture Journal*, *22*, 166.

Keller, F. B., Schoch, D., Stier, S., & Yang, J. (2017). How to manipulate social media: Analyzing political astroturfing using ground truth data from South Korea. Paper presented at the Eleventh International AAAI Conference on Web and Social Media, Montréal, Québec.

Köffer, S., Riehle, D. M., Höhenberger, S., & Becker, J. (2018). Discussing the value of automatic hate speech detection in online debates. Paper presented at the Conference Proceedings, Multikonferenz Wirtschaftsinformatik: Data Driven X-Turning Data Leuphana, Germany.

Kofoed, J., & Staksrud, E. (2019). "We always torment different people, so by definition, we are no bullies": The problem of definitions in cyberbullying research. *New Media and Society*, *21*(4), 1006–1020.

Kowalski, R. M., & Fedina, C. (2011). Cyber bullying in ADHD and Asperger syndrome populations. *Research in Autism Spectrum Disorders*, *5*(3), 1201–1208.

Kowalski, R. M., Morgan, C. A., Drake-Lavelle, K., & Allison, B. (2016). Cyberbullying among college students with disabilities. *Computers in Human Behavior*, *57*, 416–427.

Kurniasih, N., Abdillah, L. A., Sudarsana, I. K., Yogantara, I., Astawa, I., Nanuru, Freedom, R., Miagina, A., Sabarua, J.O., Jamil, M., Tandisalla, J., Duan, E., Rupilele, F. G. J., Utama, M. D., Laisila, M., Ahmar, A. S., & Rahim, Robbi. (2018). Prototype application hate speech detection website using string matching and searching algorithm. *International Journal of Engineering and Technology*, *7*(2.5), 62–64.

Magu, R., & Luo, J. (2018, October 30–November 1). *Determining Code Words in Euphemistic Hate Speech Using Word Embedding Networks*. Paper Presented at the Proceedings of the 2nd Workshop on Abusive Language Online. Brussels, Belgium.

Mantilla, K. (2015). *Gendertrolling: How Misogyny Went Viral*. Santa Barbara: Praeger.

Mathew, B., Dutt, R., Goyal, P., & Mukherjee, A. (2018, 4 December). Spread of hate speech in online social media. Retrieved from https://arxiv.org/pdf/1812.01693.pdf.

Michael, K. (2017). Bots trending now: Disinformation and calculated manipulation of the masses. *IEEE Technology and Society Magazine*, *36*(2), 6–11.

Miró-Llinares, F., Moneva, A., & Esteve, M. (2018). Hate is in the air! But where? Introducing an algorithm to detect hate speech in digital microenvironments. *Crime Science*, *7*(1), 1–15.

Müller, K., & Schwarz, C. (30 November 2018). Fanning the flames of hate: Social media and hate crime. Retrieved from http://dx.doi.org/10.2139/ssrn.3082972

National Coalition Against Censorship. (2 July 2015) *Is Reddit Moving Away from Free Speech Roots?* Retrieved from https://ncac.org/news/blog/is-reddit-moving-away-from-free-speech-roots.

O'Hara, K., & Stevens, D. (2015). Echo chambers and online radicalism: Assessing the Internet's complicity in violent extremism. *Policy and Internet*, *7*(4), 401–422.

Oboler, A., & Connelly, K. (2018). Building SMARTER Communities of resistance and solidarity. *Cosmopolitan Civil Societies: An Interdisciplinary Journal*, *10*(2), 91–118.

Olweus, D., & Limber, S. P. (2018). Some problems with cyberbullying research. *Current Opinion in Psychology*, *19*, 139–143.

Ovejero, A., Yubero, S., Larrañaga, E., & Moral, M. d. l. V. (2016). Cyberbullying: Definitions and facts from a psychosocial perspective. In R. Navarro, S. Yubero, & E. Larrañaga (Eds.), *Cyberbullying Across the Globe: Gender, Family, and Mental Health* (pp. 1–31). New York: Springer.

Popa, B. (2008, 8 May 9.30am) *Hackers Attack Epilepsy Website, Cause Serious Seizures: The Epilepsy Foundation Got Hacked*. Retrieved from https://news.softpedia.com/news/Hackers-Attack-Epilepsy-Website-Cause-Serious-Seizures-85063.shtml.

Radicalisation Awareness Network. (2017). *RAN Guidelines for Effective Alternative and Counter-Narrative Campaigns (GAMMMA+)*. Brussels: RAN Centre of Excellence.

Ramadge, A. (2009, 23 October 4.38pm). *Anonymous Attack Targets Epilepsy Sufferers*. Retrieved from https://www.news.com.au/technology/anonymous-attack-targets-epilepsy-sufferers/news-story/702ed0bbf0b49dd63aaee33f295ba1d4?sv=8ac25908490d23fa0024d6b5c82d4ff7.

Reddit. (2019). Reddit Content Policy. Retrieved from https://www.redditinc.com/policies/content-policy.

Reddit CEO Steve Huffman. (2015). Let's talk content. AMA. Retrieved from https://www.reddit.com/r/announcements/comments/3djjxw/lets_talk_content_ama/.

Reynolds, L., & Parker, L. (2018). *Digital Resilience: Stronger Citizens Online*. London: Institute for Strategic Dialogue.

Rieger, D., Schmitt, J. B., & Frischlich, L. (2018). Hate and counter-voices in the Internet: Introduction to the special issue. *SCM Studies in Communication and Media*, *7*(4), 459–472.

Schäfer, F., Evert, S., & Heinrich, P. (2017). Japan's 2014 general election: Political bots, right-wing internet activism, and Prime Minister Shinzō Abe's hidden nationalist agenda. *Big Data*, *5*(4), 294–309.

Schieb, C., & Preuss, M. (2016, 10 June). Governing hate speech by means of counter-speech on Facebook. Paper presented at the 66th ICA Annual Conference, Fukuoka, Japan.

Schroeder, J. (2018, 15:26 EDT, 23 January 2018). Mother calls for stricter hate speech rules against disabled on Twitter after pro-abortion poster surfaces with photo of her DAUGHTER who suffers rare brain disorder and facial deformities. Retrieved from https://www.dailymail.co.uk/news/article-5302779/Fury-pro-abortion-poster-pictures-disabled-child.html

Selkie, E. M., Fales, J. L., & Moreno, M. A. (2016). Cyberbullying prevalence among US middle and high school–aged adolescents: A systematic review and quality assessment. *Journal of Adolescent Health*, *58*(2), 125–133.

Soral, W., Bilewicz, M., & Winiewski, M. (2018). Exposure to hate speech increases prejudice through desensitization. *Aggressive Behavior*, *44*(2), 136–146.

Twitter. (2019). *Hateful Conduct Policy*. Retrieved from https://help.twitter.com/en/rules-and-policies/hateful-conduct-policy.

"Uhgio" (2019, 13 May). Having retards compete as athletes is pointless. Retrieved from https://www.reddit.com/r/insanepeoplefacebook/comments/bo0gce/having_retards_compete_as_athletes_is_pointless/.

Wagenseil, P. (2008, 31 March). Hackers Flood Epilepsy Web Forum With flashing lights. Retrieved from https://www.foxnews.com/story/hackers-flood-epilepsy-web-forum-with-flashing-lights.

Wells, M., & Mitchell, K. J. (2014). Patterns of Internet use and risk of online victimization for youth with and without disabilities. *The Journal of Special Education*, *48*(3), 204–213.

Wells, M., Mitchell, K. J., Jones, L. M., & Turner, H. A. (2018). Peer harassment among youths with different disabilities: Impact of harassment online, in person, and in mixed online and in-person incidents. *Children and Schools*, *41*(1), 17–24.

Williams, J. L. (2017). *Media, Performative Identity, and the New American Freak Show*. Cham, Switzerland: Springer.

Willingham, A. J. (2018, 8:21 PM ET, Wed February 7, 2018). Why the mom of a child with a facial deformity fought to take down just one cruel tweet. Retrieved from https://www.cnn.com/2018/02/07/health/sophia-weaver-natalie-facial-deformities-advocates-medically-fragile-kids-trnd/index.html

Wu, B. (2015). Doxxed: Impact of online threats on women including private details being exposed and "swatting." Plus Greg Lukianoff on balancing offence and free speech. *Index on Censorship*, *44*(3), 46–49.

"YeezyDiseezy" (2019) Saying "retard" is not hate speech. Retrieved from https://www.reddit.com/r/unpopularopinion/comments/a4k46g/saying_retard_is_not_hate_speech/.

YouTube. (2019). Hate speech policy. Retrieved from https://support.google.com/youtube/answer/2801939?hl=en.

Zhang, Z., & Luo, L. (2018). Hate speech detection: A solved problem? The challenging case of long tail on Twitter. *Semantic Web* (Preprint), 1–21.

Zilber, A. (2016, 17 December 5:24 pm). *Newsweek Reporter Claims Trump Supporter*. Sent Him a Video of a Strobe Light Flashing to Intentionally Trigger His Epilepsy. Retrieved from https://en.mogaznews.com/World-News/290092/Newsweek-reporter-claims-Trump-supporter-sent-him-a-video-of-a-strobe-light-.html

3 Towards a conceptual and experiential understanding of disablist hate speech

Acceptance, harm, and resistance

Leah Burch

Research has shown that many disabled people experience disablist hate speech on a regular basis. However, current legislation across the globe is unable to effectively recognise or challenge this failure and thus continues to exclude the experiences of many disabled people. This chapter works with both conceptual and experiential accounts of disablist hate speech to challenge this exclusion. First, I propose that a more holistic conceptualisation of hate is needed in order to capture and reflect the everyday experiences of disabled people. Next, I offer reflections of such experiences, as storied by disabled people, and consider the multiple ways that disablist hate speech is expressed and the diverse forms that this expression may take. Drawing upon the results of a preliminary research project, this chapter attempts to forge links between conceptual debates and everyday realities in order to generate a more nuanced understanding of disablist hate speech that is informed by and through lived experience. In so doing, I draw upon some of the ways in which disablist hate speech is experienced, perceived, and, at times, internalised. Importantly, I draw attention to the resistive practices employed every day by disabled people as a means of challenging disablist attitudes, and thus confronting disablist hate speech.

Recent years have witnessed a toxic combination of financial instability and political campaigning which have created widespread narratives of conflict, disagreement, and blame. In the United Kingdom (UK), where the research for this chapter occurred, the financial crisis of 2007/8 has hardened expectations of productivity, independence, and economic contribution. Following the British election of a conservative-led, Coalition government in 2010, and subsequently, the Conservative party in 2015, a series of changes to the way in which welfare support is awarded and distributed has sought to create a 'big society matched by big citizens' (Government, 2010). To do so, the government promised to 'create a fairer welfare system where benefits are capped to the level that makes work pay' Conservatives, 2015, p. 3) in order to protect the financial stability of 'hard-working taxpayers.' Those occupying positions of power have been able to draw upon the notion that 'we are under threat' to bring into existence, 'the collective' who are situated in opposition with Others (Reicher, 2012). Through a process of homogenization, stories of financial instability have generated an alignment between the 'I' and 'we' against the 'you' and 'them' (Ahmed, 2004). In turn, we have witnessed a growing 'benefit stigma' which is driven by the perception that those who receive welfare support are both underserving and unable (Baumberg et al., 2012). Carefully scripted and emotionally charged stories of hate and resentment towards disabled people have sustained strict population divisions and created the ideal scapegoats for politicians and media outlets (Glaeser, 2005).

Media representations of welfare recipients as 'scroungers' and 'cheats' who simply take from the 'hardworking taxpayer' are suggested to have nurtured a particularly hostile environment for disabled people (Briant, Watson, & Philo, 2011, 2013; Burch, 2018; CRPD, 2016; Garthwaite, 2011). Stories of austerity have focused on those perceived to be contributing to the financial instability of the population: the hardworking taxpayers at the heart of the conservative narrative. The pervasive feeling of disgust that has underpinned much political and media discussion of the welfare system have served to perpetuate the expectations of the neoliberal citizen. In what Goodley, Lawthom, and Runswick-Cole, (2014, p. 981) term 'neoliberal-ableism,' we have been 'expected to overcome economic downturn and respond to austerity through adhering to ableism's ideals [and] its narrow conceptions of personhood.' This narrative is easily absorbed by those citizens who, through fear of becoming associated with the subordinated group (Wendell, 1996), take up the values and expectations of neoliberal-ableism, adhering to a strict work regime, while at the same time demonstrating frustration towards those who are not perceived to do so. These frustrations contribute to, and normalise, disablist preconceptions which position disabled people as unable, inferior, and unworthy (Leah Burch, in press).

The absorption of disablist language into our everyday social discourse is an important point to consider. Hate crimes do not occur in a vacuum, but are socially and relationally embedded encounters that take place within the ordinariness of everyday life. Hate cannot solely be explained in terms of the beliefs and actions of extreme bigots, but rather uncomfortably, an emotion that is expressed and enacted by ordinary people in their everyday lives (Iganski, 2008). These ordinary expressions of hate become accepted and normalised as routine features of everyday life for those perceived to be 'different' (Chakraborti, 2017, 2018). For many disabled people, instances of hate represent a constant 'drip, drip, nag, nag effect' of 'low-level harassment' (EHRC, 2011, 2012, 2017). Findings from Mencap's 'Stand by Me' campaign suggest that these incidents become part of 'normal life' for many disabled people, and ones that they are expected to try to avoid (Mencap, 2011). Indeed, the ongoing project #ImWithSam has reported that incidents such as verbal and physical attacks, threats, and accusations of paedophilia can make disabled people feel scared, less confident, and more likely to stay within the confines of their own house (Dimensions, 2016). These 'low-level' incidents are often so regular that the boundaries between what is and is not acceptable become blurred. It is reported that many disabled people, and particularly those with learning difficulties, find it difficult to recognise hate incidents which in turn, contributes to low levels of reporting (Simmonds, Burke, Ahearn, & Kousoulis, 2018).

While a number of wide-scale research projects have highlighted the high level of 'bullying', 'name-calling', and harassment of disabled people (Brookes & Cain, 2015; Quarmby, 2008, 2011; Sherry, 2010), as well as recognise the relevance of disability to 'cyber-hate' (Alhaboby, Al-Khateeb, Barnes, & Short, 2016), very few articles specifically draw up the language of 'disablist hate speech'(Burch, 2018; Burnap & Williams, 2015, 2016).While derogatory and insulting, disablist hate has often been cloaked under the terming of 'banter' (Levin, 2013) and therefore not recognised for the personal, social, and cultural harms that it can create. In addition to the dismissal of 'hate' under the pretence of banter, disablist hate has been questioned over whether or not it exists at all (Sherry, 2010). As a result, such phenomena have often been left outside of wider discourses of hate. As this chapter will explore in more detail, the way in which we frame our understanding and meaning of 'hate' alters how we interpret and define the realities that people are experiencing. Therefore, this edited collection of chapters is a much-needed addition to wider conversations concerning disablism and disablist hate speech.

In this chapter, I hope to contribute to this small field of thought by exploring some conceptual and experiential understandings of hate speech. First, I grapple with the ambiguity surrounding the meaning of hate speech and offer a more holistic approach that is more flexible to the everyday experiences of disabled people. Next, I consider some of the stories shared by participants in the research project, and reflect upon how hate speech is understood, experienced, and also resisted. Doing so, I hope to forge greater links between the conceptual debates and everyday realities of hate speech in order to generate a more nuanced understanding of disablist hate speech that is informed *by* and *through* lived experience.

Conceptual understandings of disablist hate speech

The concept of hate speech has been debated by academics and policy-makers on an international scale. Developing from a multitude of disciplinary backgrounds, discussions have grappled with ongoing conceptual issues, such as how we might define, classify, measure, and regulate hate speech in the modern world. In particular, a recurring point of contention refers to the question of 'hate' itself, specifically concerning what this emotion means and how it might be enacted. In the following section, I consider the conceptual understanding of hate speech as it has been developed within and through these distinct disciplinary terrains. Importantly, I will outline how these understandings are relevant to the lives of disabled people, and thus seek to provide a more specific conceptual framing of disablist hate speech.

Disagreements regarding what 'hate' means has contributed to a vast amount of conceptual ambiguity. The concept of hate is suggested to be a slippery and elusive term that complicates the way in which we define and recognise hate crime and hate speech in practice (Chakraborti & Garland, 2012). There have been inconsistencies defining what hate crime means, as well as incongruities surrounding different 'victim' groups (Chakraborti, 2018). In addition, while the inclusion of the term 'hate' suggests a level of seriousness and significance, and thus urgency to respond, it is equally argued that hate is rarely recognised as the underlying motif of these particular crimes (Mason-Bish, 2013). According to Kiska (2013, p. 110), these ongoing conceptual tensions have created a term which 'seems to be whatever people choose it to mean. It lacks any objective criteria whatsoever.' While there is no universal definition, it is plausible to infer some key characteristics that do suggest some consistencies regarding the meaning and understanding of this term.

Hate speech may be defined as the expression of derogatory vocabularies (Iganski & Levin, 2015) and personal prejudices that aim to dehumanise the target (Tsesis, 2002) and provoke discrimination (Taylor, 2012). Hate speech preserves unequal power relations by denigrating the *Other* while simultaneously bolstering the superiority of the speaker. In turn, hate speech enables the construction and reconstruction of strict identity boundaries.

As Ahmed (2004, p. 49) suggests, 'Hate is involved in the very negotiation of boundaries between selves and others, and between communities, where "others" are brought into the sphere of my or our existence as a threat.'

These divisionary constructions are increasingly important within the traditional cultural trend to homogenise certain Others as threats to the moral social order, as illustrated in the introduction to this chapter. What Bauman (1989) referred to as a process of 'making invisible the very humanity of the victim,' shows how it was, and remains to be, possible to homogenise marginalised groups based upon negative assumptions prescribed by the majority. Research suggests that the use of homogenisation within cultural discourses makes it easier to feel and commit hate towards others, as their sense of individual humanity is removed (Sternberg & Sternberg, 2008) and their moral worth diminished. The category of the human shifts according to the moral and social values that one sees necessary; 'the human is a normative convention' (Braidotti, 2013, p. 26). Homogenisation thus creates an opposition to the category of the human, a group of marked identities that fail to meet the expectations and criteria of the human figure. Disabled people have historically been cast outside of this human boundary (Mollow, 2012) making the expression of hate speech particularly important to consider. Indeed, while hate speech may be directed towards an individual, the attack is likely to be aimed at the widespread denigration of a whole identity group. Disablist hate speech, from this perspective, represents the discursive and symbolic dehumanisation of disabled people as a marked-out group.

With these distinct, yet interrelated understandings of hate speech in mind, Maussen and Grillo's (2014) three characteristics of hate speech offer the most useful conceptualisation for this chapter. According to these authors, hate speech is directed towards an individual based upon their identity; it intends to, or results in, the stigmatisation of the target's identity group; and it causes the identity group to be perceived as undesirable and unworthy (Maussen & Grillo, 2014). Such a perspective allows for a reconsidering of the broader and more ambiguous concept of hate and the diverse ways that this can be discursively expressed towards disabled people.

A broader understanding accommodates and recognises everyday experiences of disablist hate speech, and not simply as an extreme articulation of prejudice or aggressive encounter (Sorial, 2015). Yong (2011, pp. 394–402) proposes four different types of speech that may be considered under the label of hate speech. The first, targeted vilification, is vilificatory speech which intends to wound, insult, or intimidate the target. Diffuse vilification, like the former intends to insult or intimidate, yet does so in the form of symbolic speech directed to wider audiences, rather than individuals or small groups. Third, political advocacy for exclusionary and/or eliminationist policies relates to the implementation of certain policies that result in further discrimination. Finally, adverse assertions of fact and value are defined as the expression of personal opinions regarding *Others*. Often, this type of speech is protected under the argument for free speech, which maintains the value of truth, discovery, democracy, and autonomy. Considering the diverse types of speech identified within the remit of hate speech is important, as it enables a more holistic approach to recognising the diverse ways that hate speech is expressed and the different harms it can enact.

An increasing field of work has sought to establish the harms of hate speech as a means of conceptualising what it is, and how it should be addressed (Gelber & McNamara, 2016; Iganski, 2008; Simpson, 2013; Waldron, 2012). Based upon research conducted with indigenous and ethnic minority communities in Australia, Gelber and McNamara (2016) present two different types of harms, constitutive and consequential. The first, constitutive harms, are those rendered in the 'saying' of hate speech and are of particular relevance to the psycho-emotional impacts of hate speech. That is, hate speech can cause existential pain for those targeted by it, such as feeling hurt, disempowered, and silenced (Gelber & McNamara, 2016). According to Waldron (2012), these harms impede one's sense of human dignity and subjective worth, therefore providing a case for legal recognition and regulation. Such hate speech expresses contempt towards someone's identity, which in turn, is likely to impede the target's own sense of identity. It is for this reason that Chakraborti (2015) has suggested that hate crimes 'hurt' more than other crimes. The findings from this research support this point, and these will be discussed in the following section of this chapter.

Consequential harms describe the effects of hate speech after it has been expressed. Relating to social harms such as inequality and discrimination, consequential harms maintain population divisions through the denigration of *Other* groups. In this way, consequential harms impact large groups of people, in particular those who may identity with the targeted individual's identity group (Bell & Perry, 2015). Hate speech sends out a terroristic message that certain people are not welcome within particular areas, and are therefore at risk of danger if they impede this discursive-locational contract (Iganski, 2006). As a result, individuals that identify with particularly marginalised groups may be subject to 'locational imprisonment', that is, feeling unable to move within certain spaces due to the fear of being targeted (Iganski, 2006). Simultaneously, hate speech acts as confirmation of stereotypes against particular members of society and therefore, the development of a cultural tolerance of discrimination (Nemes, 2002).

These consequential harms thus refer to the hardening of public attitudes and reproduction of marginalising stories and practices and, as discussed earlier, can easily be related to the scapegoating of disabled people within the context of austerity. It is within the embodied constitution of the ordinary, hard-working taxpayer as the '*real victim*' where hate becomes a shared cultural feeling towards the Other (Ahmed, 2004). Such harms, with their collectivising outcome, demonstrate how disablist hate speech contributes to structures of power within our society, which continue to place disabled people, among other marginalised groups, at the bottom of the hierarchy.

The research project

The findings discussed in this project are drawn from an Economic and Social Research Council (ESRC) funded research project[1] conducted as part of a Master's degree in Social Research at the University of Leeds. This was a small-scale preliminary project aiming to generate some preliminary insights and questions for the proceeding PhD project. Specifically, the project sought to gain a better understanding of the meaning and relevance of hate speech to the everyday realities of disabled people. It seems that the academic pursuit to effectively frame the boundaries of hate and create a clear and workable concept, has simultaneously dislocated the term to some extent, from the everyday realities of people's experiences. Chakraborti (2016, p.580) argues that a string of academic theorising of hate has created a concept that is 'too complex, too ethereal, and too detached from the everyday realities of victims.' Similarly, Gelber and McNamara (2016) note that the lack of experiential knowledge guiding discussions regarding hate speech has contributed to a highly theoretical and conceptual string of debates. Thus, this research seeks to listen to and (re)present the stories told by disabled people regarding their own experiences of hate speech. While academic debate has been fruitful to understanding the issue of hate speech, the focus on experience aims to present new directions and opportunities for taking these discussions and developments forward. In this way, this research begins with the experience of disability and, in line with this edited collection of works, seeks to confirm the relevance of hate speech to the lives of disabled people.

The project worked with four self-identified disabled people recruited through *Daisy Inclusive UK.* Semi-structured interviews sought to provide an open and reciprocal space where participants were invited to share stories and reflections of their own experiences and understandings of hate speech. While the practice of telling such emotive stories can be ethically challenging, it is equally suggested to be self-empowering (Elliott, 2005). In this way, the use of storytelling appealed to the participatory potential of research where participants are given time and space to reclaim the right to narrate their own lives (Morris, 1992). As a research tool, storytelling emerged as an empowering and emancipatory tool which invited participants to embark upon their own journey of meaning-making (Clandinin & Rosiek, 2007; Dorries & Haller, 2001), as well as valuing such a journey as a unique contribution to the research project. Following transcription, narrative analysis was employed as a means of capturing the lived realities of participants and the meanings attached to such experiences. This method of analysis aimed to interpret the way in which people perceived reality, made sense of their worlds, and performed social actions (Pheonix, Smith, & Sparkes, 2010, p. 3). Through this narrative interpretation, it was then possible to produce a longer story of analysis that thematically collated the narratives of participants. In the following section of this chapter, I explore some of the themes that arose throughout the analysis. This includes a consideration of the diverse ways that disablist hate speech is understood and responded to.

"The kind of thing you expect on the playground": Understanding and defining hate speech

Reflecting some of the wider conceptual inconsistences associated with the label of hate speech, participants demonstrated some difficulty in articulating a neat definition of what constitutes hate speech in their everyday lives. Participants offered general understandings of hate speech as 'horrible' (Arial), 'stereotypical' (Fred Smith; Raymond), and 'derogatory, nasty names' (Fred Smith). Building upon this, Raymond described hate speech as a means of labelling and marking out difference. This suggests that hate speech is understood in terms of problematisation, whereby certain individuals are marked out as different, and thus deemed to occupy an 'outsider status' (Perry, 2009). Similarly, Ariel discussed the role of hate speech as focusing on what is perceived to be 'wrong' with the targeted individual. Simply being different does not necessarily indicate that someone will be the target of hate crime or hate speech, but it is the problematisation of this difference that is key (Chakraborti, 2015).

Disablist hate speech should be understood as part of wider social processes of disablism, whereby 'a hierarchical structure of power in society [is] based upon notions of "difference", with the "mythical norm" at the top and those who are "different" assigned subordinate positions' (Hall, 2018, p. 75). This process of identity demarcation is bound to the relationship of stigma (Brown, 2013) and explains how acts of hate are justified when the target is presented as unworthy (Tsesis, 2002). Noted by Medina (2013), such a process has negative epistemic consequences, allowing members of the dominant group to have distorted images of themselves as 'knowers.' Hate speech is therefore understood to contribute to, as well as constitute, an oppressive construct disability, to which disabled people are distorted and stereotyped as merely putative subjects (Abberley, 1987).

The analytical work presented here draws connections between the theoretical understandings already developed and the personal understandings of hate speech offered by participants. In a similar way, participants presented their own journey of meaning-making, drawing upon already established terminology in order to help them to define hate speech in relation to their own experience. Collette, for example, referred to hate speech as 'bullying' and 'the kind of thing you expect on the playground', and Ariel referred to it as 'abuse, plain and simple it's abuse.' While the language of 'bullying' and 'abuse' still presents hate speech as negative, such concepts have been criticised as reducing the level of violence inherent in the expression of both hate speech and hate crime (Ralph, Capewell, & Bonnet, 2016). It is argued that the reference to 'abuse' or 'bullying' decriminalises the act of hate and results in a paternalistic response to challenging this, such as safeguarding (Sherry, 2010, 2017). The language that is used to describe and define hate speech raises important questions about how language moves between different layers of understanding, and more specifically, between academia and everyday life. As discussed in the previous section of this chapter, the way in which we understand hate speech, and the significance that we attach as a result, generates different responses and protections.

Aligning to the difficulty in defining hate speech with clarity and confidence, participants presented slight unease with explicitly relating the term to their own experiences. Collette, for example, expressed caution at being seen to 'exaggerate your situation.' Similarly, although Raymond classified hate speech as a form of 'disabled discrimination,' he also warned that it would be 'wrong to look for discrimination.' These reflections present the difficulty in recognising and defining what exactly constitutes hate speech, and how this differs from incidents that disabled people are expected to, or have been accustomed to, simply accepted as a routine part of everyday life. Many disabled people may not recognise certain incidents to be inherently hateful due to the normalisation of these types of experiences (Smith, 2015). As Collette explained, 'you start to think that is [hate speech] is the norm.' It is, she argues, 'just another straw on the back.' Relating to other research findings (EHRC, 2017; Richardson et al., 2016), the normalisation of these experiences not only complicated the way in which it was conceptually perceived, but equally, responses to it. Ariel explained that 'no-one's reporting it because that's what you get all your life' and Raymond suggested, 'if I reported everything that happened to be over the years, then I'd be doing not much else.' Crucially, the normalization of hate speech presented by participants blurs boundaries between what is and is not acceptable, confuses attempts to define what hate speech is, and thus places the impetus on self-management and regulation as a means of dealing with and responding to hate speech individually. It is perhaps unsurprising, then, that participants found it much easier to reflect upon the harms, rather than the definition of hate speech.

'If you are mentally tortured, it sticks with you': The harms of hate

When discussing the harms of hate speech, participants made a distinction between those that affected them personally, and those that had wider social consequences. Discussing wider social harms, or consequential harms (Yong, 2011), participants spoke about the dominance of negative social attitudes towards disability that dominate our current society. Specifically, not only had participants demonstrated the normalisation of hate speech in their everyday lives, but they noted wider cultural acceptance and more specifically, ignorance towards this reality. Collette described disablist hate crime being 'last on the agenda' and Raymond suggested that 'it's not taken as seriously as everything else.' For him, this lack of social response related to the assimilation of derogatory and disablist language into 'normal speech,' noting that 'around hate crime, it's all still open season on the disabled.' Supporting this point, Collette noted how terminology such as 'mong' and 'flid' had become 'everyday language.' Similarly, Ariel described,

> when people use words, erm, such as spaz, retard, they're all stuff that are used every day, all the time… They don't think that they're doing anything wrong because they don't see it as wrong, because they just see it as normal.

Like Levin (2013), participants point to the social acceptance of disablism as a natural feature of society, rather than one that provokes concern.

Focusing particularly upon the context of austerity and the welfare system, Fred Smith discussed the implications of an 'anti-disability campaign' which had created a particularly hostile environment for disabled people. This campaign, well documented within academic research (Briant et al., 2013; Burch, 2018; Garthwaite, 2011) and in the introduction of this chapter, has reinvigorated long-standing distinctions between 'deserving' and 'undeserving' populations (Patrick, 2016). Such representations have, according to Raymond, demonised disabled people by presenting them as 'useless' and 'a drain on society.' Drawing upon the understanding of hate speech as one concerned with identity formation, this 'anti-disability campaign' has determined 'the very negotiation of boundaries between selves and others,' bringing the 'other' figure in as proof of 'our' existence (Ahmed, 2004, p. 49). As Raymond meticulously explained:

> I think when society is struggling like it is with austerity, and people are struggling, they look for reasons. They look for reasons why they're struggling, why they haven't got any money, why they can't pay the bills, why they haven't got a job, why they, why the housing situation's horrible… we've been conditioned by the people that run this country to look at each other… you haven't got this job because of the disabled, you haven't got this job, and then we tear on each other.

Evident within Raymond's explanation of how disabled people have been made a scapegoat to much larger stories of financial instability, there is a sense of violence that is inherent to his description. His suggestion that we 'tear on each other' draws upon the physical act of pulling something apart with force. This description implies that while the negotiation of boundaries through hate speech is symbolic, such relationships become embodied by social actors. They are felt within the everyday negotiations of our minds and our bodies within the surrounding social space. The construction of disability as a marker of deviance and inferiority within the welfare state carries significant consequences for the way in which populations are divided. Such divisions are fundamental to the expression of hate speech as this notion of deviance is 'necessary for the symbolic (re)affirmation of collective sentiments and the ritual (re)enforcement of moral boundaries'

(Williams & Bendelow, 1998, p. 47). The danger, of course, is that these boundaries are affirmed within the minds and bodies of those targeted.

Through the telling of their stories, participants reflected upon some of the personal harms that they had experienced as a result of hate speech. Importantly, participants drew upon the distinction between 'verbal' and 'physical' hate not as a means of hierarchising harms, but demonstrating the constitutive harms (Gelber & McNamara, 2016) of both types of hate. For Collette:

> hate crime is a horrible thing, and speech is nowhere as bad as shoving a knife in you or setting fire to your house, or whatever people do, but it still can be as hurtful because it still messes with your head.

The psychological violence of hate speech is made clear in Collette's reflections on her own experiences. Not violent in the typical sense of 'shoving a knife in you' or 'setting fire to your house,' Collette describes the psycho-emotional violence she has encountered. More traditional conceptualisations of violence have tended to privilege expressions that are physical, while excluding verbal or symbolic acts from definition. For example, Cudd (2006, p.87; emphasis added) defines violence as 'the intentional, forceful infliction of *physical* harm.' This type of definition has maintained a hierarchy of oppression that perceives physical violence as the most serious form of violence (Capewell, Ralph, & Bonnett, 2015; D. Meyer, 2010). Hate speech, within this conceptualisation, is perceived as little more than an indication of further, more violent acts of harm, rather than innately violent in itself. While the expression of hate speech may, in fact, foreshadow a physical act of hate crime, participants in this research suggest that hate speech in itself is harmful. For Ariel, dismantling this hierarchy is important as hate speech can have long-lasting psychological harms. She explains that 'sticks and stones may break my bones, but words do so much more… If you are mentally tortured, it sticks with you.' Here, Ariel urges us to rethink the traditional boundaries of violence discussed above, and recognise the long-lasting emotional violence that can occur as a consequence of hate speech. Such violence, it is suggested, demonstrates the psycho-emotional disablism inherent to disablist hate speech.

Psycho-emotional disablism refers to the internalisation of oppression resulting from the accumulation of disablist encounters (Thomas, 1999). Such encounters shape 'what people can *be,* as well as affecting what they can *do* as a consequence' (Thomas, 2004, p. 38). Thus, from this approach, the process of disablement can operate within individual minds and bodies, moving within and between the outside and the inside of our bodies. Experiences of disablement contribute to how our personal subjectivities are relationally shaped and sculpted by the surrounding social world. As Mol and Law (2004 cited in Titchkosky, 2007) explains, 'we all *have* and *are* a body… as part of our daily practice, *we also do (our) bodies.* In practice, we enact them.' From this understanding, the experience of hate speech within the everyday lives of disabled people contributes to the ways in which disabled minds and bodies interact with that social world in the future. As reported by participants, hate speech impeded their sense of self, dignity, and their confidence. For Collette, hate speech made her feel 'isolated' and 'helpless,' and Raymond said that it would 'break me sometimes.' In her own words, Ariel described a particularly pertinent reality of this process of internalisation and psycho-emotional disablism for her:

> when someone digs you a hole and throws you in it, well in your mind you're gonna keep slowly scratching out of that hole until you get to the point where you hit rock bottom and you can't scratch anymore.

Here, Ariel offers a vivid reflection on how the psycho-emotional disablism that occurs as a result of hate speech, can result in sensually felt bodily and psychological restrictions.

Important to consider, however, is that while hate can hurt, it can also be resisted. Indeed, due to the diversity of experiences of having an impairment within a disabling world, disabled people have a particularly unique body of knowledge of the surrounding social world (Siebers, 2013; 2014). While experiences of hate speech can result in long-lasting psychological harms, they can simultaneously lead to complex means of responding to, and resisting, disablism. The embodiment of harmful and disabling experiences creates an opportunity for resistance. In the words of Merleau-Ponty (1962, p. 206), 'we are in the world through our body… by thus remaking contact with the body and with the world, we… rediscover ourselves.' It is this embodied process of rediscovery and resistance that the following section explores.

"Make them laugh, they'll listen and if they listen, they learn": Resisting hate

Any holistic account of oppression should, for Wendell (1996), also recognise means of resistance. Resistance appeals to the confrontation of normative structures which have traditionally sought to position particular identities as inferior to others (Medina, 2013). For participants, resistance was evident in the refusal to see themselves as subjects of tragedy (Thomas, 1999b) and instead, as educative beings able to disrupt narrow ideas about disability that stem from a lack of knowledge. 'We are scared of things we don't understand, people don't understand difference' (Fred Smith). Specifically, both Raymond and Ariel discussed the implications of a segregated education system, which limits interactions between disabled and nondisabled children. As Raymond explained, 'it's about educating children and stopping the divides at a young age… you've gotta be exposed to people that are different than you.' Greater diversity within the school system is suggested to 'stop the divides at a young age' (Raymond) as well as to generate an appreciation of the diverse gains that disabled learners and teachers bring to the classroom (Bolt, 2017).

In its wider context, education plays a role in the everyday encounters between disabled and nondisabled people. In particular, humour was described as a response to hate speech which, in turn, presented an opportunity to challenge oppression through education (Sorensen, 2008). Acting like 'a comedian' enabled Raymond to challenge the views of others as it created 'a space for actually having conversations about disabled, in a humorous way' (Raymond). Humorous conversations are vital in order to engage others with disability, as Fred Smith explained: 'I'll make something funny out of anything, because, make them laugh, they'll listen, and if they listen, they learn.'

To this end, it is suggested that humour is a means of instigating honest conversations about what it means to be disabled (Reid, Stoughton, & Smith, 2006) by 'switch[ing] the comic gaze outwards towards disabling social norms and critiq[ing] disabling stereotypes' (Lockyer, 2015, p. 1406). Disability comedy, as enacted and explored by participants, provides a route to education, 'because it *re-presents* disability, potentially leading to changes in social behaviour' (Reid et al., 2006, p. 639). That is, it *re-presents* disability as a source of knowledge, rather than construction of wider disablism. Disability humour functions as a resistive device by educating others about alternative ways of *being* in the world and therefore stretching normative imaginations of the human mind and body.

While the use of humour is presented here as a device for educating others, and in turn challenging expressions of disablist hate speech, participants presented more disabling encounters with humour. Raymond in particular, warned of self-depreciation when reflecting upon how he previously used humour in an attempt to pass off hate speech, rather than address it. Similarly, Collette suggested the need to 'have a laugh at yourself, you have to sometimes.' It may be that humour provides a means of managing disablist hate speech, with both resistive and self-depreciating results. As Raymond explained, 'The verbal towards me, I've had it over the years, you know, you know the names I've been called. I always try to deal with it with a bit of humour.' The risk of self-depreciation through the management of hate speech in humorous ways thus presents the danger of reinforcing to the majority that certain stereotypes are open to ridicule (Ellithorpe, Esralew, & Holbert, 2014).

While the experience of humour is not straightforward, it may still be perceived as a means of managing and confronting disablist hate speech as it attempts to bridge gaps between disabled and non-disabled people (Lockyer, 2015) as well as erase the notion of disability as a taboo (Stronach & Allan, 1999). Such humour enables the formerly oppressed individual to take ownership of the stereotypes used against them (Sorensen, 2008). Thus, while the power and outcome of humour is unpredictable (Meeus & Mahieu, 2009; Reid et al., 2006), disability humour is presented to have enabled participants to take control of situations that aim to reduce their sense of power, disrupt social hierarchies, and presents new ways of engaging and being in the world around. This disruption of power is vital to challenging disablist hate speech, as well as exposing wider systems of disablism. Indeed, disability disrupts power relations to assert the productivity of resistance that is able to push against the docility that power strives for (Beckett, Bagguley, & Campbell, 2016). Moreover, humour presents the management of one's own emotions based upon knowledge about the social world, in order to control a situation where emotions are no longer at risk (Meyer, Salovey, Caruso, & Cherkasskiy, 2011; Salovey & Meyer, 1990). Disability emerges, then, not simply as a socially constructed identity, but a mind and body of knowledge (Siebers, 2014) that has developed unique and novel ways of navigating a disabling social world.

While it is imperative to continue to research the ways in which disablist hate speech is expressed and the context in which it emerges, it is equally important to harness the diverse ways in which disabled people are resisting these disablist expressions.

Conclusion

In this chapter, I have offered some preliminary thoughts regarding some of the ways that disabled people might understand, conceptualise, and respond to disablist hate speech. While the findings are based upon the stories of a small number of participants, these stories have been fruitful to thinking more critically and reflectively about what we mean and understand when we talk about disablist hate speech.

Importantly, the findings demonstrate the need to think about hate speech as it operates in the everyday lives of disabled people. While the literary background of hate speech is theoretically complex, it continues to lack conceptual clarity. Such ambiguity parallels the difficulty participants faced when attempting to articulate a neat and concise definition of hate speech. Indeed, while participants were able to talk about hate speech, they expressed difficulty in drawing conceptual boundaries around it. In particular, the normalisation of these types of experiences seemed to have blurred the boundaries between what is and is not acceptable behaviour (Hollomotz, 2013). In turn, it can mean that it is easier for individuals to accept incidents like hate speech as part of their everyday life. As Mark Brookes (in Brookes & Cain, 122015, p. 91) explains, 'I had been underestimating how often I had been a target… I often just try to ignore it and move on, because it is over so quickly.' The acceptance and lack of recognition of these incidents, however, will continue to contribute to the significant under-reporting of disablist hate (Emerson & Roulstone, 2014).

It is also important to recognise that while the act of hate speech may be over very quickly, participants in this research described their long-lasting impacts. Such harms have been conceptualised using the work of Carol Thomas on psycho-emotional disablism in order to detail the intricate ways that hate speech is disabling, 'by shaping individuals' "inner worlds," sense of "self" and social behaviours' (Thomas, 2007, p. 72). Participants reported feelings of disempowerment and lack of confidence (Reeve, 2014) as a result of their experiences of hate speech. This process of psycho-emotional disablism is thought to contribute to the epistemic violence inherent to the expression of hate speech (Medina, 2013) as targeted individuals begin to see 'themselves and their lives through the stigma' (Brown, 2013, p. 154). These harms are particularly relevant to wider work on hate crime which documents the everyday navigation and management that individuals make in order to avoid situations where hate arises (Iganski & Lagou, 2018; Iganski, 2008; Perry, 2018).

The austerity policies which often scapegoat disabled people are an element of the structural background to disability hate speech and must be challenged. But individual responses to disablist hate speech also deserve more attention. Importantly, participants in this research were keen to discuss the more affirmative ways that they responded to experiences of hate speech. In particular, the use of humour and education were presented as methods of not only coping with hateful experiences, but also challenging the very disabling attitudes that underpin them. Humour, for example, offered participants the opportunity to take ownership of stereotypes traditionally used against them (Sorensen, 2008) while also providing a means of (re)presenting disability in ways that can help to eradicate the notion of taboo (Reid et al., 2006; Stronach & Allan, 1999). Such a response enabled participants to engage others in meaningful and honest conversations about disability. The resistive strategies discussed by participants demonstrates that the *effects* of hate crime are not determined, but rather best understood by listening to the voices of those at the centre (Ahmed, 2004). By reflecting upon personal experiences of hate speech, participants demonstrated their unique knowledge of the social world, and the personal navigations they carried out in order to *be* within this social world. In this way, participants are presented as '*productive bodies* capable of activities that change the nature of their lives' (Burkitt, 1999, p. 2; emphasis in original). Gaining a greater insight to the ways in which disabled people are already challenging disablist hate in their everyday lives is crucial in order to work more effectively *with* disabled people. Such an approach would allow us to tap into and develop innovative means of resisting hate crime that have relevance and utility to the realities of hate crime experienced by disabled people in their everyday lives.

Note

1 ESRC Grant Number ES/J500215/1.

References

Abberley, P. (1987). The concept of oppression and the development of a social theory of disability. *Disability, Handicap and Society*, *2*(1), 5–19.

Ahmed, S. (2004). *The cultural politics of emotion* (1st ed.). Edinburgh: Edinburgh University Press.

Alhaboby, Z., Al-Khateeb, H., Barnes, J., & Short, E. (2016). 'The language is disgusting and they refer to my disability': The cyberharassment of disabled people. *Disability & Society*, *31*(8), 1138–1143.

Bauman, Z. (1989). *Modernity and the Holocaust*. Cambridge: Polity Press.

Baumberg, B., Bell, K., Gaffney, D., Deacon, R., Hood, C., & Sage, D. (2012). *Benefits stigma in Britain*. Retrieved from https://wwwturn2us-2938.cdn.hybridcloudspan.com/T2UWebsite/media/Documents/Benefits-Stigma-in-Britain.pdf

Beckett, A., Bagguley, P., & Campbell, T. (2016). Foucault, social movements and heterotopic horizons: Rupturing the order of things. *Social Movement Studies*, *16*(2), 169–181.

Bell, J., & Perry, B. (2015). Outside looking in: The community impacts of anti-lesbian, gay, and bisexual hate crime. *Journal of Homosexuality*, *62*(1), 98–120.

Bolt, D. (2017). Enabling the classroom and the curriculum: Higher education, literary studies and disability. *Journal of Further and Higher Education*, *41*(4), 556–565.

Braidotti, R. (2013). *The posthuman*. Cambridge: Polity Press.

Briant, E., Watson, N., & Philo, G. (2011). *Bad news for disabled people: How the newspapers are reporting disability*. Glasgow: Strathclyde Centre for Disability Research and Glasgow Media Unit.

Briant, E., Watson, N., & Philo, G. (2013). Reporting disability in the age of austerity: The changing face of media representation of disability and disabled people in the United Kingdom and the creation of new 'folk devils'. *Disability & Society*, *28*(6), 874–889.

Brookes, M., & Cain, D. (2015). A different reality. In R. Shah & P. Giannasi (Eds.), *Tackling disability discrimination and disability hate crime* (pp. 90–97). London: Jessica Kingsley.

Brown, L. (2013). Stigma: An enigma demystified. In L. Davis (Ed.), *The disability studies reader* (4th ed., pp. 147–160). London: Routledge.

Burch, Leah. (in press). 'The stuff of nightmares': Representations of disability on the online bulletin board, Reddit. In D. Garrasi & J. Johanssen (Eds.), *Disability, media, and representations: Other bodies*. London: Routledge.

Burch, L. (2018). 'You are a parasite on the productive classes': Online disablist hate speech in austere times. *Disability and Society*, *33*(3), 392–415. https://doi.org/10.1080/09687599.2017.1411250

Burkitt, I. (1999). *Bodies of thought: Embodiment, identity and modernity*. London: Sage Publications.

Burnap, P., & Williams, M. (2015). Cyber hate speech on twitter: An application of machine classification and statistical modeling for policy and decision making. *Policy and Internet*, *7*(2), 223–242. https://doi.org/10.1002/poi3.85

Burnap, P., & Williams, M. (2016). Us and them: Identifying cyber hate on Twitter across multiple protected characteristics. *EPJ Data Science*, *5*(11), 1–15. https://doi.org/10.1140/epjds/s13688-016-0072-6

Capewell, C., Ralph, S., & Bonnett, L. (2015). The continuing violence towards disabled people. *Journal of Research in Special Educational Needs*, *15*(3), 211–221. https://doi.org/10.1111/1471-3802.12112

Chakraborti, N. (2015). Re-thinking hate crime: Fresh challenges for policy and practice. *Journal of Interpersonal Violence*, *30*(10), 1738–1754.

Chakraborti, N. (2016). Mind the gap! Making stronger connections between hate crime policy and scholarship. *Criminal Justice Policy Review*, *27*(6), 577–589. https://doi.org/10.1177/0887403415599641

Chakraborti, N. (2017). Responding to hate crime: Escalating problems, continued failings. *Criminology & Criminal Justice*, *18*, 1–18.

Chakraborti, N. (2018). Framing the boundaries of hate crime. In Nathan Hall, A. Corb, P. Giannasi & J. Grieve (Eds.), *The Routledge international handbook on hate crime* (pp. 13–23). London: Routledge.

Chakraborti, N., & Garland, J. (2012). Reconceptualising hate crime victimisation through the lens of vulnerability and "difference". *Theoretical Criminology*, *16*(4), 499–514.

Clandinin, J., & Rosiek, J. (2007). Mapping a landscape of narrative inquiry. In J. Clandinin (Ed.), *Handbook of narrative inquiry: Mapping a methodology* (pp. 35–76). London: Sage.

Conservatives. (2015). *The Conservative Party Manifesto 2015*. London: Conservatives.

CRPD. (2016). *Inquiry concerning the United Kingdom of Great Britain and Northern Ireland carried out by the Committee under article 6 of the Optional Protocol to the Convention*. CRPD.

Cudd, A. (2006). *Analyzing oppression*. Oxford: Oxford University Press.

Dimensions. (2016). *#ImWithSam – experiences of hate crime*. Reading. Dimensions UK. Retrieved from https://www.dimensions-uk.org/get-involved/campaigns/say-no-autism-learning-disability-hate-crime-imwithsam/

Dorries, B., & Haller, B. (2001). The news of inclusive education: A narrative analysis. *Disability & Society*, *16*(6), 871–891. https://doi.org/10.1080/09687590120084001

EHRC. (2011). *Hidden in plain sight: Inquiry into disability-related harassment*. EHRC.

EHRC. (2012). *Out in the Open: Tackling disability-related harassment, a manifesto for change*. EHRC.

EHRC. (2017). *Tackling disability-related harassment: Final progress report 2017*. EHRC.

Elliott, J. (2005). *Using narrative in social research*. London: Sage.

Ellithorpe, M., Esralew, S., & Holbert, L. (2014). Putting the 'self' in self-depreciation: When deprecating humor about minorities is acceptable. *Humor*, *27*(3), 401–422.

Emerson, E., & Roulstone, A. (2014). Developing an evidence base for violent and disablist hate crime in Britain: Findings from the life opportunities survey. *Journal of Interpersonal Violence*, *29*(17), 3086–3104.

Garthwaite, K. (2011). 'The language of shirkers and scroungers?' Talking about illness, disability and coalition welfare reform. *Disability & Society*, *12*(2), 369–372.

Gelber, K., & McNamara, L. (2016). Evidencing the harms of hate speech. *Social Identities*, *22*(3), 324–341.

Glaeser, E. (2005). The political economy of hatred. *The Quarterley Journal of Economics*, *120*, 45–86.

Goodley, D., Lawthom, R., & Runswick-Cole, K. (2014). Dis/ability and austerity: Beyond work and slow death. *Disability & Society*, *29*(6), 980–984.

Government, H. (2010). *The coalition: Our programme for government*. London: Crown Copyright.

Hall, Nathan. (2018). Understanding hate crimes: Sociological and criminological perspectives. In N. Hall, A. Corb, P. Giannasi & J. Grieve (Eds.), *The Routledge international handbook on hate crime* (pp. 69–80). London: Routledge.

Hollomotz, A. (2013). Disability and the continuum of violence. In A. Roulstone & H. Mason-Bish (Eds.), *Disability, hate crime and violence* (pp. 52–64). Oxon: Routledge.

Iganski, Paul. (2006). Free to speak, free to hate? In L. Morris (Ed.), *Rights: Sociological perspectives*. London: Routledge.

Iganski, Paul. (2008). *Hate crime and the city*. Bristol: Policy Press.

Iganski, P., & Lagou, S. (2018). The personal injuries of 'hate crime.' In N. Hall, A. Corb, P. Giannasi & G. D. Grieve (Eds.), *The Routledge international handbook on hate crime* (pp. 34–46). London: Routledge.

Iganski, Paul., & Levin, J. (2015). *Hate crime: An international perspective*. New York: Routledge.

Kiska, R. (2013). Hate speech: A comparison between the European Court of Human Rights and the United States Supreme Court jurisprudence. *Regent University Law Review, 25*, 107–161.

Levin, J. (2013). Disablist violence in the US: Unacknowledged hate crime. In A. Roulstone & H. Mason-Bish (Eds.), *Disability, hate crime, and violence* (pp. 95–105). London: Routledge.

Lockyer, S. (2015). From comedy targets to comedy-makers: Disability and comedy in love performance. *Disability & Society, 30*(9), 1397–1412.

Mason-Bish, H. (2013). Conceptual issues in the construction of disability hate crime. In A. Roulstone & H. Mason-Bish (Eds.), *Disability, hate crime and violence* (pp. 11–24). London: Routledge.

Maussen, M., & Grillo, R. (2014). Regulation of speech in multicultural societies: Introduction. *Journal of Ethnic and Migration Studies, 40*(2), 174–193. https://doi.org/10.1080/1369183X.2013.851470

Medina, J. (2013). *The epistemology of resistance: Gender and racial oppression, epistemic injustice, and the social imagination.* Oxford: Oxford University Press.

Meeus, W., & Mahieu, P. (2009). You can see the funny side, can't you? Pupil humour with the teacher as target. *Educational Studies, 35*(5), 553–560.

Mencap. (2011). *Stand by me: Ending disability hate crime together.* London. Mencap [online] Retrieved from https://www.mencap.org.uk/sites/default/files/2016-07/How%20to%20stand%20by%20me.pdf Accessed 3 September 2019.

Merleau-Ponty, M. (1962). *The phenomenology of perception.* London: Routledge.

Meyer, D. (2010). Evaluating the severity of hate-motivated violence: Intersectional differences among LGBT hate crime victims. *Sociology, 44*(5), 980–995. https://doi.org/10.1177/0038038510375737

Meyer, J. D., Salovey, P., Caruso, D., & Cherkasskiy, L. (2011). Emotional intelligence. In R. Sternberg & S. Kaufman (Eds.), *The Cambridge handbook of intelligence* (pp. 528–549). Cambridge: Cambridge University Press.

Mollow, A. (2012). Is sex disability? Queer theory and the disability drive? In R. McRuer & A. Mollow (Eds.), *Sex and disability* (pp. 285–313). Durham: Duke University Press.

Morris, J. (1992). Personal and political: A feminist perspective on researching physical disability. *Disability, Handicap and Society, 7*(2), 157–166.

Nemes, I. (2002). Regulating hate speech in cyberspace: Issues of desirability and efficacy. *Information & Communications Technology Law, 11*(3), 193–220. https://doi.org/10.1080/1360083022000031902

Patrick, R. (2016). Living with and responding to the 'scrounger' narrative in the UK: Exploring everyday strategies of acceptance, resistance and deflection. *Journal of Poverty and Social Justice, 24*(3), 245–259. https://doi.org/10.1332/175982716X14721954314887

Perry, B. (2009). The sociology of hate: Theoretical approaches. In B. Levin (Ed.), *Hate crimes Volume 1: Understanding and defining hate crime* (pp. 55–76). Westport, CT: Praeger.

Perry, Barbara. (2018). Exploring the community impacts of hate crime. In Nathan Hall, A. Corb, P. Giannasi, & J. Grieve (Eds.), *The Routledge international handbook on hate crime* (pp. 47–59). London: Routledge.

Pheonix, C., Smith, B., & Sparkes, A. C. (2010). Narrative analysis in aging studies: A typology for consideration. *Journal of Aging Studies, 24*(1), 1–11. https://doi.org/10.1016/j.jaging.2008.06.003

Quarmby, K. (2008). *Getting away with murder: Disabled people's experiences of hate crime in the UK*. London: Scope.

Quarmby, K. (2011). *Scapegoat: Why we are failing disabled people*. London: Portobello Books.

Ralph, S., Capewell, C., & Bonnet, E. (2016). Disability hate crime: persecuted for difference. *Journal of Special Education*, *43*(3), 215–232.

Reeve, D. (2014). Psycho-emotional disablism. In C. Cameron (Ed.), *Disability studies: A student's guide* (pp. 122–125). London: Sage.

Reicher, S. (2012). From perception to mobilization: The shifting paradigm of prejudice. In J. Dixon & M. Levine (Eds.), *Beyond prejudice* (pp. 27–47). Oxford: Wiley.

Reid, K., Stoughton, E., & Smith, R. (2006). The humorous construction of disability: 'Stand-up' comedians in the United States. *Disability & Society*, *21*(6), 629–643.

Richardson, L., Jill, J. B., Colin, B., Aida, G., Julian, M., Richardson, L., … Himmerich, J. (2016). 'I felt that I deserved it' –Experiences and implications of disability hate crime. *Tizard Learning Disability Review*, *21*(1), 80–88. https://doi.org/10.1108/TLDR-03-2015-0010

Salovey, P., & Meyer, J. D. (1990). Emotional intelligence. *Imagination Cognition and Personality*, *9*(1), 185–211.

Sherry, M. (2010). *Disability hate crimes: Does anyone really hate disabled people?* Surrey: Ashgate.

Sherry, M. (2017). Disability and hate crime. In *Lecture presentation at Leeds Beckett University*. Leeds.

Siebers, Tobin. (2013). Disability and the theory of complex embodiment – For identity politics in a new reigster. In L. Davis (Ed.), *The disability studies reader* (4th ed., pp. 278–297). New York: Routledge.

Siebers, T. (2014). Returning the social to the social model. In *Non-normative positivisms: Towards a methodology of critical embodiment*. Minneapolis, MN: Wordpress.

Simmonds, R., Burke, C., Ahearn, E., & Kousoulis, A. (2018). *A life without fear? A call for collective action against learning disability hate crime*. London: Mental Health Foundation.

Simpson, R. M. (2013). Dignity, harm, and hate speech. *Law and Philosophy*, *32*(1), 701–728. https://doi.org/10.1007/s10982-012-9164-z

Smith, M. (2015). Disability hate crime – A call for action. In R. Shah & P. Giannasi (Eds.), *Tackling disability discrimination and disability hate crime* (pp. 299–324). London: Jessica Kingsley.

Sorensen, M. (2008). Humor as a serious strategy of nonviolent resistance to oppression. *Peace & Change*, *33*(2), 167–190.

Sorial, S. (2015). Hate speech and distorted communication: Rethinking the limits of incitement. *Law and Philosophy*, *34*(1), 299–324. https://doi.org/10.1007/s10982-014-9214-9

Sternberg, R. J., & Sternberg, K. (2008). *The nature of hate. The nature of hate*. New York: Cambridge University Press. https://doi.org/10.1017/CBO9780511818707

Stronach, I., & Allan, J. (1999). Joking with disability: What's the difference between the comic and the tragic in disability discourses? *Body & Society*, *5*(4), 31–45.

Taylor, R. (2012). Hate speech, the priority of liberty, and the temptations of non ideal theory. *Ethical Theory and Modern Practice*, *15*(3), 353–368.

Thomas, C. (1999a). *Female forms: Experiencing and understanding disability*. Buckingham: Open University Press.

Thomas, C. (1999b). Narrative identity and the disabled self. In M. Corker & S. French (Eds.), *Disability discourse* (pp. 47–56). Buckingham: Open University Press.

Thomas, C. (2004). How is disability understood? An examination of sociological approaches. *Disability & Society*, *19*(6), 569–583.

Thomas, C. (2007). *Sociologies of disability and illness: Contested ideas in disability studies and medical sociology*. Basingstoke: Palgrave Macmillan.

Titchkosky, T. (2007). *Reading & writing disability differently: The textured life of embodiment*. Toronto, ON: University of Toronto Press.

Tsesis, A. (2002). *Destructive messages: How hate speech paves the way for harmful social movements*. New York: New York University Press.

Waldron, J. (2012). *The harm in hate speech. Political studies review*. President and Fellows of Harvard College. https://doi.org/10.4159/harvard.9780674065086

Wendell, S. (1996). *The rejected body: Feminist philosophical reflections on disability*. New York: Routledge.

Williams, S., & Bendelow, G. (1998). *The lived body: Sociological themes, embodied issues*. London: Routledge.

Yong, C. (2011). Does freedom of speech include hate speech? *Res Publica*, *17*(4), 385–403. https://doi.org/10.1007/s11158-011-9158-y

Part II

The personal impact of disability hate speech

4 Disability hate speech

"They think they can call me anything"

Armineh Soorenian

Introduction

This chapter explores the issue of disability hate speech within the broader context of disability hate crime in the United Kingdom (UK). It discusses the possible motivations behind disability hate speech and the reasons why little focus has been given to this strand of disability hate crime in British criminal law both in terms of its recognition and trial. Insights will be shared as to why even the moderate versions of hate speech like name calling, which are criminal offences under the Criminal Justice and Public Order Act are not being enforced, instead simply being left unreported and classed as "just what happens" to disabled people (Criminal Justice and Public Order Act, 1994). The chapter concludes by recommending ways of responding more effectively to these crimes, including raising awareness of the damaging impact of disability hate speech.

Laws and practices concerning disability hate crime in the UK

The UK Equality Act (The Equality Act 2010, p. 7) defines "disability" as a "physical or mental impairment and the impairment has a substantial and long-term adverse effect on his or her ability to carry out normal day-to-day activities." With this definition in mind, a total of 13.9 million individuals are disabled in the UK (Department of Work and Pensions, 2018). In their daily interactions, disabled people are often targeted because of perpetrators' prejudicial attitudes. The United Nations Convention on the Rights of Persons with Disabilities (United Nations, 2008 Article 16 – Freedom from exploitation, violence and abuse) highlights this problem and demands appropriate responses, stating: "State parties shall take all appropriate legislative, administrative, social, educational, and other measures to protect persons with disabilities, both within and outside the home, from all forms of exploitation, violence, and abuse, including their gender-based aspects."

Notwithstanding this international obligation, disabled people in the UK are known to experience more harassment and hate than their nondisabled counterparts (Emerson & Roulstone, 2014). Targeting people because of certain characteristics which render them vulnerable (be it because of age, impairment, gender, "disability" status, or any other protected characteristics), where prejudice cannot be discounted from such targeted abuse is a key definitional feature of a "hate incident," and where a law is broken, a "hate crime" (Citizens Advice, 2018). The "discriminatory oppressive or abusive behaviour" based on values and norms of a minority group of people, perceived threats or "social strain" and limited access to resources related to an age of economic downturn and social instability may be considered as "disablism" (Quarmby, 2008, p. 9). In this context, the perpetrators' perceived motivations generally reflect a prejudice created by linking disability benefits with impairments, an assumption of the group definition of the victim, a negative construction of perceived difference.

As a manifestation of disablism, "disability hate crime" was introduced into section 146 of the Criminal Justice Act in (2003), becoming law in 2005 (Criminal Justice Act, 2003). The Crown Prosecution Service (CPS) defines a hate crime as "any criminal offence which is perceived by the victim or any other person, to be motivated by hostility or prejudice, based on a person's disability or perceived disability; race or perceived race; or religion or perceived religion; or sexual orientation or perceived sexual orientation or transgender identity or perceived transgender identity." (Crown Prosecution Service, 2016). That said, the CPS guidance also states that "there is no legal definition of hostility, so we use the everyday understanding of the word which includes ill-will, spite, contempt, prejudice, unfriendliness, antagonism, resentment and dislike" (Crown Prosecution Service, 2017).

"Disability" is one of five centrally monitored strands of hate crime, the others being race, religion/faith, sexual orientation, and gender identity. However, a "disability hate crime" is not a separate offence in law. Where there is not an identifiable criminal offence, the police refer to and record some cases as "hate incidents." Section 146 of the Criminal Justice Act creates a sentencing provision, which puts a duty on courts to increase the sentence of any offence where there is evidence of hostility towards the victim because of disability (Criminal Justice Act, 2003). In these instances, the establishing of aggravation due to disability-related hostility should be treated as more serious than an incident where such factors are absent. To establish disablist "hate crime" in law, it is expected that either disability-related hostility is displayed, or hostility based wholly or partly on a motivation particular to a person's "disability" is demonstrated (Criminal Justice Act, 2003) where hostility has been established through words or actions, there is no requirement for hate crime to be established through motivation. As such bullying and hate speech are not seen as a crime in English law unless explicitly accompanied by a primary offence-assault, like affray, vandalism, or property offences (Roulstone, Thomas, & Balderston, 2011).

In the British context, official statistics released by the Home Office in 2018 indicated that between 2011/12 and 2017/18, the number of disability hate crimes reported have increased by more than 300%, from 1,748 to 7,226 (Home Office, 2018). Still, it is thought that this is under-reported when compared to the Crime Survey for England and Wales (Home Office, 2018). It is believed that the difference may be due to the respondents of the Crime Survey basing their response on their perceived vulnerability. This is likely to be a reason why the estimate of disability hate crime is higher in the Crime Survey than the number of these offences recorded by the police. It is unclear, however, if the numbers demonstrate an increase in incidents or an increase in the awareness, an increased willingness of individuals to report crime, or increased diligence by police. Regardless, the proportion of these hate crimes being classified as hate speech, involving harassment and bullying, and the corresponding charges is undocumented. Disability hate speech can take the form of unwelcome comments (written or spoken) or conduct as verbal abuse, being shouted at, name calling, offensive graffiti, or online posts. The lack of attention to and recognition of such crimes is alarming and is despite the fact that hate speech has the potential to cause mental distress, physical harm, insecurity, intruding an individual's privacy and dignity, and contribute to an offensive, humiliating, hostile, intimidating, and degrading environment.

Disabled people often rely on social media to feel less isolated and to join virtual communities. Despite this, over recent decades, the advancement in digital communication facilitated through virtual environments has created and reinforced an online context for disablist vulnerable situations. The anonymity of offenders has exposed disabled people to online offences (Wells & Mitchell, 2014). Cyber-harassment refers to these anti-social offences, defined as intimidating and unwanted contacts via electronic means that triggers fear and distress (Dreßing, Bailer, Anders, Wagner, & Gallas, 2014). Internet hate crimes including such disability-related incidents as disability hate speech are starting to be recognised and victims are being encouraged to report these crimes to the police (National Police Chiefs' Council, 2015). Charity organisation Leonard Cheshire contacted police forces in England and Wales, using the Freedom of Information Act to obtain data about online disability hate crime between 2016/17 and 2017/18. Almost three quarters of the forces responded. Leonard Cheshire found that there had been a total of 313 disability hate crimes recorded in 2017/18, compared to 235 offences in the previous year, an increase of almost a third (Leonard Cheshire, 2019).

In the UK there are a number of legislative acts to respond to cyber-harassment. These include Malicious Communications (1988), Criminal Justice and Public Order Act (1994), the Protection from Harassment Act (1997), Crime and Disorder Act (1998), Communications Act (2003), and Equality Act (2010) (Crown Prosecution Service, 2016). In addition, when disability is taken into account, the harassment could also be addressed under the Disability Discrimination Act (1995), Section 127 for disability hate crime (Crown Prosecution Service, 2016). The complexity of the legal remedies available and additional acts in this field, however, can contribute to the challenges in supporting victims and managing responses (Alhaboby, Haider, al-Khateeb, & Short, 2016).

When a police officer is unable to understand and apply the complicated law of disability hate crime, or identify learning disabilities and autism, there will be potential for further tragedies, where appropriate responses are not forthcoming soon enough. The confidence of the police in their abilities to detect and determine if an incident was hate-related is much higher than the confidence of the disability community, and those who have had contact with people with various impairments (Richardson et al., 2016).

The experience of disability hate crimes

Victimisation of disabled people has reached a new and higher level of concern. With the continuous emerging of electronic communications vulnerable situations are more easily created. Prejudice, relating disability with impairment, and the use of the disability to coerce victims into closer contact are only a few of the differences in the impact and experiences of disability hate speech between disabled and nondisabled victims. Sin, Hedges, Cook, Mguni, and Comber (2009) emphasise that this type of violence not only has a traumatic impact on the disabled individual, but also generates fear within the broader community of disabled people. Whether the incidents of victimisation are serious and criminal or lower level, repetitive attacks or one-off events, they all have a powerful and long-lasting impact on the quality of victims' lives. Most commonly, victims change their lives in some way to avoid incidents occurring again, rather than authorities dealing with the situation to provide safety.

Despite a sharp increase in the number of disability hate crimes reported in the UK in recent years, the proportion of these hate crimes being classified as hate speech, involving harassment and bullying, and the corresponding charges is unclear. As a victim of such crime expressed: "For some reason society feels that, because somebody is different, that they have a free pass to just ask anything and it's downright rude" (Snowdon, 2017). The lack of recognition of such crimes is despite the fact that hate speech has the potential to cause physical harm, mental stress, anxiety, or insecurity, violating an individual's dignity, and/or creating an intimidating, hostile, degrading, humiliating or offensive environment.

The prejudicial aggression shown in all types of disability hate, whether incidence or crime, can range from "banal" or mundane prejudicial actions (Equality and Human Rights Commission, 2011), and intimidating stares to opportunistic street crime, being taunted, bullied, physical harassment, and sexual assault. Being shouted at and victimised for occupying wheelchair spaces on the bus, using disabled parking spaces at shopping centres, being pushed past in public places, including shops, cafes, and pubs, being abused inside and outside care facilities, and exploitation and violence within institutional care, day centres, and individual's homes are all too common examples of disability hate crime (Beadle-Brown et al., 2014; Hunter, Hodge, Nixon, Parr, & Willis, 2007; Sin et al., 2009). Damage to disabled people's homes, gardens, access ramps, as well as adapted cars have also been reported (Richardson et al., 2016). These incidents can be multiple, sometimes occurring extensively and over a long period of time (Equality and Human Rights Commission, 2016), and other times they can indeed be one-off events. There is often no reciprocal arrangements, relationship or interdependency between the victims and their perpetrators, although Thomas (2011) argues they may be known to live within the same neighbourhood. In the cases of people with learning difficulties, robbery, being held captive, and even murder is more prevalent, whereas wheelchair users are likely to be tipped out of their wheelchairs and robbed (Thomas, 2011). Nevertheless, the commonality of all these events is about one person having control over another.

While disability hate crime tends to be more common in areas of high deprivation (Macdonald, Donovan, & Clayton, 2017), a disabled person's risk of being abused and/or harassed is largely dependent on their own and their friends' identities and the places they live and frequently visit (Sin et al., 2009). Risk factors such as the type of impairment (learning difficulty and/or mental health issues), intersectional identities (being a woman and/or belonging to an ethnic minority group), and low socio-economic status heightens significantly the likelihood of being a victim. According to Mind (2007), mental health service users are 11 times more likely to be victimised and experience intimidation compared with nondisabled people. Motivations to commit a hate crime range from hate, stigma, jealousy, stereotypes such as life not worth living (Clements & Read, 2008), and accusations of fraud in cases of invisible impairments (Quarmby, 2015). To situate these specific assumptions, the attention should be focused on media stereotyping of disabled people as "scroungers," as well as segregated living and charity discourses. In terms of print media,

Briant, Watson, and Philo (2011) reported an increase in the number of articles about the claimed "burden" that disabled people are alleged to place on the economy; some articles even blaming incapacity benefit claimants causing the recession. The vitriolic approach adopted by some of the media coverage in the period following the Comprehensive Spending Review is at best questionable and at worst deeply offensive and damaging. This has had adverse effect on disabled people's own feelings of security and safety, and has added to their sense of isolation.

Being disabled often is a risk factor in becoming a victim of hate speech and cyber-harassment generally, and being vulnerable to unwanted attention. This type of harassment can exacerbate the impact of impairments (including mood disturbances, anxiety, deterioration of existing impairments, and health conditions), and sometimes lead to suicide or suicidal attempts. Where people with learning disability or autism are the victims, the onus tends to be on them to avoid people, places and times associated with the occurrence of victimisation (Richardson et al., 2016) with a greater impact on their social life and career paths as they might be forced to restrict access to their places of study, work, and socialisation. The effect of the resulting marginalisation on disabled people's confidence, social inclusion, and participation in the community needs not be overlooked as most disabled people will go out of their way to avoid certain people and places. Smith (2015, pp. 37–38) contends "Disabled people restructure their lives to minimize real and perceived risk to themselves even if they have not experienced targeted violence personally."

A culture which creates and maintains structures and practices that disable and exclude people with impairments promotes a view that disabled people are worthy of contempt and hostility (Walker, 2010). Victims of disability hate crime generally come to believe that these events are part of their lives; victimisation is just what happens for a person with learning disabilities or autism, and that they "deserved it" (Richardson et al., 2016). This is how such incidences have been "normalised," even mundane experiences for many disabled people in the UK (Chakraborti, Garland, & Hardy, 2014). Disabled people's families, friends, and support workers can also become victims by association. They may be indirectly impacted, when supporting their loved ones after incidents. Additionally, families may be forced to change their lifestyle and behaviour – to be extra vigilant, with a significantly negative impact on their stress levels and physical and mental health.

This was, perhaps best reflected in Fiona Pilkington's story. In 2007, Pilkington killed herself and her daughter Frankie, who had learning difficulties, following a hate campaign in which local youths in the Leicestershire area targeted Frankie's learning disability. Local police recorded Ms Pilkington's complaints as evidence of anti-social behaviour, not as an on-going hate crime concern and "cry for help" (Sturcke, 2010). Subsequently, the investigation revealed that police had not responded properly to repeated calls by the family reporting harassment (Independent Police Complaints Commission, 2011). Similarly, in McCarthy's study (2017), many people (including police, doctors, nurses, health visitors, social workers, and support workers as well as the women's family and friends) knew that women with learning disabilities were experiencing cruelty, humiliation, servitude, exploitation, and theft broadly labelled as domestic violence. Yet, arrests, charges, prosecutions, and convictions were uncommon, signalling to the perpetrators that they are immune from repercussions.

It is not surprising then to learn that the reasons why little focus has been given to disability hate speech in British criminal law both in terms of its recognition and trial is because many disabled people are reluctant to report the regular harassment they experience as a hate crime. This is because they do not recognise it as such, do not believe it will be taken seriously by the police and others, they have previous poor experiences of reporting, or fear of reprisal because it involves someone they know (Sin et al., 2009). Where victimisation is reported, there have been systemic institutional failures that nurture a culture of disbelief and prevent such incidents from being dealt with effectively, where police have been also unsympathetic, ineffective and even unkind (Equality and Human Rights Commission, 2011). Contacting the police and potentially going to court may also be distressing for many disabled people.

Furthermore, disabled people's organisations do not tend to pay much attention to domestic violence, whilst women's refuges are not necessarily focused on violence against disabled women (Thomas, 2011). Poor access to reporting centres, disused centres, and a lack of professional clarity as to just what can be treated a disablist hate crime/allegation are some of the key barriers to reporting a disability hate crime (A Roulstone & Thomas, 2009).

Many disabled people, especially those with learning difficulties and autism, do not recognise or use the term "hate crime" to refer to their experiences. The lack of a clear, common definition of disability hate crime and use of the term "hate" can be difficult for many people with learning disabilities or autism. In Alhaboby et al.'s study (2016), the majority of participants perceived a lack of awareness, training, and education, when they asked for support from victim support groups, police, or healthcare professionals. Notions of vulnerability are still being used to negate claims of disablist hate crimes (Roulstone et al., 2011). The practicality of a concept of crime that is motivated by negative constructions of perceived difference has been challenged because it may lead to a "special needs" approach, which works to perpetuate, instead of understanding and alleviating cultural differences of disability (Thomas, 2011).

Collecting evidence of hostility in general is complex, especially so when it is disability-related. The practice of the police and CPS is known to lack in relation to gathering the evidence, which would be needed in order to regard a defendant's behaviour as an aggravating feature, for example, displaying hostility relating to disability (HMCPSI, HMIC, & HMI Probation, 2013). The weak legal and policy constructions of disablist hate crimes have militated against a full and fair response (Roulstone et al., 2011). Relying on a perception of hostility towards the victim and proving the motivation of the hostility as the definition of disability hate crime could be difficult to identify for both victim and police. Disabled people's resignation and acceptance to referring to disability hate speech as just what happens to them, justifying the violence – makes it more challenging to discover whether or not they see the events as being motivated by a prejudice based on their impairment or disability. This in itself, is likely to present an obstacle to reporting.

Responding more effectively

In the current testing, with financial times for public and third sector agencies, there is little permanent core funding for work in this field, a situation that is likely to continue, and the attention in funding has shifted from hate crime to knife crime (Roulstone et al., 2011). This exclusionary social context reflects and extends social prejudices around disability, itself a factor in disability victimisation. Yet, not doing anything to tackle disability victimisation is not an option. Public agencies have a statutory duty to take reasonable steps to protect all citizens. The social and economic benefits of bringing an end to the isolation and exclusion of all disabled people, including people with learning disabilities or autism, should be a key priority. Financial pressures should not be seen as barriers to tackling disability hate crime. A number of measures may be achieved at little or no cost through pooling resources, partnerships, changing attitudes through example, developing different ways of working and training. Recommendations outlined here can be implemented to work in this direction.

Training and direct experience influenced by self-perceived police confidence and competence at effectively managing disability hate crimes must be created and maintained. These need to include recognition of disability hate speech, and the identification of people reporting victimisation possibly having a learning disability or autism. The training must help to decipher whether there is evidence of hostility towards a person's impairment, and whether the victims are repeatedly been targeted and abused. Being able to communicate effectively, meeting the communication needs of the victims, responding effectively to incidents, and acquiring sufficiently detailed evidence to investigate and charge individuals must also be key features of these programmes. The involvement of disabled people's organisations in the creation, development, and delivery of these training programmes can also go a long way to shifting attitudes towards protecting the rights of disabled hate crime victims.

Advocacy, self-advocacy, the support of disabled people's organisations and similar groups, and the provision of accessible information about the positive and negative aspects of relationships can all help to reduce disabled people's vulnerability to exploitation and harm from those who they hope would love them. Victims need to be empowered and helped to understand that they need not and should not put up with victimisation. The right peer support mechanisms need to be put in place to demonstrate that, given the right situations, disabled people are not vulnerable and dependent (Thomas, 2011). Community centres, churches, schools, and colleges all have a role in challenging negative assumptions, supporting victims, and reinforcing their empowerment through effective policies for responding to bullying or hate speech.

Considering many incidents go without being reported to the police, it is unlikely that social services would necessarily be aware of the victims' isolation, inability to leave their abusers due to lack of support. Since those who are more able and need less support are more likely to experience victimisation (Beadle-Brown et al., 2014), and that these experiences impact on community participation and well-being more generally, care assessments should take into account previous and future vulnerability to victimisation. During routine health checks, general physicians (GPs) and practice nurses could ascertain whether their disabled patients have been subjected to or fear victimisation. In this way, hard data must be recorded and then shared between the various agencies involved – the police, the local authority, the medical professionals, community learning disability teams, housing providers, and any third sector organisations involved in the overall support of the target population. Victims need to be enabled to access other types of support, including specialist victim support, counselling, and therapies for victims with autism and learning disabilities. Accessible places of refuge must be provided in various commercial and business premises to create a safe space, and appropriate help and support, such as mental health first aid, could be offered by trained staff.

Individuals and their family/carers need to be informed and clarified about what a hate crime is within the law, as well as possible prevention strategies and where to go to report and receive support after an incident. The following case in point is a positive recent move in this direction. Celebrity Katie Price, in response to her son being targeted with degrading and abusive comments online, launched a campaign to make online abuse of disabled people a criminal offence, via an e-petition. Members of Parliament (MPs) backed the campaign, recognising that current laws were not fit for purpose. The petition's committee consequently launched an inquiry into online abuse and put forward a number of key recommendations, including: "Social media companies need to review their processes and provide advice and support for those who identify as needing additional protection." (Schofield, 2019).

Following this, a debate was held in the House of Commons on 29 April 2019, where it was revealed by Margot James, the Minister for Digital and the Creative Industries, that

> The Law Commission has been asked to complete a wide-ranging review of hate crime legislation in order to explore how to make hate crime legislation more effective, including whether it is effective in addressing crimes targeting someone because of their disability.

She also noted that this review was unlikely to be completed within the current session of Parliament; however, there is nothing stopping a private Member's Bill to address this in the meantime (Hansard Debate, 2019).

Furthermore, attention must be paid to the subtleties of language and its interpretation – the issue of vulnerability needs to be addressed (McClimens & Brewster, 2017). Disabled people may be targeted because of perceived vulnerability rather than a motivation of hatred, but this should not lead to a reduction in police or prosecutorial responses. There needs to be change within the criminal justice and community safety systems, which recognise that hostility towards disabled people, triggered by a perception of vulnerability, is a complication of hatred. A helpful approach that takes account of long-term health conditions and the way in which people with such conditions are discriminated against is the social model of disability; it provides a way of looking beyond the individual for causes of discrimination and targeted crime (Roulstone et al., 2011). The social model also facilitates a redefinition of "disability" in a way that is aligned with the approach of British disabled people's organisations. The social model suggests that disabled people are disabled by social, cultural, attitudinal, environmental, and other barriers, rather than their impairments (Barnes, 1992).

Currently, the victim, the police, or a witness are required to detect that what is happening may be based on hostility related to disability before hate crimes are recorded. More effective means of reporting disability hate speech, such as more accessible forms, helplines, and third-party reporting systems are needed. Conventional reporting methods such as the phone may not be accessible for many disabled people. More appropriate responses to disability hate speech based on the objective assessment of the offence itself could also be developed. Police services can adopt more consistent practices for acquiring best evidence so that prosecutions of perpetrators can follow. Any increased awareness and understanding of disability hate speech needs to extend to other agencies such as the CPS and the judiciary, so that improvements in the police response are in turn standardised, supported, and followed through in prosecuting and sentencing policies and practices.

Mapping encounters and spaces could help to identify potential contextual and interpersonal "triggers" of harassment and violence, in some way addressing the limitations of current hate crime data and recording individual incidents

(Hall, forthcoming). This could then reshape the ways in which the police and local authority agencies interpret and address hate crime, from the current focus on increasing reporting of incidents and prosecutions to prevention strategies, to identify and intervene in spaces and relations where hostility is likely to occur. Disability hate crime reporting needs to be matched by more harsh sentences and a greater connection between reported and sanctioned hate crime.

There is also a need for more research. As yet little is researched and documented about how disabled people perceive, experience, react to, and report disability hate speech and cyber-harassment – how different these experiences are from other types of disability hate crimes or nondisabled victims' experiences.

Conclusion

Disability hate speech as an important strand of disability hate crime remains largely invisible, especially when compared to religious or racial hate speech, which is frequently reported in the media. Its existence is frequently denied and disabled victims who report it are routinely ignored or are dismissed outright as unreliable witnesses. Consequently, those who offend via disability hate speech often go unpunished and public awareness of these incidents remains low. Lack of understanding could severely limit disabled people's human rights in being afforded a secure, safe, public space. Writing and evidence on disablist hate speech is not legally, academically or publicly as yet as extensive – reflecting both the relatively recent recognition of disablist hate speech in the UK and the absence of key policy endeavours linked to specific disablist hate-motivated incidences. The targeting of disabled people for hate speech needs further research.

A wider approach to prevention and support is therefore needed involving a number of agencies in addition to the police. Vision and leadership are needed to take positive steps to make disabled people's communities safer for them by tackling all types of hate incidents and crimes, providing effective support to victims and families. An urgent policy and practice review is therefore required to ensure disabled people gain the fullest protection of the law and that where hate speech occurs they are accounted for in official statistics. In an era of public financial austerity, where underlying inequality is unlikely to be responded to, by collaborating with disabled people themselves, statutory bodies need to gain a better understanding of the context of discrimination in which disabled people live, through policy making and appointing more disabled people into public life, including the criminal justice system.

References

Alhaboby, Z., Haider, M., al-Khateeb, B. J., & Short, E. (2016). The language is disgusting and they refer to my disability: The cyberharassment of disabled people. *Disability & Society*, *31*(8), 1138–1143.

Barnes, C. (1992). *Disabling imagery and the media: An exploration of the principles for media representations of disabled people*. Derby: The British Council of Disabled People.

Beadle-Brown, J., Richardson, L., Guest, C., Malovic, A., Bradshaw, J., & Himmerich, J. (2014). *Living in fear: Better outcomes for people with learning disabilities and autism (Main report)*. Canterbury: Tizard Centre, University of Kent.

Briant, E., Watson, N., & Philo, G. (2011). *Bad news for disabled people: How the newspapers are reporting disability*. Glasgow: Strathclyde Centre for Disability Research and Glasgow Media Unit, University of Glasgow.

Chakraborti, N., Garland, J., & Hardy, S. J. (2014). *The Leicester hate crime project*: Briefing Papers, No. 1: *Disablist hate crime*. Leicester: University of Leicester.

Citizens Advice. (2018). *What are hate incidents and hate crime?* Retrieved from https://www.citizensadvice.org.uk/law-and-courts/discrimination/hate-crime/what-are-hate-incidents-and-hate-crime/

Clements, L., & Read, J. (2008). *Disabled people and the right to life: The protection and violation of disabled people's most basic human rights*. London: Routledge.

Crown Prosecution Service. (2016). *Impact and dynamics of stalking and harassment*. Retrieved from http://www.cps.gov.uk/legal/s_to_u/stalking_and_harassment/#a05a

Crown Prosecution Service. (2017). *Hate crime*. Retrieved from https://www.cps.gov.uk/hate-crime

Department of Work and Pensions. (2018). *Family resources survey: Financial year 2016/17*. Retrieved from https://www.gov.uk/government/statistics/family-resources-survey-financial-year-201617

Dreßing, H., Bailer, J., Anders, A., Wagner, H., & Gallas, C. (2014). Cyberstalking in a large sample of social network users: Prevalence, characteristics, and impact upon victims. *Cyberpsychology, Behavior, and Social Networking*, *17*(2), 61–67.

Emerson, E., & Roulstone, A. (2014). Developing an evidence base for violent and disablist hate crime in Britain: Findings from the life opportunities survey. *Journal of Interpersonal Violence*, *29*(17), 3086–3104.

Equality and Human Rights Commission. (2011). *Hidden in plain sight: Inquiry into disability-related harassment*. Equality and Human Rights Commission.

Equality and Human Rights Commission. (2016). *Causes and motivations of hate crime*. Retrieved from https://www.equalityhumanrights.com/en/publication-download/research-report-102-causes-and-motivations-hate-crime.

Hall, E. (2019). *A critical geography of disability hate crime*. *Area 51*(2), 249–256.

Hansard Debate. (2019). *Online abuse*. Retrieved from https://hansard.parliament.uk/commons/2019-04-29/debates/65420802-6952-4830-9CF3-1B4001FFE0EA/OnlineAbuse

HMCPSI, HMIC, & HMI Probation. (2013). *Living in a different world: Joint review of disability hate crime*. London: HMCPSI, HMIC, and HMI Probation.

Home Office. (2018). *Hate crime, England and Wales, 2017 to 2018*. Retrieved from https://www.gov.uk/government/statistics/hate-crime-england-and-wales-2017-to-2018

Hunter, C., Hodge, N. S., Nixon, J., Parr, S., & Willis, B. (2007). *Disabled people's experiences of antisocial behaviour and harassment in social housing: A critical review*. London: Disability Rights Commission.

Independent Police Complaints Commission. (2011). IPCC report into the contact between Fiona Pilkington and Leicestershire Constabulary 2004–2007. Independent Investigation Final Report, *IPCC Reference*: 20009/*016872*. London: Independent Police Complaints Commission.

legislation.gov.uk. (2010). The Equality Act 2010. Retrieved from https://www.legislation.gov.uk/ukpga/2010/15/contents

legislation.gov.uk. (2003). Criminal Justice Act 2003. Retrieved from https://www.legislation.gov.uk/ukpga/2003/44/contents

legislation.gov.uk. (1994). Criminal Justice and Public Order Act 1994. Retrieved from https://www.legislation.gov.uk/ukpga/1994/33/contents

Leonard Cheshire. (2019, 11 May). *Reports of online disability hate crime soar by 33%*. Retrieved from https://www.leonardcheshire.org/about-us/press-and-media/press-releases/reports-online-disability-hate-crime-soar-33

Macdonald, S. J., Donovan, C., & Clayton, J. (2017). The disability bias: Understanding the context of hate in comparison with other minority populations. *Disability & Society*, *32*(4), 483–499.

McCarthy, M. (2017). 'What kind of abuse is him spitting in my food?': Reflections on the similarities between disability hate crime, so-called 'mate' crime and domestic violence against women with intellectual disabilities. *Disability & Society*, *32*(4), 595–600.

McClimens, A., & Brewster, J. (2017). Intellectual disability, hate crime and other social constructions: A view from South Yorkshire. *Journal of Intellectual Disabilities*. https://doi.org/10.1177/1744629517730181.

National Police Chiefs' Council. (2015). *Internet hate crime*. Retrieved from http://www.report-it.org.uk/reporting_internet_hate_crime

Quarmby, K. (2008). *Getting away with murder: Disabled people's experiences of hate crime in the UK*. London: Scope.

Quarmby, K. (2015). *Disability hate crime motivation survey – Results*. Retrieved from https://katharinequarmby.wordpress.com/

Richardson, L., Beadle-Brown, J., Bradshaw, J., Guest, C., Malovic, A., & Himmerich, J. (2016). "I felt that I deserved it" – Experiences and implications of disability hate crime. *Tizard Learning Disability Review*, *21*(2), 80–88.

Roulstone, A., & Thomas, P. (2009). *Hate crime and disabled people*. Manchester: Equality and Human Rights Commission and Breakthrough UK.

Roulstone, A., Thomas, P., & Balderston, S. (2011). Between hate and vulnerability: Unpacking the British criminal justice system's construction of disablist hate crime. *Disability & Society*, *26*(3), 351–364.

Schofield, C. (2019). *Here's everything you need to know about Harvey's Law and what it means for disabled people*. Retrieved from https://www.yorkshireeveningpost.co.uk/read-this/harveys-law-means-for-disable-people-explainer/

Sin, C. H., Hedges, A., Cook, C., Mguni, N., & Comber, N. (2009). *Disabled people's experiences of targeted violence and hostility*. Manchester: Equality and Human Rights Commission.

Smith, M. (2015). Disability hate crime – A call for action. In P. Giannasi & R. Shah (Eds.), *Tackling disability discrimination and disability hate crime: A multidisciplinary guide* (pp. 36–53). London: Jessica Kingsley Publishers.

Snowdon, K. (2017, 23 October). Disability hate crime reports surge, and campaigners think media portrayals have "Demonised" people. Retrieved from https://www.huffingtonpost.co.uk/entry/disability-hate-crime-reports-increase-53-home-office_uk_59e60f9ee4b0a2324d1df159

Sturcke, J. (2010, 16 March). *Police under investigation over Fiona Pilkington case*. Retrieved from http://www.guardian.co.uk/uk/2010/mar/16/police-under-investiation-fiona-pilkington

Thomas, P. (2011). "Mate crime": Ridicule, hostility and targeted attacks against disabled people. *Disability & Society*, *26*(1), 107–111.

United Nations. (2008). *United Nations convention on the rights of persons with disabilities*. New York: United Nations General Assembly.

Walker, P. (2010). *Frankie Boyle meets his match.* Retrieved from http://www.guardian.co.uk/society/2010/apr/08/frankie-boyle-downs-syndrome

Wells, M., & Mitchell, K. J. (2014). Patterns of Internet use and risk of online victimization for youth with and without disabilities. *The Journal of Special Education, 48*(3), 204–213.

5 Very bad bedside manner

Medical professionals and hate speech

Sheri Wells-Jensen and Claire Wells-Jensen

Introduction

Experience is important. Context is important. Environment is important. No utterance is made in isolation. Where, to whom, how, why, and when we say things matters as much as, or more than, the words spoken. Each time I speak, everything within and around me influences the words I choose, how I string them together, what I leave out and what I emphasize, all filtered through my very particular understanding of the world around me. Then that message passes out of my controlled space and into the arcane territory that is another person's very particular understanding of the world around her, and I can only hope that she received the message I intended to send. Sociolinguists, philosophers, and activists like Hymes (1962), Austin (1975), Grice (1975), and Elgin (2009) have spent their professional lives struggling to describe the myriad shifting and interlocking factors that weave through and around everything we say, shaping how it will be received.

Such analysis is complicated under the best of circumstances, and when examining hate speech, defined by Parekh (2012) as speech that "affects an individual's dignity, reputation or status in society," the circumstances are decidedly *not* the best. The topic is important, and a false analysis could do real damage. We have to be wakeful and strategic, seeking first to do no damage. The hope is, of course, that accurate work can help us understand hate speech and uncover ways in which we can work toward eliminating it.

In the ideal world, blind and visually impaired people should be able to count on ophthalmologists as allies, but this is rarely the case. This chapter highlights the disabling environment that blind people encounter when visiting an eye doctor. Next, the chapter will highlight the disablist attitudes displayed by health care professionals in such environments. It will also discuss the effects of such attitudes in terms of psycho-emotional disablism (see other chapters in this volume). Finally, the chapter will suggest that while disablist language about blindness might not officially or legally be recognized as hate speech, its message – that it is better to be dead than blind – is effectively the same. In this way, disablist language needs to be recognized as a previously unrecognized form of hate speech, since it wounds and invalidates its victims. The fact that the speakers (and sometimes the blind listeners themselves) often do not perceive what is said as "hateful" makes this a particularly interesting, and insidious, scenario.

Establishing the context

Imagine I (Sheri) am in the hallway of an office building. The door before me, which opens inward, bears a small plastic rectangle with a braille room number on it; I find it (after some searching) affixed to the centre of the door itself. Pausing there to locate and read the number means that I will be in the way of anyone wishing to enter or leave that room, so I try to be quick. There is a larger plastic rectangle above the room number which most likely indicates the name of the office's current inhabitant, but its surface is featureless: there are not even raised print letters for me to trace with my fingers. I rely on the number alone as evidence that I have reached the right place. It's probably right, but I would have appreciated the extra information on that other sign.

I open the door and step in. As I've been given no information about the layout of the room now before me, I pause in the doorway to listen. There is a TV across the room diagonally to my left. Sometimes, TVs play propaganda for the "benefit" of the people waiting in the outer office, but this one has its volume dulled to unintelligibility, so it's useful as a landmark, but not as a source of information about which office I'm in. I can hear that there is a wall to my right, so altogether I imagine that I have a handle on the rough size and shape of the room, but I don't yet know where the reception desk is. I make a hypothesis that it's on the wall I'm facing, somewhere to the right of the TV perhaps. I step in, allowing the door to fall closed behind me, and make my way across the room, weaving through an assortment of chairs, some of which contain people whose feet I touch with my cane as I go. If there is a clear path from the door to the desk, I'm clearly not on it. But I cross the room with a few murmured apologies and locate the desk by listening for the sound of typing. The receptionists (I think maybe there is more than one; it is an awful lot of typing) say nothing as I pause there; I am not certain if they are busy, or if I am in the wrong place, or if perhaps they are turned away from me and cannot see me.

Eventually, someone from behind the desk says: "Can I help you?" and I give my name and the reason I'm there, relieved to learn at last (based on their lack of surprise) that I am in the right place. I am handed a sheaf of printed forms, which I cannot read, and a discussion begins about how I will fill these out. This problem has apparently never occurred to them before. A second receptionist joins the first, and we determine eventually that I can go over this information orally with somebody later on. I don't know who this person will be, if he or she will be accurate (or able to spell), and I'm not sure if we will have any privacy while my information is discussed, but I feel pressured to let all this go. The process will clearly be an inconvenience for them.

After this, despite the inexpertly given directions, I find a place to sit. Although I hear the pages of magazines turning around me, there is nothing for me to read while I wait. I spend some time paying attention to the people coming and going around me and locate the door to the inner office on the wall to the left of the desk, right beside the TV where I thought it probably had to be. This takes about two minutes. After that, I go back to listening to other people turn pages and wishing I'd brought my own supply of reading material. Finally, my name is called, and I get up and walk to the door. When I get there, the receptionist has no idea what to do to get me through the door and on into the inner sanctum: Should she lead me by the hand? Walk backwards in front of me? Get behind and push me? I give her the 30-second tutorial on how to guide a blind person, and she takes tiny nervous steps down the hall with me holding her elbow, unnecessarily narrating each slight turn as we pass along the hallway.

We pass through a doorway, and I wait to find out if this is another reception area, a room with a table and chair, or something else. There is an uneasy pause. She's thinking something over. "Right in front of you," she begins, and then spins around, puts an arm around my waist and another on my shoulder, more or less in waltz position, and pulls me forward. She hasn't said so, but she's trying to get me to sit down in a chair. I extract myself from her grasp, rearrange my clothing, and sit down. "Oh, good job," she says, and she pulls my cane from my hand, wondering aloud where she should put it. I get up, reclaim it from her, stow it behind the chair and sit back down. There's another pause, and then I hear her tennis-shoed feet carry her away from me, back out into the hallway. I'd wager, at this point, that we are both equally exhausted.

This, for me, is a description of a fairly typical visit to an ophthalmologist – a specialist in diseases of the eye.

Medical offices in general, and ophthalmologists' offices in particular, are notoriously bad at accessibility. This is perhaps to be expected. As medical personnel whose personal and professional goals are to search for cures for all kinds of blindness, they default to a medical model of disability (Davis, 2017; Fisher & Goodley, 2007). I am a totally blind adult who does not have, or seek, any prospect of vision-restoring treatment; I am a conundrum at best, and evidence of failure at worst. They aren't quite sure what to do for or with me and treat my simple request for antibiotic drops as somewhat odd. My consistent experience with ophthalmologists' offices has been that the environment is never welcoming.

By way of illustration, in my decades of frequenting these offices, I have never found any of the following:

- Names of the ophthalmologists in braille or raised letters on the outer office door;
- Any attempt (before I arrive or after I enter) to orient me to the layout of the office;
- A staff member comfortable guiding blind people – or capable of giving clear verbal directions;
- Anything for me to read in the waiting room;
- Braille pamphlets about blindness from consumer organizations;
- Any kind of adaptive technology beyond eyewear which is for sale;

- An established method via which blind people can fill out their own paperwork independently;
- Accessible information about medications;
- Braille business cards;
- Any means of writing notes (such as dates of future appointments) in braille for patients – or even a plan for emailing that information;
- Braille signage within the office itself;
- Accessible tactile models of the human eye;
- A blind employee of any kind at any level.

There is no indication in the physical or interpersonal environment of the office to suggest that blind people are expected to show up or are in any way welcome. If we do show up, perhaps in a panic-stricken search for a miracle cure or some kind of despondent final visit, it is clearly expected that some sighted person will be completely in charge. The professional goal for ophthalmologists is to prevent or reverse loss of eyesight. Taking this mandate seriously, and aware of the fact that they have to engage in some degree of marketing to attract and retain patients, they eliminate any evidence of the possibility of blindness from their physical environment. Blindness is the enemy to be eradicated, and the environment communicates that this has been well and thoroughly done.

Although this may comfort sighted patients with minor eye problems and encourage those who are worried about losing their vision, the cumulative effect on patients who are already blind is palpable. This is of course not "speech" in a strict or legal sense; rather, it is the disablist nonverbal background of the speaker and perhaps the listener as well – and precisely because it is background, its impact is difficult to attend to.

It might be natural to expect that professionals who deal regularly with matters pertaining to vision would be inclined to put small accommodations in place. The fact that this is *not* done is significant. What the patient infers from this low-level disablist message will vary, but it will not go unnoticed. The professional, on the other hand, has clearly established that he need not make any effort to change his usual routine. This is his territory; he is fully in charge and comfortable. Nothing else need be done, and because the superficial circumstances are unremarkable – even perhaps elegant – it is difficult to find fault. The professional is fulfilling his role just as is expected, and the patient, it is assumed, should do the same. If there is a patina of privilege coating the otherwise sanitized surfaces in the office, it goes unmentioned.

What is said

There are, of course, eye care professionals who are steadfastly courteous. But as medical personnel, they are strongly drawn toward a medical model of disability. The "disease" (in this case blindness) is the principal problem, and their calling is to seek the "cure." (Consult Davis, 2017 and Fisher & Goodley, 2007 for further discussion of the medical model and its more humane alternatives).

In this context, where blindness is profoundly undesirable – representing, as it does, professional and perhaps personal failure – it is not unusual to find impassioned discourse. Patients must be saved from the enemy, and the enemy is blindness. To fail to do this is tragic, perhaps even shameful. Doctors would insist that their first priority is to do no harm. However, it is difficult to read the following quotation from Dr. Henry Marsh, a noted British neurosurgeon, without recoiling: "Leaving somebody completely blind after surgery (it has happened to me twice) is a peculiarly unpleasant experience. It feels worse than leaving them dead" (Marsh, 2017, p. 242).

First, there is his peculiarly self-absorbed perspective, in which the blindness somehow has happened to *him* primarily, rather than to his patients. Then comes the centrepiece: the very clear statement that blindness feels *worse than death*, that complete surrender to the disease is such an unbearable and tragic loss that even if the patient could be saved, perhaps she *should not be*. He makes no attempt to soften that statement, and there is no way it can be misunderstood. It is not the arrogance, the ignorance, or even the extreme eugenic overtone that makes this hate speech. It is the unquestioned and unquestionable social authority of the speaker, lending force to his words in the minds of blind and sighted readers alike. He is the authority on this topic. If the neurosurgeon has said it, then it must be true – because he, after all, is an expert; he knows all about the eye and the brain and about what can go wrong. His colleagues, his staff, his neighbours, people in general and (perhaps most cruelly) his patients accept his words as truth. *It is better to be dead than blind.* Such comments reflect a broader attitude that disability disqualifies people from participation and recognition in society and that if disability was eliminated altogether, the world would be a better place (Garland-Thomson, 2012).

Hate speech and medical charities

Another contingent deeply invested in the destruction of blindness are the assortment of charities which have "curing blindness" as their philanthropic target. These agencies have two inextricably intertwined goals which affect the way they communicate: to cure blindness. That is not to say that the search for medical progress is anything but admirable, and there is obviously nothing wrong with campaigns to prevent or reverse blindness in and of themselves. People can and should get regular eye exams, just as they can and should get vaccinations, go to the dentist, and wash their hands before eating, and there are campaigns advocating for these things which do a great deal of good.

Unfortunately, however, the goals of raising money and either finding a cure or performing individual surgeries to counteract eye diseases are sometimes more important than accurate, respectful representations of the abilities of real blind people.

Their depictions of blindness and blind people assume that the blind person receives no training in any adaptive blindness skills and is unable to invent even the simplest solutions for herself. Furthermore, although social support and educational systems for blind people in developing nations are much less substantial than those in wealthier nations, it is still inaccurate to state that blindness, rather than poverty, is to blame. In this context, the stereotypical helpless and (crucially) profoundly grateful blind adult or child is welcome, but the independent, active, joyful blind person cannot be. Regardless of how many years have passed since the onset of blindness, the blind person in this world of discourse remains frozen in time, eternally defeated and frightened, without the agency or impulse to work through even the simplest problems.

The sighted audience is invited to "imagine how it feels," or in some scenarios (such as the ill-conceived "How Eye See It" campaign from the Foundation Fighting Blindness) to actually dare to put on a blindfold themselves for as much as two or three minutes while attempting some familiar task, and to reflect afterward on "what it's like to be blind." (For a discussion of the differences between the incompetence of sighted people wearing blindfolds versus the abilities of a blind person with skills and experience, consult Silverman (2015). For a video in reaction to the "How Eye See It" campaign, go to https://youtu.be/jQid1NzFsvk (Wells-Jensen, 2016).

The "imagine how it feels" approach offers two related possibilities. One is to exploit the audience's fear of blindness by emphasizing themes of helplessness, isolation, and loss:

- "... as his sight declined... his daughter began to spend most of her time watching over him."
- "It's not unusual for him to trip or fall."
- "As his vision grew worse [he] no longer spent time with other children."
- "[She was] just sitting at home unable to work or even play with her grandchildren."
- "[He was] doomed to a life of darkness."

These are straightforward messages of disdain for blind people and their abilities. They function as hate speech, as they insult blind people and state that we are useless, unloved, and pathetic. And, once again, these messages are powerful because they are accompanied by the high social status associated with medical personnel and philanthropists.

Another approach is to emphasize the joy and relief that comes with the cure, which seems at first glance to be a more "positive" message. However, the underlying assumptions are equally hostile, and in fact are more insidious.

Elgin (2009), building on the philosophical and linguistic work of writers like Austin (1975) and Hymes (1962) demonstrates how verbal attacks can be backgrounded within utterances, making them more difficult to address directly. For example, a professional might say that "Children who have their sight restored... can play with friends, succeed in school, and pursue their dreams." The unstated assertion in the background is that blind children cannot play with friends, will fail at school, and cannot pursue dreams. This is the background to the utterance – presumed to be shared by both participants in a conversation, without being stated explicitly. For a blind individual to object to such a statement and to simply assert that they can succeed in these areas leaves the wider negative message unchallenged – one that disparages and devalues all blind people. (Consult Tannen, 2007 and Elgin, 2009 for further discussion of metamessages and the effect of this kind of verbal violence.)

Once this type of rhetorical pattern has been pointed out, it is easy to find analogous examples of similar "hidden" verbal attacks:

- Message: "Those who have their sight restored are given an average of 50 years of sight, allowing them to learn, play, and build bright futures." Underlying assumption: Blind adults cannot learn, cannot play, and have no future.
- Message: The dream of restoring sight is "offering hope to millions of Americans." Underlying assumption: To be blind is to have no hope.
- Message: "They can recognize their families again." Underlying assumption: Without sight, it is (bizarrely) impossible to identify even your own family members. (The blind can't recognize voices?)
- Message: "They can now enjoy some of life's simple joys like reading." Underlying assumption: The joyless blind people cannot read.
- Message: "They finally get their lives back." Underlying assumption: Blind people don't have lives. (Again, perhaps we are better off dead.)

The cumulative effects of disabling environments, verbal aggression, and eugenic messages about disabled lives being worthless are incredibly destructive. Psycho-emotional disablism takes a toll, as reflected in the following statement "I thought about taking my own life; I was useless to myself; I was useless to others. I stayed at home. I cried."

Conclusion

There are certainly *direct* acts of hate speech against blind people – many worse than the example provided by Dr. Marsh. Even the word "blind" itself is commonly used to mean "ignorant" or "clueless." However, the more frequent forms of hate speech issue thick and fast from "well-meaning" professionals who derive their livelihood from their "battle" with blindness. Despite the fact that linguistic analysis clearly reveals the verbal attack within the utterance, this kind of rhetoric is normalized and the intent praised as philanthropic. My instinct that I, Sheri, have been attacked is dismissed. I am perceived as oversensitive and misinformed.

This is a particularly insidious form of gaslighting. Strong, capable, loving, productive blind adults are told that we are submissive, isolated, miserable creatures who can contribute little or nothing to society. We are only shadows of who we could be, and we need able-bodied people to rescue us and solve our problems.

When we understand this and when we are able to identify hate – no matter how it is disguised – we can deal with it directly. We can name it. We can point it out. We can explain how it functions. We can work with both medical professionals and charitable organizations so they stop attacking the people they are meant to serve. And maybe, if we can do all these things, we will draw a little closer to eliminating it.

References

Austin, J. L. (1975). *How to do things with words*. Oxford: Oxford University Press.

Davis, L. J. (2017). *Beginning with disability: A primer*. London: Routledge.

Elgin, S. H. (2009). *The gentle art of verbal self-defense*. New York: Fall River Press.

Fisher, P., & Goodley, D. (2007). The linear medical model of disability: Mothers of disabled babies resist with counter-narratives. *Sociology of Health & Illness*, *29*(1), 66–81.

Garland-Thomson, R. (2012). The case for conserving disability. *Journal of Bioethical Inquiry*, *9*(3), 339–355.

Grice, H. P. (1975). Logic and conversation. In P. Cole & J. L. Morgan (Eds.), *Syntax and semantics* (Vol. 3: Speech Acts, pp. 41–58). New York: Academic Press.

Hymes, D. H. (1962). The ethnography of speaking. In T. Gladwin & W. C. Sturtevant (Eds.), *Anthropology and human behavior* (pp. 13–53). Washington, DC: Anthropological Society of Washington.

Marsh, H. (2017). *Admissions: Life as a brain surgeon*. New York: Thomas Dunne Books.

Parekh, B. (2012). Is there a case for banning hate speech? In M. Herz & P. Molnar (Eds.), *The content and context of hate speech: Rethinking regulation and responses* (pp. 37–56). Cambridge, MA: Cambridge University Press.

Silverman, A. M. (2015). The perils of playing blind: Problems with blindness simulation and a better way to teach about blindness. *Journal of Blindness Innovation and Research*, *5*(2). Retrieved from https://nfb.org/images/nfb/publications/jbir/jbir15/jbir050201.html

Tannen, D. (2007). *You just don't understand: Women and men in conversation*. New York: William Morrow.

Wells-Jensen, S. (2016). *Dr. Sheri Wells-Jensen: #HowEyeSeeIt*. Retrieved from https://youtu.be/jQid1NzFsvk

6 Everyday ableism and hate speech

A tale of three encounters in one day

Damian Milton

Introduction

When trying to understand autism and autistic ways of being one will quickly come across the controversies that exist between various "stakeholder" groups and positionalities, with autistic voices often at odds with those of non-autistic parents and practitioners. Once thought of as a rare disorder, the concept of autism has expanded in recent decades to encompass a wider range of people. Much academic work in this area along with practice models are dominated by a medicalised and psychological framing of "deficits" in one's actions in the world and interactions with others. Such a framing can lead to the stigmatising of autistic people as less than fully "human" in their sense of self and membership of society, rather than as ways of being. This framing has also led to autistic people being "spoken for" instead of at the core of decision-making processes regarding autistic people, as individuals and as a community.

The subversion of autism as a construct by autistic activists and scholars can be set against a backdrop however of cultural discrimination, stereotyping, and othering. At its most violent, the "othering" of autistic people can lead to all kinds of abuse, from subtle forms of "gaslighting" to blatant ableism and hate speech. One can see these forms of abuse as being embedded within cultural expectations of normativity and resultant stigmatisation of those deemed outside of these parameters. Living with the consequences of a stigmatised identity can lead to alienation, social isolation, and a negative spiral of psycho-emotional disablism (Milton & Moon, 2012), where social disablement infiltrates one's psychological and emotional well-being. Autistic people thus have to navigate social life, knowing (and in some cases not) that their ways of being are not accepted within the realms of hegemonic normalcy, often resulting in attempts to mask one's difficulties that can further exhaustion as well as potentially impact their sense of self.

Hate crimes both impact on the individual targeted as well as wider community life (Sherry, 2003), as they indicate intolerance and a lack of safety for disabled people, further spreading fear and othering. Hate crimes are often perpetrated by strangers with no previous connection with their victims (McPhail, 2000), which is suggestive of the act being perpetrated on the assumption of someone being characterised by a stigmatised identity of a collective group. Upon being the victim of a hate crime, however, autistic people may also be less willing to engage with a complaint of criminality, especially if they have had negative encounters with the criminal justice system in the past.

Disablism can be said to refer to discriminatory, oppressive and abusive behaviour targeted at disabled people (Quarmby, 2008). Hate speech and hate crimes can thus be seen as forms of disablism regularly encountered (Sherry, 2010). The wider social victimisation of autistic people and those with learning disabilities is well documented in research (Chakraborti, Garland, & Hardy, 2014; Emerson & Hatton, 2008; Gravell, 2012). Richardson et al. (2016), through using a survey method as well as focus groups and interviews, looked into hate incidents toward autistic people and those with learning disabilities, including wider forms of victimisation. 46% of their sample had been victimised and many also talked of historical abuse and bullying. National surveys such as by Emerson and Hatton (2008) found a figure of 32%. In both these samples, those deemed more "able" participants experienced more serious incidents of victimisation.

The nature of such negative social experiences ranges from disapproving stares to criminal assault, and Richardson et al. (2016) found that multiple incidents of victimisation were common and often sustained over a period of time. The most common age of instigators of abuse were teenagers (61%) with half of the respondents saying that the perpetrator was known to them. Although "mate crime" is not the main topic of this paper, bullying and victimisation by so-called "friends" can be a common experience. In the accounts of victims and carers, police were often said to be often unsympathetic and/or ineffective, whilst others had much more positive accounts of responses by the police. Yet most incidents were left unreported. In this research, family carers were also often "victims by proxy" of such disablism. Richardson et al. (2016) found that through a history of victimisation, it can lead to something of a self-fulfilling prophecy (Becker, 1963); of feeling that this is "just what happens" to autistic people and those with learning disabilities; and as pointed out by Richardson et al. (2016), is likely to lead to less reporting of incidents to authorities:

> Whether the incidents were serious and criminal or lower level, repetitive harassment, they all had a long lasting and powerful impact on the quality of life of the people concerned
>
> (Richardson et al. 2016: 87).

Aut-ethnography

Although differing in one major respect from aut-ethnography, "aut-ethnography" (Milton, 2014) is fundamentally the same in other respects, in the sense of being a form of self-reflective qualitative method exploring personal experience in relation to wider social theory and social issues. Whereas aut-ethnography often seeks to construct a coherent narrative of self over time, an "aut-ethnography" analyses snippets or fragments of experience and their relation to wider socially situated contexts, yet without the constraint of telling a coherent story.

This is to reflect my own fragmented and shifting "rhizomatic" sense of meaning-making as an autistic person.

Three encounters in one day

The three fragments utilised for this aut-ethnographic case study happened to occur on the same day in the south-east of England. This has not been dubiously constructed for dramatic effect or to try and conform to the coherent story of an "aut-ethnography," but is a reflection of what for me in hindsight could be described as just a "bad day." This may be minimisation, but that is something we can return to later. For those who like a story – the three encounters all occurred on a trip my son and I had taken to an appointment at a medical centre. Yet this is somewhat beside the point.

Fragment one

My son and I were walking to a train station. Usually a pleasurable activity, especially with the prospect of a train ride that my son tends to like. My son and I are both autistic, yet he is also classified as having a severe learning disability. When out for a walk something we sometimes do is hold each other by our little fingers. This can be a surprisingly useful form of communication, such as applying the smallest of pressure can indicate wanting to stop. Whilst merrily on our way I heard a shout from behind: "Are you f***ing gay or something?" This remark angered me for obvious reasons, yet being in an immediately compromising and stressful situation, my abilities to process what to say was limited. I turned around to angrily see three teenagers and somewhat shouted: "He is my son!" Upon reflection I am not sure that this was necessarily the best choice of words, yet it seemed to create enough dissonance for the teenagers to turn away and not engage further.

This encounter illustrates the ways in which autistic behaviours are often subjected to a hostile gaze – and in this case hate speech which read autistic interactions as homosexual ones (themselves subject to hateful assumptions). Homophobia was directed at us as autistic people because our relationship was identified as non-normative. Such prejudice demonstrates the overlapping nature of hate. The completely unprovoked hostility represented an attack on both my son and me. Moreover, such utterances psychologically wound. Hate speech harms its victims.

Fragment two

My son and I arrived for an appointment at a medical clinic. Although this clinic should have had information at hand that both my son and I were autistic, what we were to encounter would not be the most "autism-friendly." Instead, it was a disablist encounter. Upon arrival the receptionist was quite busy, and I kept turning around to see if my son was okay, as he was exploring the reception area and there were automatic doors where he could easily go through them and potentially get himself into danger. When I did try and converse with the receptionist, they remarked: "It helps if you keep eye contact when talking to someone." I was immediately flabbergasted, but somehow explained how my son was autistic and I needed to keep an eye on him. I did not disclose at that moment that I was also autistic.

This disablist policing of social interactions (accompanied by judgmental and critical comments) is common for autistic people. It is a form of discipline, a reminder that autistics are constantly judged and criticised by people who are non-autistic and have no interest in accepting different forms of human interaction. Again, the critical gaze of disablism takes an emotional toll – it is a form of psycho-emotional disablism that wears autistic people down, a reminder that the social environment is hostile in many ways. Coming on top of the previous hate speech, the effect of such disablism is to demean and belittle.

But as the previous fragment also illustrated, autistic people demonstrate resistance to this oppression. Upon sitting in the reception area, I noticed my heartbeat was very high and that I was highly stressed, something that I generally need to keep to a minimum to minimise other unwanted adverse events potentially happening. Thankfully, I noticed that the clinic was undergoing a review and there were feedback cards to fill in. Doing this about what had just happened managed to bring my stress down somewhat.

Fragment three

My son and I had just boarded our train to return home and found seats. Suddenly there was a loud banging at the train window, and a fairly young drunken man holding a beer can shouted "F***ing weirdos!" before stumbling away again. Again, disablist hate speech was directed at us as two autistic people in an unprovoked and unexpected context. The element of surprise – as well as the fact that they were outside the train – limited any opportunity to respond. The insult – weirdos – is not just a generic slur. In this context, it is disability hate speech. It is symbolic violence aimed at diminishing our sense of human dignity. Like other forms of hate speech, it involves a wound that strikes deep.

Such an encounter on its own would potentially be enough to send me into something of a panic attack, let alone after the other events that had previously happened that day, yet I had to hold things together for the sake of my son's safety. Needless to say, I was more than relieved when we did eventually return home. The broader social environment, filled with disablism and disability hate speech, offered terror rather than inclusion and victimisation rather than safety.

Nobody else on the train or the train platform reacted to this event at all in any way that I could see.

Reflection and discussion

In the events described here, the first and third acts could be considered hate speech, infused with a bias that discriminates against people due to them being perceived as belonging to a stigmatised category (McPhail, 2000; Sherry, 2003), and also as open verbal abuse. The first fragment consists of a random attack based on the observance of behaviour (finger-holding between two males). One could say in this instance that othering occurred, but through a stigmatising of a group that I would not identity as belonging to. Yet the verbal attack was also framed as a question. Perhaps this framing shows an insecurity as to what exactly the young person had seen and why, and they had jumped to the nearest available stigmatised group to categorise us in? What this showed to me was that discrimination on the grounds of perceived sexuality had a very similar pattern to that originating in disablism, at least on this occasion. The third fragment shows a categorisation and othering based squarely in a kind of disablism which is, no doubt, all too familiar to autistic people, the tag of being a "weirdo." Many autistic people take pride in their eccentricities and one friend of mine proudly wears a "weird pride" badge from time to time, yet of course this is not to invite attacks for forming such an identity, but to fight against regular slurs on being perceived as acting against expected behavioural norms.

The damage sustained by the second of these acts was somehow more pernicious to me though than either of the others. As the event was an indication of an assumed normativity with resultant ableist "micro-aggressions" that happen frequently in social life, usually without sanction, and yet diminishing those on the receiving end of them. It is such widespread and unquestioned ableism in society that is so persistent and destabilising. All of these actions came from people who were total strangers to my son and me, signifying through our ways of being that we are somehow perceived as not "normal" and judged accordingly as members of one stigmatised collective group stereotype or another (McPhail, 2000). The perpetuation of such social dynamics leads on to a negative spiral of psycho-emotional disablism, which is at the very least "hard to navigate" a way out.

In these incidences, I was both a victim of hate speech or micro-aggressions as well as a victim by proxy (Richardson et al. 2016). It is perhaps doubtful that I would have experienced all of these events had I not been accompanied by my son. Whereas I may be able to "mask" some of my ways of being so as to lessen the chances of being attacked in some social situations, this affordance is not accessible to my son, whose non-normative actions attract attention. It should also be stated here though that high levels of masking obviously has its own potential downsides in regard to well-being.

Scior and Werner (2015) suggested that direct contact with marginalised groups was the most impactful approach for changing social attitudes toward them. It would certainly help if autistic people were less segregated or not represented as "exotic others" within the media. To make an impact on the embedded everyday ableism rife in contemporary social life though would take a monumental cultural shift from where we find ourselves today.

References

Becker, H. (1963). *Outsiders: studies in the sociology of deviance.* New York: The Free Press.

Chakraborti, N., Garland, J., & Hardy, S. J. (2014). *The Leicester hate crime project*: Briefing Papers, No. 1: *Disablist hate crime*. Leicester: University of Leicester.

Emerson, E., & Hatton, C. (2008). *People with learning disabilities in England*. Lancaster: Lancaster University.

Gravell, C. (2012). *Loneliness and cruelty: People with learning disabilities and their experience of harassment, abuse and related crime in the community*. London: Lemos and Crane.

McPhail, B. A. (2000). Hating hate: Implications of hate crime legislation. *Social Service Review*, *74*(4), 635–653.

Milton, D. (2014). Becoming autistic: An aut-ethnography. *Cutting Edge Psychiatry in Practice*, *4*, 185–192.

Milton, D., & Moon, L. (2012). "And that, Damian, is what I call life-changing": Findings from an action research project involving autistic adults in an on-line sociology study group. *Good Autism Practice*, *13*(2), 32–39.

Quarmby, K. (2008). *Getting away with murder: Disabled people's experiences of hate crime in the UK*. London: Scope.

Richardson, L., Beadle-Brown, J., Bradshaw, J., Guest, C., Malovic, A., & Himmerich, J. (2016). "I felt that I deserved it" – Experiences and implications of disability hate crime. *Tizard Learning Disability Review*, *21*(2), 80–88.

Scior, K., & Werner, S. (2015). *Changing attitudes to learning disability: A review of the evidence*. London: Mencap.

Sherry, M. (2003). *Don't ask, tell or respond: Silent acceptance of disability hate crimes*. Hamilton, ON: Disabled Women's Network Ontario.

Sherry, M. (2010). *Disability hate crimes: Does anyone really hate disabled people?* Surrey: Ashgate.

7 Hate speech and dwarfism

The influence of cultural representations

Erin Pritchard

Introduction

There remains widespread confusion of what the appropriate term is to refer to someone with dwarfism. This confusion is exacerbated by cultural representations of people with dwarfism. Heider, Scherer, and Edlund (2013) suggest that cultural beliefs about people with dwarfism are largely media driven. Dwarfism has strong links to the entertainment industry. Most people will not have encountered someone with dwarfism in society, but will be able to recall seeing them in some form of entertainment, such as within a film or television show, where it can be almost guaranteed that their dwarfism was the main attraction. According to Adelson (2005), throughout history and in the present day, people with dwarfism have been a popular form of entertainment, not so much for any talents, but rather due to their small stature. Their small stature is deemed an oddity that is used to amuse others. This can shape how others perceive them. Dwarfism is a rare impairment. It is unlikely that you are going to meet many people with dwarfism in society across your lifetime. As most people do not know any people with dwarfism outside of the entertainment industry, it influences how they are perceived, including what names are associated with them.

There are many terms used to describe someone with dwarfism, including, but not limited to: person with dwarfism, person of short stature, dwarf, little person, and person of restricted growth. Haller, Dorries and Rahn (2006) suggest that the terms used to refer to a group of disabled people are important to consider as they can affect how others perceive them and their own self-perception. Most people with dwarfism accept any of these terms, although this can depend on where you are in the world. For example, little person is favoured in the US, yet it can be met with hostility in the UK as this term is also used to refer to children. It is therefore considered infantilising and contributing factor to the patronising comments they often receive within society. Sometimes the term 'dwarf' is also deemed distasteful by people with dwarfism, due to it connection to particular representations, including within fantasy stories and films. What is also problematic about this term is that the pluralised version is often mistakenly written as 'dwarves' instead of 'dwarfs'. The latter refers to someone with dwarfism, whilst the former was devised by Tolkien to refer to mythical creatures featured in stories such as *Lord of the Rings*. The term 'person with dwarfism' uses person-first language, placing less significance on the person's impairment and signifies that they human. Whilst that may seem obvious, it is unfortunately important to emphasise that people with dwarfism are humans as opposed to mythological beings. Person with dwarfism indicates that their impairment is part of their identity, but does not represent all of their identities, allowing them to be more than just a person with dwarfism.

The one term that the almost all people with dwarfism never use and find offensive is 'midget'. People with dwarfism and their associations often refer to it as the 'm word'. Referring to the term as the 'm word' aids in showing their objection to it and encourages avoidance or censorship. However, due to the influence of freak shows and present-day entertainment, 'midget' is often used as a term to refer to people with dwarfism. It was within the freak show where the term 'midget' originated in 1865. The term 'midget' was used to refer to people with proportionate dwarfism, but in today's society the term is used as a derogatory slur towards most people with dwarfism, including those with disproportionate dwarfism. The term 'midget' embodies and represents a historical disdain for people with dwarfism. Whilst the freak show disappeared at the turn of the 20th century, the term 'midget' has not.

'Midget' remains a popular term used to describe people with dwarfism within the entertainment industry, especially within lowbrow entertainment, as with the examples of 'midget wrestling' and 'midget tossing'. As well as in the entertainment industry, 'midget' is also used as a name for a variety of products, which gives it an acceptability and a constant presence within society. This is unfortunate for people with dwarfism as they endure the unwanted social repercussions from the term's popularity.

This chapter aims to demonstrate why 'midget' should actually be seen as a form of hate speech due to its origins and the way it is used towards people with dwarfism in society. Seglow (2016) argues that constant signs of hate speech impacts upon a person's reputation, self-respect, and dignity. The use of the term 'midget' can signify to the person that their impairment is still deserving enfreakment and mockery and that nothing has really changed since the freak show era. It argues that the word dehumanises people with dwarfism and continues to perpetuate the myth that they are a form of entertainment. The first part of this chapter focuses on the origins of the term in the Victorian freak show. It explores the oppressive origins of the term, which both dehumanises people with dwarfism and constructs them as figures of entertainment, ridicule, and Othering by nondisabled people.

Moving on, the next part of the chapter focuses on how the freak show has left an unwanted and harmful legacy in terms of encouraging the term to be used in society, from lowbrow entertainment to a myriad of products. This of course gives the term a popularity that has implications for people with dwarfism in society, including name-calling (Pritchard, 2017). Drawing on empirical data, the chapter shows some of ways the term has affected the social experiences of people with dwarfism and how they respond to them, such as the avoidance of particular spaces. The last part of this chapter shows how people with dwarfism and their associations are protesting against the use of the term 'midget' and calls for more attention to be given to their reasoning. It argues for the term 'midget' to be recognised as a form of hate speech and for its use to be removed from the entertainment industry, the media, products, and subsequently society.

Origins – The freak show

One of the most famous entertainment venues featuring people with dwarfism was the Victorian freak show. The freak show was a popular form of entertainment where people would go to see those whose body differed from the norm. The purpose of the freak show was to expose those whose body deviated from the norm in a way that their physical traits dominated the entire person on exhibit (Thomson, 1996, p. 61). The height of someone with dwarfism was his or her only reason for being on display. Their height was exaggerated and made more prominent in order to ensure that their one identity that differed significantly from the norm was exposed as an oddity. For example, people with dwarfism were often exhibited next to people with gigantism (whose own height was artificially raised) in order to exaggerate both of their sizes. The differences between the freak show performers were exploited for the financial benefit of the owners, who encouraged people to see them as sub human.

Most people will be familiar with the freak show as a historical phenomenon. Since its demise, the freak show has been popularised in films such as *Freaks (1932)*, and most recently, *The Greatest Showman (2017)*. It has also been propagated within television shows, such as *American Horror Story: Freak Show* (2014, 2015), as well as within a large selection of academic and non-academic literature. Adelson (2005) recalls how after having her daughter who was born with dwarfism went searching for literature on dwarfism, the only books that she found were on the freak show. Books are a form of reference that shape our knowledge about a particular subject. This is problematic as the nonacademic books are likely to use terminology relating to the freak show, including 'midget'. Even some of the academic books on the freak show refer to people with dwarfism as midgets. Whilst this may have been the correct term to use in the freak show, there is no correction made by the authors to indicate that the word is offensive to people with dwarfism. This gives the term an acceptance in society, including within academic where new knowledges are formed.

'Midget' is a term that originates from the freak show in order to separate those with disproportionate dwarfism (dwarfs) from those with proportionate dwarfism (midgets). Those with a proportionate body size were preferred over people with disproportionate dwarfism, as they were deemed to have more perfectly formed features. Tom Thumb, who had proportionate dwarfism and was referred to as a midget, was one of the most written about celebrities in the 19th century (Bogdan, 1988). His celebrity status aided in popularising the term.

The labelling of those with proportionate dwarfism as midgets is where the confusion of the term's acceptability in modern society arises from. However, the term 'midget' has no medical connotations, but is the result of terminology that emphasises and dehumanises a person's diminutive stature. The terms used in the freak show were usually a mixture of medical terminology and 'show-world hype' (Bogdan, 1988, p. 3). 'Midget' is derived from the term 'midge', a type of insect also known as a gnat or sandfly. This is not a desirable term to be associated with, as it affiliates people with dwarfism with unwanted pests and creatures that are not human. The addition of the suffix 'et' placed additional emphasis on their short stature which could then be exploited by the freak show owner. Using the example of the freak show, where disabled people were exhibited in a similar way to animals at a zoo, Shakespeare (1994) suggests that disabled people are often affiliated with animals. This is because their humanity is not unconditionally accepted. In the freak shows, those who were deemed fully human were the paying audiences and the owners of the show.

The exploitation of people deemed freaks helped to reproduce the prejudices and discrimination that were critical in their formation in the first place (Gerber, 1993). During the freak show era, disabled people did not have any rights or laws to protect them from discrimination. The freak show aided in the social oppression and exploitation of disabled people, who are were at that time and in some cases continue to be a powerless minority group. For many people with particular impairments, if they were not employed within the freak show, they would have likely been put into asylums or workhouses. Thus, they were exploited in order to avoid such places. This created an unfair situation for disabled people, who were forced to either live in dire conditions or exploit their impairment to escape such a cruel fate. Either way, unfair power relations within society which oppressed disabled people shaped their destiny.

The freak shows began to decline with the rise of disability rights and equality. 'Today the notion of the freak show that displays the bodies of disabled people for profit and public entertainment is both repugnant and anachronistic, rejected but nevertheless recent and compelling in memory' (Thomson, 1996, p. 58). Whilst the freak shows have almost disappeared and great strides have been made in terms of better employment opportunities available for disabled people, including people with dwarfism, the shows continue to influence how dwarfism is perceived in society. According to Backstrom (2012, p. 683), 'the disability rights movement has not been successful in eliminating the freak show discourse that surrounds certain extreme bodies.' People with dwarfism continue to be exploited within the entertainment industry, where the word 'midget' retains popularity. The origins of the term 'midget' within the freak show has filtered into the rest of society and remains a common (though unacceptable) term to use in the present day.

Present-day use

People with dwarfism continue to be used for entertainment purposes, simply because of their impairment. This form of entertainment is very similar to the freak show, in the sense that both the freak show and present-day lowbrow entertainment uses the dwarf body as nothing more than something to be objectified and ridiculed. Apart from some objection amongst a few associations for people with dwarfism (which will be explored further on), there has been no objection to lowbrow entertainment that incorporates people with dwarfism and the language they use. 'Midget' is often a term that coincides with lowbrow entertainment featuring people with dwarfism, allowing it to remain popular and unchallenged:

> Midgets are great, everybody should have one.
>
> (Jimmy Kimmel, cited in Adelson, 2005)

In the entertainment industry, terms that are deemed to be offensive are thought to be banned from use. People understand that if a term is censored within the media, then it will not be tolerated within society. However, if a term is still prevalent within the media, then its acceptance within society will flourish. According to Haller et al. (2006), the media's use of certain terms can make them more memorable for the audience. This aids in continuing their popularity within society. What is also problematic in Jimmy Kimmel's remark is that he is positioning people with dwarfism as a commodity. Merish (1996) points out that those in the freak show were positioned as objects, not subjects. This implies that they are powerless and subhuman, which allows the nondisabled person to have control over them, including the ability to decide what terms to use to refer to them.

In the above quote, replace the word 'midget' with another derogatory term associated with a different minority group, and consider what the implications there would be for the American television host and comedian Jimmy Kimmel. Would he still be a revered celebrity or would he be taken off air? This all depends upon which term you have thought of. If it is a term relating to a racial minority group, then it is likely that Jimmy Kimmel would be taken off air. There would rightly be a whole media frenzy berating his comment. Some words that constitute hate speech have received more attention than others (Delgato & Stefancic, 2004). Whilst certain terms, especially those referring to specific ethnic groups have gained widespread attention in terms of being recognised as hate speech and being removed from use, others have not. Martin (2010) argues that jokes towards racial minorities are less tolerated than jokes towards disabled people. This also includes the type of language used towards each group. Kimmel's reference to people with dwarfism as midgets and his further dehumanisation of them as pets, something you can own, was met with no media hostility. This is because mocking people with dwarfism, and regarding them as a spectacle reminiscent of the freak show is still widely accepted within society.

It needs to be recognised that there are some dwarf 'entertainers' who have aided in perpetuating the misconception that people with dwarfism are figures of fun and that it is acceptable to call them midgets. Adelson (2005) suggests that because most members of the public do not know any people with dwarfism personally, their impressions are formed by what they see in popular culture. These representations in popular culture are partly encouraged by dwarf entertainers. The dwarf entertainers collude with a misrepresentative and oppressive narrative of the impairment and the lives of people with it. This is problematic as according to Ablon (cited in Adelson, 2005) only 1% of people with dwarfism partake in the entertainment industry – and the scripts are usually framed by nondisabled people in ways that enfreak people with dwarfism for the entertainment of other nondisabled people. This means that the minority of dwarf entertainers get to represent the majority of people with dwarfism and collude with the power of (almost exclusively) nondisabled producers and writers. The enfreakment of people with dwarfism onstage always spills over onto people's offstage lives (Bogdan, 1988). Whilst it is (arguably) 'permissible' to stare and laugh at a person with dwarfism on stage, it is not acceptable to do this off stage. However, in practice the comedic enfreakment continues in society, where people fail to recognise that dwarfism is an impairment as opposed to a form of entertainment.

Outside the entertainment industry, the term 'midget' is also used as part of a name for a myriad of items, including confectionary and cars. The term is used to denote that the particular item is small for its group. Hate speech can also take a more tangible form, such as monuments, flags, or sports mascots (Delgato & Stefancic, 2004). The use of the term on many branded items allows its presence to be maintained within society. In the UK, a popular brand of confectionary called 'Midget Gems' can be found in most supermarkets and sweet shops. These sweets were invented by the Lyons confectionary company in the 1930s. Since then other brands, including supermarket own brands, have also produced their own version of the sweets, increasing their popularity. Ben-Moshe (cited in Haller et al., 2006, p. 65) points out that even when derogatory disability terms are not directed at an actual group of disabled people, they still perpetuate stigma in relation to disability.

According to Delgato and Stefancic (2004), hate speech is intended to be (and has most effect when it is) seen by a large audience. Midget Gems, along with other items that adopt the term 'midget', are found in everyday spaces, such as shops. These items promote an aversive message that people with dwarfism are inferior and do not belong. If it is acceptable to name a packet of sweets Midget Gems, then why not a person? I am going to break away for a moment and share one of the worst experiences I have had as a woman with dwarfism. I was in New York and was walking to the subway. My friend (of average stature) was walking a few paces behind me. She noticed a teenager trying to get a photograph of me, so she put her hand over the lens. Because the girl could not a get a photograph of me she went back to her friends who started shouting, 'Come here midget', 'I want a photo of you midget', 'Come back here midget!'. There were also some sexually explicit words shouted at me, but I have left them out to not cause offence.

This may be one of the worse encounters, but there plenty of other past experiences of people calling me midget, including as a child and up to the present day. Am I being 'overly PC' for trying to discourage this? Imagine experiencing someone calling you a midget, then you go into a shop and see on display a packet of Midget Gems. Then you go home and turn on the television and hear an average-sized presenter telling an amused audience jokes about midgets.

It acts as a reminder that your impairment is amusing to other people and that you are inferior. Because of these messages you feel out of place and devalued within society. You know that because of these constant messages, the next time you go out you know you will probably have to endure someone calling you that name once again.

Someone who goes out and buys a packet of Midget Gems is not necessarily trying to cause any offence in the same way a person shouting midget at a person with dwarfism is. However, it provides the term with legitimacy, an acceptability, and a constant presence within society.

Oi, midget! Social implications

The constant presence of the term *midget* within the media and as a name for products has implications for people with dwarfism in society, including name-calling and being perceived as a figure of fun. According to Haller et al. (2006), what disabled people are called forms part of their identity. Using a term that is derived from the freak show is a continuation of the way people with dwarfism are associated with being a form of entertainment for others. This is problematical for people with dwarfism who do not partake in lowbrow entertainment, as they are associated with the dwarf on stage:

> I used to be called Bridget the midget. When I was growing up a song came out called 'Bridget the midget' and of course everyone at school would call me Bridget the midget for ages… It was on *Top of the Pops* [British music show] and really popular. From then on, it became acceptable to use that term because it had been seen on the television.
>
> (Jade)

As dwarfism is a rare impairment, seeing someone in the media with dwarfism being called a midget can influence its use towards others. Jade was the only person with dwarfism at her school. This automatically makes her stand out and connects her to the dwarf entertainer who promoted the term 'midget'. Using the term 'midget', which has its origins in an era when people with dwarfism were promoted as oddities, reproduces such perceptions.

The continual use of disablist terms in the media contributes to the discriminatory attitudes and practices within society (Barnes, 1992). Using the term 'midget' within the media encourages the term's use in society and provides it with an appearance of legitimacy and acceptability. According to Barnes, disabling terms in the media reinforce society's misconceptions about disabled people. As it is a term that is popular within the media, then it is likely that they are being compared with a derogatory representation of dwarfism. Pritchard (2017) argues that how people with dwarfism are represented within the media will result in unwanted attention for people with dwarfism in society, including name-calling. Furthermore, in their study, Shakespeare, Thompson, and Wright (2010) found that 77% of their participants, who all had dwarfism, had been on the receiving end of verbal abuse. 'Midget' is a derogatory term and is often shouted at them in the street by strangers:

> Everywhere I go they just say, 'that's a midget.'
>
> (Myraar)

In the context of 'that's a midget' the phase is dehumanising and objectifying. The phase can denote that the person is a figure of fun that is permissible to treat in the same way as the entertainers with dwarfism. The person has no other identity and is perceived as a separate species.

Labels associated with a person's impairment focus attention on their most apparent characteristic, whilst all other identities remain absent (Longmore, 1985). This is especially problematic when that label/impairment is associated with derogatory stereotypes. When someone calls a person with dwarfism a midget, they are mocking that person, deeming them intolerable and portraying them as an outcast within society. They perceive their dwarfism to a spectacle, which does not fit in with the norm. There is no other identity to them, except for being 'a midget'. Delgato and Stefancic (2004) argue that hate speech can result in the victims withdrawing from society. The unwanted attention they receive can influence how people with dwarfism navigate the built environment, including avoiding particular spaces:

> I don't go to McDonalds [fast food chain], you get a lot of young people there and they can be just awful. They all like to have a good giggle at you with their friends and you will always get that one person trying to show off by calling you some name like midget.
>
> (Amanda)

The negotiation of spaces represents power. Pritchard (2014) found that people with dwarfism often avoid certain spaces within the built environment in order to minimise the amount of unwanted attention they receive, including verbal abuse. Avoiding spaces due to other people's behaviour demonstrates inferiority and being unaccepted within society. It validates the impact a word can have on a person's wellbeing, as well as their safety.

Shakespeare et al. (2010) studied people with dwarfism and found that over a third of their participants had experienced mental health problems because of the unwanted attention they received in society. Finding their own way to minimise these encounters aids in reducing mental health issues. However, it denies people with dwarfism full engagement with the built environment. The avoidance of particular spaces demonstrates an unequal power relation and a state of vulnerability. Shakespeare et al. found that 63% of their participants felt unsafe when out. This name-calling people with dwarfism fear may turn into something more serious.

Waseem and Hovy (2016) suggest that hate speech can lead to hate crimes. Furthermore, Craig (2002) points out that people who experience hate crimes may avoid the area where the incident took place in order to enhance their safety:

> I still go into pubs near where I live, but I wouldn't risk going to pubs in other areas. I am always worried that it could start off with name-calling and then turn into physical abuse.
>
> (Grace)

Avoiding a place where they are more likely to encounter unwanted attention acts as a safety strategy. It indicates that the term 'midget' could lead to a dangerous situation for people with dwarfism, but at the same time demonstrates fear and powerlessness. The real solution should not be for people with dwarfism to avoid certain spaces, but for the catalysts to these encounters to be removed. This can be done through recognising the term 'midget' as a form of hate speech.

At first glance, it may be difficult to consider the term 'midget' as a form of hate speech, as it does not denote that a person calling someone with dwarfism a midget actually hates them. According to Roulstone, Thomas, and Balderston (2011, p. 354), the term 'hate' itself is very emotive and hate may well not be the motivation for the often low-key, frequently repeated forms of bullying and intimidation that disabled people experience. For people with dwarfism, it is more that other people are influenced by cultural representations of them that encourage them to be devalued as opposed to hated. However, according to Parekh (2012, p. 37), hate speech includes the use of 'degrading, threatening, harassing or stigmatizing speech which affects an individual's or a group's dignity, reputation and status in society'. The term 'midget' ticks all of these boxes. Firstly, it degrades and stigmatises the person with dwarfism as it shows them to be sub-human. Secondly, it is both harassing and threatening as it is an offensive term, which people with dwarfism are often subjected to by people who are usually bigger than them. Third, it is often accompanied by harassment, ridicule, or even threats of violence.

Challenging words

As the way dwarfism is perceived is socially constructed, it can also be deconstructed through challenging these representations and the terms we use. Numerous disability groups have fought hard to adopt a name that is respectful and challenges derogatory stereotypes associated with them (Dajani, 2001). Challenging representations and using appropriate terminology, that is not associated with a time that deemed people with dwarfism to be spectacles, can help people with dwarfism become equal members of society. Some associations for people with dwarfism have become proactive in challenging the term 'midget':

> It was a term [midget] that kept getting used again and again, I was objecting to several programmes on television and the advertising standards agency,

> and they just said it was a term that's not offensive. We know it is, but we as a group had not communicated that effectively to the wider world so it needed some sort of authority. So what I decided to do was I went and said in the committee [of the Restricted Growth Association] was, can we pass a resolution guys that we as a group are definitely not happy with being called midget and it was passed without exception. It was unanimous, every hand in the room shoot up and said we agree that we as a group of people do not want to be called this word.
>
> (Naomi)

Naomi is a member of the Restricted Growth Association (RGA), a charity for people with dwarfism based in the UK. Little People of America (LPA) also point out that 90% of their member's state that the term should not be used to refer to people with dwarfism (Little People of America, 2015).

Challenging the use of the term 'midget' illustrates Longmore's (1985, p. 422) suggestion that 'the refusal to accept a stigmatized social identity aids in asserting pride and in recognising themselves as fully human, which helps to challenge the subordinate social role that the term encourages'. Refusing to accept the term 'midget' is a protest against the view that people with dwarfism are subordinate and spectacles. Linton (cited in Haller et al., 2006, p. 65) argues that it is important to take control of what terminology is used to describe disabled people, as it can reinforce dominant cultural views of disability. A term that is associated with the freak show only serves to perpetuate the myth that people with dwarfism are a form of entertainment.

Little People of America have also challenged a number of institutions that have used the word 'midget', including Universities and high schools who have used the term for their mascots in sports. Delgato and Stefancic (2004) point out that numerous American high schools and sports teams use derogatory racial names and logos, which cause upset to the affiliated racial minorities. Some of these protests by the Little People of America have met with success, whilst others have not. For example, Freeburg Community High School in Illinois have kept their nickname 'the Freeburg Midgets', despite protests.

According to Haller et al. (2006), the dominant members of society, including nondisabled people and the media, often resist changes in language, deeming it being overly 'politically correct'. This ignores the reasoning for changes in language, such as challenging negative stereotypes, which the dominant groups within society will not face. Relying on the person or institution to stop using the term does not guarantee success. This is because they tend to act surprised that their logo or mascot is causing offence, or try to defend themselves by claiming that someone from the minority group within their fraction finds it acceptable (Delgato & Stefancic, 2004).

For example, 'midget wrestling' is a name developed and used by average height promoters, and its acceptance is reinforced through the dwarf entertainers that perform under the name. Dwarf entertainers and nondisabled people, including those employed within the media continue to have more power in determining what terminology is acceptable, whereas it should be up the person(s) who are impacted by the term. Barnes (1992) claims that it is difficult to banish disablist terms from social use, including within the media, because nondisabled people devise many of these terms. As demonstrated, the term 'midget' is derived from the freak show, which was managed by nondisabled people. In addition, when products such as Midget Gems have been given their name they have so by non-disabled people, who are not impacted by the name. This demonstrates that the average-sized person gets to determine what terminology is associated with people with dwarfism, creating an unequal power relation.

A hierarchy of impairments is also created when terms associated with some minority groups are more accepted than others:

> I've had editors say to me you can't censor words when I was trying to explain that the term 'midget' is an equally offensive term like 'nigger' to a black person or 'faggot' to a gay person. Yet, neither of those words would make the air with ease that the term 'midget' does across mainstream channels.
>
> (Naomi)

All minority groups have a particular term that is highly offensive to them as it is used as an insult by those who wish to offend. However, not all are given the same tolerance by the media. According to Kruse (2002, p. 176), 'using the term midget towards a dwarf [sic] is the same as calling a person of African descent a nigger'. Whilst this parallel will make some people feel uncomfortable, it demonstrates how some terms are more acceptable to use than others, despite them both being offensive to their respected minority group. The acceptance of derogatory words associated with one minority group, alongside the condemnation and censorship of others, creates a hierarchy of minority groups, of hate speech, and of oppression. For better equality, all minority groups should be respected when they deem a certain term to be derogatory. This equality can be achieved through recognising those terms as hate speech.

Conclusion

The disappearance of the freak show during the 20th century indicates some improvement in the representation and public treatment of disabled people. Despite the improvement for disabled people in general, the use of the term 'midget' demonstrates that the legacy of the freak show remains strong and that people with dwarfism are still being impacted by the freak show. Adopting a term that originated within the freak show demonstrates how little progress we as a society have made in terms of providing equality for people with dwarfism.

When people call someone a midget, more often than not the reason for it reflects how people are encouraged to perceive people with dwarfism in the entertainment industry, which is usually as an inferior being that is constructed as a figure of fun, as opposed to a disabled person. Banishing the word 'midget' from the media and society is one of the first steps in recognising people with dwarfism as actually people and not as spectacles reminiscent of the freak shows. To do this, the word must first be recognised as a form of hate speech, which is not acceptable to use within the media or anywhere else. The media can both encourage the use of negative terminology or challenge it. If the word 'midget' is used in the media, it aids in increasing the term's popularity and encourages its use. On the other hand, if it is not used it demonstrates it unacceptability and reduces its popularity.

To recognise 'midget' as a form of hate speech is difficult when it is used freely in society. The continual use of the term in the media helps to strengthen the term's popularity and use in society. What makes it even more difficult is that some dwarf entertainers encourage the use of the term. This gives the term acceptability, as people with the impairment are using it. It is easy, if not lazy, to carry on using the term because a few dwarf entertainers do. The majority of people with dwarfism, who are not in the entertainment industry, and strongly oppose the term, are ignored. This is because they challenge the nondisabled person's view towards them. The views of people with dwarfism in society should be given more consideration, as opposed to those who are unaffected by the term.

References

Adelson, B. (2005). Dwarfs: The changing lives of archetypal 'curiosities' – And echoes of the past. *Disability Studies Quarterly*, *25*(3). http://dx.doi.org/10.18061/dsq.v18025i18063.18576

American Horror Story: Freak Show. (2014). Netflix, 8 October.

American Horror Story: Freak Show. (2015). Netflix, 14 January.

Backstrom, L. (2012). From the freak show to the living room: Cultural representations of dwarfism and obesity. *Sociological Forum*, *27*, 682–707.

Barnes, C. (1992). *Disabling imagery and the media: An exploration of the principles for media representations of disabled people*. Derby: The British Council of Disabled People.

Bogdan, R. (1988). *Freak show: Presenting human oddities for amusement and profit.* Chicago, IL: University of Chicago Press.

Craig, K. M. (2002). Examining hate-motivated aggression: A review of the social psychological literature on hate crimes as a distinct form of aggression. *Aggression and Violent Behavior*, *7*(1), 85–101.

Dajani, K. F. (2001). What's in a name? Terms used to refer to people with disabilities. *Disability Studies Quarterly*, *21*(3), 196–209.

Delgato, R., & Stefancic, J. (2004). *Understanding words that wound.* Boulder, CO: Westview Press.

Freaks (1932). [DVD] (1932) Directed by Tod Browning. USA: Metro-Goldwyn-Mayer [Viewed 21 December 2018].

Gerber, D. A. (1993). Interpreting the freak show and freak show. *Disability, Handicap & Society*, *8*(4), 435–436.

Haller, B., Dorries, B., & Rahn, J. (2006). Media labelling versus the US disability community identity: A study of shifting cultural language. *Disability & Society*, *21*(1), 61–75.

Heider, J. D., Scherer, R. C., & Edlund, J. E. (2013). Cultural stereotypes and personal beliefs about individuals with dwarfism. *The Journal of Social Psychology, 153*(1), 80–97.

Kruse, R. (2002). Social spaces of little people: The experiences of the Jamisons. *Social and Cultural Geography, 3*(2), 175–191.

Little People of America. (2015). *LPA issues statement to abolish the 'm' word.* Retrieved from https://www.lpaonline.org/the-m-word

Longmore, P. K. (1985). A note on language and the social identity of disabled people. *American Behavioral Scientist, 28*, 419–423.

Martin, N. (2010). A preliminary study of some broad disability related themes within the Edinburgh Festival Fringe. *Disability & Society, 25*(5), 539–549.

Merish, L. (1996). Cuteness and commodity aesthetics: Tom Thumb and Shirley Temple. In R. G. Thomson (Ed.), *Freakery: Cultural spectacles of the extraordinary body* (pp. 185–203). New York: New York University Press.

Parekh, B. (2012). Is there a case for banning hate speech? In M. Herz & P. Molnar (Eds.), *The content and context of hate speech: Rethinking regulation and responses* (pp. 37–56). Cambridge, MA: Cambridge University Press.

Pritchard, E. (2014). *The social and spatial experiences of dwarfs in public spaces*, Unpublished PhD thesis. Newcastle University.

Pritchard, E. (2017). Cultural representations of dwarfs and their disabling effects on dwarfs in society. *Considering Disability Journal*, 1, 1–31.

Roulstone, A., Thomas, P., & Balderston, S. (2011). Between hate and vulnerability: Unpacking the British criminal justice system's construction of disablist hate crime. *Disability & Society, 26*(3), 351–364.

Seglow, J. (2016). Hate speech, dignity and self-respect. *Ethical Theory and Moral Practice, 19*, 1103–1116.

Shakespeare, T. (1994). Cultural representation of disabled people: Dustbins for disavowal? *Disability & Society, 9*(3), 283–299.

Shakespeare, T., Thompson, S., & Wright, M. (2010). No laughing matter: Medical and social experiences of restricted growth. *Scandinavian Journal of Disability Research, 12*(1), 19–31.

The Greatest Showman (2017). [DVD] Directed by Michael Gracey. New York: Lawrence Marks Productions [viewed 21 December 2018].

Thomson, R. G. (1996). Introduction: From wonder to error—A genealogy of freak discourse in modernity. In R. G. Thomson (Ed.), *Freakery: Cultural spectacles of the extraordinary body* (pp. 1–19). New York: New York University Press.

Waseem, Z., & Hovy, D. (2016). *Hateful symbols or hateful people? Predictive features for hate speech detection on Twitter.* Paper presented at the Proceedings of NAACL-HLT 2016, San Diego, CA.

Part III

Disablist hate speech within a geopolitical context

8 Hate speech targeting Sami people with disabilities

Line Melbøe and Hege Gjertsen

Introduction

In essence, research on hate speech has focused on single groups (Nadim, Fladmoe, & Wessel-Aas, 2016). However, according to research on harassment, it sometimes occurs as interactions between group affiliations, thereby exposing some people to added risk (Buchanan & Fitzgerald, 2008). Consequently, studies of hate speech should also examine the interactions between various group affiliations (Nadim et al., 2016). In this chapter, we elaborate on the phenomenon of hate speech targeting individuals with a double minority-group affiliation, Sami people with disabilities, from an intersectional perspective.

The Sami are the indigenous people of Sapmi, a territory including northern parts of Norway, Finland, Sweden and Russia. The majority live in Norway, where the Sami population is estimated to be 40,000 (Dagsvold, Møllersen, & Stordahl, 2016). Over the last decade, we have seen an increased focus on discrimination targeting Sami (Bals, Turi, Skre, & Kvernmo, 2010; Hansen, Melhus, Høgmo, & Lund, 2008) and disabled people (Tøssebro, 2016; Vedeler, 2014) in Norway. However, research focusing hate speech targeting either the Sami (Midtbøen & Lidén, 2015) or people with disabilities (Olsen, Vedeler, Eriksen, & Elvegård, 2016) is scarce, and no research has addressed hate speech targeting Sami people with disabilities. According to our studies focusing on the situation of Sami people with disabilities, this group experiences bullying and hate speech because of both their Sami background and their disability (Gjertsen, Melbøe, Fedreheim, & Fylling, 2017; Melbøe, Johnsen, Fredreheim, & Hansen, 2016). There are several categories of hate speech, and these are interrelated. The chapter elucidates how Sami people with disabilities experience hate speech in different ways as members of an indigenous group and as persons with disabilities.

In accordance with our participants' descriptions of how they have experienced hate speech related to *both* being Sami and having a disability, one might conclude that belonging to more than one marginalized group can cause a "double handicap" (Brooks & Deegan, 1981) or "double discrimination" (Habib, 1995). However, this "additive" way of thinking does not adequately explain the phenomenon of hate speech experienced by the participants in our studies. Instead, as designated by Fekjær (2010), the combination of different statuses sometimes seems to carry greater significance than their sum. Thus, membership in two stigmatized groups does not necessarily cause increased harassment only but also makes the harassment take on different qualities (Buchanan & Fitzgerald, 2008). In this chapter we through an intersectional perspective attempts to capture the meaning of belonging to different groups at the same time and how this can affect experiences with hate speech in various ways, based on the situation (Grönvik & Söder, 2008).

The Sami

Historically, the Sami engaged in reindeer herding, farming, and fishing (Lund, Brustad, & Høgmo, 2008). However, today the majority has adopted a more Western lifestyle characterized by modern professions, trades, and dietary habits (Sjölander, 2011). Moreover, an increasing share of Sami people have relocated from core Sami areas and now live in urban areas (Selle, Semb, Strømsnes, & Nordø, 2015). From the mid-nineteenth century until World War II, the Sami were subjected to a strong assimilation policy whereby Norwegian authorities made vigorous efforts to acculturate them into Norwegian society. For example, the use of the Sami language was banned in Norwegian schools, and many Sami children were sent to boarding schools to remove them from their cultural and linguistic backgrounds and to facilitate their assimilation. Parallel to the authorities' Norwegianization policy, the Sami personally experienced stigmatization, discrimination, and everyday racism (Minde, 2005). In recent decades, there has been a Sami ethnic and cultural revival with increased use of the Sami language and customs and the establishment of Sami institutions such as a Sami parliament, college, and research centres (Turi, Bals, Skre, & Kvernmo, 2009) and the passage of the Sami Act (Ministry of Local Government and Modernisation, 1987). The Norwegian government has officially declared and ratified the Sami as indigenous people of Norway (ILO Convention No. 169, 1989). Hence, Sami people, according to the Convention, have the right to exercise control over their way of life and to maintain and develop their identity, language, and religion within the framework of the Norwegian state. Today, Sami people, in general, are treated as equals in Norwegian society (Pedersen & Høgmo, 2012), but they still experience more bullying and ethnic discrimination than the majority Norwegian population (Hansen et al., 2008).

Norwegian welfare policy

Compared to many other countries, Norway has a rather comprehensive welfare policy. The aim of the social security system in Norway is to ensure an acceptable standard of living for everyone. This is done, for example, through a universal minimum pension, while the health policy intends to remove differences in health conditions and mortality between different social groups (Stamsø, 2009). The welfare provision has a universal nature, which means that all citizens are equally entitled to a decent standard of living and full citizenship rights (Saunes,

Hansen, Tomic, & Lindahl, 2017). According to the Health and Care Services Act (Ministry of Health and Care Services, 2011), all Norwegian citizen inhabitants have a legal right to home healthcare services, regardless of age, gender, socio-economic status, or other differences. However, some benefits are means-tested or selective, for example, disability benefits. The public sector has the main responsibility for welfare production (Loga, 2018). The Ministry of Health and Care Services is organized, managed, and financed primarily by Norwegian municipalities. Political documents and legislation underline that people with disabilities are entitled to enjoy the same living conditions and quality of life as the rest of Norway's population.

Based on international rankings, Norway in general performs very well in many measures of well-being, and Norwegians are, in general, more satisfied with their lives than the average, relative to most other countries (see for example OECD, 2017). Furthermore, the health status in Norway is good with a high life expectancy and sound health compared with the average in Organisation for Economic Co-operation and Development (OECD) countries (Saunes et al., 2017). However, research on living conditions of people with disabilities has revealed that this group experiences poorer living conditions compared to the Norwegian population in general in regard to housing, education, employment, income, health, social relations, and self-determination (Gjertsen et al., 2017; Kittelsaa, Wiik, & Tøssebro, 2015; Söderström & Tøssebro, 2011). Since people with disabilities are a heterogeneous group, living conditions will vary; however, people with intellectual disabilities are one of the groups found to have the poorest living conditions in several areas.

Regarding discrimination and the ability to participate, Norway ratified the United Nations Convention on the Rights of Persons with Disabilities (CRPD) in 2013. The rights of Norwegians with disabilities are also protected through several national laws and policies, the main one being the Equality and Anti-Discrimination Act prohibiting discrimination. This law functions to promote equality and equity, to ensure all citizens the same opportunities and rights to societal participation, to increase accessibility, and to ensure that social and physical environments are accessible (Ministry of Children and Equality, 2017). Nevertheless, people with disabilities experience discrimination related to work, housing, education, and other aspects of their lives more often than nondisabled people.

The data

This chapter relies on data from two studies performed by the Institute of Social Education (ISE) at UiT, the Arctic University of Norway. One is a qualitative study of the life situation of Sami people with disabilities (Melbøe et al., 2016), and the other is a quantitative survey of living conditions among people with intellectual disabilities in Sami areas (Gjertsen et al., 2017). The first was commissioned by the Nordic Welfare Centre (NVC) and the second by the Norwegian Directorate for Children, Youth, and Family Affairs (Bufdir) and the NVC. Both studies were conducted in accordance with the National Ethical Committee for the Social

Sciences and approved by the Norwegian Social Science Data Service. However, when we were invited to participate in this book about hate speech, we performed a new analysis on the data from the two studies, this time examining them to illuminate the phenomenon of hate speech targeting Sami people with disabilities.

The qualitative study focused on the life situation of Sami people with disabilities and was conducted from 2014–2015. The study included 31 semi-structured interviews with people with disabilities and a Sami background and/or their next of kin or caregivers. The selection included children, youths, adults, and elderly people (7–88 years old). The study focused on the situations of 10 females and 21 males with a variety of impairments, including sensory (e.g. sight and/or hearing), physical (e.g. paralysis), or cognitive (e.g. learning disability) challenges. Pseudonyms were used for all participants to protect their privacy and for confidentiality.

In 2017, the ISE conducted a study of living conditions among persons with intellectual disabilities in Sami areas in Norway. A total of 93 persons, 16 years and older, responded to the survey; 57% were men and 43% women. Most of the participants had a mild or moderate intellectual disability, and a few had a severe or profound intellectual disability. A third of the sample had a Sami background. We examined whether there are differences in the living conditions of persons with intellectual disabilities with and without a Sami background, and we compared their living conditions to those of people with intellectual disabilities in Norway, in general, as well as with the living conditions of the Norwegian population in general. In addition to different dimensions of living conditions and quality of life, the study focused on bullying. This was the first living-conditions survey in Norway for which persons with intellectual disabilities could answer the questionnaire themselves and the first living-conditions survey among this group to focus on the meaning of having a Sami background. The questionnaire included mainly fixed-response categories, but also had several open-ended questions.

How we define "hate speech"

This book chapter applies an understanding of the concept of hate speech that aligns with that of the LDO (2015, p. 5). Here, hate speech is understood as:

> degrading, threatening, harassing or stigmatising speech, which affects an individual's or group's dignity, reputation and status in society by means of linguistic and visual effects that promote negative feelings, attitudes and perceptions based on characteristics such as ethnicity, religion, gender, disability, etc.

However, neither of the two studies this chapter is based on has explicitly used the term hate speech. Although hate speech has been a punishable offence since 1970, the hate speech term is seldom used in Norway. As emphasized by Olsen et al. (2016 and in this volume), "hate" is perceived as a very strong word in Norway and implies something severely negative, and thus even informants who have experienced serious harassment hesitate to use this term.

When we base this chapter on findings from our studies revealing bullying and discrimination of Sami people with disabilities, it is because we argue that bullying, discrimination, and hate speech are related. This sort of overlap between hate speech, bullying, and discrimination research is described, for example, by Eggebø and Stubberud (Eggebø & Stubberud, 2016). Both hate speech and bullying include offensive actions in an asymmetrical relationship, and both might cause uncertainty, fear, and anxiety for those targeted (Nilsen, 2014). Nonetheless, much of the research on bullying does not necessarily question the actual content of the offensive speech, which makes it impossible to determine whether the offence is discriminatory or not, a premise for classifying the bullying as hate speech (Eggebø & Stubberud, 2016). However, in our qualitative study, especially, we have data that clearly reveal that the content of bullying has discriminatory characteristics. For example, some are told that they are "being stupid as a Sami," while others are tormented for their physical appearance such as having a harelip or other characteristics caused by their impairment/ diagnoses.

Even if we assert that some of the bullying demonstrates hate speech, in this chapter we use the terms bullying and harassment as well as hate speech. The main reason for this is that bullying was the main concept applied in our studies, and thus, for both methodological and ethical reasons, we will continue to refer to it as such. Moreover, as pointed out by Olsen et al. (2016), there is no clear demarcation between what constitutes hate speech and what is "just" an unpleasant experience. By using the concepts of bullying and harassment in addition, we hope to present a more complete picture of the experiences of Sami people with disabilities with offensive actions than if talking strictly about hate speech. Experiences of violence are not included in our definition of hate speech in this chapter, although such experiences are part of the picture drawn by the participants in both studies. By using an intersectional perspective, we intend to capture the complexity of the concept of hate speech.

In the living-conditions survey, we operationalize "bullying" by asking the respondents if, during the previous year, they have experienced someone saying hurtful, negative remarks to them or threatening to hurt them (Gjertsen et al., 2017). Since the questionnaire had to be easy for the respondents with intellectual disabilities to understand, there were only "yes" and "no" choices to respond to the questions. The informants could, however, elaborate on their answers using their own words when we asked open questions.

In the qualitative study of the life situations of Sami people with disabilities, the participants freely described their experiences of bullying and discrimination. Common to the stories told by our informants was their experience of something unpleasant inflicted by others, such as threatening, harassing, or stigmatizing speech.

The extent of hate speech

The findings from our quantitative study reveal that persons with intellectual disabilities are victims of bullying and violence more often than the general population. Furthermore, women are more vulnerable than men, and those with a Sami

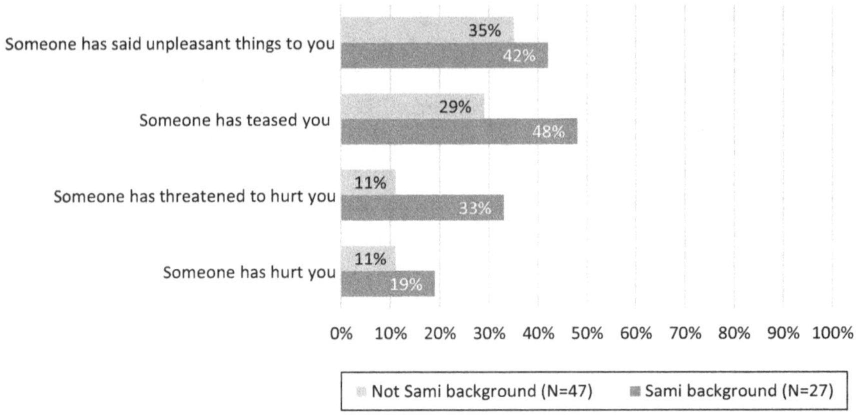

Figure 8.1 During the last year, have you experienced something like what we have described?

background are at even greater risk of being victims of bullying and violence than those without a Sami background. More than one-third of the respondents in the survey (37%) have experienced others making unpleasant remarks to them, and almost half (47%) have experienced being teased. In the survey, 17% report that someone has threatened to harm them, and 14% report that they have been harmed by others. A considerably higher proportion of persons with a Sami background have experienced the different types of bullying described compared to those without a Sami background. Figure 8.1 shows that while 42% of those with a Sami background have experienced hate speech, the percentage of those without a Sami background reporting the same experience was 35%.

About one-third (33%) of the respondents with a Sami background reported that lately they have been afraid of being beaten or bullied when travelling alone near their homes.[1] Only 17% of those without a Sami background reported the same experience.

In our qualitative study of Sami people with different types of impairments, about half of the informants talked about bullying and harassment, even if we did not ask specific questions about these. This supports the findings from the living-conditions study that indicate that experiences with hate speech among Sami people with disabilities are commonplace.

Hate speech motivated by ethnicity and disability

We will now present examples of experiences with degrading, threatening, harassing, and stigmatizing speech suffered by Sami persons with disabilities, and we will particularly consider the characteristics this kind of speech is based on.

Several of the participants in our qualitative study described experiences of harassment and bullying due to their impairment. One of these is Laila, an adult woman with an intellectual disability. She questions how people at different places meet her: "They say I am handicapped ... Are they allowed to say that?" Klaus, an adult man with a physical impairment, describes how peers violated him at school by calling him a *cripple,* etc. An adult woman with a hearing impairment, Berit, was bullied in school because she did not master speech as well as others. Her peers called her *dumb* and accused her of not understanding anything at all. Moreover, Berit described how others later tormented her for getting a hearing aid, how she tried to hide it so that others could not see it, and, in the end, how she wrecked the hearing aid herself by stepping on it because she was so tired of being bullied.

Per, an adult man with a hearing impairment, referred to his experiences of harassment due to his impairment even from the staff at school. He described how he was treated:

> I was presented almost like intellectual disabled when I started school ... My father was furious and my mother very disappointed. When I had finished my Master [*sic*] degree, she visited the headmaster and confronted him.

Several of the participants in our qualitative study reported bullying and harassment because of their Sami background. Being accused of "being stupid as a Sami" is an insult experienced by several. One of those who was repeatedly submitted to this kind of comment at school was Knut, a young boy with Attention Deficit Hyperactivity Disorder (ADHD). His mother described how he is easily provoked due to his diagnosis, which his peers found very amusing and thus bullied him. In this way, Knut ended up being bullied because of both his ethnicity and his disability. One of the other participants who described experiencing harassment and bullying motivated by her Sami background was Rakel, a young woman with a psychiatric impairment. She referred to how:

> It was not very easy to come from a very little Sami school at the age of twelve. The environment was pretty much harder than I was used to ... not physical ... but I was called Sami bastard and that sort of thing. And when we should draw each other, I was drawn as a reindeer and that sort of thing.

Paradoxically, while Rakel's peers in a mainstream Norwegian school bullied her for being Sami, she had actually transferred from the Sami school she had attended earlier because her peers there bullied her for not being Sami "enough." According to Rakel: "That was partly the reason we moved. Because there (at the old school) the bullying focused on we did not keep reindeer." However, Rakel is not the only one who described harassment from other Sami children due to not being Sami "enough."

Per, who was mentioned previously, did not have a chance to learn Sami in school, even though he came from a Sami-speaking family. This was because the teachers did not think he would be able to learn both Norwegian and Sami. Per described how, when he tried to talk to other Sami people in public, he was sometimes threatened with a beating or told to "get the hell out of here" when they realized that he did not speak the Sami language. Nicolai, an adult with a physical impairment, reported being bullied by other Sami because of his Sami background. He was bullied primarily about his Sami characteristics such as high cheekbones. According to Nicolai, the Sami who bullied him, even if they came from Sami families, often did not define themselves as Sami. Nicolai stated that he thinks their behaviour is related to their own earlier experiences of being victims of bullying.

Per, Rakel, and Nicolai's experiences of bullying and harassment focusing on their Sami background by other Sami are not unique. Høgmo (1989; 2005) claimed that the strongest Sami discrimination takes place within combined Norwegianized Sami and Norwegian local communities, and that it is often persons with a Sami background themselves who inflict the most humiliating discrimination. Høgmo (2005) argued that such discrimination is not caused by hate targeting the Sami but rather is a reaction to attitudes in the majority community. Thus, disparaging speech about Sami reduces the focus on the perpetrators' own ethnic background (A. Høgmo, 2005, pp. 19–20). However, while this explanation aligns with Nicolai's experience, it does not explain why other Sami pupils harassed Rakel for not having reindeer, etc.

The reason for the Sami pupils' harassment of Rakel might actually be quite the opposite. In the Sami revitalization process following the long assimilation period, the Sami elite have focused on distinguishing between the Sami and the Norwegian, holding onto the idea of the Sami as "a traditional and genuine common culture" (Gaski, 2008, p. 234). Consequently, Rakel and others who do not necessarily have these traditional visible cultural traits, such as speaking the Sami language, keeping reindeer, etc., might experience not being perceived as "real" Sami or "Sami enough." To Sami with disabilities, this is problematic, as they, like Rakel, risk exclusion from both the Norwegian majority and the Sami minority, not being fully accepted by either and thus not really belonging anywhere.

Marit, an elderly woman with an intellectual disability, describes another example of harassment because of her Sami background. She refers not only to how, as a pupil decades ago, she was forbidden to wear Sami clothing at the boarding school but also how even her mother had been met with anger from the staff when she visited Marit at school wearing traditional Sami clothing, known as the gákti. Wearing the gákti today can still be a cause for harassment and even hate speech, as this visible cultural trait makes it possible for others to identify who is a Sami. Klaus, an adult man with a physical impairment, describes experiencing hate speech recently when he was travelling to Oslo, the capital of Norway, and wore the gákti. He describes how, suddenly, an adult on the other side of the street shouted: "Get lost and go back up north where you belong. You have nothing to do here at the south!" Briefly summarized, Sami people with disabilities seem to experience bullying and harassment sometimes because of their Sami background, sometimes due to their disability, and at times as a combination of both.

As pointed out by Soorenian in this volume, for many victims, hate speech occurs so often that it is regarded as something that just happens to them. We find this kind of normalization and denial present in the qualitative study among Sami people with disabilities. While bullying at school, according to some participants, was taken seriously, others experienced that bullying was ignored and silently accepted. The normalization of hate speech targeting both disabled and Sami people may both reinforce the overlaps and intersectionality of hate speech and make it more difficult to recognize. Furthermore, as Burch (2018) pointed out, people employ different practices of resistance to challenge hate speech. Most of those who related stories about bullying at school seemed to perceive it as something they had to expect and that nothing could be done about it. Several of the informants did not express anger because of what someone had done or said to them or because no one tried to stop the bullying. Burch (2018) discussed how hate speech harms its victims in complex ways through the internalization of hateful attitudes. This may be the case among our informants as well.

Where does hate speech take place and who are the perpetrators?

Hate speech targeting Sami people with disabilities happens at different places. In our studies, the most frequently reported location for these experiences is *school* and especially primary school. The participants have attended different kinds of schools, such as Sami schools and boarding schools (especially the elderly participants), mainstream, and special schools. They reported experiences of being bullied in all these settings and across different periods of time, that is, from the 1950s when our eldest participants went to school until today. The experience of bullying and harassment at school was especially difficult for those attending boarding schools, as they had to stay at school all week long. Thus, they were exposed to bullying and harassment both during the day and in their free time.

Moreover, Kai, another adult man with a cognitive impairment, reported harassment even from the staff at the boarding school. He described how the staff at his school, for example, regularly initiated and organized snowball fights between the Sami boarding pupils and the Norwegian-speaking pupils who lived nearby at home. During these fights, staff deliberately joined the Norwegian-speaking team in a match against Sami pupils, who were in the minority. Kai referred to how he and his best friend ended up practising martial arts in their leisure time in order to be able to defend themselves.

Other participants described how staff at boarding schools, although not necessarily participating in bullying, offered very little support. Olaus, an elderly man with a physical impairment, reported that pupils could not expect any support from staff when it came to bullying: "The housewife was really harsh … It was no use to complain to her … Once I was told that if I did not stop complaining I would be spanked." Moreover, Kai described how, according to traditional Sami upbringing, children were expected to solve their own problems, which meant that it was no use complaining at home about harassment and bullying that took place at school. Even though there is now only one Sami boarding school remaining in Norway, our young participants talked about extensive bullying and harassment even today in mainstream schools. This is serious as Sami pupils with impairments have to attend school every day since education is compulsory for 10 years in Norway.

Some of the participants also reported being targeted by harassment and bullying out in society in general. One of these was Ragnar, an elderly man with a psychiatric impairment. He talked about such experiences: "Especially earlier, not as much the last twenty years, in our village. There has been extensive bullying from the Norwegians targeting us Sami … Even today there is still a lot of hidden racism." Unfortunately, Ragnar's experience is not unique. Sami people, especially adults and the oldest, are to a certain degree used to being discriminated against and stigmatized because of their Sami background. Sami people living in mixed communities with mainly Norwegian inhabitants are more exposed to such attacks than those living in mainly Sami communities (Hansen et al., 2008). This means that there seem to be geographic variations in the occurrence of hate speech, bullying, and harassment targeting people of Sami background. The likelihood of experiencing hate speech because of having a Sami background is much higher in areas with a dense Sami population than in core Sami populated areas, as the assimilation policy did not weaken Sami culture as much in these areas as in other parts of Norway.

Furthermore, in our study of living conditions among people with intellectual disabilities, several of the adults told stories about bullying, harassment, and threats at sheltered workshops or at group homes.[2] In the survey, a higher percentage of respondents living in group homes reported being afraid or worried (30%) compared to those not living in group homes (21%). This may be related to the fact that many people living in group homes are insecure when it comes to other residents (Hansen & Grødem, 2012). Some of the respondents told us that they were afraid of or had experienced harassment or being beaten by co-tenants in the group home where they live. One of the informants with an intellectual disability talked about not feeling safe at home: "There is just one person in the group home who is bad. I have talked about it. I am afraid that he will beat me or say something."

According to our studies, Sami people with impairments also experience harassment within the welfare system, for instance from nurses, doctors, etc. Berit, a woman with a hearing impairment who was mentioned earlier in the chapter, described a visit to her home by the local health nurse (who was also Sami) after Berit had her first baby. The nurse spoke to Berit in Sami, a language Berit had not had an opportunity to learn as she was forced to learn Norwegian in school. Berit described the visit:

> I asked her (the local health nurse) to speak Norwegian as I couldn't speak Sami. She became very angry and said, "You come from a Sami village and can't speak Sami!"

Our studies show that Sami people with disabilities experience hate speech at places where they expect to feel safe. Olsen et al (2016) found a similar situation in their study of hate speech directed toward disabled people in Norway. However, Sami people experience this even more often. This draws a sad picture of everyday life for many Sami people with disabilities.

As Sherry (2010) pointed out, it is often assumed that hate crimes (including hate speech) are senseless, irrational, and random "stranger crimes." However, he emphasized that, according to research, very often the perpetrators of disability hate crimes are "people directly in their lives," referring to the victims. This is also the case in our studies, where the participants reported that very often, it is people they know who bully or harass them. Among those mentioned are classmates, co-tenants where they live, and people at work or professionals within welfare services. Several specifically pointed out that their "friends" are actually the ones bullying or harassing them. It is particularly important to be aware of this when it comes to persons with intellectual disabilities, as they are especially at risk for the phenomenon of "mate crime" (Roderick, 2014). Mate crime implies that someone "makes friends" with a person and then abuses or exploits the relationship. Many persons with intellectual disabilities find it challenging to establish friendships, which makes them more likely to accept any "friendship" offered, even though it may turn out to be dysfunctional or even abusive. Moreover, because of their impairments, some people with intellectual disabilities might also have problems reporting that someone is exploiting their friendship, harassing them, etc. Thus, it is important to be aware and to pay special attention to hate speech targeting this group.

In short, Sami people with disabilities seem to experience hate speech at all kinds of places, including in public such as in the street, and at what have been perceived as relatively safe or protected locations such as at school, at work, or where one lives. Furthermore, hate speech is used by both individuals from the Norwegian majority and individuals from the Sami minority, by strangers and by people the victims know, and by people with and without disabilities themselves.

The consequences of hate speech

Experiences of hate speech have serious and various consequences for Sami people with disabilities. In the living conditions survey, we find a correlation between bullying and poor mental health. The term "mental health" was operationalized by four questions about mental health issues. We asked the respondents if they often struggle with sadness/loneliness/anger/feeling afraid. The response choices were "yes" or "no."

We found that people with intellectual disabilities both with and without Sami background have poorer mental health compared to the population in general. Previous studies have found the same (Hove, 2009; Söderström & Tøssebro, 2011). Both Hove (2009) and Olsen et al. (2016) stressed that people with intellectual disabilities who are exposed to bullying have a higher risk for developing depression and feelings of sadness.

Further, we found that people with intellectual disabilities and a Sami background have poorer mental health than those without a Sami background. We examined different variables in the statistical analysis and found that among

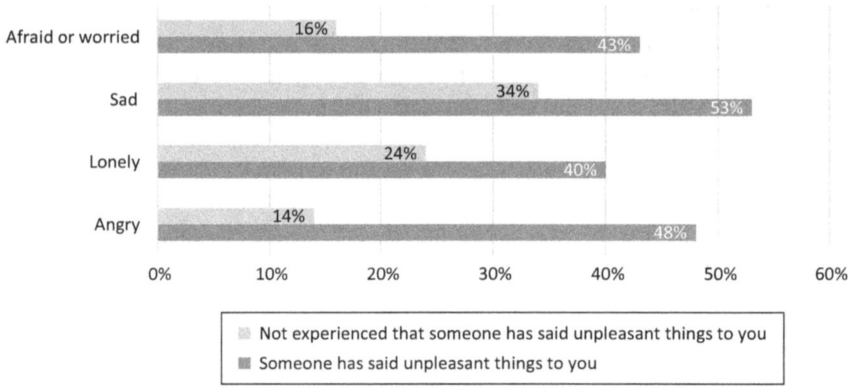

Figure 8.2 Do you usually struggle with feeling afraid or worried/sad/angry?

others bullying corresponded to poor mental health. The respondents, both with and without Sami background, who had been bullied report poorer mental health than those not experienced bullying. Figure 8.2 illustrates how 43% of those reporting that someone has said unpleasant things to them, are usually afraid or worried. Only 16% of those not having experienced this report similarly. A higher proportion of those who report that someone has said unpleasant things to him or her, also more often feel angry, lonely, and sad than those who had not been bullied. As shown in Figure 8.2 the respondents with Sami background are more exposed to unpleasant comments than those without. This corresponds to the findings of Hansen and Sørlie (2012), who revealed that Sami people are at higher risk for poor mental health than others because of the bullying they endure.

In our qualitative study, participants also reported that bullying caused mental stress. For example, Barbro, a young Sami woman, described how, after years of extensive verbal and physical bullying at school, she was admitted to a psychiatric ward as a teenager. The mother of Knut, a young Sami boy with an ADHD diagnosis, described how years of extensive harassment and bullying because of being Sami resulted in them taking him out of school for months, involving him in traditional reindeer-herding activities instead. According to his mother, her son had considered taking his own life, but after months of taking part in reindeer herding instead of being at school, he became a happy boy again. In the end, Knut actually chose to move to be with his family in another town in order to continue his education.

Hate speech also affects the relationships Sami people with disabilities have to others. When we asked one adult informant from the living-conditions study if there were something else he/she wanted to add regarding school, the response was as follows:

> I have been called a lot of unpleasant things which I can talk a lot about. I have been beaten, I have so many strange experiences with other people, that

> I haven't been able to relate to someone when it comes to relationships and such things. I can't do it.

Previous studies conducted among ethnic minority people underline that hate speech directly harms the mental health of its victims (Katharine Gelber & McNamara, 2016; Hansen, 2010a,b). Some participants stressed that they especially experienced offensive statements in the media, such as on radio, television and/or on the Internet, targeting the Sami as a minority group as exhausting and a burden. For example, Johan, a reindeer herder, pointed to newspaper headlines regarding permissions to establish mining, snowmobile trails, etc., stating that the Sami are old-fashioned and out of step with modern society, thereby hindering development. Wherever he goes in his spare time, people confront him with such headlines or court trials and want to discuss these, and he feels that he must continually defend reindeer herding, Sami interests, and the traditional Sami way of life. Essentially, these kinds of statements do not necessarily qualify as hate speech as this concept is often limited to more offensive forms of stigmatizing, discriminatory, or degrading statements. As underlined by Chakraborti and Garland (2012), the use of the concept "hate" might indicate that hate speech includes only very extreme statements, which means that we might overlook subtler but just as harmful expressions of prejudice.

However, similar to Nadim, Fladmoe, and Enjolras (2016), we argue that, in order to decide whether a statement qualifies as hate speech or not, it must be interpreted in the context in which it is presented. For example, what Johan and other Sami experience as offensive statements probably varies depending on whether these are presented in serious newspapers, radio programs or TV broadcasts or by private individuals on Facebook or other social media. The limit of what they perceive as offensive statements most likely occurs in "serious" media rather than in private contexts, for instance, on someone's Facebook page. Furthermore, for Johan and other Sami, the number of statements also seems to be a determinant for whether they perceive statements as offensive or not. This aligns with Chakraborti's (2010) claim that, to the targeted person or group, it is just as much the sum of many small and less serious offences that has consequences over time. In Norway, news constantly focuses on conflicting interests between the Sami minority and the Norwegian majority, especially concerning the right to natural resources. It is possible that some statements in these debates concerning conflicting interests might be defined as hate speech, as Sunde (2013) argued that, within political discourse, aggressive and intolerant statements in social debate are included in the understanding of hate speech.

Undoubtedly, some media coverage of Sami topics promote hatred targeting the Sami people and are perceived as offensive. Although these statements in different media might not qualify as hate speech, they are the cause of what the literature refers to as minority stress (Nadal et al., 2011), as described by Johan and others among our participants. This phenomenon underscores how even small experiences of discrimination at all levels have the potential to make members of a minority group feel marginalized in society and experience "minority stress"

(Nadal et al., 2011), where it can be defined as an additional burden individuals from stigmatized groups are exposed to due to their position (Bjørkman, 2012, p. 10). According to Klaus, an adult man with a physical impairment, he deliberately chooses not to read or comment on media coverage regarding the Sami on certain websites and other online media because he knows that these often include racist comments, etc. One might define this as a democratic problem since the amount of harassment at these websites actually limits participation in public debates regarding issues important to Klaus and other Sami.

Furthermore, as a result of more than a century of subjection to forceful assimilation by which Norwegian authorities have attempted to erase Sami culture and language, elderly Sami in particular have experienced extensive harassment and discrimination from the majority society. Consequently, to protect their children from such harassment, many parents have denied them access to their Sami identity and the Sami culture, and not allowed their children to reveal their Sami background in public settings. For example, when Ante was a pupil going on a school excursion decades ago, his parents expressly instructed him not to light the bonfire too quickly because doing so would disclose being Sami (traditionally, Sami have lived close to nature and been competent at tasks like lighting a fire). The fear of degrading and threatening comments related to the assimilation process have, according to Mikkel, up until now made many Sami refrain from teaching their children about their language and culture, with the result that some loathe their Sami background and heritage. The practice of hiding their Sami background and resisting passing on the language and culture described here is undoubtedly a consequence of the historical assimilation process with the discrimination, oppression and hate speech it resulted in.

An intersectional perspective on hate speech

Research primarily addresses either hate speech in general (Gagliardone, Gal, Alves, & Martinez, 2015; Katherine Gelber, 2002) or focuses on targeting specific marginalized groups, such as people with disabilities (for example Burch, 2018; Sherry & Neller, 2016) or people with minority ethnic background (for example Baez, 2002; Daniels, 2008). Hence, there is little knowledge about how the combination of membership of two such marginalized groups can affect hate speech experiences and the consequences of such. Thus, we will now take an intersectional perspective, and discuss three examples that illustrate how the combination of being Sami and having a disability can elicit distinct experiences of hate speech.

On several occasions, Per has been threatened and told to stay away by other Sami when they realize that he does not speak Sami. This harassment or hate speech is not motivated by his hearing impairment, but rather by the perpetrators being provoked by his inability to speak the Sami language and thus not perceived as a "real" Sami. Per is not the only Sami who has encountered hate speech or harassment because of not speaking Sami. However, his impairment was the reason that professionals denied him the opportunity to learn Sami in the first place; they did not expect that he would be capable of learning two languages – an incorrect assumption, since he later learned to speak English very well. Per experienced these negative comments and the related exclusion to an even harsher degree because they came from individuals from his own ethnic group and hindered him from taking part in his own culture.

Knut's story is another example of how the characteristics of ethnicity and disability interact. At school, peers bully Knut and accuse him of being "stupid as a Sami." Yet Knut's impairment (ADHD) makes him easy to provoke and causes his strong emotional reactions. Consequently, it is actually Knut's impairment that makes it so tempting for his peers to harass him.

At first glance, one might doubt whether intersectionality is a relevant perspective when analyzing these two examples of hate speech. The content of the hate speech in these situations does not aim at *both disability and Sami background*, and hence does not reflect what Andersson, Ivert and Mellgren (2018) describe as intersecting motives. However, it is the combination of disability and Sami background, that make both Per and Knut targets of hate speech. Even if the hate speech against Knut is motivated specifically by his Saminess, his impairment is what triggers his strong reactions and motivates his peers to torment him. Per is subjected to hate speech for not being perceived as Sami enough as he does not speak Sami, but it is his hearing impairment that is the reason for his lack of language skills. An intersectional perspective provides the possibility to analyze both situations and show how the intersectionality of being Sami *and* disabled affect the situations and provide the grounds for hate speech. This is something that people who belong to only one of these groups do not experience. Thus, occasionally what creates space for hate speech is the interaction between disability and Saminess, and not the fact of being Sami and disabled.

The third example illustrates how the combination of Saminess and disability not only *causes* hate speech, but also *affects the consequences* of such. Kai has been tormented because of both his impairment and his Sami background and describes how cultural issues have had an impact on how he deals with this. He points to how, according to traditional Sami upbringing, people expect Sami children and youth to solve their own problems, including experiences of harassment or hate speech. This practice can prevent young Sami with disabilities from reporting such experiences. Second, traditional Sami child-rearing practices emphasize fostering inner strength and hardiness, using teasing as a training method to obtain this (Javo, Alapack, Heyerdahl, & Røsnning, 2003). This custom might make it difficult for Sami children to identify where the boundary lies between teasing as a part of traditional upbringing and hate speech. Third, the Sami people have a long history of discrimination due to a strong government assimilation process that has tried to replace the Sami culture with the Norwegian (Minde, 2005), which might make them extra sensitive to hate speech. Fourth, some people with disabilities experience hate speech so often that they seem to accept this as something that just happens to them (Soorenian, this volume), which might prevent them from reporting these experiences. This tendency was found in a previous study, which suggested that victims of hate crimes tend to refrain from reporting these experiences due to the normalization of violence (Andersson & Mellgren, 2015).

Briefly summarized, this combination of factors might make it difficult for young Sami with disabilities to understand that the hate speech experienced is not acceptable, and thus prevent them from reporting it. This is very unfortunate, as it may imply a lack of action to stop or prevent hate speech and hinder welfare services from providing victims with adequate support. The latter is of particular concern, as exposure to hate speech can potentially cause long-term psychological consequences such as anxiety, depression, sleeping problems, insecurity, and low self-confidence (Eggebø & Stubberud, 2016).

This chapter has revealed how Sami people with disabilities experience hate speech motivated by both their ethnicity and disabilities. However, according to our analysis based on an intersectional perspective, Sami people with disabilities do not necessarily experience "double discrimination" (Habib, 1995). As highlighted in the last three examples, the interaction between categories, rather, seem to form distinct experiences of hate speech.

Notes

1 This includes those answering "yes, very" and "yes, a little" to this question.
2 Many people with intellectual disabilities live in group homes with other people in need of help. These may be people with different kinds of and degrees of intellectual disabilities but can also be people with mental illnesses (Kittelsaa & Tøssebro, 2011). They have their own rooms or apartments. Nevertheless, they often have to share some spaces with other residents, for example, the kitchen and living room. Services are often organized and provided in connection with these group homes.

References

Andersson, M., Ivert, A.-K., & Mellgren, C. (2018). When there is more than one motive: A study on self-reported hate crime victimization among Swedish university students. *International Review of Victimology*, *24*(1), 67–81.

Andersson, M., & Mellgren, C. (2015). Anmälningsbenägenhet vid utsatthet för hatbrott. *Socialvetenskaplig Tidsskrift*, *3*, 283–301.

Baez, B. (2002). *Affirmative action, hate speech, and tenure narratives about race, law, and the academy*. London: Routledge.

Bals, M., Turi, A. L., Skre, I., & Kvernmo, S. (2010). Internalization symptoms, perceived discrimination, and ethnic identity in indigenous Sami and non-Sami youth in Arctic Norway. *Ethnicity & Health*, *15*(2), 165–179.

Bjørkman, M. (2012). *Lesbisk selvtillit – lesbisk helseUtfordringer og mestringsstrategier hos lesbiske kvinner*. Ph.D. Universitetet i Bergen, Bergen.

Brooks, N., & Deegan, M. J. (1981). Women and disability: The double handicap. *The Journal of Sociology and Social Welfare*, *8*(2), 229–231.

Buchanan, N. T., & Fitzgerald, L. F. (2008). Effects of racial and sexual harassment on work and the psychological well-being of African American women. *Journal of Occupational Health Psychology*, *13*(2), 137–151.

Burch, L. (2018). 'You are a parasite on the productive classes': Online disablist hate speech in austere times. *Disability & Society*, *33*(3), 392–415.

Chakraborti, N. (2010). Crimes Against the "Other": Conceptual, operational, and empirical challenges for hate studies. *Journal of Hate Studies*, *8*(1), 9–28.

Chakraborti, N., & Garland, J. (2012). Reconceptualizing hate crime victimization through the lens of vulnerability and 'difference'. *Theoretical Criminology*, *16*(4), 499–514.

Dagsvold, I., Møllersen, S., & Stordahl, V. (2016). "You never know who are Sami or speak Sami": Clinicians' experiences with language-appropriate care to Sami-speaking patients in outpatient mental health clinics in Northern Norway. *International Journal of Circumpolar Health*, *75*(1), 32588. doi:10.3402/ijch.v75.32588

Daniels, J. (2008). Race, civil rights, and hate speech in the digital era. In A. Everett (Ed.), *Learning race and ethnicity: Youth and digital media* (pp. 129–154). Cambridge, MA: MIT Press.

Eggebø, H., & Stubberud, E. (2016). *Hate speech report two: Research on hate and discrimination report 2016:21*. Oslo: Rapport-Institutt for samfunnsforskning.

Fekjær, S. B. (2010). Klasse og innvandrerbakgrunn: to sider av samme sak? In K. Dahlgren & J. Ljunggren (Eds.), *Klassebilder: Ulikhet og sosial mobilitet i Norge* (pp. 84–97). Oslo: Universitetsforlaget.

Gagliardone, I., Gal, D., Alves, T., & Martinez, G. (2015). *Countering online hate speech*. Paris: UNESCO Publishing.

Gaski, L. (2008). Sami identity as a discursive formation: Essentialism and ambivalence. In H. Minde (Ed.), *Indigenous peoples: Self-determination, knowledge, indigeneity* (pp. 219–236). Delft: Eburon Academic Publishers.

Gelber, K. (2002). *Speaking back: The free speech versus hate speech debate*. Amsterdam: John Benjamins Publishing Company.

Gelber, K., & McNamara, L. (2016). Evidencing the harms of hate speech. *Social Identities*, *22*(3), 324–341.

Gjertsen, H., Melbøe, L., Fedreheim, G. E., & Fylling, I. (2017). *Kartlegging av levekårene til personer med utviklingshemming i samiske områder*. Tromsø: Norges Arktiske Universitet & Nordens Velferdssenter.

Grönvik, L., & Söder, M. (2008). *Bara funktionshindrad?: Funktionshinder och intersektionalitet*. Malmo: Gleerup.

Habib, L. A. (1995). "Women and disability don't mix!": Double discrimination and disabled women's rights. *Gender & Development*, *3*(2), 49–53.

Hansen, I. L. S., & Grødem, A. S. (2012). *Samlokaliserte boliger og store bofellesskap. Perspektiver og erfaringer i kommunene*. Oslo: Fafo.

Hansen, K. L. (2010a). Ethnicity, self-reported health, discrimination and socio-economic status: A study of Sami and non-Sami Norwegian populations. *International Journal of Circumpolar Health*, *69*(2), 111–128.

Hansen, K. L. (2010b). Indigenous health and wellbeing. *Circumpolar Health Supplements 2010*, *7*, 99–115.

Hansen, K. L., Melhus, M., Høgmo, A., & Lund, E. (2008). Ethnic discrimination and bullying in the Sami and non-Sami populations in Norway: The SAMINOR study. *International Journal of Circumpolar Health*, *67*(1), 99–115.

Hansen, K. L., & Sørlie, T. (2012). Ethnic discrimination and psychological distress: A study of Sami and non-Sami populations in Norway. *Transcultural Psychiatry*, *49*(1), 26–50.

Hove, O. (2009). *Mental health disorders in adults with intellectual disabilities: Methods of assessment and prevalence of mental health disorders and problem behavior*. PhD-avhandling, University of Bergen, Bergen, Norway.

Høgmo, A. (1989). *Norske idealer og samisk virkelighet : Om skoleutvikling i det samiske området*. Oslo: Gyldendal.

Høgmo, A. (2005). *Er en flerkulturell skole mulig? Oslo: Gyldendal akademisk*. Oslo: Gyldendal akademisk.

ILO Convention No. 169. (1989). *Indigenous and tribal peoples convention*. 05 Sep 1991.

Javo, C., Alapack, R., Heyerdahl, S., & Røsnning, J. A. (2003). Parental values and ethnic identity in indigenous sami families: A qualitative study. *Family Process*, *42*(1), 151–164.

Kittelsaa, A., & Tøssebro, J. (2011). *Store bofellesskap for personer med utviklingshemming: Noen konsekvenser*. Trondheim: NTNU Samfunnsforskning.

Kittelsaa, A., Wiik, S. E., & Tøssebro, J. (2015). *Levekår for personer med nedsatt funksjonsevne: Fellestrekk og variasjon*. Trondheim: NTNU Samfunnsforskning.

LDO. (2015). *Hatytringer og hatkriminalitet [Hate speech and hate crime.]*. Oslo: Likestillings- og diskrimineringsombudet.

Loga, J. (2018). Civil society and the welfare state in Norway – Historical relations and future roles. *Community Development Journal*, *53*(3), 574–591.

Lund, E., Brustad, M., & Høgmo, A. (2008). The Sami – Living conditions and health. *International Journal of Circumpolar Health*, *67*(1), 6–8.

Melbøe, L., Johnsen, B.-E., Fredreheim, G. E., & Hansen, K. L. (2016). *Situasjonen til samer med funksjonsnedsettelse*. Stockholm: Nordens Velferdssenter.

Midtbøen, A. H., & Lidén, H. (2015). *Diskriminering av samer, nasjonale minoriteter og innvanddrere i Norge. En kunnskapsgjennomgang, Rapport 2015:01*. Oslo: Institutt for samfunnsforskning.

Minde, H. (2005). *Assimilation of the Sami: Implementation and consequences* (Vol. 3/2005). Kautokeino: Resource Centre for the Rights of Indigenous Peoples.

Ministry of Children and Equality. (2017). *Equality and Anti-Discrimination Act*.

Ministry of Health and Care Services. (2011). *The Health and Care Service Act*.

Ministry of Local Government and Modernisation. (1987). *The Sami Act*.

Nadal, K. L., Issa, M.-A., Leon, J., Meterko, V., Wideman, M., & Wong, Y. (2011). Sexual orientation microaggressions: "Death by a Thousand Cuts" for lesbian, gay, and bisexual youth. *Journal of LGBT Youth*, *8*(3), 234–259.

Nadim, M., Fladmoe, A., & Wessel-Aas, J. (2016). *Hatefulle ytringer på internett. Omfang, forebygging og juridiske grenser*. Oslo: Institutt for samfunnsforskning.

Nilsen, A. B. (2014). *Hatprat*. Oslo: Cappelen Damm akademisk.

OECD. (2017). *How's life? 2017 measuring well being*. Paris: OECD.

Olsen, T., Vedeler, J. S., Eriksen, J., & Elvegård, K. (2016). *Hatytringer. Resultater fra en studie av funksjonshemmedes erfaringer. [Hate speech. Results from a study of disabled people's experiences.]* (Vol. 6/2016). Bodø: Nordland Research Institute.

Pedersen, P., & Høgmo, A. (2012). *Sápmi slår tilbake: samiske revitaliserings- og moderniseringsprosser i siste generasjon*. Kárášjohka: ČálliidLágádus.

Roderick, A. L. (2014). "A counterfeit friendship": Mate crime and people with learning disabilities. *The Journal of Adult Protection*, *16*(6), 355–366.

Saunes, I. S., Hansen, T. M., Tomic, O., & Lindahl, A. K. (2017). *Health in Norway –2017: Commentary report for OECD comparison of health in different countries*. Oslo: Norwegian Institute of Public Health.

Selle, P., Semb, A. J., Strømsnes, K., & Nordø, Å. D. (2015). *Den samiske medborgeren*. Oslo: Cappelen Damm Akademisk.

Sherry, M. (2010). *Disability hate crimes: Does anyone really hate disabled people?* Surrey: Ashgate.

Sherry, M., & Neller, A. (2016). Intellectual disability, stigma, and hate crimes. In K. Scior & S. Werner (Eds.), *Intellectual disability and stigma: Stepping out from the margins* (pp. 111–126). London: Palgrave Macmillan.

Sjölander, P. (2011). What is known about the health and living conditions of the indigenous people of northern Scandinavia, the Sami? *Global Health Action*, *4*(1), 8457.

Söderström, S., & Tøssebro, J. (2011). *Innfridde mål eller brutte visjoner?: Noen hovedlinjer i utviklingen av levekår og tjenester for utviklingshemmede*. Trondheim: NTNU Samfunnsforskning.

Stamsø, M. A. (2009). *Velferdsstaten i endring: Norsk sosialpolitikk ved starten av et nytt århundre*. Copenhagen: Gyldendal akademisk.

Sunde, I. M. (2013). *Forebygging av radikalisering og voldelig ekstremisme på internett* (827808100X). Oslo: Kompetansesenter for kriminalitetsforebygging.

Tøssebro, J. (2016). Scandinavian disability policy: From deinstitutionalisation to non-discrimination and beyond. *Alter – European Journal of Disability Research*, *10*(2), 111–123.

Turi, A. L., Bals, M., Skre, I. B., & Kvernmo, S. (2009). Health service use in indigenous Sami and non-indigenous youth in North Norway: A population based survey. *BMC Public Health*, *9*(1), 378.

Vedeler, J. S. (2014). Disabled persons' job interview experiences: Stories of discrimination, uncertainty and recognition. *Disability & Society*, *29*(4), 597–610.

9 Stereotypes fomenting hate

Perceptions, stigma, and real-world consequences for Africans with disabilities

Mark P. Mostert

In many areas of Africa, prejudicial stereotypical perceptions of persons with disabilities are generated by closely held negative social beliefs and vocabularies that drive animus and violence as a matter of cultural imperative.[1] In this chapter, I identify the influence of stigma in vocabulary surrounding the causes and perceptions of disability in Africa as a driving force in both hate speech and other forms of victimization, which can even involve murder. Stigmatizing attitudes around disability are the source of hate speech. At its most basic, stigma undergirds the Otherizing of those deemed to be of lesser value than the stigmatizers, and arises out of negative, erroneous, perceptions and fear of "the Other." I discuss this context as it related to Africans with disabilities. In Africa, there is widespread and significant stigma attached to peoples' disability characteristics; social stigma is the foundational context surrounding Africans with disabilities. Then I apply this discussion to illustrative examples of stigma related to the treatment of persons with leprosy in Nigeria and general perceptions of disability in Kenya.

Hate speech does not exist without a series of interconnected contexts – some obvious, others hidden – which together shape both the content and severity of that speech. Concomitantly, hate speech is powerful not only because of its inherent animus, but because its promulgation can result in real-world actions and consequences that are detrimental and even dangerous to targeted groups or individuals. I also discuss how stigma, vocabulary, and negative stereotypical behaviour is the link between hate speech and the devastating physical abuse and killing for the trafficking of the body parts of Tanzanians with albinism. Finally, I offer some practical suggestions at the grassroots and policy levels that may begin to stem the tide of prejudice against Africans with disabilities. These responses to hate speech may, in part or in whole, begin the process of countering the effects of stigma for Africans with disabilities so that they may take their rightful and inclusive place in African society.

The social model of disability

Over the past several decades there has been a major shift from viewing disability via the medical model to that of disability as a social construct. Historically, the medical model of disability held that disability was a medical and clinical construct intrinsic to the individual. Thus, disability was something to be examined, diagnosed, managed, and "cured" where possible. Given this orientation, the medical model concomitantly implied the supposed unconstrained abilities of nondisabled persons. Unsurprisingly, this dichotomy attributed to persons with disabilities implies a palpable sense of being incapable and dependent. In layperson's perceptions, people with disabilities were either to be pitied for their disability characteristics, celebrated as brave and resilient in overcoming their lot in life, or subjected to negative reactions because of their "abnormality." Furthermore, when persons with disabilities are expected to take sole responsibility for their individual circumstances, there is little or no emphasis on the wider obligations of society to ensure equality and human rights for those who are disabled. Additionally, this view holds that disability is a master status. Disability is assumed to be central to the individual's identity rather than as adjunct to people's innate humanness and personhood and the notion that they have more in common, not less, with their nondisabled counterparts.

Currently, a social model of disability is preferred by disability advocates and disability studies scholars for unpacking issues related to disability and society, because it emphasizes that disability is a social construct. This implies that all human beings exist on any number of continua related to their physical, psychological, and emotional makeup, creating unique individuals with an unlimited array of personal characteristics that transcend compartmentalization and fixed categories. Therefore, the social model of disability moves disability characteristics to a tangential rather than a central influence, decentralizing the primacy of any disability and its characteristics. That is, while some human characteristics may cause impairment, these characteristics are not the ultimate definer of the person in whom they reside, but are rather adjuncts to their individuality akin to any other human characteristic (Stone-MacDonald & Butera, 2014). As such, the social model of disability accepts the reality of disability, but demands social willingness and action to implement fully inclusive communities at every level. The social model demands changes in both physical and attitudinal barriers – in the cases discussed in this chapter, the social model points to the need to remove the stigmatizing attitudes that form the core of hate speech.

Social stigma and disability

A fundamental concern and of particular import to Africa relates to the idea of disability stigma and its various real-world manifestations which result in discrimination against Africans with disabilities, transcending national, ethnic, and political boundaries. The term stigma, originally from the Greek, describes a physical marking that identifies societal undesirables. Durkheim ([1895] 2013) identified stigma as a broad social phenomenon distinguishing between socially acceptable and unacceptable behaviour. In the modern era, unpacking the meanings and implications of stigma is usually ascribed to Goffman (1963) who saw stigma as a characteristic that was both an undesirable and discrediting factor to whom it was applied, thereby lowering the status of the person so labelled. Goffman notes that stigma is "the phenomenon whereby an individual with an attribute which is deeply discredited by his/her society is rejected as a result of the attribute. Stigma is a process by which the reaction of others spoils normal identity." Or, stated differently, "stigma is a socially constructed reaction to deviance from an agreed-upon set of norms, and in the case of disability, is mediated by perceptions rather than functional limitations" (Saetermoe, Scattone, & Kim, 2001, p. 699). Building on Goffman, I discuss the framework of stigma as laid out by Link and Phelan (2001) to explain the phenomenon before turning to how stigma operates among the treatment of people with albinism in Tanzania, persons with leprosy in Nigeria, and general perceptions of disability in Kenya.

Link and Phelan (2001) define stigma as "the convergence of interrelated components" (p. 367). Thus, stigma exists "when elements of labeling, stereotyping separation, status loss, and discrimination occur in a power situation that allows the components of stigma to unfold" (p. 367). This definition acknowledges that depending on social contexts, stigma might be a matter of degree ranging from mild to severe. Link and Phelan describe several components of how stigma is constructed. The centrality of these components of stigma to disablist hate speech will become apparent in this discussion.

Component 1: Labelling and differences

The roots of stigma are created when people distinguish among and label human differences. However, not all differences are labelled equally. For example, many are ignored as being socially irrelevant because these differences have little, if any, broader social consequence (e.g., one's name). However, other differences are labelled as socially significant (e.g., skin colour, sexual orientation), thereby leading to varied forms of social grouping based on perception of difference, usually negative. Furthermore, social phenomena chosen for labelling and grouping vary according to place and time (e.g., in the 19th century small foreheads and large faces were regarded as ape-like and therefore likely represented someone with criminal proclivities). In sum, stigma generates labels that become affixed to a group of persons who over time are oppressed or excluded based on the designated negative label.

Component 2: Associating human differences with negative attributes.

Here stigma is formed when labelled differences are tied to a set of undesirable characteristics that comprise a stereotype. Recently, researchers have begun to address the nature of underlying cognitive processes that support the use of categories and how said categories are connected to stereotypes. Findings have demonstrated that people often make categories and stereotypes in split-second and probably unconscious decisions, which, at least initially, serve as "shorthand" to pass judgements about the labelled group (Link & Phelan, 2001).

Component 3: Separating "us from "them"

The third component of stigma relates to its ability to separate groups of people into antagonistic categories of "us" versus "them." Here the abovementioned connection between stereotype and undesirable characteristics become the justification for the perception that the "them" are so essentially different than the "us" and that the "them" are completely different types of people almost entirely irreconcilable with the "us." This, in turn, raises the probability that "they" are so qualitatively different from the "us" that they may not even be considered human, thereby justifying many ways of treating "them" poorly or abusively. "They" are subjected to Othering – a fundamental dynamic within hate speech.

Component 4: Status loss and discrimination

As the sequence of components 1–3 accumulate, the labelled person or group accumulates a significant loss of social status and increased discrimination, resulting in the target being devalued, rejected, and susceptible to extreme ostracism and potential physical harm. This is another of the connections to hate speech (and even hate crimes). Subsequently, significant social isolation occurs further eroding basic human rights such as social inclusion. Thus, overall loss of social status means lives of inequality and oppression for those considered to be "the other." It follows that by this point, stereotyping leads to overt discrimination, on any and all fronts.

Component 5: Stigma and power

Link and Phelan further note that stigma relies on social, economic, and political power to achieve its stigmatizing aims. This power resides in the stigmatizers ("us") used against the stigmatized ("them"). What matters in terms of stigma is that the "us" group's perceptions and actions prevail over "them" in all aspects of private and public life. Inevitably, therefore, collateral damage to the stigmatized means that they are often unable to rectify discrimination because of their powerlessness. Similarly, hate speech is directed at marginalized people.

I now turn to the notion of stigma and Africans with disabilities and its applicability to hate speech.

The impact of stigma on the lives of Africans with disabilities

According to the UN, there are more than 90 million Africans with disabilities, who because of negative stereotyping, discrimination, prejudice, and hate are almost all excluded from access to education and from almost every corner of society. This situation is often exacerbated among those who are multiply disadvantaged (e.g. by being disabled, female, a child, etc.).

There are at least two foundational reasons undergirding stigma of people with disabilities in Africa: an immense lack of information about the causes and characteristics disability, and stereotypical animus preventing full inclusion of persons with disabilities in the wider society (Eide, Khupe, & Mannan, 2014). This stereotypical animus is expressed and reproduced through hate speech which has terrible effects on the lives of people with disabilities.

Cultural beliefs and values

There is little doubt that across the continent many cultural attitudes and beliefs negatively affect how persons with disabilities are perceived. These attitudes and beliefs are usually forged by an amalgam of ignorance, superstition, poverty, negative stereotyping and self-preservation. This toxic mix plays out in various levels of discrimination from relatively mild (e.g., name calling, threats) to severe (e.g., physical violence, killing). For example, in Ghana, Ashanti men with physical disabilities are prevented from becoming chiefs, and nondisabled chiefs can be destooled if they become disabled. Furthermore, children with visible disabilities are often killed or abandoned. Cultural prejudice is expressed not only through hate speech but even though hate crimes.

In other African contexts, a child with a disability is perceived as a curse upon the whole family, or at least a cause of social shame and embarrassment. Other negative cultural beliefs connect disability to taboo maternal or relatives' behaviour, or to a general sense of supernatural evil meted out as punishment to wayward humans (Eide et al., 2014). Therefore, it is not surprising that the vast majority of Africans with disabilities are marginalized, discriminated against, and almost always excluded from the societies and communities in which they live – even if they seek high-level social involvement such as entering politics. For example, in Kenya it is unlawful for people with visual or hearing problems to become President as the constitution stipulates that the President read English and Kiswahili without Braille or sign language.

Having said that, not all cultural beliefs about disability in Africa are negative. For example, among the Chagga in East Africa those with physical handicaps are valued as pacifiers of evil spirits and in Benin they are often selected as law enforcement personnel. The Turkana of Kenya perceive children with disabilities as a gift from God to be well cared for or risk the deity's wrath (Eide et al., 2014). However, negative connotations attached to disabilities are much more prevalent. These negative connotations are always active in hate speech.

Disability and poverty

Tangentially, other forms of discrimination that may result in highly negative abusive, or hate speech connected to disability relate to those with disabilities who are poverty stricken (especially females, children, and youth). This is especially telling, seeing as a significant proportion of all disabilities are preventable and are linked directly to poverty (Parnes et al., 2009). For example, economic poverty might lead to poor or no medical care (either preventative, responsive, or rehabilitative), which increase disability prevalence. This is exacerbated, as noted below, by disability bias and negative attitudes from medical and other support personnel should such services be available.

Education

Education is a crucial aspect for increasing social and economic status, even more so for Africans with disabilities who are often shunned from the workforce for no other reason than negative perceptions of their disability characteristics. The United Nations Educational, Scientific, and Cultural Organization (UNESCO) estimates that more than 90% of children with disabilities in the Global South do not attend school. Of the 10% that do attend school, only half of these complete their primary education (Koszela, 2013). This translates to literacy rates for adults with disabilities at around 3%. However, the concomitant reality is that African children and youth without disabilities are two or three times more likely to attend school than their disabled peers (Parnes, et al., 2009). These circumstances are exacerbated by an overall bias among teachers towards those with disabilities. The vast majority of teachers in Africa have little to no training in special education. This deficit, combined with cultural biases, creates a deep sense of suspicion even among those tasked to educate students with disabilities. Various forms of Othering and hate speech can therefore be reinforced in schools.

Disability and gender

In Africa, stigma is intertwined with both disability and gender. Thus, females with disabilities are doubly disadvantaged and even more so as children. Females with disabilities are also more likely to be subjected to domestic and public violence. Unsurprisingly, they have higher mortality rates than their male counterparts, and, as adults, are almost always employed at rates far lower than men with disabilities. Even when employed, the stigma of disability almost guarantees that employers and coworkers are likely to engage indiscriminative behaviour, including negative, abusive, or hate speech.

I now turn to three illustrative cases of stigma among Africans with disabilities and their connections to hate speech: (a) people with albinism in Tanzania, (b) persons with leprosy in Nigeria, and (c) general perceptions of disability in Kenya.

People with albinism in Tanzania

The stigma of albinism in Tanzania begins with the birth of the child who is clearly and immediately different, given that the parents are black and the child white (Thuku, 2011). For many Africans, albinism's characteristics are believed to be caused, among others, by the mother's extramarital activity with a white person, having shaken hands with a person with albinism, or having shared a meal with someone with albinism. Albinism, therefore, is believed to be a curse visited on the family; being positioned as cursed is a crucial component of hate speech against people with albinism. In many cases babies with albinism, especially among the Maasai, are either killed or abandoned to die. In other cultural communities, for example, the Digo of northeastern Tanzania, babies with albinism are subjected to an elaborate "death ritual" whereby an infant is dropped into a lake to see if it will survive – its subsequent death being proof of its sub-humanness (Under the Same Sun, 2013). The Othering in hate speech is often reproduced in hate crimes.

Those with albinism who survive are often subjected to hate speech that positions them as witches, and cultural beliefs explain their characteristic reddish eyes as having been burned by the sun. They are also often regarded as lazy as they avoid working in the heat of the day to protect their vulnerable skin from sunburn. In some instances, these negative and deadly stereotypes follow people into adulthood. For example, the Sekuma of northwestern Tanzania allow persons with albinism to grow to adulthood, but some of those with albinism are then designated to be buried alive with a deceased Sekuma chief (Under the Same Sun, 2013).

The maltreatment, abuse, and murder of Tanzanians with albinism garnered international attention in 2008 with high-profile international reports that they were being killed or maimed for various body parts ostensibly to be used for good luck charms or as ingredients in potions thought to have magical qualities. However, the killing of Tanzanians with albinism began earlier, in October 2006, in and around the city of Mwanza on the shores of Lake Victoria. It is also of note that this region of Tanzania has the highest per-capita number of witchdoctors in the country (Dave-Odigie, 2010). They play an important part in the hate speech against people with albinism.

In 2008, the Tanzanian government intervened in response to pressure from the international community. In a significant symbol of solidarity with Tanzanians with albinism, then-President Kikwete appointed a woman with albinism, Al-Shymaa John Kwegyir, to the National Parliament as a way of raising awareness of the albinism problem and to give Tanzanians with albinism a political voice at the highest levels of government. In January 2009, Kikwete's government banned all traditional healers and witchdoctors from practising their trade, some of which involved using albino body parts in various potions and for lucky charms. Enforcement, however, was difficult given that traditional perceptions around albinism were (and are) so deeply entrenched in the communal psyche. Subsequent to the banning of witchdoctors, the Tanzanian government declared the killing of persons with albinism to be a capital crime (Bucaro, 2010).

As in other forms of hate speech, the targeting of Tanzanians with albinism focuses on an already marginalized and excluded group whose isolation makes it easier for them to be targets of humiliation, victimization, mutilation, and killing. This exacerbates an already dire set of circumstances for this population which encompasses, among others, (a) serious health issues, especially related to sun exposure and skin cancer, (b) their voluntary or involuntary withdrawal from the community as a result of ostracism or as a result of psychological or physical abuse, (c) a concomitant sense of low self-worth and a deep sense that society devalues them, (d) discrimination against their family and friends for being associated with the person with albinism, (e) the inability to participate fully (or even partially) in broader social settings, (f) denial of the right to marry, (g), employment discrimination, and (h) a concomitant denial of their most basic human, educational, and legal rights.

Persons with leprosy in Nigeria

Leprosy stigma is still a global phenomenon, especially in the developing world. In many countries, stigmatizing attitudes towards persons with leprosy are as high as 80% in the general population despite there often being a high level of understanding of the real causes and treatment of leprosy. Thus, this empirical knowledge does not necessarily correlate with more positive attitudes towards those who have the disease. There are generally four mediating factors related to the fear of leprosy, namely, (a) visible deformities, (b) perceived incurability and chronic course of the disease, (c) perceived infectiousness, and (d) perceived "bad origin" of disease. Furthermore, given that leprosy is also a "visible" disease, it follows that persons with leprosy are among the groups most likely to self-isolate and be reluctant to seek treatment of the condition (Wong, 2004).

As is the case of stigma attached to albinism in Tanzania, the stigma attached to leprosy in Nigeria reveals similar areas of misperception, oppression, denial of human rights, and even hatred (Gussow & Tracy, 1970). While many Nigerians reveal a great or lesser accurate view of leprosy and its causes, the stigma attached to leprosy is still undergirded by traditional negative beliefs. For example, some Nigerians believe that leprosy is caused by supernatural forces or as a result of a witchcraft curse preempted by the breaking of some form of social taboo (e.g., having sex with a menstruating female). Other negative perceptions of leprosy include reduced chances of getting married to someone with leprosy or increased divorce rates when a spouse contracts the disease, or that the condition is hereditary. Furthermore, prejudicial perceptions of difference and Otherness are emphasized by those who point to the visible effects of the disease (particularly in advanced cases) and use it to reinforce not only the notion of "us versus them," but also that those with leprosy are less than human and are to be shunned. Hate speech is part of this process. Perhaps the greatest fall-out here is that persons with leprosy might delay seeking medical treatment, having self-isolated due to their diminished social status and attacks on their humanity.

A significant finding related to stigma, hate speech, and leprosy is related to how the disease is viewed among different religious groups in Nigeria. For example, there is evidence that leprosy stigma is higher among Nigerian Christians who generally perceive leprosy as a punishment for sin, and lower among Muslims who often accept leprosy as being part of God's will. Further, as with many medical and other disabilities, stigma attached to leprosy is not limited to the person with the disease alone, but is often extended to the entire family, thereby complicating their social status within the community even further. This leads to a wide array of missed opportunities, especially those related to (a) acquiring life and employment skills, (b) employment, (c) participation in family and community life, (d) access to preventative and treatment healthcare, (e) access to and participation in educational pursuits, (f) rejection by the family and the wider community, etc. (van Brakel & Miranda-Galarza, 2013).

General perceptions of disability in Kenya

Approximately 10% of the Kenyan population embodies some form of disability (Ingstad & Grut, 2007) and of this number approximately 25% are children of school-going age. As is the case with albinism and leprosy, disability in general in Kenya is viewed as being caused by any number of negative forces. For example, many Kenyans believe that a disability is a curse from a supernatural or mysterious otherworldly force (Ogechi & Ruto, 2002), or as a result of witchcraft spells placed either upon the family or the individual with disabilities (Monk & Wee, 2008). In the larger social context, there is a widespread belief that taboo activities such as adultery or incest can result in a child born with disabilities. Others believe that disability is simply the deliberate plan of an unseen deity. Also, there is a widespread belief that disability can result from some broken taboo by the mother (e.g., eating eggs during pregnancy) or other closely related family members (Monk & Wee, 2008).

Some beliefs resulting in stigma and hate speech are even more specific. For example, among the Nandi, killing an animal without provocation during a wife's pregnancy is believed to cause disability in the newborn child, while among the Abagusii, children born with cleft palates are thought to be the result of parents making fun of someone with a disability (Ogechi & Ruto, 2002). It must also be noted, however, that as in Tanzania and Nigeria, not all traditional beliefs are negative. For example, many families of children with disabilities are supportive and caring, and in many instances, people with disabilities are allowed to take part in important ritual events. In other communities, it's the disability itself that ensures that the community cares for and values the person with disabilities, For example, certain tribes believe that the person with a disability is the sacrificial lamb to evil spirits, and that taking care of said person ensures that no other evil will befall the community. Others such as the Turkana hold that children with disabilities are actually a gift from God and that they should be well taken care of to avoid the wrath of the supernatural for not taking care of their disabled charges (Stone-MacDonald & Butera, 2014).

Other Kenyans believe that disability is a punishment meted out to parents of children with a disability. In this regard, studies conducted among the Maasai reveal that mothers often see their children with disabilities as defective and have been known to expose their infants to harsh conditions to precipitate their demise (Hsieh, 2012). Other stigmas are attached to both family and community perceptions of disability. For example, a person with a disability is often viewed as less able to contribute to the greater economic good of the family and community. Such persons are therefore not only seen as a financial and resource liability internally, but also by the larger community resulting in the shaming of the family with a member with disabilities and a concomitant probability that the family member with a disability is kept isolated from the larger community based on shame and loss of social status. These cultural practices result in many people hating the family member who is disabled.

Given the conditions related to the stigmatization of people with disabilities in Tanzania (albinism), Nigeria (leprosy), and Kenya (general disability issues) it is imperative that strategies be developed to mitigate stigma's considerable influence.

Ways forward

While not specifically addressing the issue of hate speech, Heijnders and van der Meij (2006) provide a useful analytical framework of stigma reduction strategies at several levels from micro to macro: (a) intrapersonal (treatment, counselling, cognitive-behavioural therapy, empowerment, group counselling, self-help, advocacy, and support groups), (b) interpersonal (care and support, home care teams, community-based rehabilitation), (c) organizational/instructional (training programs, revised policies), (d) community (education, contact, advocacy, protest), (e) governmental/structural (legal/policy interventions, rights-based approaches). These strategies may address some of the precursors to hate speech, but their efficacy needs to be carefully analyzed.

Intrapersonal level interventions

At this level, the primary focus is on changing individual behaviour via knowledge, encouraging more positive self-perceptions, personal empowerment, and economic support to reinforce and maintain positive attitudes and behaviour. The literature in this regard is mixed as to efficacy, with some studies reporting efficacy under certain conditions while other studies indicate limited efficacy overall. Self-help, advocacy, and support groups seek to provide support among people with disabilities to develop positive self-identity, self-esteem, and an array of coping skills. As with other aspects, the literature in this area is very limited, but generally tend to indicate that these interventions are effective, at least to some extent.

Interpersonal level interventions

Here the idea is to modify the environment in which people with disabilities reside, especially in terms of the impact of social support and networks on health status and behaviour. For care and support, generally assumed to be positive and helpful, there is some research indicating that people receiving such care and support may actually run the risk of emphasizing the negative aspects of disability. Home care teams are generally viewed as helpful, especially in terms of modifying positive behaviour towards the person with disability being cared for. However, there is no research specifically establishing efficacy or inefficacy of the home care team idea. Community-based rehabilitation uses community development to rehabilitate and equalize opportunities for social integration of people with disabilities. Again, the research literature is scant here with only vague indications that community-based rehabilitation, let alone modifying of the environment for increased inclusivity, engenders positive outcomes for people with disabilities.

Organizational/institutional level

This level seeks organizational change to modify health and stigma-related aspects of organizations whose makeup does not accommodate or consider persons with disabilities, usually by utilizing training programs or the development of new organizational policies that are more disability-friendly. Surprisingly, for training programs and institutional changes, the literature reveals very few indications of efficacy or inefficacy. For strategies focusing on changing organizational structures to accommodate people with disabilities there is, as in other areas, no solid documentation of efficacy.

Community level

Here the aim is to increase knowledge related to specific disability conditions and to address stigma within specific community groups. Education is usually the first strategy, singly or in combination with other strategies, to reduce disability stigma. Clearly, "educational strategies" cover a wide variety of approaches and the literature here, as in other areas where literature exists, shows mixed efficacy results. In addition, the notion of contact refers to encouraging positive interactions between the public and persons with disabilities at the point of contact to reduce disability stigma. The limited literature here shows some positive findings while also noting that there are some dangers involved; for example, that disclosing one's disability status could have negative follow-on effects. Advocacy programs and strategies seek to promote the rights of persons with disabilities at the national and governmental level by advocating for changing laws and policies that are unfavourable to persons with disabilities. There is, apparently, no literature that has examined the effects of advocacy at this level. Finally, the idea of protest is to actively confront and challenge disability stigma of individuals, groups, and organizations/governments by peaceful protest and public opposition to those stigmas. There is no literature addressing protest efficacy in improving the lot of persons with disabilities.

Educational programs to alleviate stigma

There is little doubt that educational programs to erase stigma attached to disabilities must take into account as a first premise the role of cultural perceptions, beliefs, values, and actions that feed the disability stigma in the first place and how these vectors influence the course of programmatic goals and objectives (Stone-MacDonald & Butera, 2014) and that stigma-reduction educational programs must be carefully matched to the unique culture, community, and mindset of the population to which it is applied.

Of particular interest here is building a corpus of research around effective and empirically tested knowledge-based strategies. That is, strategies that provide a major pushback against disability stigma, replacing them with empirically based knowledge. However, this is easier said than done. For example, in Nigeria, once medical interventions proved highly effective in treating and preventing leprosy, it was assumed that stigma toward the disease and those who carried it would diminish. However, that was not the case. Similarly, "health education" efforts – educating people about the true medical causes and sequelae of disease did not necessarily translate into lower levels of stigma, most certainly because these campaigns were either too generic or failed to take into account local social and normative nuances in the communities in which they were introduced (Gussow & Tracy, 1970).

There are other documented examples of well-meaning but ultimately unsuccessful strategies related to disability. For example, the historic use of a biomedical approach of "early detection and cure" (or management of the disability) was not successful in many areas, probably, as noted above, because it did not consider cultural factors related to stigma and disability (van Brakel & Miranda-Galarza, 2013). Additionally, in developing countries (including Africa), many health professionals hold negative, stereotypical, and mythical views of disability despite their medical training. Such negative biases mean that those with a disease, especially in more advanced and visible stages, might be turned away from hospitals and clinics, or subject to insensitive handling.

Other sigma reduction strategies include, for example, (a) encouraging and using nondiscriminatory language, beginning with people-first language (person with a disability vs. a disabled person, etc.), (b) integrating services for people with disabilities into the general health care system rather than having them in separate (and often unequal) settings, (c) encouraging the mass media to provide less negatively biased and sensational reports about persons with disabilities, (d) teaching self-advocacy skills to people with disabilities, (e) changing negative language to more positive and accurate representations (e.g., changing the term "leprosy" to its medical term, "Hansen's Disease"), (f) providing medical and psychosocial counselling to people with disabilities to increase their self-help and self-advocacy skills, (g) conducting emancipatory research (i.e., encouraging people with disabilities to have more prominent roles in the research process), (h) integrating disability awareness into all public institutions, (e.g., schools, government departments, the public health sector, etc.), and (i) encouraging community self-support groups, etc.

Overall, however, there is very little empirical research evaluating the many programs assumed to reduce disability stigma in Africa and even less attention paid to identifying gaps in this rather meagre database (Wong, 2004).

Nongovernmental and other grassroots organizations

Church missionaries and religious institutions, alongside nongovernmental organizations, have dominated services and support for Africans with disabilities with regard to stigma elimination. However, these well-meaning efforts were often seen as not taking fully into account local perceptions, beliefs, and communal knowledge of disability; a first step to starting a conversation that will eventually reduce disability stigma and hate speech.

The need for more empirical research

There is little doubt that the need for more empirical research around stigma and disability is sorely needed across a wide array of topics in every African country (e.g., research about the impact of traditional beliefs and stigma, conducting censuses for establishing an accurate picture of the extent of disability countrywide, research on the extent of resources for every aspect of every disability, the connection between illness and attached stigmas, physical vs. intellectual disabilities, mild vs. severe disabilities, the bidirectional relationship between disability and poverty, etc.) Generally, the research base is scattered and unfocused, although pockets of fairly deep research do exist (e.g., research related to specific diseases causing medical and other disabilities, and research on certain social aspects of disease and disability). Perhaps of immediate concern is that there is very little to no research related to the stigmatizers (or the perpetrators of disability hate speech) with the available literature being overwhelmingly in favour of studying the victims of stigmatization. Additionally, there needs to be a holistic research approach to stigma reduction which incorporates relevant theoretical, behavioural, psychosocial, and cultural models as a means of providing a comprehensive framework for deeper investigations.

Building empirical research databases will have the cumulative effect of providing meta-answers to vexing problems in the area of disabilities and is also entirely necessary in order to form the undergirding sound base upon which national policies can be devised, articulated, and implemented.

In terms of research design, given the heavily embedded nature of disability stigma, a combination of quantitative and qualitative approaches seems best, as well as the incorporation of a transdisciplinary approach to examine stigma and hate from a variety of interconnected methods and disciplines. Furthermore, qualitative and other ethnographic approaches may be best suited to the uncovering of deep understandings of stereotypical perceptions and attitudes, their contribution to disability stigma, and in explaining the complex interactions at work psychologically, emotionally, and intellectually among both the stigmatized and stigmatizers. In terms of quantitative research, there is a significant need for randomized controlled trials to establish which stigma reduction strategies work better than others and also to establish the validity and reliability of any formal assessment quantitative instruments.

Advocacy

By definition, stigma attached to persons with disabilities means that they are invariably seen as having low or no social status. Clearly, full participation in civic life is a major path toward empowerment and higher social status. Perhaps the most effective way to enhance social status and fuller inclusion in society is the ability of disability advocates, persons with disabilities themselves, and their organizations to advocate for their unqualified inclusion at all levels of society. Such advocacy, over time, will allow these entities to gain and build on political power to the point that they will have a national influence on those who are able to provide support and resources for those with disabilities, including their governments and international entities offering such support (Koszela, 2013).

Such advocacy, of course, is only attained incrementally and is especially taxing among Africans with disabilities who may have, over the course of their lifetimes, been socialized into accepting their lowly lot in life and who often do not possess the requisite tools to make the transition from being oppressed and downtrodden to being empowered and politically influential. That said, there are encouraging signs that the advocacy movement continues to grow and is ever more vocal in the demands for equals rights, treatment, and societal participation (e.g., the Secretariat of the African Decade of Persons with Disabilities, the Southern African Federation of the Disabled, and Disabled People's Organizations, etc. (Ingstad & Grut, 2007).

Socio-economic rehabilitation

Africans with disabilities are almost always among the most poverty-stricken because they are discriminated against, ostracized, denied entry or advancement in the workforce, and generally have to rely on survival by the kindness of others or by begging. Socio-economic rehabilitation refers to the idea of people with disabilities, or those generally in poverty, becoming empowered enough to engage in economic activity that enhances their lives and allows them to provide for themselves and even others. This, in turn, boosts self-esteem, promotes a goal-directed sense of self-efficacy, and reciprocally enhances the person with the disability's status among nondisabled members of the community.

Collaborating with religious leaders

Van Brakel and Miranda-Galarza (2013) suggest that another avenue for combating disability-related stigma is to collaborate with community religious leaders, given that these leaders usually have significant standing in their communities and therefore may well be able to influence and change social attitudes towards persons with disabilities. While it is true that some religious leaders may reinforce negative disability stereotypes, particularly related to the causes of disability, it is equally true that these leaders can promulgate positive attitudes (e.g., from

Biblical or Koranic texts) and valid information related to disabilities to end many of the myths surrounding disability. Equally, concerted efforts must be made to reduce the influence of traditional healers and witchdoctors who perpetuate damaging myths, stereotypes, and fear of disability (Under the Same Sun, 2013).

Conclusion

Given that stigma, either overtly or covertly, underlies and forms perceptions for Africans with disabilities, it must, as a matter of course, be significantly reduced or completely eliminated as a significant precursor to acts of hate and hate speech. As noted, a careful examination of extant strategies designed to reduce stigma are, at best, partially effective, ineffective, or devoid of enough empirical evidence to make solid decisions as to which strategies should be used and which should be discarded. More attention, research, and advocacy are needed to identify strategies for countering both disability stigma and disability hate.

Note

1 While person-first language is generally accepted, this can vary from one cultural context to another.

References

Bucaro, S. (2010). A black market for magical bones: The current plight of east Africa Albinos. *Public Interest Law Reporter*, *15*(2), 131–140.

Dave-Odigie, C. P. (2010). Albino killings in Tanzania: Implications for security. *Peace Studies Journal*, *3*(1), 68–75.

Durkheim, E. ([1895] 2013). *The rules of sociological method and selected texts on sociology and its method.* Basingstoke: Palgrave Macmillan.

Eide, A. H., Khupe, W., & Mannan, H. (2014). Development process in Africa: Poverty, politics, and indigenous knowledge. *Africa Journal of Disability*, *3*(1–14), Article No: 75.

Goffman, E. (1963). *Stigma: Notes on the management of a spoiled identity*. Upper Saddle River, NJ: Prentic-Hall.

Gussow, Z., & Tracy, G. S. (1970). Stigma and the leprosy phenomenon: The social history of a disease in the nineteenth and twentieth centuries. *Bulletin of the History of Medicine*, *44*(5), 425–449.

Heijnders, M., & van der Meij, S. (2006). The fight against stigma: An overview of stigma-reduction strategies and interventions. *Psychology, Health, and Medicine*, *11*(3), 353–363.

Hsieh, N. A. (2012). *Of curses and cows: Barriers to the realization of special needs education in Kenyan Maasai communities*. Boston, MA: Blue Kitabu Research Institute.

Ingstad, B., & Grut, L. (2007). *See me, and do not forget me*: *People with disabilities in Kenya*. Oslo: SINTEF Health Research.

Koszela, K. (2013). *The stigmatization of disabilities in Africa and the developmental effects. Independent Study Project (ISP) Collection. 1639*. Retrieved from https://digitalcollections.sit.edu/isp_collection/1639

Link, B. G., & Phelan, J.C. (2001). Conceptualizing stigma. *Annual Review of Sociology, 27*, 363.

Monk, J., & Wee, J. (2008). Factors shaping attitudes towards physical disability and availability of rehabilitative support systems for disabled persons in rural Kenya. *Asia Pacific Disability Rehabilitation Journal, 19*(1), 93–113.

Ogechi, N. O., & Ruto, S. J. (2002). Portrayal of disability through personal names and proverbs in Kenya: Evidence from Ekegusii and Nandi. *Wiener Zeitschrift fur Afrikastudien, 3*, 63–82.

Parnes, P., Cameron, D., Christie, N., Cockburn, L., Hashemi, G., & Yoshida, K. (2009). Disability in low-income countries: Issues and implications. *Disability and Rehabilitation, 31*(14), 1170–1180.

Saetermoe, C. L., Scattone, D., & Kim, K. H. (2001). Ethnicity and the stigma of disabilities. *Psychology & Health, 16*(6), 699–713.

Stone-MacDonald, A., & Butera, G. (2014). Cultural beliefs about disability in East Africa. *Review of Disability Studies: An International Journal, 8*(1), 295–304.

Thuku, M. (2011). Myths, discrimination, and the call for special rights for persons with albinism in sub-Saharan Africa. *Intercultural Human Rights Law Review, 5*, 1–24.

Under the Same Sun. (2013). Retrieved from https://www.underthesamesun.com

van Brakel, W. H., & Miranda-Galarza, B. (2013). Infectious diseases: A case study of leprosy-related stigma. In P. W. Corrigan (Ed.), *The stigma of disease and disability: Understanding causes and overcoming injustices* (pp. 139–164). American Psychological Association.

Wong, M. L. (2004). Designing programmes to address stigma in leprosy: Issues and challenges. *Asia and Pacific Disability Rehabilitation Journal, 15*(2), 3–12.

10 Amputation of disability as hate speech pattern in Poland

Beata Borowska-Beszta

Disability hate speech is still not recognized in Poland as a significant social, legal, or political issue. The reason for this refusal to admit the presence of disability hate speech in Poland can be directly linked to the Communist period from 1945 to 1989 and its after-effects – widespread prejudices which remain today. Communist ideology involved amputating disabled people from the rest of society as a result of the Marxist-Leninist doctrine that glorified "socialist man." Disabled people were not regarded as compatible with an ideology that promoted itself as developing a more evolved level of humanity. In Poland, Communist ideology subjected disabled people to open repression, scorn, shame, and isolation. Disability hate speech in Poland cannot be understood without understanding this background of Communist oppression.

This chapter explains how the unique experiences of Communist oppression in Poland have shaped both historical and contemporary disability hate speech. No previous studies have highlighted the specific dynamics of disability hate speech associated with Communist ideology in a post-Socialist country. While disability hate speech has been the subject of foreign sociological studies on disability (Sherry, 2010), the concept of "disability hate speech" and its links to Communist ideology have not been recognized, even where hostility to disability has been recognized as an issue by Polish pedagogues studying school violence (Tłuściak-Deliowska, 2017), bullying in general (Plichta, 2010) or risk behaviours and cyberbullying towards people with intellectual disabilities (Plichta, 2017).

The chapter demonstrates that the Kremlin ideology required the social amputation of disabled people from the community. The language of "amputation" is important because it presents an incredibly cruel, personal, vicious social dynamic in a scientific, clinical, medical tone. The social amputation of disabled people occurred in many ways. Disability was regarded as incompatible with the higher development of humanity under Communism (known as "socialist man"), so there was a concerted effort to amputate any recognition of disability in the lives of people. The phenomenon and experience of disability was amputated from people's lives and from social history. Hostility to the presence of disability meant that disability simply could not be publicly admitted, and disabled people were forcibly cut off from the rest of society. More accepting views of disability were censored because they were not considered consistent with Marxist-Leninist ideology.

The amputation of disability occurred on many layers, including in symbolic and linguistic representation, propaganda, community exclusion, and in academic and media coverage. In the symbolic layer, disability was the legibly negated value of a given person, which required elimination or amputation. At the linguistic level, disability required a symbolic technique of amputation of "lameness" (as it was called at the time) through the process of "productivization." In propaganda, disability was either framed as a social pathology alongside other forms of deviance which must be eliminated, or it was used to demonstrate the success of the socialist system when an "invalid" was "productivized" and could achieve superhuman feats. In terms of amputation from the community, disabled people were denied representation in the public space and disability hate crimes were effectively encouraged. Positive and humanistic representation of disability phenomena was silenced either in the press or in specialist academic literature. Disability was presented rather as something to be combated and eliminated.

The Communist legacy

The Polish pattern of hate speech towards people with disabilities must be traced to the cultural background of the Communist domination of Poland which forced it to be dependent on the USSR from 1945 until 1989. Communist hate speech towards people with disabilities was framed by the political, cultural, and ideological concept of a *new labour man*, or *socialist man*, which was a central element of Marxist-Leninist ideology. In Communist ideology, the new socialist man was by definition nondisabled; those who were disabled were regarded openly as a lower form of life. The Communist authorities emphasized the ideal properties of the "new Tovarishch": a devoted, highly skilled worker who achieved supernatural results measured by standard percentages, often above 100%. The new labour man was devoted to (and controlled by) the Communist Party. Being a worker and a member of the Communist Party was a privileged entity in the social ladder of Communist Poland. On the other hand, the presence of disabled citizens was regarded as incompatible with the Communist ideal. The Communist system's "solutions" to the problem of disability included propaganda, censorship, hatred towards the despised population, and institutionalization.

In the practice of propaganda, brainwashing, and censorship, the aim was to achieve power over the citizenship. The Polish philosopher Kołakowski (1983) (and see also Michalewska-Pawlak, 2010, p. 118) wrote that the features positively valued in Communism are:

> servility, cowardice, lack of initiative, readiness to listen to superiors, readiness to inform, indifference to public opinion and public interest. Negative traits are, on the contrary, the ability to initiate, care for common issues, insist on the criteria of truth, fitness and social benefit regardless of the interests of the party apparatus.

Michalewska-Pawlak further characterized the leadership of the Communist Party as "mostly people with low moral qualifications, unscrupulous opportunists" (2010, p. 120).

The Communist system sought to weaken traditional Polish values, such as the influence of the family and the Catholic Church and the Polish emphasis on the ability of citizens to question those in power. Because the socialist system is designed to ensure that citizens are subjected to total social and political control, the power of the family, churches and other associations was attacked by the Communists. Bogucka identifies degrading effects of the Marxist-Leninist ideological system on the personality of Poles: "the state destroyed the trust between people, the ability to associate and cooperate, (and) forbid the functioning of civic organizations, in their place to organize licensed organizations" (Bogucka quoted in Michalewska-Pawlak, 2010, p. 24).

Freedom of speech and the opportunity to publicly criticize the system was impossible in a society characterized by constant censorship and propaganda from the Communist Party. The monopolistic Communist Party dominated social life and family life and incapacitated citizens and made them assume a passive, Homo Sovieticus (Tischner, 1992). Michalewska-Pawlak notes:

> all media remained under the control of the authorities, which created a special office for propaganda purposes, dealing with preventive censorship. Every ideology based on the slogans of freedom and equality creates the myth of a new man, ready to live in a social community based on collective principles. The formation of a 'citizen' with the right identity and attitude was to stabilize changes and testify to their inviolability.
>
> (2010, p. 116)

Challenges to the status quo were met with repression. Social life was controlled and monitored in every dimension by the monopolistic Communist Party, using the means of oppression in various fields, including limiting or eliminating freedom of speech, using ideological propaganda in the media, and requiring all levels of education to be consistent with Marxist-Leninist ideology. Anything that questioned Communist propaganda about the alleged huge economic and sociocultural successes of the system was censored.

Socialist apparatchik amputates disability

Communist authorities could not tolerate disability (especially intellectual or psychiatric disorders) to be publicly recognized alongside the new "socialist man." Brenk points out that disability was considered shameful and incompatible with an ideal socialist state – meaning that there were no efforts at integration. Indeed, "people with intellectual disabilities were treated with contempt, and institutions for the mentally ill were called 'houses of madmen'" (Brenk, 2015, p. 317). Such denigration of disabled people was a key element of the Communist regime – while the "socialist man" was valorized, the disabled person was demonized. One was a Communist hero, the other a parasite.

Under the Communist regime, citizens were divided into clear categories: those who brought about production (workers) and those who do not raise anything. The Communist ideal was based on the idea of a "working man." There was a prevailing cultural pattern of stigma associated with unemployment; placing people outside of the workforce in the social margins of the People's Republic of Poland. The motto "who does not work does not eat" was built on a stigmatizing social relation to "freeloaders." Disabled people who did not work were often placed among this category of freeloaders, and their contributions to society (and sometimes, their value in life) was questioned.

In practice, the amputation of disabled people from society involved their total isolation. As Witkowski (1993, p. 8) writes:

> In our country, for decades, people have been dissuaded from meeting disabled people on the street, in the store, at the office, at work. Special centers were created for them, I would say ghettos, stressing the greatness of the system that provides such practical solutions.

Borowska-Beszta (2012) has also noted the ways people with disabilities were not visible in public spaces in the Communist period. Exclusion generates the denial of rights as well as social and political invisibility. The effects of such state-sponsored prejudice against disabled people were profound. Hate speech against disabled people resulted in dehumanization and violence against persons with disabilities in institutions (Tarkowska, 1997). Kowalik (1996) notes that people with disabilities experienced negative attitudes, distancing, devaluation, de-legitimization, and discrimination. Such hate speech can be found both in the official propaganda of the Kremlin and in censorship imposed on colonized Poland.

Academic life was also strongly immersed in the propaganda of Marxist-Leninist ideology and the censorship of content which did not correspond to it. Amputation of disability also occurred within academic literature, including the humanities, social sciences, and other fields. These publications did publish material about the presence of disability, since choices over publication were determined by ideological prejudices rather than the scientific merit of the research. But Communists engaged in systematic censorship of academic content incompatible with official ideology. The channels of spreading propaganda and censorship included the media, but they also occurred in the science, education, and rehabilitation sector for the disabled. Some scientific publications concerning, inter alia, issues of disability were censored, in line with the indoctrination of the Communist state. As a result, scientific publications rejected all content that could undermine the Communist foundations of social life, such as the "ideal man" – thereby creating a culture of insulting disabled people and their families.

The Communist system did occasionally recognize disability in another way: when it used the idea of the "productivization of invalids" in its propaganda.

Communist ideology suggested that some people – "invalids" – could overcome their disability and prosper because of Communism, to the point where they developed superhuman capacities. Bednarowicz (1946, p. 101) notes that Communist ideology promoted the idea that invalids should be "restored to society as useful individuals." The restoration of their roles – beyond their previous abilities – served propaganda functions.

Communist propaganda stressed the successes of the "productive war invalids." Rusinek (cited in Brenk, 2015, p. 320) provides a historical record of such propaganda:

> Citizen Władysław Marszałek, blind and with the left upper limb amputation, an employee of the State Linen Industry Works in Nowa Sól reaches 205% of the standard norm; his companion of work with these establishments was blind and with the amputation of the right upper limb, citizen Józef Ozga, also reaches 205% of the norm; citizen Stanisław Zając, 100% disabled, blind, employed in a carton factory in Krakow, makes 200% of the standard norm.

Such exaggerated figures served a role in the propaganda and ideology and were used by the authorities to promote the benefits of the socialist system. Messages about invalids being productivized were laced with other themes about the merits of professional training provided under socialism, the benefits of socialism in terms of trade unions and politics, and the importance of building class consciousness among the working class (Szymańska, 1948). Lipkowski, a scholar and special educator, wrote:

> in our country, the aims of education are consistent with the ideology of socialism and aim to achieve a level of education and training that would be best adapted to the growing needs and progress of culture and civilization of socialist society. Special pedagogy, as a unit of general pedagogy, cannot determine and pursue goals contrary to the objectives of general pedagogy, it results from Marxist axiology, which treats every human individual, that is also the retarded, as a value in itself, regardless of the values existing outside it.
>
> (Lipkowski, 1980, p. 43)

Despite the indication that the "retarded individual" is a valued person, the practice of everyday life in Communist Poland indicated advanced discriminatory practices and the exclusion of disabled people from public spaces of social life.

Another consideration for the authorities concerning disability was their estimation of the degree to which a person could successfully be indoctrinated. If people belonged to certain disabilities that were not able to be easily indoctrinated (such as the intellectually disabled or the mentally ill), they were segregated, marginalized, excluded, isolated, and amputated from public space and public discourse. Amputation of disability was conducted alongside the existing censorship of uncomfortable or shameful content by the authorities.

There was a hierarchy of disability during Communist times in Poland until 1989, and people with intellectual disabilities and profound mental illness experienced the most severe violation of rights and marginalization. They were treated with contempt and their personal dignity was not recognized, because their disabilities were identified with social pathology. There were significant problems when the first attempts to create support associations of people at that time wanted to be constituted with the "mental retardation." Krystyna Mrugalska, mother of a boy with cerebral palsy, an educator, a social activist for the disabled people in the Communist era in Poland, founder of the Polish Association for People with Mental Retardation, recalls:

> The first circles of parents of children with intellectual disabilities arose in People's Poland in the 1960s and this was a unique social movement at that time – genuinely bottom-up, determined in achieving goals, energetic, creating a new social quality, not licensed by the state. It must be remembered that parents organized themselves in a time when their children were not covered by school duty, because nobody imagined that "such children" can learn, have no benefits or entitlements. They did not exist in social awareness and authorities. Parents from the first seven established circles started from a simple form of support for their daughters and sons – the organization of summer camps and small rehabilitation teams. They collected money mainly at workplaces. Attempts at contacts with the authorities in those days generally ended in failure – when one of the parents of the circle in Silesia went to the voivodeship secretary to agree and support the fundraising for rehabilitation, he got the answer that "buy a hammer and hit your own head." In this way he would get rid of the idiotic idea that "handicapped" children need fresh air. Therefore, it took decades for the social mentality to change and a comprehensive support system to be created. Besides, it was largely created by parents. When in the early 1960s we went to the socialist authorities to agree to establish a relationship analogous to the relationship of the blind or deaf union, we heard that mental retardation is such a social pathology that cannot have its representation. It would violate the systemic doctrine of socialist society. It was agreed, however, that the parents of children with intellectual disabilities can do something for them and on this basis they were allowed to "hug" to one of the licensed organizations, if that one wants us.
>
> (Borowska, 2014)

The degree of hate speech – suggesting that a parent of the disabled child should hit himself on the head with a hammer because of having ideas or raising public awareness – was not just one man's opinion. It reflected the broader Communist attitude to profoundly disabled people who they believed could not contribute to the system through employment. The effects of such widespread policies of hate are still being felt today.

Śliwerski (2017, p. 40) adds that "Polish pedagogy is still catching up with the times of the PRL (Polska Rzeczpospolita Ludowa), the period of internal censorship and the iron curtain in relations with the world of capitalist science."

Andrzej Wojciechowski, professor of art, academics, and teacher who developed and implemented presence of the disabled artists in public spaces of Toruń by organizing the *Atelier* for Developing the Creative Activities of the Disabled People, and who organized regular art exhibitions in the 1970s and 1980s until the present, wrote openly about the reality of bullying and humiliation towards people with disabilities continuing in the 1990s, after Poland regained its sovereignty (Wojciechowski, 2001).

Hate speech in Poland today

Garwol (2016) writes that "the Polish legal system, unlike Austrian, British or American, does not contain the concept of 'hate speech'" (p. 305), despite the existence of crimes against people with disabilities that have been analyzed by Polish courts. Rogalska and Urbańczyk (2017) highlight the current lack of specificity in the term "hate speech" in Polish legal language, although the authors add that the phenomenon is a permanent element of jurisprudence and the doctrine of law. Matlak (2017, p. 105) concludes that

> there is no expressive hate speech in the Polish Penal Code, but indirectly two articles are concerned: 256 of the Penal Code 'who incites hatred on the basis of national, ethnic, racial, denominational differences or because of their denomination – up to 2 years in prison' and 257 of the Penal Code 'who publicly insults a group of people or an individual because of their national, ethnic, racial, religious affiliation, or because of their lack of religious denomination – up to three years in prison.'

Definitions created by Polish researchers in the fields of humanities (Matlak, 2017) and the social sciences (Rogalska & Urbańczyk, 2017) are diverse in terms of the groups they include as well as the nature of hate speech. Its ontological scope is imprecise, according to Matlak (2017), who emphasizes the multiplicity of concepts and understanding of the phenomenon in Poland. The author writes,

> until now, there has been no uniform definition of hate speech that would allow us not only to define a category, but to solve the terminological problem associated with its use and create a lasting conceptual network. The ontological status has not been determined, which makes it difficult to determine the subject of the research.
>
> (p. 101)

Matlak (2017) links the use of hate speech to the experience of propaganda – an issue that Poles know too well. Similarities between hate speech and propaganda include the way hate speech is persuasive in its character, is an element of public language and a set of linguistic means, and is often aggressive, populist, propagandist, provocative, pauperized, vulgar, offensive, contemptuous, characterized by stereotypes, prejudices, and colloquialisms (p. 107). Matlak (2017, p. 107) emphasizes that

> the language of propaganda aims to create a picture of reality that accomplishes the goals of the propaganda sender… (it is based on) emotionality, dogmatism, bipolarity and frequent inconsistency… Hatred based on unverifiable assumptions and generalization combined with exaggeration and unreliability is the basis for the definition of hate speech.

Hate speech is also used to discredit the opponent.

Even though there is no clear legal definition of hate speech, and disability is often excluded from the list of protected categories, academics in Poland do recognize the harm that such speech inflicts. Śledzińska-Simon (2010, p. 93) writes that "hate speech can intimidate, threaten to humiliate, insult, and also consolidate stereotypes and lead to discrimination and even physical violence." As this chapter has shown, hate speech can be a powerful weapon in amputating disabled people from the community and denying them opportunities for inclusion, rights, and respect. The patterns of shame, disgust, and prejudice which were circulated throughout Polish society under Communist colonization continue to have lasting effects today. For instance, the lack of discussion about disability issues, and the continuing absence of disabled in many public spaces, demonstrate that these problems need to be addressed more effectively. Media coverage is also problematic. Analyzed the weekly women's magazine *Your Style* in 1990–1991 (shortly after Poland regained its sovereignty) and counted totally only two articles on disability issues. This example also indicates that the amputation of disability phenomena from the media has lasted from the previous political system.

Conclusion

Disability hate speech during the Communist period in Poland revealed a peculiar dimension: the amputation of disabled people from the community, from the media, and from academic texts in social sciences omitting the voice of people with disabilities. This amputation occurred because people with profound disabilities did not match the Communist ideal of "socialist man" as they did not work. They were stigmatized, isolated, and demonized. The disability rights movements of other countries were not possible against this background of Communist colonization, marked by constant propaganda, censorship, and repression of dissent. Hate speech was not illegal – it was almost encouraged as a part of the demonization of anyone who did not work. Using an instrumentalist approach, anyone who was not working was not contributing to society, so their entire value in life was questioned. They were physically and ideologically amputated from society.

The Communist state system was so oppressive that it is still difficult in post-Socialist Poland to promote notions of disability rights. The deinstitutionalization process for people with intellectual disabilities and mental illness, which was present in other countries such as the United States in the 1970–1980s, was not possible under the Communist regime and progress to inclusion has been much slower than elsewhere. The hate speech which dominated the representation of disability under the Communist regime delayed the processes of integration and inclusion of people with intellectual disabilities and mental illness. The linguistic patterns of hate speech occurred (and helped justify) the physical exclusion of people with disabilities from the community. Negative propaganda about disability resulted in exclusionary, oppressive, hateful behaviour to people with disabilities. The long-lasting effects of this amputation demand re-education programs, so that the needs of people with disabilities can be addressed and their rights acknowledged.

The amputation of disabled people from public spaces blocked the voice of advocates, perpetuated social stigma, created isolation and promoted a lack of understanding of the needs of people with disabilities. Someone with a disability that prevented him from working (the core tasks required by Marxist-Leninist ideology) was a non-grata personage, which is why they found in segregated institutions. Hate speech meant that the value of disabled people's lives was questioned: "What good are they if they cannot work?" Such social utilitarianism was a major mechanism for social devaluation. Assuming that someone's value as a human being is linked instrumentally to their capacity to work and "produce" was used as a justification for taking people with profound disabilities away from the community and putting them into segregated institutions.

Hate speech dictated by the Communist system in Poland perpetuated discrimination and has left lasting effects today. The practices of social isolation prevented communication and mutual learning between disabled and nondisabled Poles. Additionally, it caused a delay in the progress of inclusion: policies such as normalization and deinstitutionalization which occurred in the United States in the 1970s did not occur in Poland until twenty years later.

References

Bednarowicz, E. (1946). Pierwszy Ogólnopolski Zjazd kierowników referatów i oddziałów spraw inwalidzkich powiatowych i wojewódzkich władz administracji ogólnej. *Praca i Opieka Społeczna*, *2*, 96–104.

Borowska, M. (2014). *Dawno temu w PRL...upośledzenie było, niezgodne z doktryną socjalizmu*. Retrieved from http://niepelnosprawni.lublin.pl/dawno-temu-w-prl-uposled zenie-byloniezgodne-z-doktryna-socjalizmu/

Borowska-Beszta, B. (2012). *Niepełnosprawność w kontekstach kulturowych i teoretycznych*. Kraków: Wyd. Impuls.

Brenk, M. (2015). Aktywizacja osób niepełnosprawnych w propagandzie Polski Ludowej lat 1946–1956. In M. Kowalski, A. Knocińska & P. Frąckowiak (Eds.), *Reintegracja – Edukacja – Adaptacja. Aktywizacja zawodowa i społeczna osób zagrożonych wykluczeniem* (pp. 312–322). Gniezno: Gnieźnieńska Szkoła Wyższa Milenium.

Garwol, K. (2016). Hejt w internecie–analiza zjawiska. *Edukacja-Technika-Informatyka*, *7*(4), 304–309.

Kołakowski, L. (1983). *Kłopoty z Polską*. Warszawa: Wydawnictwo Przedświt.

Kowalik, S. (1996). *Psychospołeczne Podstawy Rehabilitacji Osób Niepełnosprawnych.* Warszawa: Wyd. Interart.

Lipkowski, O. (1980). Podstawy pedagogiki specjalnej In A. Hulek (Ed.), *Pedagogika rewalidacyjna* (pp. 52–59). Warszawa: PWN.

Matlak, S. (2017). Status ontologiczny mowy nienawiści. *Naukowy Przegląd Dziennikarski, 4*, 101–111.

Michalewska-Pawlak, M. (2010). *Obywatelskość demokratyczna jako idea normatywna w koncepcjach polityczno-programowych polskiej opozycji w latach 1980–1989*. Gdańsk: Europejskie Centrum Solidarności.

Plichta, P. (2010). Uczniowie niepełnosprawni intelektualnie jako ofiary i sprawcy agresji rówieśniczej – kontekst edukacyjny. In J. Pyżalski & E. Roland (Eds.), *Bullying a specjalne potrzeby edukacyjne – Podręcznik metodyczny* (pp. 1–23). Łódź: WSP/ Centrum Badań Behawioralnych Uniwersytetu Stavanger.

Plichta, P. (2017). *Socjalizacja i wychowanie dzieci i młodzieży z niepełnosprawnością intelektualną w erze cyfrowej*. Toruń: Wydawnictwo Adam Marszałek.

Rogalska, E., & Urbańczyk, M. (2017). Złożoność zjawiska mowy nienawiści w pozaprawnym aspekcie definicyjnym. *Studia nad Autorytaryzmem i Totalitaryzmem, 39*(2), 117–135.

Sherry, M. (2010). *Disability hate crimes: Does anyone really hate disabled people?* Surrey: Ashgate.

Śledzińska-Simon, A. (2010). Decyzja ramowa w sprawie zwalczania pewnych form i przejawów rasizmu i ksenofobii jako trudny kompromis wobec mowy nienawiści w Unii Europejskiej. In A. Bodnar, G.-G. Aleksandra, R. Wieruszewski & M. Wyrzykowski (Eds.), *Mowa nienawiści a wolność słowa. Aspekty prawne i społeczne*. Warszawa: Wolters-Kluwer

Śliwerski, B. (2017). Paradygmaty współczesnej pedagogiki jedności w Polsce. *Przegląd Badań Edukacyjnych, 2*(25), 39–58.

Szymańska, H. (1948). Zadania opieki społecznej na obecnym etapie. *Opiekun Społeczny, 9*, 320–325.

Tarkowska, E. (1997). Ludzie w instytucji totalnej: przypadek domów pomocy społecznej w Polsce. In A. Gustavsson & A. Zakrzewska-Manterys (Eds.), *Upośledzenie w społecznym zwierciadle*. Warszawa: Wyd. Żak.

Tischner, J. (1992). *Etyka solidarności oraz homo sovieticus*. Kraków Znak.

Tłuściak-Deliowska, A. (2017). *Dręczenie szkolne. Społeczno-pedagogiczna analiza zjawiska*. Warszawa: Wydawnictwo APS.

Witkowski, T. (1993). *Rozumiec problemy osób niepelnosprawnych: (13 rodzajów niepelnosprawnosci)*. Warszawa: Małe Dzieło Boskiej Opatrzności.

Wojciechowski, A. (2001). *Obecność. Teksty zebrane* Toruń: Uniwersytet Mikołaja Kopernika.

11 Disability under austerity

Do some forms of political rhetoric constitute disability hate speech?

Lisa Davies

Introduction and background

What I am writing here, in consideration of whether some forms of political rhetoric constitute disability hate speech, is a personal account supported by research. I am a disabled woman, person, of the nonwalking, wheelchair-using variety. Here, as in much of my current scholarly work, I forgo a predilection to objectivity (Mercer, 2002; Salzman, 2002; Stanley & Wise, 1993). I acquired my primary impairment at birth. Disability hate and disability hate speech have been an aspect of my experience even before I as an individual was capable of conscious thought or memory. My parents had to cope with the tide of medical and social negativity that comes with the decision to parent and love a disabled child. Much of this negativity was and is founded upon prejudice, and comes from a place of fear, disgust, and yes, hatred. I feel confident based on my experience in asserting that the hostility I encounter as a disabled person has increased under austerity. A 2014 survey by disability charity Scope found that over four-fifths (85%) of the British public believed and acknowledged that disabled people face prejudice (Aiden & McCarthy, 2014). This suggests that my experience is not without a degree of credence. A further understanding I have acquired is that because I am disabled, I am not wanted or welcome in the world. My impairment makes me an outsider, and my inclusion, my status as a citizen, is highly conditional. The words of Kitchin (1988) help to contextualise how I feel as a disabled person when I attempt to access the social world:

> The ideological messages to disabled people that are inscribed in space through the use of segregationist planning and inaccessible environments are clear "you are out of place," "you are different." As a result, forms of oppression and their reproduction within ideologies leads to distinct spatialities with the creation of landscapes of exclusion, the boundaries of which are reinforced through a combination of the popularising of cultural representations and the creation of myths.
>
> (Kitchin, 1988, p. 351)

Alongside the fact that as a disabled person I am unwelcome in the social world, as represented in the organisation of social environments, which can be explicit or implicit, hate speech on the basis of disability further ratifies my exclusion. It is another method by which I am made to "know my place" and understand that I am "out of place" (Kitchin, 1988). On occasion hate speech is overtly expressed, it exists in the everyday utterances of friends, relatives and strangers, is encountered in a variety of settings. There is, in my experience, so much disability hate speech that as a disabled person you become numb to it as a means of survival. Of course, much of the disability hate speech I encounter is covert and insidious, so much so, that I would have to work hard to convince even an empathetic, understanding non-disabled person that many of the things people say to me are indeed hate speech, and by continuation a crime. Many people I meet do not understand that some of the utterances they make, either to me, or about me, are hate speech (Deal, 2007), much that is prejudiced and based on hate is far too easy to rationalise and account for.

Political rhetoric under austerity: The impact of austerity on disabled people

In this chapter, I aim to use a broad socio-political understanding of the concept of disability hate speech, demonstrating that under austerity, disability hate speech is a key element of victim-blaming, scapegoating, and demonising. I am not going to look at cases prosecuted (or not) through the legal system. Instead, I am going to demonstrate how this practice occurs by looking at two examples of political rhetoric that were forwarded by members of the Conservative government, which may be considered to varying degrees as examples of disability hate speech. The examples I will use to illustrate my argument are comments made by Conservative MP Philip Davies in 2011 and by Chancellor Phillip Hammond in 2017. My socio-political analysis of disability hate speech is committed to discussing the impact of such language and the policies and practices which surround it. I will discuss the broad impacts of such austerity policies and hate speech on disabled people collectively, but also reflect on the personal impact of such hate speech on me as a disabled person.

My argument is that when politicians stand up in parliament and make prejudicial arguments for paying disabled people less than nondisabled people, or when they suggest that the inclusion of disabled people in the workforce is, even in part, to blame for a poor performing economy, it is disability hate speech. In addition, doing so from their position of power only serves to make hate speech of this kind socially acceptable to some members of society. Whilst the government may publicly condemn the hostility and abuse disabled people experience (Equality and Human Rights Commission, 2011, 2017), using disability hate speech to justify the government's austerity policies encourages others to do the same.

In June 2011, Conservative MP Philip Davies, stood before the House of Commons and argued that disabled people could legally be paid less than the minimum wage if it would help them obtain employment. He stated, "If an employer is looking at two candidates, one who has got disabilities and one who hasn't, and they have got to pay them both the same rate, I invite you to guess which one the employer is more likely to take on" (Stratton, 2011).

In December 2017, the Chancellor, Phillip Hammond, argued that the increased participation of disabled people in the workforce was part of the reason explanation for the slow economy:

> It is almost certainly the case that by increasing participation in the workforce, including far higher levels of participation by marginal groups and very high levels of engagement in the workforce, for example of disabled people – something we should be extremely proud of – may have had an impact on overall productivity measurements.
>
> (Slawson, 2017)

In my view, both of these examples of political rhetoric express prejudice towards disabled people. The timing and social context is important in making the case that such rhetoric is indeed hate speech. Both of these political speeches were delivered during a period of austerity. In 2010 the coalition Lib Dem and Conservative government embarked on a program of austerity cuts to public services to reduce public expenditure. The publicly stated justification for these policies was the 2008 banking crisis and a need, the government argued, to reduce the country's debt. Academics such as Briant, Watson, and Philo have argued that the government is "using the financial crises to legitimate these cuts" (2013, p. 875). Similarly, Taylor-Gooby and Stoker (2011) comment that the financial crisis is being used as an excuse for a massive restructuring of welfare systems and public services.

A number of writers have noted and asserted the multiple detrimental impacts that the range of cuts implemented under austerity have had upon disabled people (Cross, 2013; Duffy, 2014; Mendoza, 2015; O'Hara, 2015). In "Counting the Cuts," Duffy asserts that:

> Disabled people in poverty bear a burden which is more than four times the (modal) average... The reason that cuts have been targeted in these areas is not moral or economic – it is political. It's easier to scapegoat disabled people and people in poverty. Disabled people and people in poverty have no effective political representation.
>
> (Duffy, 2014, p. 17; 21)

In her book, *Austerity Bites,* Mary O'Hara outlines the comprehensive impact of the cuts on disabled people, which she unequivocally asserts as even worse than the impact upon nondisabled people:

> The harm and inequity experienced by sick and disabled people was incontrovertible and it was pervasive. As the months passed in 2012 and 2013 it was abundantly clear that the radical upending of the entire social security structure that was causing so many problems for nondisabled people was also

> the primary culprit behind the suffering of people with disabilities-only often to a much greater degree. And this new political world order did not occur in a vacuum… All of these efforts [of activists] served to highlight what even a few years earlier would have been regarded as inconceivable – that rather than showing adults and children with disabilities the respect they deserve, the government was breaking the most fundamental of social contracts, hellbent as it was on cutting vital benefits and services regardless of local objections backed by solid evidence of the misery their policies were foisting on people.
>
> (O'Hara, 2015, p. 142; 145)

Alongside acknowledging that the cuts unfairly target disabled people, O'Hara asserts that the imposition of austerity and the ideas that underpin it are not an organic occurrence or an accident, but a conscious act designed to maintain and increase inequality. Based on my personal experience of austerity as a disabled person, and the reading and research I have done on the subject, I agree. As Briant, Watson, and Philo (2013) comment, the motivation to implement such cuts is not exclusive to the Conservative government, Labour, too, sought to cut spending on disability. However, the actual implementation of these cuts by the Conservative government is new. Since 2010, the think tank Demos has been documenting the impact of austerity on disabled people. The financial losses to disabled people projected by Demos' research are stark and imply a bleak future for those disabled people, like me, who are in receipt of state support:

> Our research reveals disabled people are bearing the brunt of the austerity measures, losing an estimated 28.3 billion by 2017/2018. While striking, these calculations will invariably be an underestimate of the true impact of the cuts – as we opted for the most conservative estimates on the more unknown elements of reform.
>
> (Wood, 2013)

Davies' political rhetoric is particularly hateful when examined alongside the austerity policies which so profoundly negatively impact the lives of disabled people. Therefore, a socio-political analysis of disability hate speech is essential: the rhetoric that is featured in this piece functions to provide an emotional justification for the policy of austerity, the removal of what are vital financial and social supports from disabled people. Furthermore, such rhetoric is and must be simple and readily understood by most, so that it is widely communicated and gains social traction; people are less likely to repeat an idea if it is too complex or they do not understand what is being said. Arguably, the simplicity of such hateful rhetoric is one aspect that makes it so dangerous.

Davies' is giving voice to long-held prejudices and attitudes that many disabled people, (myself included) have experienced, and which have played a role in preventing them from finding employment (Muscular Dystrophy Campaign, 2010) – that their work is not of the same value as nondisabled people.

Additionally, Davies is capitalising on the existence and prevalence of those prejudices in an attempt to create a context in which the labour of disabled people is not only literally devalued, but this devaluation is socially acceptable. His comments further undermine the chances of disabled people to obtain employment and thereby improve their own financial situations by attempting to create a context in which disabled people are paid less than nondisabled people for work they do. That is particularly egregious and hateful, especially when you consider that the employment rate for disabled people in Britain is 47.6%, as compared to 79.2% for nondisabled people (Equality and Human Rights Commission, 2017).

In forwarding such rhetoric, Davies is playing his part in making an already difficult task, that of obtaining employment, even harder, in effect, he is creating an additional barrier. An additional degree of hate is identifiable when you consider that Davies' is a member and representative of the very same Conservative government, that through its austerity policies, is removing vital financial support from disabled people. This is being accomplished through a number of its reforms, including use of the Work Capability Assessment as a method of deciding who is and isn't "fit for work" and therefore entitled to Employment and Support Allowance or not, and, in practice, reducing the number of people entitled to the benefit:

> The government needs to deliver a test that is fit for purpose. Most disabled people want to work they face significant barriers such as a lack of skills and experience, confidence and even negative attitudes from some employers. The work capability assessment ignores all this it's a tick-box test of someone's medical condition.
>
> (Hawkes cited in O'Hara, 2015, p. 154)

Phillip Hammond's comments that the inclusion of more disabled people in the workforce serves as part explanation for slow economic productivity is another attempt to scapegoat disabled people and create a political climate of resentment, animosity and hate. It is an attempt which does not survive the smallest of scrutiny, particularly when you consider that only 47.2% of disabled people are actually part of the workforce (Equality and Human Rights Commission, 2017). As with Davies' comments, his analysis is simplistic and lacks even a cursory understanding of the barriers to work that disabled people face. To blame one particular group, even partially, for poor economic figures, is to ignore the impact of a financial crisis on the economy and the already flawed nature of the economic system we live under (Mendoza 2015). It is also to ignore the impact of his own government's austerity policies on that same economy (O'Hara, 2015).

Political rhetoric and disability hate speech in justification of welfare reform

The comments of Davies and Hammond are both focused on the subject of productivity through work and contribution to the economy. Implicit within them is the historically held and still-prevalent idea that disabled people are unproductive, or less productive than their nondisabled peers (Kitchin, 1988). In these examples, the value of disabled people as humans is predicated on their ability, or perceived lack thereof, to contribute financially or economically to society. Representing disabled people in this way is cogent to the government's agenda because within the highly simplistic political discourse of austerity, if you accept that disabled people are unproductive, then disabled people are "undeserving" and the removal of financial and social support through a broad range of cuts and reforms becomes rational (Garthwaite, 2011). This is a representation that disabled people are required to confirm, through deficit-based assessments in order to qualify for support (Grover & Piggott, 2007). In a sense, disabled people are compelled to damage their own reputations in an attempt to obtain vital financial support.

Removing money and other forms of support from disabled people is not politically popular, and is considered a political risk (E. Briant et al., 2013); creating and repeating the perception that disabled people are unproductive economic burdens to society is a means by which the government seeks to direct and control the political discourse in respect of welfare reform. It is a rationalisation of government policy through disablist hate speech, where the notion of disabled people as unproductive burdens (similar in some ways to eugenic ideologies) is a weapon to derail a disability rights agenda. In the disability hate speech of austerity and in deficit-based assessments for disability benefits, there is no implicit recognition of the need to remove disabling barriers. As Burch (2018) argues in her analysis of online disablist hate speech, employing examples from the chat room Reddit, "Representations of welfare dependency create a meta-narrative of disability as an economic expense to the rest of society" (p. 399).

Burch's work is an indication of the impact and effectiveness of such rhetoric in terms of convincing people to believe, adopt, and repeat it. Her work helps to illustrate that such rhetoric encourages hostility and hate toward disabled people. Welfare reform supported by this type of rhetoric incites anger in people, it is divisive, and attractive to some people, because it provides a simple answer to a complex issue. It also gives people somebody to hate. Indeed, in a number of the examples from Burch's research, hate is predicated on Conservative rhetoric of productivity, and the idea that disabled people are unproductive and economically burdensome:

> The use of "parasites" as a means of identifying and marking out disability is supported by the relationship between welfare and employment, to which the first is presented as inferior to the latter. Making this connection, one user argues that "you are a parasite on the productive class", thus confirming that the disabled figure is not only unproductive, but burdensome to those who are productive. Indeed, one user explains the importance of productivity, suggesting that "if you want anything in life, you have to work for it."
>
> (Burch, 2018, p. 401)

Political rhetoric of this type is also proliferated through newspapers and other media outlets, the majority of which support the Conservative government.

Disabled people are frequently represented as "underserving claimants," "cheats," and as economic burdens or drains on the economy (Briant, Watson, & Philo, 2011; Briant et al., 2013). Burch adds:

> To justify these changes to welfare, politicians and media outlets have adopted a strategic narrative. That is, they have expressed pity for "hardworking taxpayers" who have been portrayed as the real victims of financial instability. At the same time, we have witnessed a surge in vitriolic welfare rhetoric that brands welfare recipients, and many disabled people, as "scroungers," "cheats," and "scum."
>
> (Burch, 2018, p. 393)

Research into media representations of disabled people under austerity by Briant, Watson, and Philo (2013) drew similar conclusions in arguing that evidence indicates in terms of their representation disabled people are a new "folk devil," and that they are first to feel the impact of austerity measures which were established by the coalition government, and justified in part by the global economic crisis with the aim of meeting the targets of the OECD (Organisation for Economic Co-operation and Development). Media representations of the kind I discuss here are in part intended to make the removal of support from a social group that has, historically at least, elicited a degree of empathetic reaction from the general public, more palatable to that same group. Those who regard such rhetoric as accurate are less likely to object to the removal of support from disabled people or speak in opposition to austerity. Indeed, the research I have discussed in this section can be taken as an indication of the extent to which people join in, repeating the various media narratives in respect of disabled people and thereby proliferating and disseminating such views and increasing hostility and social division.

Personal experience: Policy as an expression of disability hate speech

Acknowledging that disability hate speech can also be expressed through writing, Conservative policy in respect of welfare reform acts as a further expression of the hatred this government has for disabled people. They need not even speak. Their political perspective is conveyed at every stage of the assessment process for benefits such as Employment and Support Allowance (ESA) and Personal Independence Payment (PIP). I have direct, lived, and have contemporary experience of this. Assessments are often of no benefit to me at all, and any financial support I receive is highly conditional, such that, if I could obtain employment that provided me an income I could live on, I would gladly not claim ESA or PIP. I do so out of financial necessity. I have been trying to secure financially viable employment for most of my adult life. The government is placing responsibility for finding employment onto disabled individuals, and doing little to encourage inclusive working practices or make workplaces accessible, whilst simultaneously making the eligibility criteria for benefits like ESA and PIP harder to satisfy.

Briant, Watson, and Philo provide an insightful overview of the outcome and function of the political rhetoric discussed in this chapter:

> The new and recently introduced Fitness to Work tests, which are designed to "reactivate" disabled people, have raised the threshold of "ability" and many of those previously classified as disabled are now seen as being fit for work. Those previously classified as disabled are described in the popular media and in political discourse as people who have taken illegitimately from the taxpayer and cheated "genuine" claimants. This is in turn being used to fuel claims for even tougher tests to push people off benefits. Rather than the responsibility bearing on the state to ensure demand in the job market for disabled people and inclusive employment practices, disabled people are themselves being blamed for their perceived failure to secure employment.
>
> (2013, p. 886)

I have been assessed more times under Conservative austerity than at any other time in my life. I find assessments acutely distressing, and they are a contributory factor in my own depression. I have been required to fill in an ESA50 (Capability for Work questionnaire) multiple times in the past few years, and each time I have to send medical evidence restating the fact that I still can't walk, there is still no cure for my condition, and I still can't do the things they have asked me previously. Repetition, repeatedly having to focus on and write about myself in terms of deficits, and having to acknowledge that I'm only going to get worse is one of the many reasons I find them harmful and distressing:

> A work capability form (ESA) just landed on my doorstep, the mood of my weekend has changed and I have yet another form to fill in. I am going to nickname myself "Ms no days off" from now on, how many times do I have to tell someone what I'm doing before they leave me and my family in peace. #sogladIameducated… for approximately the second time in three months I have survived trial by ESA. The success of my form filling skills was confirmed by the fact my money was there to collect this morning and I did not get called for the medical assessment I've heard so many lovely things about. I think this means I am good at pathologising my own body for the purpose of my own financial survival.
>
> (Private Journal Entry 2015: 11; 20)

I have also recently been transferred from Disability Living Allowance (DLA) to PIP. This process involved having to reassert my entitlement to an allowance that I have been on for years, as with ESA, I could have lost vital financial support. As with ESA, I had to fill in another lengthy form and provide medical evidence of my impairment and other medical conditions. Many of the questions on the ESA and PIP forms are identical, but both are treated as separate processes, so I was required to provide the same information again. For PIP, I also had to attend a medical assessment. Due to my previous personal experience of assessments I now will not and do not attend, without someone present who I trust to witness what occurs.

The fact that I am actually disabled, is no longer enough to reassure me that everything will be ok. Based on my experience, I do not trust assessors to exercise equitable judgement. It is not uncommon to have personal information I provide as part of the assessment process used as an argument against my need for what I am applying for:

> I filled in the PIP form yesterday, it hurt me physically and psychologically, repeatedly considering my own predicament in the way required by the form causes me acute distress and is humiliating. I also can't write for long periods without pain… Being forced to fill in the PIP form, and having my right to the same amount of money I've been considered eligible for more than 20 years questioned has once again made me painfully conscious of the extent of my own unhappiness. The last two days have been horrible, I had a nightmare last night and I'm not sleeping very well. My anxiety levels are high. I'm posting the PIP form tomorrow. I'm going to send it signed for because I don't want it to go missing and have vital money stopped, and believe me, they would, they have done this before now for a lot less and because of organisational incompetence… The PIP situation has reaffirmed for me the fact that the mental, psychological and practical costs of receiving state support are too high, and I would do many things not to have to go through another assessment ever again in my life.
>
> (Private Journal Entry 2015: 195; 196; 197)

I am not alone in regarding assessments as distressing; many disabled people and their supporters have reached similar conclusions having been through the ESA and PIP assessment processes. In the research on portrayal of disabled people in the media, the idea that welfare support was easily obtained free money was commonly found and repeated (E. Briant et al., 2011; E. Briant et al., 2013). This does not reflect my experience or the experience of the disabled people who I feature here. A report by Burgess entitled "Assessing the Assessors" concluded the following of the Work Capability Assessment:

> The WCA is abusive. It causes harm and damages health, especially mental health. The WCA is disrespectful; it treats people as unreliable, feckless or fraudulent. WCA reports are woefully inaccurate, they are influenced, not by objective judgements, but by a system that wants to save money and meet targets. The WCA process is callous and inhumane. Instead of respecting disabled people's need for accessibility the WCA seems prejudiced against disabled people. The WCA seems to promote unprofessional practice. The WCA seems designed to cause, hardship and poverty.
>
> (Burgess et al., 2014, p. 4)

They are invasive in ways many people don't understand or too easily dismiss. Repeated deficit-based assessments have caused me permanent psychological damage. The example of "Nicola" from Akers' (2016) study, entitled "How Does it Feel to be Assessed" articulates one aspect of my experience:

> Everybody just deals with it, you just carry on around and nobody makes a fuss. So that's how I've looked at it. I've always s looked on the positive side, I can't do that, but I can do that. Whereas just filling this form, I just found horrendous. It made me face what I couldn't do… But as I say, it made me, look at what I couldn't do and have to write it down. It was so much. No I can't do this, no I can't do that, well yes I can do that, but have to do it this way or I have to alter the way I do it in my house, because my house has everything planned how I need it… But what… when I came to fill in this new form... I mean it's so invasive... so… really makes you look into what you can do and what you can't do.
>
> (2016, p. 12)

I know from experience that state financial support is far from "free" and is in fact highly conditional and restrictive – this is particularly true of ESA. Much of the harm and damaged caused to myself and other disabled people goes unacknowledged because our injuries are not physical.

Conclusion

There is perhaps not a clearer indication of the hatred the Conservative government has for disabled people than the combination of their rhetoric, such as that forwarded by Davies and Hammond, and their welfare reform policy, forwarded under austerity. Rhetoric informs policy, policy informs rhetoric. The proliferation of such rhetoric in the media is a factor in increased hostility towards disabled people. As part of their concluding remarks in their research Briant, Watson, and Philo (2013) draw a direct link between rhetoric, policy, and a rise in hostility towards disabled people. They note that this moral panic is affecting both perceptions of disabled people, and disabled people's perceptions of themselves. Adding, that disabled people feel dually threatened by changes to their benefits and changes in reporting. They affirm that the use of pejorative terms coupled with misrepresenting the levels of fraud risks raising already high levels of hostility targeted towards disabled people (Equality and Human Rights Commission, 2011). Importantly, they observe that increased media coverage is consciously linked to the forwarding of a particular political policy and the production of mass concern about fraud and misclaiming stems from deliberate political intervention. At a personal level, I am encouraged by research which acknowledges the conscious, intentional nature of rhetoric and policy, particularly in an academic context. Furthermore, in my daily life I encounter too many people prepared to assume the government is ignorant of the impacts of their policies on people, and as someone whose own life has been detrimentally affected by austerity from a number of perspectives, this is both a source of frustration and something I find hard to believe. I chose in this piece to focus on my own and others experiences of welfare because the rhetoric I have discussed provides an emotional justification for cuts to welfare.

Burch too acknowledges the negative impact of such coverage reflecting that it is likely to impact the relationship between disabled and nondisabled people:

> These representations are detrimental, as the portrayal of disabled people as a financial drain on society and a personal burden to "taxpayers" is likely to impact the relationship between disabled and nondisabled people.
>
> (2018, p. 393)

The Committee on the Rights of Persons with Disabilities (CRPD) has suggested that such political rhetoric proliferated through mass media campaigns may have contributed to a rise in disability hate crime (United Nations Committee on the Rights of Persons with Disabilities, 2016, p. 14). I have experienced disability hate crime myself and that experience formed part of my rationale for writing this piece, and in line with the CRPD's assertion that such rhetoric may have contributed to a rise in disability hate crime, I find it difficult to see how such rhetoric has not been a factor in the rise at some level.

References

Aiden, H. S., & McCarthy, A. (2014). *Current attitudes towards disabled people*. London: Scope.

Akers, C. (2016). *How does it feel to be assessed?* Sheffield: Centre for Welfare Reform.

Briant, E., Watson, N., & Philo, G. (2011). *Bad news for disabled people: How the newspapers are reporting disability*. Glasgow: Strathclyde Centre for Disability Research and Glasgow Media Unit, University of Glasgow

Briant, E., Watson, N., & Philo, G. (2013). Reporting disability in the age of austerity: the changing face of media representation of disability and disabled people in the United Kingdom and the creation of new 'folk devils'. *Disability & Society*, *28*(6), 874–889. doi:10.1080/09687599.2013.813837

Burch, L. (2018). 'You are a parasite on the productive classes': Online disablist hate speech in austere times. *Disability & Society*, *33*(3), 392–415.

Burgess, R., Duffy, S., Dilworth, N., Bence, J., Blackburn, W., & Thomas, M. (2014). *Assessing the assessors–The work capability assessment's culture of contempt*. Sheffield: Centre for Welfare Reform.

Cross, M. (2013). Demonised, impoverished and now forced into isolation: The fate of disabled people under austerity. *Disability & Society*, *28*(5), 719–723.

Deal, M. (2007). Aversive disablism: Subtle prejudice toward disabled people. *Disability & Society*, *22*(1), 93–107.

Duffy, S. (2014). *Counting the cuts: What the government doesn't want the public to know*. Sheffield: Centre for Welfare Reform.

Equality and Human Rights Commission. (2011). *Hidden in plain sight: Inquiry into disability-related harassment*. London: EHRC.

Equality and Human Rights Commission. (2017). *Being disabled in Britain: A journey less equal*. London: EHRC.

Garthwaite, K. (2011). 'The language of shirkers and scroungers?' Talking about illness, disability and coalition welfare reform. *Disability & Society*, *26*(3), 369–372. doi:10.1080/09687599.2011.560420

Grover, C., & Piggott, L. (2007). Social security, employment and incapacity benefit: Critical reflections on a new deal for welfare. *Disability & Society*, *22*(7), 733–746.

Kitchin, R. (1988). 'Out of Place', 'Knowing one's Place': Space, power and the exclusion of disabled people. *Disability & Society*, *13*(3), 343–356.

Mendoza, K. A. (2015). *Austerity: The demolition of the welfare state and the rise of the zombie economy*. Oxford: New Internationalist.

Mercer, G. (2002). Emancipatory disability research. In C. Barnes, M. Oliver & L. Barton (Eds.), *Disability studies today* (pp. 228–249). Cambridge: Polity Press.

Muscular Dystrophy Campaign. (2010). *Right to work: The Trailblazers' employment report*. Retrieved from www.mdctrailblazers.org/assets/0000/4485/Trailblazers_Right_to_work_webcopy.pdf

O'Hara, M. (2015). *Austerity bites: A journey to the sharp end of cuts in the UK*. Bristol: Policy Press.

Salzman, P. C. (2002). On reflexivity. *American Anthropologist*, *104*(3), 805–813.

Slawson, N. (2017). *Philip Hammond causes storm with remarks about disabled workers*. Retrieved from https://www.theguardian.com/politics/2017/dec/07/philip-hammond-causes-storm-with-remarks-about-disabled-workers

Stanley, L., & Wise, S. (1993). *Breaking out again: Feminist ontology and epistemology*. London: Routledge.

Stratton, A. (2011, 17 June). *Tory MP Philip Davies: Disabled people could work for less pay*. Retrieved from https://www.theguardian.com/society/2011/jun/17/tory-philip-davies-disabled-people-work

Taylor-Gooby, P., & Stoker, G. (2011). The coalition programme: A new vision for Britain or politics as usual? *The Political Quarterly*, *82*(1), 4–15.

United Nations Committee on the Rights of Persons with Disabilities. (2016). *Inquiry concerning the United Kingdom of Great Britain and Northern Ireland Carried out by the Committee under Article 6 of the Optional Protocol to the Convention*. Geneva: UNCRPD.

Wood, C. (2013, 27 March). *Destination unknown*: April 2013. Retrieved from www.demos.co.uk/blog/destinationunknownapril2013

12 Hate speech by carers

Exploring an Australian case

Mark Sherry and Solomon Amoatey

In September 2018, the Australian Broadcasting Commission (ABC) published an audio recording of the apparent beating and verbal abuse of a 14-year-old autistic boy by the carers employed to assist him. There are a number of sounds that indicate the boy is bashed by the carers, and this case would likely have been prosecuted as a disability hate crime in many jurisdictions. However, it was not – indeed, not a single charge was laid against the carers. That seems a profound injustice. This chapter will largely focus on the disablist hate speech which occurred in the incident (even though the absence of disability hate speech laws in Australia meant that this also was not prosecuted). By focusing specifically on the disablist hate speech which occurred in this particular case, the chapter will demonstrate the connections between disability hate speech, danger, harm, and pain. It will also suggest that it is necessary to move beyond individual-level responses, and to consider the broader sociopolitical context of disablism (and systemic failures in the service and criminal justice systems) when discussing such incidents. It will highlight the importance of the background of Australian disability policy in understanding such incidents.

Like many types of abuse, verbal aggression that demonstrates disability hatred is a foreboding sign of physical aggression. The assaults on the autistic teen were preceded by a threat – "I'm gonna bash you." This threat undoubtedly provoked fear in the victim, who makes sounds which may represent the word "no" (although his profound communication makes his limited verbal utterances difficult to understand). One of the two carers on the video states, "I just wanna f***ing beat these kids without any risk." This is an important element of the incident, both because it demonstrates the awareness of the carer that there are potential punishments for such acts (which he calls "risks"), but also because it further underlines the links between (and impact of) hateful words and threatening intentions.

Disabled people are often blamed when they are the victims of physical assault, disability hate crime, or disablist hate speech (Shakespeare, 2012). In the case under discussion, the carers began by blaming the victim for the assault and their verbal abuse. At the same time, they use a racist slur alongside this victim-blaming. The carer states: "Stupid f***, stop hitting yourself… you f***ing wog." These terms – the disablist reference to being "stupid," the swearing, the blaming of the victim for the violence, and the racial slur via the use of the word "wog" – are indeed gross and offensive. The vitriol which was contained in the hate speech aimed at this autistic teen is tangible. Being described as a "wog," in Australia, is a racist term which developed to refer to a person who is Italian, Greek, or Lebanese; it involves an experience of Otherness that separated these people from other Australians (Sala, Dandy, & Rapley, 2010; Tsolidis & Pollard, 2009). These so-called "carers" did not verbally take responsibility for the attack; instead, they blamed the victim (adding another layer of injury) and told him to "stop hitting yourself."

Officially, there are safeguards built into the disability system in Australia to prevent such violence and to respond promptly and seriously to such incidents. But unofficially, as this case demonstrates, such policies can mean very little in practice. The perpetrators of this disablist hate speech and assault were fired and reported to the police, but they were not charged with any crimes. Being fired from the agency is a very light punishment when one considers the magnitude of the attack on the disabled victim. They were able to register to work with disabled people in other states and in fact became carers in the aged care system, leaving serious concerns over the fate of their other clients in future. This is particularly relevant when one considers the link between advanced age and disability and the over-representation of disabled people in nursing homes in Australia, which of disability advocates have opposed for decades (Sherry, 2003, 2006).

While it is true that disability hate speech is often accompanied by assault and other crimes, it has been suggested that low-level insults are perhaps a more frequent element of disablist hate crimes (Tyson & Hall, 2015). This is an important insight which should not be forgotten in discussing such crimes – there is a continuum of victimization. Perry (2009) points to a "pyramid of hate," but it is also important to remember that one incident can contain multiple levels of victimization. Although this case was never officially prosecuted, it will be suggested in this chapter that it involved both disablist hate speech and a violent disability hate crime (assault). The reason for regarding these acts as disablist crimes (even though there are no disability hate crime laws in Australia) is that Australia is a signatory to the Convention on the Rights of Disabled Persons and the vast majority of international laws would identify such acts as criminal violations of human rights. Although disablist hate speech often occurs in isolation, it is important to also note that there are clear links between hate speech and violent victimization in some cases. In such circumstances, disablist prejudices are expressed in the commission of more violent acts (Sherry, 2010).

The language used to describe verbal attacks on disabled people is contested and contextual. For instance, people may choose to describe it as "bullying," "emotional abuse," "verbal abuse," "harassment," or "disablist hate speech." For instance, Novin, Brokhof, and Rieffe (2018, p. 1) use the term "bullying" to describe the process where "children are repeatedly and intentionally attacked, humiliated and/or excluded by an individual or group." However, they do not explore the nature of the relationship between disability and bullying, leaving open the possibility that some forms of "bullying" are specifically disablist, with unique disability-related characteristics. For this reason, the term "disablist hate" has been used in other studies (Burch, 2018; Chakraborti, Garland, & Hardy, 2014; Emerson & Roulstone, 2014; Roulstone, Thomas, & Balderston, 2011; Taylor, 2017). The key point being emphasized by these other studies is that when verbal abuse is directed specifically around disability, it is disability hate speech. It is clear that such verbal aggression and disability hate speech leaves psychological scars. These scars are particularly hard to identify and respond to effectively when the person is minimally verbal or nonspeaking (Murphy, O'Callaghan, & Clare, 2007), such as the victim in the case under discussion in this chapter.

There are clear connections between the hate speech evident in the case under discussion and the broader concept of verbal abuse, defined by Mouton et al. (2010, p. 206) as "the infliction of mental anguish through yelling, screaming, threatening, humiliating, infantilizing, or provoking intentional fear" (p.206). The literature on disability and abuse clearly demonstrates that victims of verbal and emotional abuse frequently experience severe anxiety, sleeplessness, post-traumatic stress disorder, damage to their self-esteem, feelings of powerlessness, insomnia, self-injurious behaviours, and problems with anger (Chatzitheochari, Parsons, & Platt, 2014; Mepham, 2010; Murphy et al., 2007). Studies of children with autism, the impairment of the victim in this case, report higher rates of verbal abuse and bullying than other children (Bitsika & Sharpley, 2014; Bitsika, Sharpley, & Bell, 2013; Symes & Humphrey, 2010). Novin, Brokhof, and Rieffe (2018) indicate that boys with autism are between three and four times more likely to experience bullying and victimization than other boys.

Unfortunately, Australian literature on safeguarding disabled people often ignores the specific situation of those who are nonverbal or minimally verbal, such as the victim in this case (for instance, Ottmann, McVilly, & Maragoudaki, 2016). These victims cannot advocate for themselves, given their combination of speech and cognitive impairments. Such impairments may give carers more power (and more confidence) in committing acts of abuse, hate speech, and hate crimes. Disabled children are particularly at risk, as are those with high support needs with regard to personal care and those who are profoundly intellectually disabled (Hassouneh-Phillips, 2005; Kamavarapu, Ferriter, Morton, & Völlm, 2017; Kendall-Tackett, Lyon, Taliaferro, & Little, 2005). Direct care staff with no qualifications (who are the majority of workers in institutional settings) are more likely than others to engage in abusive behaviours (Kamavarapu et al., 2017).

Professionals and service providers in the disability area have ethical and legal obligations to report abuse. The carers in the case under discussion in this chapter were clearly aware of the risk that others would report them. After the victim's injuries became obvious, they spoke about being "careful" about what they said and plotted to find explanations for his cuts and bruises. They realized the need to explain the victim's injuries and together fabricated an excuse. One carer said, "We'll just say he slipped over. If he did, f*** I hope I didn't graze bra." This explanation was endorsed by the other carer, who commented, "We'll say he slipped. Slipped on that. That looks grazed." This excuse – that the victim fell – is a direct example of the degree to which perpetrators of violent abuse will engage in victim blaming. It also invokes images of frail disabled people, liable to falls, reinforcing an image of vulnerability commonly that attributes blame for any misfortune to the impairments of the victim. The carers also blamed the victim for the cut on his nose, which they describe as a "graze." One comments, "We'll just say he's f***ing rubbing his nose on the blanket it must have been itchy," to which the other replied, "Yeah, yeah, that's what we'll say. That's it."

Satisfied with this lie, one of them comments, "Can't make a full story, just have to make sense." This comment explains a lot about the "vulnerability" of nonspeaking or minimally communicative disabled people to abuse, which can be covered up by carers working in collaboration. A culture of abuse has been noted before as an element of institutional life (Sherry, 2010); this scenario perfectly illustrates such practices. But this question of "vulnerability" deserves significant exploration. "Vulnerability" is a major theme in the literature about disablist hate crime and hate speech. Many disability studies scholars believe that it is a mistake to frame such crimes in terms of "vulnerability" since the term seems to connect the embodiment of disabled people to their crime victimization. Roulstone, Thomas, and Balderston (2011) argue that the trope of vulnerability is attached to crimes against disabled people and is placed on the other end of a continuum of offender motivation, opposite to hate.

On the other hand, Burghardt (2013) believes that a more complicated notion of vulnerability might emerge by acknowledging the phenomenology of impairment as well as acknowledging the broader social constructions highlighted by other scholars. (In some ways, Burghardt's argument is similar to Thomas' (2007, p. 88) recognition of the reality of the effects of impairment(s) on the activities of everyday life: "being an adult with an impairment(s) may mean that one has a greater than average need for assistance with daily tasks such as dressing, washing, cooking and travelling to the shops.") This need for assistance is sometimes exploited by abusive carers or family members. It can be, and often is, covered up or denied by abusers (and when the disabled person is communicative, they are often gaslighted).

The widespread attribution of virtuous characteristics to carers (such as kindness and altruism) is an important reason why they are not automatically assumed to engage in hate speech. However, as the case under discussion demonstrates, disabled people can certainly be hated and despised, and even carers can display such hostility. These prejudices may escalate to criminal acts. Many studies confirm that abuse and other forms of victimization by carers (particularly in institutions) is alarmingly common (Hutchison & Stenfert Kroese, 2015; Kamavarapu et al., 2017; McFarlane et al., 2001; Mirfin-Veitch & Conder, 2017).

But the case being discussed in this chapter also suggests that the bodily or cognitive impairments of their client (including his inability to report the crime) emboldened the perpetrators. Impairment experiences effect both the need for assistance and the capacity to resist or report abuse – this assault occurred in the context of changing the clothes of the disabled person. It starts with the carer commanding the disabled victim to "Get your pants off." This conversation moves immediately into disability hate speech: the disabled person is called a "spac" (short for "spastic") within seconds. The carer states, "Get undressed you stupid spac. Put your pants on." The disabled victim fails to comply immediately, prompting the carer to comment, "It's pretty sad that you are not listening." The second carer then tells the first to "Pull him up, pull him up" as he also orders the disabled person to "Stand up!"

Having a close relationship to the perpetrator of a hate crime (or hate speech) is sometimes regarded as a unique element of disability hate crimes, as opposed to other hate-motivated incidents (Chakraborti & Garland, 2009). This situation applies to these acts – these carers were in a trusted and powerful position, so close to the disabled person that they were involved in feeding, dressing, helping the person out of bed, and other intimate activities. The use of hate speech by carers and family members occurs because of the wider context of disablist attitudes and practices, from which they are not immune. Disablism promotes an image of disabled people as passive and dependent and fails to grasp the interdependency of such relationships (Thomas, 1999). In terms of living in nursing homes, such disablism may be reinforced by institutional cultures of neglect/abuse, impersonal/bureaucratic responses to human needs, and the lack of safeguards and advocacy for disabled people.

Many people in the care system, and particularly in nursing homes and group homes, are socially isolated. This isolation is a risk factor for abuse because it can embolden perpetrators when they feel no one will notice or report their behaviour. As well, specific cultural stereotypes and prejudices about cognitive impairment place disabled people like this victim at heightened risk of abuse (Sherry & Neller, 2016). Both historically and today, people with cognitive impairments face insulting and degrading slurs including labels such as "mentally defective," "feeble-minded," "idiots", "morons," "imbeciles," and "retards" (Eisenberg, Glueckauf, & Zaretsky, 1999; Siperstein, Pociask, & Collins, 2010; Walmsley, 2000). The specific insults associated with intellectual disability change from time to time, from place to place, and from culture to culture, but it is clear that there have been widespread forms of prejudice and stigma associated with cognitive impairments in many different countries and across many different time periods (Adnams, 2010; Chen & Shu, 2012; Kavanagh et al., 2014; Njenga, 2009; Scior, Addai-Davis, Kenyon, & Sheridan, 2013).

Some research seems to suggest that people with cognitive impairments experience higher rates of stigma and prejudice than many other disabled people. (For more on the relationship between stigma and hate speech, see the chapter by Mostert in this volume). This disparity between the stigma experienced by different impairment groups is often considered a part of a hierarchy of disability: people with impairments related to the mind are more likely to experience negative social reactions, and social distancing by others, than those with physical impairments (Werner, 2015). For instance, one study asked people what they would do if a large group of people with severe cognitive impairments moved next door to them, and large numbers of people indicated that they would move residences (Van Alphen, Dijker, Bos, Van den Borne, & Curfs, 2012). Two of the factors which influence such decisions are the stigma associated with "severe" impairments and the perceived threat of a large number of people with cognitive impairments. Other homeowners regarded people with intellectual disabilities as "outsiders" and expressed both anxiety and rage over the possibility of them entering the neighbourhood. Such resistance to community integration is sometimes attributed to low levels of awareness in the community about intellectual impairment (Scior, 2011).

One of the most influential studies of the prejudices surrounding disability (in particular intellectual disability) was a report conducted on behalf of the US President's Committee on Mental Retardation in 1969 (Wolfensberger, 1969). This study highlighted the nature of the stigma experienced by people with intellectual disabilities, who were unfortunately called "retardates" in the report. (Today, the word "retard" is so offensive and so full of hate that disability organizations refuse to use it and call it "the r word.") Despite this outdated language, this report identified a number of negative stereotypes associated with the stigma attributed to people with intellectual disabilities. It recorded stigma based on the following stereotypes: they are sick, subhuman, a menace, an object of pity, a burden of charity, and/or they are the "Holy innocent." Each of these stereotypes Others disabled people and separates them from the rest of the population. But it is too simple to merely attribute disablist behaviours and speech simply to a series of stereotypes. To fully understand the phenomenon of disability hate speech and hate crime, one must look at the wider sociopolitical context in which these acts occur. Two aspects of this wider context which are relevant to the case under discussion in this chapter are the level of institutional abuse in Australia and the lack of sufficient individual and systemic advocacy.

The sociopolitical context of disablism in Australia

There is a long history of testimony, and disability advocacy, around the abuse of disabled people in Australia. One of the most significant records of such abuse can be found in the Royal Commission into Institutional Abuse which was conducted from 2013 to 2017 (Royal Commission into Institutional Responses to Child Sexual Assault, 2017). The Royal Commission received 161 submissions regarding disability abuse, as well as additional information from 35 sources. The limitation of the Royal Commission was that it only looked at institutional abuse, and in particular child abuse. Such terms of reference excluded the vast majority of disabled people (who live in the community rather than residential institutions such as nursing homes) and also meant that the alarming rates of abuse experienced by disabled adults was not even considered. Nevertheless, it heard reports of significant disability abuse in these institutional settings.

The Royal Commission into Institutional Responses to Child Sexual Assault (2017, p. 75) stated:

> Children with disability have been at significantly greater risk of sexual abuse compared to the general population... vulnerability is heightened if society regards the child with disability as "different", so that the child is treated as

> the "other", excluded from mainstream settings, and discriminated against... Due to increased contact with health, education and other support services, and dependency on professionals, children with disability have more often been in high-risk institutional settings. Depending on their individual needs, children with disability may spend more time in institutional settings than children without disability, and more time alone with unknown adults at a younger age than other children. Children with intellectual disability, communication impairments, behaviour difficulties and sensory disability have been found to be particularly at risk of all forms of abuse.

The Royal Commission also concluded that there were additional challenges for disabled children (and adults) who reported sexual abuse, including blaming their abuse on their impairment, not being regarded as a credible source of information, being regarded as incapable of experiencing harm (minimizing their experience of distress and suffering from such abuse), and parents not being informed about their child's sexual abuse. Additionally, service organizations around child sexual abuse were often unskilled in dealing with the specifics of disability abuse, and the needs of disabled clients. On multiple levels, these disabled children were failed. Disability services were unskilled in dealing with sexual assault and sexual assault services were unskilled at dealing with disability issues.

Unfortunately, the Royal Commission tended to rely on a rather simplistic embodied notion of "vulnerability" to describe the victimization of disabled children. This approach meant that it did not acknowledge (let alone explore) disablist prejudices of offenders and did not specifically situate disabled people's victimization in the context of multiple systemic failures of social welfare support. Soldatic and Pini (2009) argue that federal disability policies in Australia were historically shaped by the politics of "disgust" – where disability was soaked in shame, clouded in prejudice, and measured in terms of the "deservingness" of disabled people for disability support. The need to challenge such a neoliberal agenda was certainly not considered by the Royal Commission into institutional abuse.

The Royal Commission into Institutional Responses to Child Sexual Abuse was of limited use in assessing the overall magnitude and nature of disability abuse in Australia. First, the incidence of impairment increases with age; most impairments are not congenital. The limited focus on children meant the abuse experienced by disabled people as adults was beyond the scope of the Inquiry. Second, the Royal Commission only looked at abuse in institutions, and not in the wider community, where disability abuse is also prevalent. Regardless, it was still an important record of the victimization of many disabled people.

Another major recognition of disability abuse was a previous Senate Inquiry into disability abuse, which concluded:

> Violence, abuse and neglect of people with disability is both widespread and takes many forms… the evidence presented from people with disability, their families and advocates, showed that a root cause of violence, abuse and

> neglect of people with disability begins with the de-valuing of people with disability. This de-valuing permeates the attitudes of individual disability workers, service delivery organisations and most disturbingly, government systems designed to protect the rights of individuals.
>
> (Senate Community Affairs References Committee, 2015, p. xxvi)

The Senate Inquiry heard many personal stories of abuse from disabled people, family members and advocates and it noted that some of these disabled people died as a result of violence or neglect. Often disabled people provided evidence in camera, both because of the intimate and personal nature of their testimonies and also because they feared retaliation for speaking out:

> Witnesses told of their fear of speaking out about abusers who had continued daily access to their homes as disability service workers. Evidence was also presented that showed a propensity for reports to service providers about violence and abuse to be ignored, swept under the carpet or treated as a "workplace issue" rather than a crime.
>
> (Senate Community Affairs References Committee, 2015, p. xxvi)

The Department of Social Services made a submission to the Senate Inquiry which provided statistics for the National Disability Abuse and Neglect Hotline from July 2012 to December 2014. Of the over 400 cases reported to this one source, the largest category (with 65) was psychological abuse, followed by physical neglect (60) and physical abuse (57) (Department of Social Services, 2015, p. 6). However, disability advocates indicated that these numbers were "the tip of the iceberg."

The Senate Inquiry not only recommended a specific Royal Commission into disability abuse, but also highlighted the need for the active involvement of disabled people and their allies. It recommended that the terms of reference for such a Royal Commission should "be determined in consultation with people with disability, their families and supporters, and disability organisations."

Unfortunately, the Federal Government's immediate response to this recommendation was to refuse to implement the recommendation for a Royal Commission. In response, Disabled People's Organisations Australia (which represents four national peak bodies: the National Ethnic Disability Alliance, First Peoples Disability Network, Women With Disabilities Australia and People With Disability Australia) submitted a petition demanding such a Royal Commission. Hundreds of community groups and academics from across Australia signed the petition to support this demand. The petition stated unambiguously, "Only a Royal Commission has the weight, the investigative powers, the time and resources to open the doors to the many "closed" institutions and residential environments, and expose Australia's shameful secret" (Disabled People's Organisations Australia, 2015).

Some of the points emphasized in the submissions from Disabled People's Organizations Australia are worth noting in this discussion of the sociopolitical context of disablism. They stressed that disabled people experience higher rates of abuse than nondisabled people, that disabled women experience higher rates of sexual abuse, that disabled children experience three times as much child abuse as nondisabled children, that abuse frequently happens in settings which are supposed to provide care, and that disabled people's experiences of criminal victimization are often dismissed because they are not regarded as reliable witnesses. The intersectional nature of disability abuse was also highlighted by these groups, and seemingly ignored by the government.

A more recent ABC *Four Corners* report called "Fighting the System" described the institutional and systemic barriers faced by disabled people and their families when abuse occurs. The program revealed disturbing stories of maltreatment and sexual and physical abuse, which was unpunished because the criminal justice system was unable to properly support disabled witnesses. A disability advocate told the program, "Parents should not be trusting service providers and they must do due diligence all the time, because the evidence is that it's very unsafe and there's a lot of risk" (ABC Four Corners, 2017). As this program highlighted, the response of both disability service providers and police to disablist victimization is often woefully inadequate.

A 2018 report by the New South Wales Ombudsman confirmed the systemic failure to address cases of disability victimization in community settings. The report indicates concern that abuse and neglect of disabled people was commonly reported, but there was no agency equipped to investigate noncriminal acts (such as the disability hate speech discussed in this chapter). It states that "there is no other agency that has the powers to investigate allegations that do not reach a criminal threshold, and that can play a lead role to marshal a coordinated interagency response to address the critical issues" (NSW Ombudsman, 2018). This report specifically considered 206 cases of alleged abuse and neglect and found people living in "atrocious conditions." It also found that victims were denied the supports they needed when they were isolated from the community. The Ombudsman concluded, "in my view, it is imperative that a comprehensive safeguarding approach for vulnerable adults is developed" (Foreword, NSW Ombudsman, 2018).

Major service providers have been exposed by disability whistleblowers, such as Karen Burgess' revelations that Australia's largest autism service provider, Autism Spectrum Australia, had ordered a coffin-like box to place agitated clients (Toscano & Donelly, 2015). This box was not used on clients because Burgess stopped it and reported it, but her own experiences highlighted the retaliation that whistleblowers experience – she was fired on the day her employer heard of the report to authorities. The Victorian Government has also ordered an investigation into another autism organization, Autism Plus, for ignoring the sexual abuse of disabled people in its group homes (Branley & Besser, 2017). Lifestyle Solutions, another major disability organization, is also under investigation for a number of deaths of disabled people in its care (Besser, Toft, McGregor, & Branley, 2017).

Clearly, there is a major need for widespread changes to the disability system that involve enhanced investigation of abuse, additional safeguards, systematic reform, increased advocacy and protection funding, and improved criminal justice responses.

Another important political concern is that Australian disability policy is dominated by the National Disability Insurance Scheme (NDIS), which provides individual funding for disabled people to arrange appropriate services and supports. Unfortunately, the NDIS was designed to frame disabled people as individual consumers and focused on neoliberal concerns such as "facilitation of choice" rather than a rights-based framework which focused on both community change as well as individual empowerment (Carling-Jenkins, 2014). In addition, and perhaps more importantly, there are two other major flaws with the NDIS: the vast majority of disabled people in Australia are excluded from it, and the funds allegedly designed for disabled people have not been spent. These unspent funds have been returned to the coffers of the Government, which has used the unspent funds to accrue a budget surplus, thereby reinforcing broader neoliberal policies, which themselves harm disabled people. For further discussion of the ways in which neoliberal policies harm disabled people, see Sherry (2014). The NDIS funds were allegedly designed to ensure that disabled people's rights were secured in Australia; it is an indictment on the Federal Government that these funds have not been used for this purpose. Instead, as this chapter has demonstrated, disabled people's rights are under attack.

Additionally, there is no guaranteed funding for disability advocacy through the NDIS, either at the systemic or individual level. This funding had previously been a safeguard for disabled people's rights (and freedom from abuse or support in reporting abuse). In New South Wales, the Premier announced an end to funding such advocacy, leading to a major campaign by disability advocates. It was successful to a degree – such funding is now guaranteed in that state until 2020 (Knaus, 2018). Similar concerns about the future of funding for disability advocacy have been voiced by disability advocates in other states.

Another important element of the Australian political context (particularly relevant to the case which has been the focus of this chapter) has been identified by Didi, Soldatic, Frohmader, and Dowse (2016, p. 166): Australia has no specific legal, administrative, or policy framework that addresses the protection, investigation, or prosecution of violence against disabled people, and women with disabilities are particularly harmed by these institutional and policy failures. When forms of violence that are unique to disabled women (such as sterilization or abuse in institutional settings) are ignored, Australia fails to meet the promise of human rights for disabled people. Moreover, when governments fail to address or prioritize such issues, they send wider messages that violent disablism is essentially tolerated at the highest levels.

Australia also lacks national disability hate speech and hate crime legislation. The first author was the keynote speaker at Australia's first national conference on disability hate crime, but the conference ended in somewhat disarray after complaints from government officials that it was politically unacceptable to use the word "hate" in relation to the victimization of disabled people (Sherry, 2003). Not only are disability hate crimes ignored, but the government also has not made any moves towards criminalizing disability hate speech, even though racist hate speech is included in national laws under the Racial Discrimination Act.

It would be remiss to conclude this chapter without recognizing that even though the case under discussion has involved a male disabled victim, disabled women in Australia are far more likely to experience abuse, harassment, and hate speech than men. The national representative body for disabled women in Australia, Women With Disabilities Australia (WWDA) has been an incredibly important organization in identifying this violence and abuse, responding to it in innovative ways, and advocating for more comprehensive policies. It has engaged in commendable advocacy, and developing/advocating for policies that are innovative, comprehensive, inclusive, and responsive to the needs of disabled Australian women. The following quote from one of the many reports written by WWDA (this time as a submission to the UN Special Rapporteur on violence against women, its causes and consequences in 2017) explains the magnitude of this problem:

> For more than two decades, women and girls with disability in Australia have consistently identified violence as the most urgent and unaddressed human rights issue they face. They have argued for national leadership and wide-ranging reforms in law, policy, programs and services to address the epidemic that is violence against them… The multiple forms and complex nature of violence perpetrated against women and girls with disability in Australia currently sit in a legislative, policy and service response vacuum. What this means in practice, is that many women and girls with disability in Australia are not afforded the same protections and responses as others, and violence against women and girls with disability – in all its forms – is allowed to flourish with impunity.
>
> (Women with Disabilities Australia, 2017)

Anyone interested in a more comprehensive picture of the entire spectrum of disability rights issues in Australia is strongly encouraged to read WWDA's publications. Their work is unparalleled anywhere in the world in terms of comprehensiveness, breadth, originality, and inclusion. Among other topics, WWDA has advocated on access to justice, ageing, citizenship and social inclusion, education, employment and income support, housing, health, information and communications technology, intersectionality, leadership, motherhood and parenting, sexuality, reproductive health and reproductive rights, sterilization, transport and travel, violence and abuse, and much more.

Conclusion

This chapter has discussed one case of disablist victimization which involved both assault and hate speech, but has focused primarily on the disablist hate speech involved in this case. It has demonstrated that such hate speech reflects much wider prejudices about disability, and that there are multiple layers of disability prejudice which need to be recognized in order to address these crimes. This multilayered problem demands serious responses on many levels: in the support for individual victims, in the funding of disability advocacy organizations, in government responses to the problem, in the criminal justice and social welfare systems, and in broader cultural attitudes towards disability.

The problem of disability hate speech demands many of the same responses as other forms of bias: developing education campaigns, promoting counter-narratives, providing adequate funding for appropriate victim support, and reforming the criminal justice and social welfare systems more generally. But it also demands a thorough challenge to widely held assumptions specifically about disability – the harms of disablism should not be underestimated. Disablism restricts the rights and freedoms of disabled people, shames and silences them, and results in the types of victimization discussed in this chapter. There is a need for specific disability-related supports as well, such as the provision of accessible and understandable information for people with cognitive impairments, challenging assumptions about disabled victims being nonreliable witnesses, and changing cultures of abuse that can infest disability service providers. The specific victimization of disabled women and girls need to be identified and addressed as well, and the chapter has noted the groundbreaking work of WWDA as a model for others.

The need for victim support in reporting carers is another lesson from the case under investigation (as well as the wider reports of disability abuse discussed in this chapter). Disabled people often depend on their abusers for assistance with the tasks of daily living. The fear of retaliation can be ameliorated somewhat if they experience more social inclusion (which would mean more people to whom who they could possibly report these crimes) and also more support from disability advocates. The lack of certainty around disability advocacy which has been discussed in this chapter is alarming when one considers its role in safeguarding disabled people. Moreover, when disabled people do report their experiences of abuse, they should be taken seriously. There should be serious consequences for offenders who engage in the type of abusive behaviours discussed in this chapter.

New and more effective ways to report disablist victimization is also necessary. While some international hate crime agencies provide telephone apps that make reporting easier, these are sadly lacking in Australia. Few disability agencies or agencies for victims of crime have even considered how such apps could be more accessible for disabled people. For those such as the autistic teen who was the victim discussed in this chapter, these apps are unsuitable given the extent of their profound intellectual and communication disabilities. This victim could not speak; he could not report the crime in any way. The scars on his body were the only way he personally communicated that something had happened to him. Fortunately, there was a recording of this incident, and there is a need for additional safeguards in disability institutions and group homes such as these recording systems. Sadly, many family members have found that recording all the events which happen in the room of their loved one is the only way they can identify abusive incidents and prevent their recurrence.

As the case discussed in this chapter demonstrates, disabled people often have pre-existing relationships with those who commit hate speech and hate crimes against them. These are not the "stranger crimes" which are often involved in other forms of hate; those who are closest to the disabled people (and indeed, those who perform intimate assistance to them) can be the perpetrators of such acts. That is not to imply that the majority of carers or family members are abusive, simply to note that there are a small number of people who engage in such acts. Disability hate speech needs to be included in hate crime legislation; while Australia includes racist hate speech in its national legislation, it fails to do so when it comes to disability. Every level of law enforcement needs to be aware of the targeted victimization involved in disablist hate speech and hate crimes, from street-level police to prosecutors and judges. If they fail to take these cases seriously, then victims will be left without justice and perpetrators will go unpunished.

The fact that the perpetrators of the disablist hate speech and hate crime in the case discussed in this chapter faced no sanctions from the criminal justice system is appalling. This autistic teenager undoubtedly suffered tremendous harm from his victimization and deserved better.

Postscript

Since this chapter was initially written, there has been an election in Australia and in the lead-up to that election, the Federal Government agreed to the demands for a Royal Commission into disability abuse. The evidence in this chapter was that such a Royal Commission is clearly needed, but events subsequent to the announcement of the Royal Commission are a reminder that there are no guarantees that such investigations will be effective, inclusive, comprehensive, and credible. One problem that has already emerged is that two of the people who were named as Royal Commissioners, John Ryan and Barbara Bennett, had previously been in leadership positions in organizations that are likely to be reported for abuse. Disability organizations have called on them to step down over these conflicts of interests and some disabled people have already said that they will not testify since they do not believe the Royal Commission is credible (Coggan, 2019). This is a travesty; so many years of advocacy have gone into making the Royal Commission a reality, and there are warning signs that it may not be as effective as it should have been. These developments are still happening as the final version of the chapter was submitted. It is too soon to tell what the results of this opposition by disability groups will be.

References

ABC Four Corners. (2017). *Fighting the system*. Australian Broadcasting Commission.

Adnams, C. M. (2010). Perspectives of intellectual disability in South Africa: Epidemiology, policy, services for children and adults. *Current Opinion in Psychiatry*, *23*(5), 436–440.

Besser, L., Toft, K., McGregor, J., & Branley, A. (2017, 27 March, 3:18 am). *Top disability services provider lifestyle solutions investigated over series of deaths*. Retrieved from https://www.abc.net.au/news/2017-03-27/disability-service-provider-investigated-over-deaths/8388050

Bitsika, V., & Sharpley, C. F. (2014). Understanding, experiences, and reactions to bullying experiences in boys with an autism spectrum disorder. *Journal of Developmental and Physical Disabilities*, *26*(6), 747–761.

Bitsika, V., Sharpley, C. F., & Bell, R. (2013). The buffering effect of resilience upon stress, anxiety and depression in parents of a child with an autism spectrum disorder. *Journal of Developmental and Physical Disabilities*, *25*(5), 533–543.

Branley, A., & Besser, L. (2017, 24 September, 11:23 pm). *Disability services provider Autism Plus to be reviewed over sexual assault claims, Victorian Government says*. Retrieved from https://www.abc.net.au/news/2017-03-28/disability-service-autism-plus-faces-sexual-assault-claim-review/8393132

Burch, L. (2018). "You are a parasite on the productive classes": Online disablist hate speech in austere times. *Disability & Society*, *33*(3), 392–415.

Burghardt, M. (2013). Common frailty, constructed oppression: Tensions and debates on the subject of vulnerability. *Disability & Society*, *28*(4), 556–568.

Carling-Jenkins, R. (2014). *Disability and social movements: Learning from Australian experiences*. Surrey: Ashgate Publishing Group.

Chakraborti, N., & Garland, J. (2009). *Hate crime: Impact, causes and responses*. Thousand Oaks, CA: Sage Publications.

Chakraborti, N., Garland, J., & Hardy, S. J. (2014). *The Leicester hate crime project*: Briefing Papers, No. 1: *Disablist hate crime*. Leicester: University of Leicester.

Chatzitheochari, S., Parsons, S., & Platt, L. (2014). *Working paper: Bullying experiences among disabled children and young people in England: Evidence from two longitudinal studies*. London: Department of Quantitative Social Science, Institute of Education, University of London.

Chen, C. H., & Shu, B. C. (2012). The process of perceiving stigmatization: Perspectives from Taiwanese young people with intellectual disability. *Journal of Applied Research in Intellectual Disabilities*, *25*(3), 240–251.

Coggan, M. (2019, 8 April, 4:47 pm). *Disability groups call for conflicting commissioners to step down*. Retrieved from https://probonoaustralia.com.au/news/2019/04/disability-groups-call-for-conflicting-commissioners-to-step-down/

Department of Social Services. (2015). *Submission to Senate inquiry into violence, abuse and neglect against people with disability in institutional and residential settings, including the gender and age related dimensions, and the particular situation of Aboriginal and Torres Strait Islander people with disability, and culturally and linguistically diverse people with disability*. Canberra, ACT: Australian Cross Disability Alliance.

Didi, A., Soldatic, K., Frohmader, C., & Dowse, L. (2016). Violence against women with disabilities: Is Australia meeting its human rights obligations? *Australian Journal of Human Rights*, *22*(1), 159–177.

Disabled People's Organisations Australia. (2015). *Royal commission now*. Retrieved from https://endtheviolence.good.do/royalcommissionnow/

Eisenberg, M. G., Glueckauf, R. L., & Zaretsky, H. H. (1999). *Medical aspects of disability: A handbook for the rehabilitation professional*. New York: Springer Publishing Company.

Emerson, E., & Roulstone, A. (2014). Developing an evidence base for violent and disablist hate crime in Britain: Findings from the life opportunities survey. *Journal of Interpersonal Violence*, *29*(17), 3086–3104.

Hassouneh-Phillips, D. (2005). Understanding abuse of women with physical disabilities: An overview of the abuse pathways model. *Advances in Nursing Science*, *28*(1), 70–80.

Hutchison, A., & Stenfert Kroese, B. (2015). A review of literature exploring the possible causes of abuse and neglect in adult residential care. *The Journal of Adult Protection, 17*(4), 216–233.

Kamavarapu, Y. S., Ferriter, M., Morton, S., & Völlm, B. (2017). Institutional abuse – Characteristics of victims, perpetrators and organsations: A systematic review. *European Psychiatry, 40*, 45–54.

Kavanagh, A. M., Krnjacki, L., Aitken, Z., LaMontagne, A. D., Beer, A., Baker, E., & Bentley, R. (2014). Intersections between disability, type of impairment, gender and socio-economic disadvantage in a nationally representative sample of 33,101 working-aged Australians. *Disability and Health Journal, 8*, 191–199.

Kendall-Tackett, K., Lyon, T., Taliaferro, G., & Little, L. (2005). Why child maltreatment researchers should include children's disability status in their maltreatment studies. *Child Abuse & Neglect, 29*(2), 147–151.

Knaus, C. (2018, 5 April 21.33 EDT). *NDIS: Gladys Berejiklian U-turns on plan to cut funding to disability groups*. Retrieved from https://www.theguardian.com/australia-news/2018/apr/06/ndis-gladys-berejiklian-backflips-on-plan-to-cut-funding-to-disability-groups

McFarlane, J., Hughes, R. B., Nosek, M. A., Groff, J. Y., Swedlend, N., & Mullen, P. D. (2001). Abuse Assessment Screen-Disability (AAS-D): Measuring frequency, type, and perpetrator of abuse toward women with physical disabilities. *Journal of Women's Health & Gender-Based Medicine, 10*(9), 861–866.

Mepham, S. (2010). Disabled children: The right to feel safe. *Child Care in Practice, 16*(1), 19–34.

Mirfin-Veitch, B., & Conder, J. (2017). "*Institutions are places of abuse*": *The experiences of disabled children and adults in State care between 1950–1992*. Dunedin: The Donald Beasley Institute.

Mouton, C. P., Rodabough, R. J., Rovi, S. L., Brzyski, R. G., & Katerndahl, D. A. (2010). Psychosocial effects of physical and verbal abuse in postmenopausal women. *The Annals of Family Medicine, 8*(3), 206–213.

Murphy, G. H., O'Callaghan, A. C., & Clare, I. C. (2007). The impact of alleged abuse on behaviour in adults with severe intellectual disabilities. *Journal of Intellectual Disability Research, 51*(10), 741–749.

Njenga, F. (2009). Perspectives of intellectual disability in Africa: Epidemiology and policy services for children and adults. *Current Opinion in Psychiatry, 22*(5), 457–461.

Novin, S., Broekhof, E., & Rieffe, C. (2018). Bidirectional relationships between bullying, victimization and emotion experience in boys with and without autism. *Autism*, 23, 796–800. doi:10.1177/1362361318787446.

NSW Ombudsman. (2018). *Abuse and neglect of vulnerable adults in NSW – The need for action*. Sydney, NSW: NSW Ombudsman.

Ottmann, G., McVilly, K., & Maragoudaki, M. (2016). "I walk from trouble": Exploring safeguards with adults with intellectual disabilities – An Australian qualitative study. *Disability & Society, 31*(1), 47–63.

Perry, B. (2009). *Hate crimes*. London: Praeger.

Roulstone, A., Thomas, P., & Balderston, S. (2011). Between hate and vulnerability: Unpacking the British criminal justice system's construction of disablist hate crime. *Disability & Society, 26*(3), 351–364.

Royal Commission into Institutional Responses to Child Sexual Assault. (2017). *Final report: Volume 01. Our inquiry*. Canberra, ACT: Commonwealth of Australia.

Sala, E., Dandy, J., & Rapley, M. (2010). "Real Italians and wogs": The discursive construction of Italian identity among first generation Italian immigrants in Western Australia. *Journal of Community & Applied Social Psychology, 20*(2), 110–124.

Scior, K. (2011). Public awareness, attitudes and beliefs regarding intellectual disability: A systematic review. *Research in Developmental Disabilities, 32*(6), 2164–2182.

Scior, K., Addai-Davis, J., Kenyon, M., & Sheridan, J. (2013). Stigma, public awareness about intellectual disability and attitudes to inclusion among different ethnic groups. *Journal of Intellectual Disability Research, 57*(11), 1014–1026.

Senate Community Affairs References Committee. (2015). *Violence, abuse and neglect against people with disability in institutional and residential settings, including the gender and age related dimensions, and the particular situation of Aboriginal and Torres Strait Islander people with disability, and culturally and linguistically diverse people with disability*. Canberra, ACT: Senate Community Affairs References Committee.

Shakespeare, T. (2012). Blaming the victim: Disability hate crime. *The Lancet, 380*(9845), 878.

Sherry, M. (2003). *Don't ask, tell or respond: Silent acceptance of disability hate crimes*. North Bay, ON: Disabled Women's Network Ontario.

Sherry, M. (2006). *If I only had a brain: Deconstructing brain injury*. London: Routledge.

Sherry, M. (2010). *Disability hate crimes: Does anyone really hate disabled people?* Surrey: Ashgate.

Sherry, M. (2014). The promise of human rights for disabled people and the reality of neoliberalism. In M. Gill & C. Schlund-Vials (Eds.), *Disability, human rights and humanitarianism* (pp. 15–26). Surrey: Ashgate Publishing.

Sherry, M., & Neller, A. (2016). Intellectual disability, stigma, and hate crimes. In K. Scior & S. Werner (Eds.), *Intellectual disability and stigma: Stepping out from the margins* (pp. 111–126). London: Palgrave Macmillan.

Siperstein, G. N., Pociask, S. E., & Collins, M. A. (2010). Sticks, Stones, and stigma: A study of students' use of the derogatory term "Retard". *Intellectual and Developmental Disabilities, 48*(2), 126–134.

Soldatic, K., & Pini, B. (2009). The three Ds of welfare reform: Disability, disgust and deservingness. *Australian Journal of Human Rights, 15*(1), 77–95.

Symes, W., & Humphrey, N. (2010). Peer-group indicators of social inclusion among pupils with autistic spectrum disorders (ASD) in mainstream secondary schools: A comparative study. *School Psychology International, 31*(5), 478–494.

Taylor, S. (2017). The challenges of disablist hate crime. In A. Haynes, J. Schweppe & S. Taylor (Eds.), *Critical perspectives on hate crime* (pp. 209–232). London: Palgrave Macmillan.

Thomas, C. (1999). *Female forms: Experiencing and understanding disability*. Buckingham: Open University Press.

Thomas, C. (2007). *Sociologies of disability and illness*. New York: Palgrave-MacMillan.

Toscano, N., & Donelly, B. (2015, October 4, 9:43 pm). *Wooden box built to "calm" autistic students at day centre*. Retrieved from https://www.theage.com.au/national/victoria/wooden-box-built-to-lock-up-autistic-people-20151004-gk0uzo.html

Tsolidis, G., & Pollard, V. (2009). Being a "wog" in Melbourne—Young people's self-fashioning through discourses of racism. *Discourse: Studies in the Cultural Politics of Education, 30*(4), 427–442.

Tyson, J., & Hall, N. (2015). Perpetrators of disability hate crime. In R. Shah & P. Giannasi (Eds.), *Tackling disability discrimination and disability hate crime: A multidisciplinary guide* (pp. 69–89). London: Jessica Kingsley Publishers.

Van Alphen, L. M., Dijker, A. J., Bos, A. E., Van den Borne, B., & Curfs, L. M. (2012). The influence of group size and stigma severity on social acceptance: The case of people with intellectual disability moving into neighborhoods. *Journal of Community & Applied Social Psychology*, *22*, 38–50.

Walmsley, J. (2000). Women and the Mental Deficiency Act of 1913: Citizenship, sexuality and regulation. *British Journal of Learning Disabilities*, *28*(2), 65–70.

Werner, S. (2015). Public stigma and the perception of rights: Differences between intellectual and physical disabilities. *Research in Developmental Disabilities*, *38*, 262–271.

Wolfensberger, W. (1969). *The origin and nature of our institutional models*. Washington, DC: President's Committee of Mental Retardation.

Women with Disabilities Australia. (2017, January). *Disabled People's Organisations Australia (DPO Australia) Submission to the United Nations Special Rapporteur on violence against women, its causes and consequences: Country Visit to Australia.* Retrieved from http://wwda.org.au/wp-content/uploads/2016/01/DPOA_Sub_SR_VAW_Jan2107.pdf

13 Hammerin' Hank, (dis)ablism, racism, homophobia, and hate speech

Stephen A. Rosenbaum

This chapter is an exploration of hate speech within an American cultural context[1]. Some countries have legal provisions regulating hate speech in the form of "artistic expression" – in books, songs, plays, cinema, electronic broadcasts, audio and visual recordings, photos, paintings, internet sites, in print and social media. For example, the Indian Penal Code prohibits the promotion of "disharmony or feelings of enmity, hatred or ill-will" between identifiable groups. India's appellate tribunals have reviewed constitutional challenges by parties asking the court to impose "reasonable restrictions" on television or documentary films on the bases of defamation or "incitement to an offence."[2] The Canadian Criminal Code bans the communication of a statement in a public place that "incites hatred against an identifiable group" and is "likely to lead to a breach of the peace."[3] Germany's Criminal Code prohibits an act that "assaults the human dignity of others by insulting, maliciously maligning, or defaming such group, segments of the population or an individual because of his belonging to such group," including an assault in the media. The German Basic Law also affords primary importance to human dignity, which cannot be outweighed by other competing rights or values, such as the right to free expression.[4] Of particular relevance, the Australian High Court has reviewed a judicially imposed suppression order against an infamous "shock jock" under a state human rights charter, balancing qualified protection of free expression against a right of privacy.[5]

In contrast, the United States has long cherished constitutional protections on freedom of expression, effectively shielding those who would promulgate hate, such as the producers and hosts of shock jock radio. The case of "Hammerin' Hank," a disabled[6] man in the *Doghouse* radio broadcast of the early 2000s, seems to come under the rubric of low-level harassment and hate speech.[7] The treatment of Hank, a mocked on-air personality, is the focus of this chapter.

The *Doghouse* radio show

It is 7 o'clock in the morning and the radio dial is tuned to 94.9, not far from sister stations on the FM frequency, beacons of cosmopolitan and progressive programming, from the Pacifica network's KPFA to National Public Radio affiliates. But, station KYLD shows no resemblance to the rest of the left-end FM family. The 94.9 *Doghouse* show is a daily party between 6 and 10 o'clock in the San Francisco Bay Area where the on-air and off-air attendees – or perhaps more accurately, eavesdroppers, the audio equivalent of voyeurs – drop in. They are African-American teenage students, Latina office workers in their 30s, white stay-at-home moms pushing 40, and Asian 20-somethings in between jobs.

Many callers will get *Doghouse* T-shirts, *Doghouse* videos and tickets to concerts and nightclubs when they say the magic words "What's Up, Doghouse?" and submit to competitive questioning or other contests. They also get a dose of hip-hop, rhythm and blues, and house music vibes. But mostly they get an earful of what the canine crew calls comedy and clowning. It is the height of lowbrow audio programming: a marathon of prank phone calls and stunts, insipid interviews, crude humour, and stream-of-conscious machismo, misogyny, and sophomoric "straight talk." The deejays would have their audience believe that some of their remarks are candid and genuine, but most of the talk is "straight" because it is explicitly and incessantly heterosexist and homophobic.

San Francisco's morning newspaper awarded the show a three-star "crass quotient" several years ago in a review of radio shows "that routinely cross the bounds of good taste,"[8] with its daily menu of testicular vernacular and anatomical allusions. Phoney phone calls, gay-baiting, and what one reporter refers to as "their relentless obsession with body functions" is always a winning recipe on the show.[9] I think it may qualify as hate speech masquerading as humor.

"They're huge," says one industry trade publication writer of the *Doghouse* show. "For what they do, they really hit the mark. They really deliver the multicultural urban marketplace we're in."[10] "No other morning show has ever had double digits in San Francisco before," boasts Jeff Vandergrift, whose shock jock alias is J.V., about *Doghouse*'s 10.8 ratings share.[11] The 10.8 rating translates approximately into 10% of all radio listeners at a given time in a region with at least 65 stations. It is no surprise, then, that the show has been sponsored by prominent businesses and airs ads from government agencies. Even the Easter Seal Society has aired an announcement about services for adults and children with disabilities. These private sponsors and government agencies may be oblivious to the *Doghouse* program content and are looking only at market share.[12]

J.V. is the egocentric and sadistic lead deejay. His sidekicks are yes man Hollywood and slightly smarter straight man Elvis. Other sycophants hang out with them at the "Wild 94" party station – Greg, the laid-back mixer, Ruth, the go-fer intern, Show Biz, the Stepin Fetchit whipping boy. And then there is Hank, better known by his *nom de radio,* Hammerin' Hank. Hank's full name is Henry Ochs, according to a December 17, 2002 broadcast. Born in Kansas in 1967, Hank attended special education classes in high school and lived in a group home in California's San Joaquin Valley for about four years – perhaps a community-care residential facility for adults with intellectual or developmental impairments.[13] With regard to the group home, Hank allegedly writes: "I would of [sic] graduated from there much earlier, but I kept getting into trouble."[14] Interestingly, the references to special education and group home were deleted from more recent web page versions.

He may even be a client of a regional center – an agency that contracts with the state "to provide fixed points of contact in the community for Californians with developmental disabilities and their families [to] have access to the services and supports best suited to them throughout their lifetime."[15]

You know there is something a little different in Hank's routines. His voice is high pitched and nasal and his speech is slow. His lines are recited from memory or heavily scripted. His breathing is labored and he punctuates many of his lines with an exaggerated, prolonged laugh. He is not your standard disabled performance artist. Nor is he your typical crip sit-down comic. Hank is a wannabe deejay and maybe he's not *wanting* as much as *being.* Or, maybe he's wanting belonging, camaraderie, coolness.

He may talk the gutter talk of J.V. or Elvis – with all the female objectification, slurs against gay men, and genital hijinks. But, Hanky – as he is sometimes called – is not as cool or glib and never will be. He suits the purposes of his creators and alleged buddies much more as a puppet or pet, catering to their puerile whims and guffawing on cue. In return, he gets to be on the radio, participate in the locker room banter with the self-styled Radio Kings, and enjoy the bad boy celebrity. On his web page, Hank answers the question "Why Radio?" with: "Free stuff, the nightclubs, and the women."[16]

Here is a typical *Doghouse* scenario with Hank: An interview subject, not wise to the Wild 94 format, is phoned up. He is the author of a new book on rock 'n roll.

> *Author*: "Where are you calling from?"
> One of the *Deejays* in background responds: "'Tardville."[17]
>
> *Hank*'s script includes retorts like:
> Wow, what a fag!
> Suck my nuts.
> And then the monkeys came out of your ass.
> Did you see the size of his c----?[18]
>
> *Author* asks Hank a question.
> *Hank* replies: "If you suck me off."
> *Author*: "Did you read my book?"
> *Hank*: "I pissed on it." [19]

Some readers may question the need for such explicit quotations here. As offensive as they are, they convey a sense of the gritty programming content to those fortunate enough to have their radios turned off to the real thing. "[T]he Doghouse continues to bring new meaning to the term 'shock radio.'"[20]Slang references to penis are usually bleeped or self-censored by the crew, who abide by some standards of acceptable reference. Still, there is a steady stream of anatomical argot. A few months earlier, crew member Show Biz was given one of the infamous consequences dished out by J.V. and gang for failure to properly perform a prank or stunt. He was told to lick Hank's anus – in the KYLD studio. Hank was instructed to tell Show Biz, "Lick my butt, bitch" and they both were hooted by the other deejays for "being gay."[21] Elvis suggested that Show Biz could "taste the meatloaf served at [Hank's] group home."[22] A few weeks later, Hank is asked to phone a restaurant to say he left something behind. A man with a heavy Spanish accent at the other end is earnestly engaged for several minutes as Hank asks him, "Have you seen my balls? … They're in a tan, fuzzy sack"

Lesbianism is tolerated and even fetishized by the Wild 94 party crew. Male homosexuality, however, is the ultimate put-down and gay-baiting is *de rigeur*. For instance, on the August 16, 2002 broadcast, junior crew member Chicken is warned that if he inserts his own finger up his anus it is a true manifestation of homosexuality. On August 22, three in-studio male contestants vying for free concert tickets are humiliated drill sergeant-style. They are called faggots, ridiculed about wearing "gay" clothing and jewelry, and two of them are ordered to kiss one another and confess their homosexual tendencies. On the December 17, 2002 broadcast, Show Biz and another male crew member are told they must tongue-kiss for 30 seconds as a consequence for failing the assignment *du jour* and then Show Biz is teased because he seems to be enjoying it. J.V. and his henchmen periodically ask studio guests to shed an article or two of clothing as part of a stunt or consequence. In the past, Hank has been summoned to play a version of strip poker on the air and submit to teasing about his genitals and poor hygiene. The crew has also had him rub the breasts of hired women.[23]

They call Hank into the on-air studio.

J.V.: "You're gonna die if you keep eating like you do... What did you eat today?... And you are *still* hungry?"

Elvis: "We can probably afford to bury you in a pet cemetery... next to another bird brain."

Next, Hank is asked to read a script to various listeners who call in. He is to give them clues to guess the answers. The name of the game is "The 'Tard Password Game." The deejays are frustrated with Hank's ability to read the script or to play the game appropriately and they quickly lose interest.

J.V.: "We should go back to shocking him. If you dick the listeners, we'll cow-Taser your ass... It's the only way you're going to learn."

Elvis: "We'll bury you at the group home... You're gonna die soon."

Later that morning, they bring some kind of commercial stun gun or baton into the studio and the deejays all dare Elvis to use the Taser on Hank – or else to use it on himself. They refer to this game as "Shock the 'Tard." They read from the instrument's instructions: "It could cause 'mental confusion.'"

Hollywood: "Not relevant. [He's already mentally confused]."

J.V., Hollywood & Ruth: "Come on, Elvis... Rip the 'tard's ass."

There follow jokes about destroying brain capacity and about being "mentally challenged." Meanwhile, Hank is all but silent as the *Doghouse* crew comment on how close they are to touching him with the Taser. On subsequent shows, other members of the crew were dared to have the Taser held to their testicles. Most agreed to be shocked, no doubt for fear of being perceived as wimps. J.V. says, "'I swear to God on my mother' that all of the show's stunts are real..."[24]

The *Doghouse's* disablist allusions go beyond Hank. They include cliché Helen Keller jokes,[25] and riddles about deaf people, persistent vegetative state, and obesity.[26] Deejay Elvis, the master prank caller, will pretend to be an irate Vietnam War vet with a laryngectomy and psychiatric disability,[27] or a man with Tourette's syndrome phoning to make a restaurant reservation[28] or to get a suit fitted.[29] Some of his supposed coprolaliac utterances include:

> Christopher Reeve Super Gimp…
> Eat it…
> Faggot Heifer…
> Son of a goddamn bitch.[30]

Show Biz himself is not immune from the cavalier disablist labeling. In a segment where the production crew are airing their workplace grievances, Elvis claims Show Biz has Attention-Deficit Disorder. On another broadcast, Show Biz croons a ditty he composed about making love to a "midget girl," with her "Midget arms / Midget legs / Midget body / And big ol' head." There are allusions to "Munchkin Land," shopping at Baby Gap and rhymes like "She's standing three feet tall / Next to my balls." There are even jokes in Spanish, as when J.V. asks: "What do you call a hooker with no legs? Answer: Consuelo." (*Con suelo* is Spanish for "on the floor). [31]

The listenership is geographically and demographically diverse, the ratings are high and the commercial sponsorship is substantial. "You have to have everybody," according to J.V.[32] Can advertisers really afford to look the other way and minimize the hate speech, well into an era of disability awareness and marketplace "handicapitalism?"[33] One reporter writes off-handedly that the *Doghouse* team has come under fire for its hazing of Hank, who he describes as a "slow-witted man."[34] The criticism has been neither vigorous nor influential, however, as Hank remains on the air in full form.

If everybody is indeed tuning in, should we accept this programming as Hank's choice to do what the other shock jocks do – talk smack, be part of the "rude is hip throng,"[35] and perhaps get paid for it – no matter how tasteless or demeaning the humor? Or, through means of education, public criticism, or consumer boycott, should we work to eliminate this form of hate speech?[36] … whether his audio antics are a product of self-determination or a form of humiliating and abusive burlesque. Perhaps surprisingly, the disability advocacy community does not speak with one voice on this issue.

Hate speech and humor

Author Tom O'Connor writes that "humor does not have to be at the expense of a disabled person, but can be a sign of identification."[37] O'Connor regards identification as a necessary part of integration into popular culture, much like identity transfer from nondisabled audience member to disabled protagonist, female to male, or adult viewer to child character. "[M]ock sentiments of political correctness" and regulations are eschewed in favor of self-deprecation and mass media acceptance of people with disabilities as human beings.[38] The "healing power" of self-deprecation is what disabled humorist David Roche employs in his stand-up comedy routine:

> When I walk on stage, the audience says with one voice: "What happened to your face?" I have encouraged them to say this, so I then explain that I was born with a severe facial disfigurement.[39]

Responding to so-called "politically correct" criticism, one filmmaker defended the inclusion of a blind character in his TV sitcom. There is a rudeness about humor, he asserts, that makes people laugh:

> Now it's getting down to the point where blind people have a society and any jokes about blind people are banned... So there's another avenue of humor cut off... But jokes like that are not meant to hurt blind people – not in a million years.[40]

O'Connor sees this as an appeal for people with disabilities to be able to laugh at themselves.[41] Complementing the theory of mutual identification is the notion that stigma or oppression will be eliminated when people perceive the fundamental similarities they share with stigmatized or oppressed people, rather than the differences.[42] One student of ethnic literature states: "The way that you show people that you're really a human being is in many cases to make people relax and laugh with you."[43] In a more recent variation, Muslim and Arab-American comics appear in comedy clubs with jokes about terrorism, racial profiling, religious customs, and international politics.[44] But, the path between good-natured laughter and mockery is not easily traveled.

The slur *queer* has been successfully reclaimed[45] by those identifying as LGBTQI. But, whereas *crip* and *gimp* have become accepted insider vernacular for people with physical disabilities, there is not a similar campaign to reclaim the epithets *retard*, *tard*, or *moron*.[46] In fact, self-advocacy organizations have celebrated that "members have fought long and hard to escape the indignity of labels... far fewer people use the derogatory terms – 'the retarded,' 'the disabled,' 'the trainable.'"[47] Even acknowledging that "insults as a form of word play"[48] may be a tolerated custom amongst members of subordinated communities, it is important to view the history and context in determining whether the name-calling is a form of acceptable humor or insider speak, or has crossed the line. Author Frederick Drimmer observes that the people who work in sideshows may jokingly refer to each other as freaks, but they recognize this as an epithet – whereas disability scholar Rachel Adams discusses people who "proudly claim the title of freak as a personal or collective mode of self-identification."[49]

Humor and resistance versus subjugation

There is not the least hint of irony or self-deprecation when derogatory terms for "mentally retarded" get bandied about by Hammerin' Hank or his fellow dogs. His vocabulary is sexual and with-it, like Kate Rigg's Chink-o-Rama talk of "Hot Asian mamas... Oriental chicks" or her "give you boys a good connection... I know how to chop your sticks."[50] But, Hank is specially cast as a person who is asexual or de-sexualized. In this respect, he shares the plight of the minstrel singer who is "a cackling stereotype – the Negro as eunuch, an object of white mirth."[51]

While fag-bashing and mocking persons with disabilities is clearly sanctioned, the *Doghouse* gang do seem to "get it" enough to steer clear generally of ethnic or racial hazing, except for the airing of unwitting phone respondents with foreign accents and the periodic razzing of Show Biz when they "talk black." And, whereas Rigg appropriates the insults and Chinese stereotypes and puns, Hammerin' Hank simply spews out crude or hateful vulgarities that are devoid of self-mockery or wit and can only be described as malicious or an assault on dignity. Just as the minstrel show allowed whites to explore fantasies that middle class culture denied them – of laziness, sexual desire, unstructured time[52] – so, too, the *Doghouse* vignettes with Hank permit an exploration of silliness and raunchiness. Only, it is supposed to be even funnier when coming from the mouth of a foolish cripple, than from one of the hipper members of the crew.

In her one-woman show, Mary Duffy, who has a limb anomaly, presents as a classic female nude and armless marble statue. Her fusion of a supposedly freakish body and aesthetic sexualized gazing suggests neither freak show nor medical school case study. Duffy is instead a museum *objet d'art* that confronts the viewer with a visual and aural monologue, taking back the oppressive language, medicalization, and shame that defined her existence as a person with a disability.[53] She recasts herself as "being whole, complete, and functional."[54]

Carrie Sandahl is a disabled performance artist who uses a street theatre and body art approach, with costume, props, and one-on-one encounters in the public sphere. Her cane, uneven gait, and white lab coat with superimposed clinical text convert her into a live medical chart, objectifying her body by the medical discourse that has been imposed on her for much of her – and other disabled people's – life.[55] Frank Moore is a performance artist with cerebral palsy "that left him spastic, unable to walk or talk, and horny for attention." Moore stages nude, erotic grope-a-thons.[56] Hank stands in contrast to the re-narrated version of disabled sexual subjectivity offered by Wade, Duffy, and Moore – a sexuality which is neither pathological, nor victimized, nor passive. Instead, the *Doghouse* portrayal of Hank's sexuality fits the conventional mold: pathetic, unattractive, and deformed – owing largely to his cognitive impairment and physical appearance.

Hank's place in the canine crowd is really more akin to "Elephant Man" John Merrick's place in upper-class Victorian society. Merrick's wish to be normal, notwithstanding his physical disfigurement, turns out to be a fantasy, as he ends up on stage in a freak show or examined in a medical school lecture hall.[57] The *Doghouse's* ringleader insists that "[t]he thing people don't see is we do take care of [Hank]. We buy him clothes, we take him to the movies and the mall."[58] This kind of paternalism is reminiscent of the attitude adopted by freak show mangers who looked after their charges, even after they retired from the side show. Hank is not really just like the other show dogs in the radio sound booth. His *shtick* is not about shared humor and storytelling, nor about the elimination of stigma. His laughter is not humorous or infectious, inviting listeners to join in. Rather, it is forced and anxious, and separates the audience from the performer.

Hank does not reclaim staring or re-narrate the disability script with liberating assertions and self-representations. Nor does he manipulate the image or direct the listener in the same way as the performers described above. Lastly, he does not control the terms of the encounter.[59] On the contrary, his script is controlled by others and it is an oppressive and mocking text he is forced to recite. His performance actually *de*-humanizes and disparages. His radio persona is really an audio version of the minstrel with huge eyes and gaping mouth, the ill-fitting clothes and "nigger" dialect. In constant motion on stage, these showmen "contorted their bodies, cocked their heads… and twisted their outstretched legs."[60] In serving to "codify the public image of blacks as the prototypical Fool or Sambo," minstrelsy had a great impact on American culture.[61]

Developmentally disabled Hank is permitted – and encouraged – to *talk* about sex, to do phallic phone play, and be titillated: "You're acting like you're about to have an orgasm," J.V. tells him on the December 17, 2002, show. He can also assume the moniker Hammerin', with its sexual connotation. But Hank is not to take part in sex, except in ways the team deems humiliating or perverted, e.g., homosexual or anal sex, or in the role of a voyeur or john. It is almost like an inverted devoteeism.[62] But, in place of a pathological attraction with the disabled body, we are treated to *Doghouse's* revulsion of the disabled, along with a fetishizing of "normal" sexual imagery, i.e., non-disabled and heterosexual.[63] His is the antithesis of "managing, deflecting, resisting or renouncing stares." Hank does not manage stigma but magnifies it. And the *Doghouse* message is: Please do stare – and gawk!

Moreover, the inquisitorial "trial by humiliation" concept, recounted below, that proved so popular with Hank the 'Tard, was instituted against crew member Nick G., who had been accused of being gay. On March 4, 2003, the deejay honchos elicited evidence such as a limp-wristed handshake, so-called gay strut, effeminate manner of speech and testimony that he listens to the unofficial queer anthem, "Y-M-C-A." In his usual fashion, J.V. dismissed it all by saying the charges would be dropped if Nick merely admitted he is gay and added, disingenuously: "You homosexual men, we give you love."

The role of ridicule

The ridiculing of cognitive disability has a long and dishonorable history. During the Middle Ages and Renaissance, some persons with mental retardation were procured for amusement for the idle and well-to-do.[64] Developmentally delayed persons, for instance, served regularly as buffoons and jesters at the dinner table of Pope Leo X, who encouraged his guests to laugh at the mean-spirited pranks played on them. In one such case, a "half-witted, hungry dwarf" seated at the pope's table was jeered while eating spoiled meat covered in sauce, believing that he was partaking in a fine meal.[65] Attitudes had not progressed much by the time of the American Revolution. A person with mental retardation was treated as the village idiot and "an object of merriment and ridicule," if they were not living at home out of public view in a back room or cellar. To be living "in the community" in that era meant to be abandoned by friends and family.[66]

Beginning in the mid-1800s, the American freak show began to exhibit human oddities on stage, including persons with mental retardation, often by casting them with slightly accentuated physical features or in costume or in an allegedly primitive milieu. In the Barnum & Bailey heyday, persons with mental and physical disabilities were exhibited "indiscriminately" with nonwhite or non-Western and exotic performers. Nativist xenophobia and anti-foreigner bias are reflected in this kind of display.[67] One activist dubs this phenomenon the "pornography of disability."[68] Displays included, for example, siblings with microcephaly, known as *pinheads*.[69] They might appear in aborigine garb and background or in Aztec motif. Also exhibited were persons of short stature, referred to as *dwarves* or *imbeciles*, who might be displayed in a South Pacific setting.[70] Professor Adams writes of the historic connection between disability and race in the sensational and exploitative exhibition of persons with disabilities and "ethnographic curiosities" or "racial freaks."[71]

Some of the freaks were said to speak unintelligible languages or gibberish or would grunt or growl on cue. They would adopt insulting names like Tik Tak, the Aztec Pinhead, or The Original Aztec Indian Midgets from Old Mexico.[72]

As with the image portrayed by the black-faced, patois-speaking minstrel, there was an emphasis on the exotic or erotic. "Very special people" was one of the terms used to describe these alleged human anomalies,[73] sounding eerily like the "child with special needs" or euphemistic "special person" bestowed today on youths with disabilities.

Supposedly, only docile and cooperative subjects could be cast as freaks, as aggressive and disorderly persons were difficult to take care of and "did not exhibit well."[74] Customers, too, were expected to assume a docile pose, after taking in the barker's monologue and "gazing at the prodigious body in awestruck wonder."[75] One commentator suggests that the gazing allowed the audience to feel "more perfect, more beautiful, less repulsive" than the exhibited human oddities.[76]

Perhaps Hank is an active participant in the role of freak and may believe that this is his only entrée into the world of radio or nightclubs or social acceptance. Like the black minstrels of yesteryear and the disabled adults who played the side shows, this young man may see this as his only opportunity to enter the world of show business – or indeed to have *any* livelihood[77] – notwithstanding changing social attitudes and civil rights and employment opportunity legislation.[78] n the words of disability studies scholar Rachel Adams, "the realities of appearance-based discrimination persist in American culture"[79] as does "the discomfort of living with a body always marked as other."[80] Historically, those who were exhibited as freaks were sometimes active in the construction of their role, as was the case with William Henry Johnson, a man with microcephaly and an intellectual disability.[81] More recently, the Florida Supreme Court struck down a statutory prohibition against freak shows, holding that "those individuals in this unfortunate condition who must rely upon such exhibitions for a livelihood should be allowed to do so."[82]

Thus, it is the conscious or unconscious attitude of an intellectually disabled man who takes on the name Hammerin' Hank to convince himself he has sex appeal, while being razzed as a retard. He is today's beefy showman named Tiny or the large woman dressed up in a dainty girl's dress and made to giggle and dance.[83] We can peek at Hank's weekly sideshow, where he fancies himself a Don Juan, but instead he must laugh, play the fool, spew vulgarities, and get aroused on command.

Freedom of choice

Viewed differently, this is a performer and an audience who – like their classic freak show counterparts – choose a form of amusement despised and disapproved by the bourgeoisie.[84] Adams notes that protests and legal battles against the sideshows were couched in terms of morality, but the subtext reflected a conflict, on the one hand, between middle-class values and on the other hand, the right for marginalized populations to be employed and for the underclass to be amused "in ways that may arouse disgust or disapproval from others."[85] Is our discomfort due to an elitist and moralistic standard imposed on Hank and the *Doghouse* listeners? Or is it because we should be combating stereotypes and prejudices relating to persons with disabilities? Perhaps the dreaded disability "PC squad"[86] that monitors speech and media for the wrong words and negative images should just accept the bathroom humor as a mode of contemporary youth entertainment. Hopefully, the bathroom door one day will be closed and young people will get out of the toilet, get culture, and develop sensitivity in some other forum. Like adolescence itself, this may be just a passing phase.

Can an argument be constructed in favor of just letting Hank be Hank? This does not mean condoning the *Doghouse* show's content. But, it does suggest that disabled people deserve the same right to be wrong as nondisabled people, and are permitted to make the same choices as their peers – even choosing to be a shock jock. I began to "monitor" *Doghouse* in an effort to listen to the radio programming to which my non-disabled teenage son was exposed. When I shared my *Doghouse* discovery with colleagues in the field of disability rights and services, a passionate debate ensued among lawyers, social service providers, and other advocates about this choice, raising questions of freedom, paternalism, and social identity.[87]

Self-determination is the watchword of the contemporary disability rights movement. The concept has been embraced by consumers, parents, practitioners, and educators, with little controversy.[88] Sometimes it is expressed in terms of *choice*[89] or "people 'speaking up' for themselves" in making and acting on lifestyle choices. One self-advocates' guide defines self-determination this way:

- I will have more control over my life.
- I will have more choice about what I do every day.
- I will have more control over my future.[90]

Another guide declares:

> Self-determination is "a ten dollar word for choice… it is another word for freedom… a life filled with rising expectations, dignity, responsibility, and opportunity… a chance to live the American dream."[91]

In addition to choice, self-determination may also embody the concepts of self-advocacy, self-regulation, problem-solving, decision-making, goal setting and independence.[92] In the California model, for example, opportunities are provided to system consumers to make choices in their own lives, including where and with whom they live, their relationships, the way they spend their time, the pursuit of their personal future and program planning and implementation.[93]

The Arc (formerly Association for Retarded Citizens) is one of the oldest advocacy and service organizations for persons with intellectual or developmental disabilities.[94] The Arc's education researcher, Michael Wehmeyer, defined self-determination as "people or peoples controlling their lives and their destinies. It is both that simple and that complex."[95] He offered a slightly different definition in an earlier article: The process by which individuals become the primary causal agent for decisions made in their life – without undue internal influences.[96] Causal agency, in turn, suggests that people take actions that are purposeful and lead to achieved ends.[97] Much of the literature is about facilitating true choice and ceding control impulses, working against a history of protection and trying to fix the disability.[98]

Maybe it should have come as no surprise when a disability rights lawyer in southern California, Maxine (a pseudonym, as are all of the names given to fellow disability activists), sent the following e-mail in response to my posting about Hammerin' Hank's anal antics on the *Doghouse*, and my suggestions of abuse:

> We are assuming, somewhat paternalistically, that the individual involved here is not capable of making his own decisions about what types of activities to participate in. Is this a conserv[atee]? Have we spoken to him? I am wary about throwing around terms like "exploitation and abuse" when we do not have more facts. [It is our role] to support an individual's freedom to choose his or her pursuits and paths, even if we view them as poor choices.
>
> We may be acting hypocritically here. I am concerned about the long-term effects of complaints to the licensing unit at the Department of Social Services. Do we want licensed facilities to start monitoring the activities of

> their residents? Slippery slope here – a breeding ground for violations of individual choice and clients' rights.

These were the responses from other lawyers and advocates:

> Maxine, it sounds like you're advocating for personal autonomy.
>
> This is not a matter for investigation.[99] Besides, what about the First Amendment and all that jazz? Not that I condone bad taste, bad press or poor judgment... I find folks like Howard Stern utterly distasteful... but, I am not forced to listen to them.[100]
>
> I'm with Maxine on this. We cannot assume that "Hank" wants protection. Maybe you could get in touch with him and check it out. I can just imagine this becoming a "poster boy" issue: "See, this is what happens when these people are let out unsupervised!" What would be the complaint against "Hank's" facility? That they let him do what he *wanted* to do? The show is appalling, right up there with dwarf-tossing and the like, and we might want to think that "Hank" can't possibly understand or appreciate being the butt of this "humor" – you should pardon the expression. But, maybe he likes the celebrity it's brought him. Or maybe he's getting paid for it!

Some of the above comments are in line with contemporary theory: self-determined behavior does not always result in successful behavior. Every decision does not turn out to be an optimal one. Nor is every choice the perfect one, or every goal the right goal. There may also be negative outcomes. Support persons – service providers, families and friends – often struggle with choices that conflict with their own judgment about what is best, e.g., when an individual chooses not to work, to spend time in an unsafe area, to eat unhealthily, or chooses an unorthodox sexual lifestyle.[101] And, many of these themes are manifested in what we know of Hank's choices: the nature of his job, unhealthy eating, and offensive sexual conduct.

Upon reading the postings about Hank from disability advocates, one regional center executive director was blunt and incredulous:

> Assuming that this is a real situation, equating anus licking with free choice and client self-determination is so incredibly stupid that it boggles my mind... Free speech, slippery slope! This is really idiotic... Is "Hank" learning that he will get approval, and air time, by allowing others to make a fool of him, to make fun of him, and his disability, like he was Quasimodo "entertaining" folks outside of Notre Dame? [Some advocates just don't] understand the difference between client rights and client abuse.

Maxine responds:

> It is indeed a hard issue, but I still struggle to see how it becomes our role as advocates to monitor choices – as opposed to not supporting them or

> contacting Hank directly to let him know that there may be better things out there for him… I know people with disabilities who choose to participate in bad taste events like these. In some instances, folks are well aware of what they are doing – at least to the extent they know they are having fun, getting paid, interacting with nondisabled peers in the community and in a work setting, and enjoying some sense of celebrity. People, disabled or not, often balance such things when making choices in their lives.

Again, self-determination theorists would recognize that making unhealthy choices is part of leading a "normal" life and that the "dignity of risk" is an experience that all people should know. "To deny any person their fair share of risk experiences is to further cripple them for healthy living."[102] As Maxine argues, this may include bad employment decisions or engaging in what others may view as an exploitative activity. Ironically, this rationale is similar to the one offered by freak show entrepreneurs in defense of their exhibitions. In a letter to sociologist Robert Bogdan, one of the remaining show operators insisted that he paid his troupe of human oddities and had an above-board business relationship with them. Bogdan posits that the proprietor "did not have to profess motives manufactured from higher ideals – curing, protecting, and serving – ideals that made the person with the physical or mental difference unsure of where he or she stood."[103]

Nevertheless, one commentator asserts that self-determination should not be equated with absolute authority by the person with a disability, or as the equivalent to chaos. Moreover, if actions are consistently unsuccessful in all aspects of one's life, then that life is not very self-determined.[104] In other words, the goal must be to present information so that the best-informed decisions can be made by disabled people for themselves.[105] One research team draws the line for intervention at the point where there are serious health and safety risks, or infringement on the rights of others.[106]

Support providers still can encourage self-determination while setting the parameters of choice, e.g., by examining alternative solutions.[107] This is certainly the aim of most transition training or habilitation programs for persons with developmental disabilities of varying severity. There is no shortage of resources and studies involving employment,[108] social skills training, friendship,[109] and sexuality and sexual expression.[110] With regard to social interactions, it is ironic that while one team of academics at San Francisco State University sought to identify inappropriate social behaviors by young adults with severe disabilities, Hank was engaging in some of those very same target behaviors across town and on the air: squeals, shouts, cheers, inappropriate greeting, name calling, touching peers in an inappropriate manner, perseverating on topic or sentence, and interrupting conversations. [111]

Actually, some of the things that Hank has written – or wrote "with support" – on his *Doghouse* web page would please proponents of person-centered planning, if recorded as social, recreational or vocational objectives in his regional center Individual Program Plan (California's version of a planning team document, which records one's choices, supports, and other decisions related to living arrangements, work, education, socialization, avocation, or leisure activities). For instance, he is "still single and still looking for a lovely girlfriend." He likes "Latin women, nightclubs, baseball games, comedy shows, and TV." In terms of job preparation and satisfaction, he "would be looking for another radio job" if he were not in radio, and he detested all of his pre-broadcasting employment. Lastly, he dislikes "mean people, some veggies, liars, and people who don't stand for the national anthem."[112]

Hank's choices for career, residential living, leisure, and personal relationships clearly are more abundant than those available in the nineteenth or early twentieth century to persons with cognitive disabilities – or racial minorities – who ventured outside their homes for social or vocational purposes. Nonetheless, social skills deficit is one of the reasons that people with developmental disabilities have a hard time making friendships, retaining jobs, or otherwise negotiating the community environment.[113] Yet, can one seriously regard the Doghouse as a supportive work environment? Its deejays are hardly skilled facilitators, much less "natural supports," notwithstanding J.V.'s assertions about "hanging out" with Hank. (Under California's developmental disabilities service system, regional center program planning teams are required to first consider services and supports for persons with developmental disabilities in "natural community, home, work and recreational settings".)[114]

The reaction to Hammerin' Hank by peer- and self-advocates stands in sharp contrast to that manifested by lawyers. "Self-advocacy," according to People First of California, "means that the members are learning how to speak for themselves and make decisions about what they want to do with their lives." Sometimes referred to as "personal advocacy," it involves "speaking out or acting on behalf of oneself or others, or on behalf of a particular issue" whether individually or in groups.[115] "Appalling!!!!!!!" was the beginning of the e-mail message sent by Martine, a long-time peer advocate and regional center client, in reading the posting about Hank and Show Biz having anal sex. Her initial suggestion was to contact regional centers and area boards (statewide monitoring and advocacy system to ensure that the legal, civil and service rights of Californians with developmental disabilities are protected),[116] as well as Protection and Advocacy's unit that investigates abuse and neglect.

Martine and another peer advocate teamed up to draft a letter of complaint to KYLD's parent company and various advertisers. The effort was not lightly undertaken and involved several weeks of vetting and fretting about the letter's contents. "I am very, very strongly opposed to any letter coming from a disability rights agency on this issue – *unless* directed to do so by 'Hank' (or his conservator – and I don't believe he is conserved) in response to some allegation of exploitation or abuse," was the e-mail reply from attorney Maxine, when I told her about the letter. "It really runs afoul of all I stand for in terms of choice and independence." She continued:

> Is it [our] role to contact "Hank" in a way that passes judgment on his life and/or criticizes his choice of employment because it does not fit a disability

> rights agenda? My suggestion would be to not contact Hank at all – or to just send him basic information about [Protection & Advocacy]. I have spoken about this issue… to numbers of co-workers and friends [who have] disabilities. Everyone, without exception, has shared my concerns about the approach taken here.
>
> What if Hank had called you before this issue surfaced internally and reported that his family thought the job was "bad for him and for other people with disabilities" and told him that unless he quit he would be kicked out of their house? You would advise Hank that he had the right to make choices in his life, even if they are – by others' standards – bad choices.

Yet, choice, if taken out of context, is problematic. For example, Professor Wehmeyer cites the case of a woman with mental retardation allowed to stand at a window in her group home all day because, it is said, that was her choice. In fact, the reason she may be standing there is because she was waiting for the companion who had earlier in the week come by to pick her up.[117]

It is also a mistake to assume that self-determination is the equivalent of just making choices – such as changing the channel on the group home TV set or switching to a new adult day program.[118] Others have warned that the trivialization of choice is one of the common misinterpretations about self-determination: "[E]namored of the philosophical connections between 'choice' and 'freedom' or perhaps connecting liberation from institutions with some notion of freedom" some "seem to extol 'choice' as a value supreme to all others."[119] The exercise of choice must be complemented by problem solving, decision-making, self-awareness and goal setting.[120] One of the first writers on the subject, Dr. Bengt Nirje, conceived of self-determination as a component of normalization, which in turn encompasses the notion of respect:

> When mentally retarded adults express their right to self-determination in public and in action, and thus gain and experience due citizen respect, they also have something to teach… to society in general… the respect due to everyone.[121]

Thus, one does not simply invoke self-determination for the sake of self-determination.

It's about dignity

The debate lined up in ways that were predictable and not so predictable: Lawyers were wary of trampling on the tarmac of First Amendment jurisprudence, but were also scrupulous about preserving personal autonomy. Under conventional legal analysis, restrictions on hate speech tend to be incompatible with the First Amendment's protection of freedom of speech. Mari Matsuda, however, cites to numerous international conventions and other democratic nations' laws which proscribe racist expression or speech. She also puts forth an argument for a narrow application of a prohibition of hate speech that preserves First Amendment values. Richard Delgado also distinguishes between the values of free expression and the use of racial insults and racist speech, and lays out the elements for filing a court action against one who uses an epithet intended to demean.[122] Disability studies scholar Mark Sherry writes that "the line between speech and conduct is difficult in practice to establish."[123] He notes that those who favor penalizing hate speech define hate crimes more expansively than free speech advocates, as they conceive of *speech* and *crime* as "part of a continuum of bigotry and prejudice" rather than discrete acts. He cites other authors who view hate speech as creating a "symbolic code for violence" or a political climate where persons with disabilities experience "oppressive silencing."[124]

Self-advocacy activists espoused the same disapproving views of Hank as a system administrator. The arguments really reflect a larger dynamic in the disability rights community – where the forces of protection are up against the forces of advocacy. (Even this description does not do justice to the nuances, e.g., advocacy *for* versus advocacy *with*). But, it is not really a question of one without the other, any more than self-determination is merely about unbridled choices.

Maxine eventually conceded that a letter to the radio station was perhaps in order – so long as it did not threaten Hank's employment or question his judgment:

> I think it is appropriate to raise concerns about the station's "pattern" of promoting negative stereotypes about people with disabilities. That can be done without being judgmental of Hank's choices (assuming he is even a real person as opposed to a non-disabled person playing a "role") and without being "paternalistic" in our approach (e.g., saying "Does Hank know what he is doing?" or "You are abusing Hank.").

In regard to this latter argument, Bogdan recounts the story of a showman who took umbrage at the efforts of a disability rights activist to ban him from the New York State Fair on the grounds that "[t]he freak show is to disabled people as the striptease is to women, as 'Amos 'n' Andy' is to blacks."[125] One of the showman's complaints was that the activist ought to have talked to *him* about being exploited: "How can she say I'm being taken advantage of? Hell, what does she want for me – to be on welfare?"[126]

There is a fine line that separates individual agency from exploitation, and the spectator may easily become what Adams calls the "unwitting accomplice,"[127] if not an avid and condescending gawker. Adams writes about a developmentally disabled person of short stature who appears in a contemporary Coney Island side show and, according to the show's producer, is proud and happy with his role. However, "[w]e could not laugh, for despite [his] concerted efforts, there was nothing funny about what we were seeing and the very act of looking… suddenly made us feel complicit in his degradation."[128] Even where the object of mirth appears to be a willing participant, it is worth inquiring if that individual has given his consent and whether we as spectators have a duty to object, or question the propriety of a given act.

As for the letter to the radio station, Maxine concludes:

> My suggestion is to ask KYLD to cease the pattern and practice and to give positive images of persons with disabilities equal time… I'd stay clear of asking for the termination of the Hank programming, because cutting negative images and incorporating positive images would remedy our concerns – while maintaining Hank's employment. I know [Protection & Advocacy] has goals around challenging negative imagery, but that needs to be done in a manner that is consistent with the values of self-determination and choice.

There was never really much discussion amongst colleagues about disability images or hate speech, beyond a cursory and resigned recognition that radio producers and entertainers have a right to free expression. There was no parallel acknowledgment that insults themselves can inflict psycho-sociological or political damage, or that hate speech may be a precursor to hate crimes. For instance, Richard Delgado asserts that "[t]he racial insult remains one of the most pervasive channels through which discriminatory attitudes are imparted… Not only does the listener learn and internalize the messages contained in racial insults, these messages color our society's institutions and are transmitted to succeeding generations."[129]

Yet, whether referred to as *mongoloid idiots* or *persons with Down's*, there is an "intimate connection" between the ways people with developmental disabilities are portrayed and the social policies concerning their rights and their supports.[130] The father of a child with a disability reminds us that "[r]epresentations matter...That's why advocates of the disabled are so concerned about polite words, popular movies, and visual and textual representations of every kind."[131] In the end, the advocates narrowly reached agreement about how to handle the portrayal of Hank, by balancing self-determination and choice against negative imagery and exploitation.

Epilogue

A letter protesting the aural representation of Hammerin' Hank – not Hank himself – was mailed to Station KYLD, its parent corporation, Clear Channel Radio and to various *Doghouse* sponsors. If past complaints (which ranged from direct complaints to station management to protests to the Federal Communications Commission and to lawsuits) were any predictor,[132] however, this simply would not carry enough weight to overturn the ratings scales. Would programmers and advertisers at least express mild disapproval? Would the general manager – or corporate CEO – order the *Doghouse* boys to work in some positive images of disabled persons?[133] How would the dogs themselves respond to the criticism? I expected the usual rationalizing, defensiveness, and back-peddling that could be served up like so much chow.

In fact, the response from the parent company essentially defended the antics as good clean fun: Everybody kids around. In his letter to the self-advocates, the regional vice president wrote: "I fully understand your concern for Hank and will discuss the use of the term 'tard' with the morning show and ask them to be more sensitive to its potential negative connotation."[134]

Several weeks later, there were references to Hank's contemplating the idea of leaving *Doghouse*. J.V. intimated that the deejays had to "sign some papers" promising to forego certain on-air activities. He stated wistfully, "This show has gotten away with more than any other show."[135] He even observed one day that "no product wants to associate" with you if you are too out of line. The latter remark was curious in light of the lukewarm reception some of the commercial sponsors gave to the complaint letter about Hank. While Coinstar, a cash service network, wrote that it would review its media planning guidelines for airing commercials, more typical was the response from department store division Macy's West: "we recognize and respect the media's right to express editorial opinions, even if it may present a view contrary to those of our customers."[136]

However, any illusions of the protest letter's impact were short-lived. Notwithstanding the radio executive's promise to talk to the boys about their language, the deejays tried to give away Hank to another station and managed to work in several references to "retard" in the process. Not long afterwards, Hank was put "on trial" during a morning broadcast.

With a mix of mockery, empathy, and pity, Deejay Elvis announced, "The Trial of the Unloyal [sic] Retard."[137] Crew members acted out the roles of prosecution and defense, and a pool of jurors was assembled. "Judge" J.V. ordered that the "lone, sorry-ass prisoner" be brought in. Shackled, Hank was "officially tried" for failing to display "loyalty, honesty, and hard work," but mainly for dissing the deejays and speaking his own mind. J.V. told Hank that in addition to being discharged, he would be killed or have a limb cut off if found guilty. Elvis added that Hank would have to go back to his old job, making tacos.

A bizarre mock hearing followed, in which Ruth the Intern was appointed as the public defender. She argued that Hank has a mental disability, which she described as hyperactivity, requiring anti-depressants that sometimes caused him to be moody or act defiantly. Moreover, if kicked off the show, he would be devastated.

Ruth: "[This show] is all he's got. He lives for radio."

While the Honorable J.V. constantly ogled her breasts, Ruth engaged in a paternalistic defense, albeit spirited and seemingly sincere. She began by asking Hank his age.

Ruth: "And, do you *act* like a 35-year-old?"
Hank (flatly): "No."
J.V.: "He's not like everyone. He's not fully there."

Ruth stated that Hank "pleads no contest" to not always following orders and doing what he is ordered to do, as he does not have "full mental capacity."

Ruth: "This is what makes him endearing to our listeners. The kids love him. Listeners love him… He'll try to do his best."[138]

"He acts on impulse," testified a station engineer, who was accused of having "mental challenges" himself.

The jurors were moved – by pity? genuine empathy? – and Hank was cleared of the charges, but admonished to try harder. Once more, Hank was objectified, infantilized, talked about in the third person – as if not present – as so often occurs around people with disabilities. Thus, the barking and tail-wagging goes on as usual at FM 94.9's *Doghouse*. And J.V. assures us, with one of his self-indulgent monologues: "It's *never* a personal issue. It's *entertainment*. It's a *show*… Some little twits try to stir things up. They just don't get it." A guest chimes in: "It's *radio*."[139]

APPENDIX

October 25, 2002

I received your letter and wanted to assure you that our relationship with Hammerin' Hank is both positive and fulfilling. Hank has been with the station for almost 10 years and is endeared by both the staff and audience. Radio is his life and it is all he has wanted to do for years and I am happy that WILD 94.9 has made him a part of the family.

As a member of the *Doghouse* morning show he is part of the inner-circle of the show and that inner-circle pokes fun at each other on a constant basis. All members, be they White, Black, Asian, short, fat, or mentally disabled have fun with each other and ALL become the focus at one time or another. All of the members have openly discussed their lives on air, which is why it is common knowledge that Hank was in a group home. The other members are the butt of jokes due to their current or past situations as well.

I fully understand your concern for Hank and will discuss the use of the term "tard" with the morning show and ask them to be more sensitive to its potential negative connotation.

On another note, we also highlight Hank's ability to outwit anyone when it comes to music. He is a master of music history and song charts and is often challenged by listeners to "name that tune" or music trivia.

Again, thank you for bringing this to my attention. We have a lot of love for Hank, he is a long-term member of our family and like a family we all poke at each other but never in a malicious or hurtful way. Hank knows he can always come talk to me when something makes him uncomfortable.

Sincerely,
Michael Martin
Regional Vice President/Programming
Northern California
Clear Channel Radio

Notes

1 An earlier version of this chapter was published as Hammerin' Hank: The right to be raunchy or FM freak show? 23 *Disability Studies Qtrly* (2003), an issue of the journal devoted to the theme of disability and humor – or "gross out" humor in this instance. A recent Facebook post attributed to Hank (né Henry Ochs) on a page marked "Radio Personality Hammerin' Hank" reads: "I'm an Autistic person, who is trying to get back into the radio business. I spent over fourteen years working at WILD 94.9 in San Francisco from January 1994 until I was let go from there in August 2008. I also… have served as a PSA Voice over talent at KRBQ(Q102). I hope to secure my next radio job very soon." https://www.facebook.com/pg/DJHammerinhank/about/ (June 21, 2019).

2 See, Indian Penal Code 1860, §§153A & 153B and Constitution of India, art. 19(2) (freedom of expression). Here the legislation is rooted in the historic communal disharmony where the identifiable groups are typically Muslims, Hindus or marginalized castes.

3 Canada Criminal Code, § 319(1) R.S.C., 1985, c. C-46.

4 Germany Criminal Code, §130. The German Basic Law is the equivalent of a Constitution.

5 *Hogan v Hinch* [2011] HCA 4, [70]-[79] (reviewing case filed under State of Victoria Charter of Human Rights and Responsibilities Act 2006, §15).

6 As with ethnic, sexual or other affiliations, disability identity labels change over time – and the nomenclature is a minefield. I am sympathetic to the argument that we should accentuate the humanity, not the impairment or disabling condition. However, for the sake of brevity and variation, I also use "disabled" as an adjective – to the chagrin of linguistically purist colleagues. Some activists actually *prefer* "disability first" over "people first" language – as an act of pride, reclaiming pejorative terms or simply out of habit. On the art and politics of labeling, see Stephen A. Rosenbaum, The alien cloak of confidentiality: Look who's wearing it now, 4 *John F Kennedy Law Review* 23, 24 n. 8 (1992) and Stephen A. Rosenbaum, Aligning or maligning? Getting inside a new *IDEA*, getting behind *no child left behind* and getting outside of it all, 15 *Hastings Women's Law Journal*, 1, 4 n. 14 (2004).

7 See Edward Hall, A critical geography of disability hate crime, 51 *Area*, no. 2, 249–256, https://rgs-ibg.onlinelibrary.wiley.com/doi/abs/10.1111/area.12455.

8 Airwaves pollution, *San Francisco Chronicle* (1997a), http://www.sfgate.com; James Sullivan, Wild dogs: Really raunchy antics that outrage listeners are part of the winning formula cooked up every morning by KYLD's doghouse team, *San Francisco Chronicle* (May 15, 1998), http://www.sfgate.com/cgi-bin/article.cgi?file=/chronicle/archive/1998/05/15/DD62431.DTL. See also, Editorial – Radio on the 'edge', *San Francisco Chronicle* (November 23, 1997b), http://www.sfgate.com/cgi-bin/article.cgi?file=/chronicle/archive/1997/11/23/ED7963.DTL .

9 Sullivan, *supra* n. 8.

10 Sullivan, *supra* n. 8 (*quoting* Sandy Skeie of *Gavin* magazine).

11 *Ibid.*

12 J.C. Penney's, Sprint, AT&T Wireless, Verizon Wireless, State Farm Insurance, McDonald's, Bank of America, Wells Fargo Bank, Macy's, Seven-Eleven, Universal Pictures, Fox TV, Six Flags Marine World, Coca Cola, Coinstar, Red Bull, Mastercard, Travelocity, Dodge, Volkswagen, Honda, Hyundai, Ford-Lincoln, Mitsubishi, Toyota & Mercury, Valvoline, Trader Joe's, Albertson's, Wherehouse Music and Corona were among the advertisers. The show has also run advertisements or public service announcements from: California's Departments of Consumer Affairs and Health Services, Children and Family Commission, U.S. Immigration and Naturalization Service, Secret Service, National Child Identification Program, Oakland International Airport and San Jose Fire Department. See discussion below and *infra* n. 33 on the phenomenon of "handicapitalism."

13 For an overview of the community care facilities and programs available in California, see Calif. Health & Safety Code §§1501 & 1502.
14 KYLD website, http://www.wild949.com/dj_hank.html (June 4, 2002).
15 Calif. Welf. & Inst. Code § 4620.
16 http://www.wild949.com/deejay_hank.html (June 4, 2002).
17 I choose to repeat the epithets here. See, e.g., Richard Delgado, Words that wound: A tort action for racial insults, epithets, and name-calling, 17 *Harvard Civil Rights-Civil Liberties Law Review* 133, 145153, 156, 180 (1982) (repetition of graphic racial epithets). For a different approach, see, Mari J. Matsuda, Public response to racist speech: Considering the victim's story, 87 *Michigan Law Review* 2320, 2329, n. 49 (1989). Invoking the words of Poet Audre Lorde, Professor Matsuda refrains from repeating slurs "in a personal effort to avoid harm to others, and to prevent desensitization to harmful words." See also, *ibid.*, n. 72 ("'the only good n----r is a dead n----r' and other obscene defamation so extreme it is not included in this endnote.").
18 See, Sullivan and Editorial, *San Francisco Chronicle, supra* n. 8.
19 August 2, 2002 broadcast.
20 Sullivan, *supra* n. 8.
21 See William Pollack, *Real boys* 219, 224 (1999) (noting the name-calling and mistreatment experienced by young men suspected of being gay). But, how does one explain a link – without comment – on the Doghouse web page to Gay Pride Day 2002 photos? http://www.wild949.com/jacor-common/globalphotos.html (September 16, 2002); Or comments by J.V. and the others deploring the murder of a local transgender youth on October 20, 2002 and several subsequent broadcasts?
22 May 17, 2002 show.
23 Sullivan, *supra* n. 8.
24 Sullivan, *supra* n. 8.
25 October 2, 2002.
26 January 2, 2003.
27 February 19, 2003.
28 November 26, 2002.
29 February 3, 2003.
30 August 1, 2002.
31 Broadcasts of September 20, 2002 and December 19, 2002.
32 Sullivan, *supra* n. 8.
33 Beth Haller & Sue Ralph, Profitability, diversity, and disability images in advertising in the United States and Great Britain, 21 *Disability Studies Quarterly* 6 (2001). See also *ibid.* at 2, 4 on the need for better recognition of the disabled consumer and accurate advertising images.
34 *Ibid.*
35 Sullivan, *supra* n. 8.
36 See e.g., United Nations Convention on the Rights of Persons with Disabilities, art. 8(b)(signatories to take measures combatting "stereotypes, prejudices and harmful practices relating to persons with disabilities"), 2515 U.N.T.S. 3 (entered into force, May 3, 2008). See also, Inter-American Convention for the Elimination of All Forms of Discrimination Against Persons with Disabilities, art. III(C) (signatory countries to undertake educational campaigns aimed at eliminating prejudices, stereotypes, and other attitudes and to promote respect for, and coexistence with, persons with disabilities) (adopted by Organization of American States General Assembly, June 7, 1999). AG/RES. 1608 (XXIX-O/99).
37 Tom O'Connor, Disability and David Lynch's 'disabled' body of work, 22 *Disability Studies Quarterly* 4 (2002).
38 *Ibid.*
39 http://www.davidroche.com/about_new.htm. Roche explains that "my shadow side – my difficulty and challenge – is on the outside, where I have been forced to deal with it…" *Ibid.*

40 O'Connor, *supra* n. 37 at 3–4 (*quoting* David Lynch, whose cinematic and TV renderings often feature major characters with disabilities, in *Lynch on lynch* (Chris Rodley ed.) 153 (1997).
41 O'Connor, *supra* n. 37 at 4.
42 *Ibid.* (*quoting* Lorita M. Coleman, Stigma: An enigma demystified, in *The disability studies reader* (Lennard Davis ed.) 228 (1997).
43 Jodi Wilgoren, Arab and Muslim comics turn fear into funny, *New York Times* (*quoting* English Professor John Lowe) (September 1, 2002). See also, O'Connor, *supra* n. 37 at 4.
44 Wilgoren, *supra* n. 43.
45 See, Rachel Adams, *Sideshow U.S.A.* 10 (2001) (noting how "critics and activists… have wrested the term queer from its original pejorative connotations, while insisting on the memory of violence and shame.").
46 See, Stephen A. Rosenbaum, When it's not apparent: Some modest advice to parent advocates for students with disabilities, 5 *UC Davis Journal of Juvenile Law & Policy* 159, 160, n. 7 (2001) on the re-appropriation of epithets and Adams, *supra* n. 45 at 227 (*quoting* activist Simi Lipton)(the words *cripple*, *gimp* and *freak* "are personally and politically useful as a means to comment on oppression because they assert our right to name our own experience"). Sociologist and disability scholar Mark Sherry has collected a number of web site addresses that demonstrate how *'tard* and *retard* have actually assumed a renewed vicious connotation. See, e.g., http://tardblog.com, http://www.menace.com/retard.html and http://www.tarddance.com/retard.html.
47 Minnesota Governor's Planning Council on Developmental Disabilities, *Shifting patterns* 27 (1992) (*quoting* a People First brochure).
48 Matsuda, *supra* n.17 at 2364. Professor Matsuda argues that the appropriate standard for determining hateful or degrading speech is the "recipient's *community* standard." *Ibid.* (emphasis added). That said, "[w]e should avoid further victimization of subordinated groups by misunderstanding their linguistic and cultural norms." *Ibid.*
49 Frederick Drimmer, *Very special people* 10 (1979); Adams, *supra* n. 45 at 136. The "blunt and unsparing" term *freak* "recalls a climate in which the misfortunes of some became sources of entertainment and profit for others." *Ibid* at 10. Professor Delgado asserts that certain insults are actually "badges of degradation even when used between friends." Delgado, *supra* n. 17 at 174.
50 Cynthia Gouw, "Pacific time" KQED-FM (June 13, 2002 San Francisco)(Transcript).
51 Francis Davis, *The history of the blues* 66 (1995). This is a reference to singer George Washington Johnson. Hank's *shtick* stands in contrast to the re-narrated version of disabled sexual subjectivity offered by performance artists Cheryl Wade and Marie Duffy – a sexuality which is neither pathological, victimized, nor passive. See Rosemarie Garland-Thomson, "Dares to stares: Disabled women performance artists and the dynamics of staring" 5 (paper presented to the Greater Bay Area Interuniversity Disability Studies Consortium, Berkeley, February 8, 2002).
52 http://www.iath.virginia.edu/utc/minstrel/zipcoonfr.html.
53 *Ibid.* at 9–11.
54 *Ibid.* at 11.
55 *Ibid.* at 11–13.
56 Will Harper, Touching our private parts, *East Bay Express* 15 (February 4, 2003).
57 O'Connor, *supra* n. 37 at 9–10 in reference to David Lynch's portrayal of John Merrick in the film version of *The elephant man*. See also, Drimmer, *supra* n. 49 at 394–95 and D. Robert Bogdan, *Freak show: Presenting human oddities for amusement and profit* 125–26 (1988).
58 Sullivan, *supra* n. 8 (interview with Deejay J.V.).
59 Garland-Thomson, *supra* n. 51 at 4–5.
60 Robert C. Toll, *Blacking up: The minstrel show in nineteenth century America* (cited in http://www.africana.com/Articles/tt_200.ht.) Even *black* minstrels eventually put

on blackface, "creat[ing] a comic mask that ridiculed an entire race." Robert C. Toll, *On with the show: The first century of show business in America (*cited in *Ibid.)* In this way, they capitalized on America's racism by playing to the white belief that they were indeed the plantation darkies they portrayed on stage – advertising themselves as "genuine Negroes." Wynton Marsalis, *Reflections on minstrelsy*, http://www.pbs.org/jazz/exchange/exchange_minstrel.htm. Thomas D. "Daddy" Rice, a white man, was recognized as the first true minstrel. He impersonated "a crippled and deformed black hostler or stable groom" while singing and dancing to a tune called "Jim Crow." Mel Watkins, *On the real side: Laughing, lying, and signifying – The underground tradition of African-American humor (*cited in *Ibid.*)

61 Watkins, *supra* n. 60.

62 Garland-Thomson, *supra* n. 51 at 5.

63 The association of freakishness with homosexuality is not a new one. A 1947 gay advocacy magazine (*Vice Versa*) asked that lesbians not be identified as *freaks*. Adams, *supra* n. 45 at 93.

64 R.C. Scheerenberger, *Deinstitutionalization and institutionalized reform* 45 (1976), *quoted in* Robinsue Frohboese & Bruce Dennis Sales, Parental opposition to deinstitutionalization: A challenge in need of attention and resolution,4 *Law and Human Behavior* 1, 33 (1980).

65 C. Hibbert, *The house of medicis* 225–26 (1975) in Scheerenberger, *supra* n. 64 at 33–34.

66 R.C. Scheerenberger, *supra* n. 64 at 4.

67 Bogdan, *supra* n.57 at 119; Adams, *supra* n. 45 at 11, 26, & 200.

68 Bogdan, *supra* n. 57 at 2 (*quoting* Douglas Biklen of the Center on Human Policy, Syracuse University).

69 One contemporary author writes that this is "an unkind but vividly accurate translation of the scientific term… usually associated with feeble-mindedness." Drimmer, *supra* n. 49 at 352.

70 Bogdan, *supra* n. 57 at 119–22

71 Adams, *supra* n. 45 at 169–70, 215.

72 *Ibid.* at 124, 127, 132.

73 *Ibid.* at 6. See generally, Drimmer, *supra* n. 49. Author Frederick Drimmer uses *special people* in lieu of the "uglier" terms *freaks* and *monsters*, but notes that *performers* is the preferred term of self-reference. *Ibid.* at 10.

74 Bogdan, *supra* n. 57 at 123.

75 Adams, *supra* n. 45 at 13. The customer, nonetheless, may have been surprised to find a return stare "often laden with resentment or hostility." *Ibid.* at 7.

76 Drimmer, *supra* n. 49 at 10 (citation omitted).

77 Adams, *supra* n. 45 at 13–14.

78 Today, Adams observes, people with disabilities "must seek new, less exploitative ways of gaining the public eye." *Ibid.* at 136. The civil rights movement, sexual revolution and counterculture have ushered in changes displacing the debate from the sideshow platform to the public square. *Ibid.* at 18. See also, Drimmer, *supra* n. 49 at 15 (noting contemporary sentiment against displaying "unnaturally formed human beings" for money).

79 Adams, *supra* n. 45 at 20.

80 *Ibid.* at 227. See also, Drimmer, *supra* n. 49 at 13 (freaks hiding from the world to avoid the punishment "inflict[ed] on those who differ from the rest in mind or body").

81 Drimmer, *supra* n. 49 at 10 (citation omitted).

82 *World Fair Freaks and Attractions, Inc. v. Hodges*, 267 So. 2d 817, 819 (1972). The statute prohibited the "exhibition for pay or compensation of any crippled or physically-distorted, malformed or disfigured person in any circus, side show or other place where admission fee is charged." The Court opined that "[t]he exhibition could actu-

ally be informative and educational of facts and occurrences that the public should see and know regarding certain deformities which result to human beings; to know of the horrors that beset mankind." 267 So. 2d at 818.

83 Bogdan, *supra* n. 57 at 114.

84 Adams, *supra* n. 45 at 13–14. My apologies to Marsha Saxton, World Institute on Disability and University of California disabilities scholar, who claims that politically conscious members of the *proletariat* may also object to this form of entertainment. Bogdan, *supra* n. 57 at 146, writes that it was not notions of dignity or self-determination that led to the demise of freak shows, but the move toward custodial institutionalization and medicalization of those with disabilities. See also, Drimmer, *supra* n. 49 at 10.

85 Adams, *supra* n. 45 at 13.

86 Professors Haller and Ralph write of Madison Avenue and Wall Street's reaction to the "politically correct" monitoring of TV ads, including inappropriate images of a man with Down's Syndrome and a woman in a straight jacket. Haller & Ralph, *supra* n. 33 at 5. They do note that the monitoring has improved advertisers' sensitivity analysis.

87 Like some of my colleagues, my son was also concerned about Hank losing his job if a complaint is registered – including any criticism expressed in this Essay. But, my most grievous error – in his view – would be in hassling the *Doghouse* team. I don't believe he has ever actually heard Hank on the air, but he is embarrassed to have any connection with me and has asked that I publish this under an alias. Interestingly, he made no reference in this discussion to his brother (my older son), who had significant cognitive and physical disabilities.

88 Carolyn Hughes & Martin Agran, Self-determination: Signaling a systems change? 23 *Journal of the Association for Persons with Severe Handicaps*, 1 (1998). Still, one researcher calls the concept elusive, with no generally accepted definition. Brian H. Abery, A conceptual framework for enhancing self-determination, in *Challenges for a service system in transition* 347 (Mary F. Hayden & Brian H. Abery eds.) (1994).

89 See e.g., Mary-Ellen Fortini & Mary FitzPatrick, The universal design for promoting self-determination, in *Restructuring for caring and effective education* (Richard A. Villa & Jacqueline S. Thousand eds.) at 575–76 (2000) (self-determination refers to development of skills and opportunities for people to make decisions, experience control and have choices in their lives and ability to make choices *about* their lives).

90 *Increasing self-determination in Arizona: The plans of the design team* (n.d.) (on file with author).

91 Minnesota Governor's Planning Council on Developmental Disabilities, *supra* n. 47 at 1 (citation omitted).

92 Hughes & Agran, *supra* n. 88 at 1 and Abery, *supra* n. 88 at 353.

93 Calif. Welf. & Inst. Code § 4502(j).

94 http://www.thearc.org/history.

95 Michael L. Wehmeyer, Self-determination and individuals with significant disabilities: Examining meanings and misinterpretations, 23 *Journal of the Association for Persons with Severe Handicaps*, 5, 8 (1998) (emphasis in original).

96 Michael L. Wehmeyer, Self-determination: Critical skills for outcome-oriented transition services, 15 *Journal for Vocational Special Needs Education,* 3–9 (1992).

97 Thomas Michael Holub, Peg Lamb & Myong-Ye Bang, Empowering all students through self-determination, in *Restructuring high schools for all students* (Cheryl M. Jorgensen ed.) 186 (1998).

98 Michael W. Smull, Some thoughts from the field: Invited response to articles on self-determination, 23 *Journal of the Association for Persons with Severe Handicaps,* 53, 54 (1998).

99 Protection and Advocacy agencies have the authority to investigate incidents of abuse and neglect involving persons with developmental disabilities. 42 U.S.C. § 6042(a)(2)(B).

100 E-mail posting. Another respondent wrote: "And then there's that pesky free speech issue…"

101 Linda M. Bambara, Christine L. Cole & Freya Koger, Translating self-determination concepts into support for adults with severe disabilities, 23 *Journal of the Association for Persons with Severe Handicaps*, 27, 29 (1998).

102 R. Perske, The dignity of risk, in *Normalization: The principle of normalization* (W. Wolfensberger ed.) 194–200 (1972), cited in Wehmeyer, *supra* n. 95 at 7. One advocacy colleague, Denise, posits that there would not be such a fuss about Hank's career choice if his impairment were *physical*. She is also doubtful that there are alternative radio programming options for people with cognitive disabilities. Conversation of April 7, 2003.

103 Bogdan, *supra* n. 57 at 268. A contemporary Coney Island Side Show exhibitor, who also emphasizes the business relationship, takes umbrage at Bogdan's criticism of freak shows: "Who's exploitative, the critic who condemns the performer [or] the producer of the show who pays him a salary?" Adams, *supra* n. 45 at 216.

104 Wehmeyer, *supra* n. 95 at 11.

105 Abery, *supra* n. 88 at 355 (one must be exposed to alternatives in order to make informed decisions).

106 Bambara *et al.*, *supra* n. 101 at 29.

107 *Ibid.*

108 See, e.g, *Annotated bibliography on supported employment* (Bonnie Shoultz ed.) 1991, Research and Training Center on Community Integration, Center on Human Policy, Syracuse University; and *Pathways to home and community: Promising practices for Indiana citizens with disabilities*, Indiana Institute on Disability and Community, Indiana University, Bloomington (2000).

109 See, e.g., Stuart J. Schleien, John E. Rynders & Frederick P. Green, Facilitating integration in recreation environments, in *Challenges for a service system in transition,* chapters 5 & 6 (Mary F. Hayden & Brian H. Abery eds.) (1994).

110 See, e.g., Statement of the Committee on Sexuality, Advocating for Persons With Developmental Disabilities, www.w3ddesign.com/committee and Russell P. Shuttleworth, Toward a constructionist approach to disability and sexuality and the inclusion of disabled people in the sexual rights movement, in *Sexual inequalities and social justice* (Niels Teunis & Gilbert Herdt eds.) (2006). Research has shown that persons with intellectual disabilities are perceived by community members as being less physically attractive and exhibiting less favorable social behaviors. Moreover, the general public's acceptance of the right to date and to marry is much lower than its acceptance of successful employment of developmentally disabled individuals. Brian H. Abery & Maurice Fahnestock, Enhancing the social inclusion of persons with developmental disabilities, in *Challenges for a service system in transition* (Mary F. Hayden & Brian H. Abery eds.) 93 (1994) (citations omitted).

111 Pam Hunt, Morgen Alwell, Lori Goetz & Wayne Sailor, Generalized effects of conversation skill training, 15 *Journal of the Association for Persons with Severe Handicaps* 250, 253 (Table 2) (1990).

112 www.wild949.com/deejay_hank.hmtl (September 28, 2002). The list of dislikes is probably the most suspect in terms of its authenticity.

113 Abery & Fahnestock, *supra* n. 110 at 93.

114 Calif. Welf. & Inst. Code § 4648(a)(2). See also, § 4512(e)–(f)(defining "natural supports" and "circle of support").

115 www.peoplefirstca.org; Abery, *supra* n. 88 at 359–60 (citations omitted). The mission of Protection & Advocacy, Inc.'s (PAI) Developmental Disability Peer/Self-Advocacy Unit is to "assist[] persons with disabilities in understanding and controlling the systems and processes which affect their lives" through peer role models. PAI, *Advocacy services plan* 8 *(2003–08), avail at.* www.pai-ca.org/pubs/540201.pdf. The non-governmental organization has since been renamed Disability Rights California.

116 Calif. Welf. & Inst. Code § 4548(d)(1).

117 Wehmeyer, *supra* n. 95 at 13. Sometimes we worry the choice is contrived, not real. One mother asked about her adult son's invitation one year to spend Christmas at *his* home – rather than his parents'. "Did his housemates… 'support his choice' to invite us over or *shape* his choice on his behalf?" Diane L. Ferguson, Relating to self-determination: One parent's thoughts, 23 *Journal of the Association for Persons with Severe Handicaps* 44, 45 (1998) (emphasis added).

118 These reflect comments actually made by focus group participants during PAI's 2002 priorities-setting process.

119 Wehmeyer, *supra* n. 95 at 14 (*quoting* D. Ferleger, The place of 'choice', in *Choice and responsibility: Legal and ethical dilemmas in services for persons with mental disability* (C.J. Sundram ed.) 64–97 (1994)). See also, Abery, *supra* n. 88 at 357 (process of making choices is only one of the abilities needed to achieve autonomy).

120 Wehmeyer, *supra* n. 95 at 13.

121 Bengt Nirje, The right to self-determination, in *Normalization: The principle of Normalization, quoted in* Hughes & Agran, *supra* n. 88 at 1.

122 Matsuda, *supra* n.17 at 2341–48. *Ibid.* at 235661; Delgado, *supra* n.17 at 175–80.

123 Mark Sherry, *Don't ask, tell or respond: Silent acceptance of disability hate crimes*, 5 (paper presented at Greater Bay Area Interuniversity Disability Studies Consortium, Berkeley, November 20, 2002).

124 *Ibid.* See, e.g., R.K. Whillock, "The use of hate as a strategem for achieving political and social goals" (1995) and Marian Corker, "The UK Disability Discrimination Act: Disabling language, justifying inequitable social participation" (2000) (full citations omitted).

125 Bogdan, *supra* n. 57 at 280.

126 *Ibid.*

127 Adams, *supra* n. 45 at 216.

128 *Ibid.*

129 Delgado, *supra* n.17 at 135–36.

130 Rachel Adams, Enabling differences: New work in disability studies, 37 *Michigan Quarterly Review,* 348, 349 (1998) (referring to portrayal by doctors, educators, politicians and *artists*).

131 *Ibid.* at 349 (*quoting* Michael Bérubé, *Life as we know it: A father, a family, and an exceptional child* 260 (1996)). See also, *supra* n. 36 on international disability convention provisions on prejudicial images and stereotypes.

132 See, e.g., Peter Hartlaub, No prank too wild in the ratings game: Costly lawsuits don't deter radio station, *San Francisco Chronicle* (December 31, 2000), http://www.sfgate.com/cgi-bin/article.cgi?file=/chronicle/archive/2000/12/31/MN112871.DTL; Jerry Carroll, KYLD gives a mom a hard time, *San Francisco Chronicle* (April 3, 1998), http://www.sfgate.com/cgi-bin/article.cgi?file=/chronicle/archive/1998/04/03/DD88340.DTL .

133 December 3, 2002 broadcast.

134 See Appendix.

135 December 3, 2002.

136 Letters of October 25, 2002 and January 16, 2003 (on file with author).

137 December 17, 2002.

138 This is consistent with the Clear Channel vice president's letter of October 25, 2002. See Appendix.

139 August 14, 2002.

References

Abery, B. H. (1994). A conceptual framework for enhancing self-determination. In M. F. Hayden & B. H. Abery (Eds.), *Challenges for a service system in transition: Ensuring quality community experiences for persons with developmental disabilities* (pp. 345–380). Baltimore, MD: Paul H Brookes Publishing Company.

Abery, B. H., & Fahnestock, M. (1994). Enhancing the social inclusion of persons with developmental disabilities. In M. F. Hayden (Ed.), *Challenges for a service system in transition: Ensuring quality community experiences for persons with developmental disabilities* (pp. 83–119). Baltimore, MD: Paul H Brookes Publishing Company.

Adams, R. (1998). Enabling differences: New work in disability studies. *Michigan Quarterly Review, 37*, 342–350.

Adams, R. (2001). *Sideshow USA: Freaks and the American cultural imagination*. Chicago, IL: University of Chicago Press.

Bambara, L. M., Cole, C. L., & Koger, F. (1998). Translating self-determination concepts into support for adults with severe disabilities. *Journal of the Association for Persons with Severe Handicaps, 23*(1), 27–37.

Bogdan, R. (1988). *Freak show: Presenting human oddities for amusement and profit*. Chicago, IL: University of Chicago Press.

Carroll, J. (1998). KYLD gives a mom a hard time. *San Francisco Chronicle*, April 3, Retrieved from http://www.sfgate.com/cgi-bin/article.cgi?file=/chronicle/archive/1998/1904/1903/DD88340.DTL

Coleman, L. M. (1997). Stigma: An enigma demystified. In L. J. Davis (Ed.), *The disability studies reader* (pp. 216–232). New York: Routledge.

Corker, M. (2000). The UK Disability Discrimination Act: Disabling language, justifying inequitable social participation. In A. Silvers & L. Francis (Eds.), *Americans with disabilities: Exploring implications of the law for individuals and institutions* (pp. 357–370). New York: Routledge.

Davis, F. (1995). *The history of the blues: The roots, the music, the people*. New York: Hyperion.

Delgado, R. (1982). Words that wound: A tort action for racial insults, epithets, and name-calling. *Harvard Civil Rights-Civil Liberties Law Review, 17*, 133–181.

Drimmer, F. (1979). *Very special people: The struggles, loves and triumphs of human oddities*. New York: Amjon.

Ferguson, D. L. (1998). Relating to self-determination: One parent's thoughts. *Journal of the Association for Persons with Severe Handicaps, 23*(1), 44–46.

Fortini, M., & Fitzpatrick, M. (2000). The universal design for promoting self-determination. In R. A. Villa & J. S. Thousand (Eds.), *Restructuring for caring and effective education: Piecing the puzzle together* (Vol. 2, pp. 575–589). Baltimore, MD: Paul H Brookes Publishing Company.

Frohboese, R., & Sales, B. D. (1980). Parental opposition to deinstitutionalization: A challenge in need of attention and resolution. *Law and Human Behavior, 4* (1–2), 1–87.

Garland-Thomson, R. (2002). *Dares to stares: Disabled women performance artists and the dynamics of staring*. Paper presented to the Greater Bay Area Interuniversity Disability Studies Consortium, Berkeley, CA.

Gouw, C. (2002). "Pacific Time" Transcript KQED-FM. June 13, 2002, San Francisco.

Hall, E. (2019). A critical geography of disability hate crime. *Area, 51*(2), 249–256. Retrieved from https://rgs-ibg.onlinelibrary.wiley.com/doi/abs/10.1111/area.12455.

Haller, B. A., & Ralph, S. (2001). Profitability, diversity, and disability images in advertising in the United States and Great Britain. *Disability Studies Quarterly, 26*(3). Retrieved from http://dsq-sds.org/article/view/716.

Harper, W. (2003). Touching our private parts. *East Bay Express*, February 8.

Hartlaub, P. (2000). No prank too wild in the ratings game: Costly lawsuits don't deter radio station. *San Francisco Chronicle*, December 31. Retrieved from http://www.sfgate.com/cgi-bin/article.cgi?file=/chronicle/archive/2000/2012/2031/MN112871.DTL

Holub, T., Lamb, P., & Bang, M. (1998). Empowering all students through self-determination. In C. M. Jorgensen (Ed.), *Restructuring high schools for all students* (pp. 49–70). Baltimore, MD: Paul H. Brookes Publishing Company.

Hughes, C., & Agran, M. (1998). Self-determination: Signaling a systems change? *Journal of the Association for Persons with Severe Handicaps*, *23*(1), 1–4.

Hunt, P., Alwell, M., Goetz, L., & Sailor, W. (1990). Generalized effects of conversation skill training. *Journal of the Association for Persons with Severe Handicaps*, *15*(4), 250–260.

Indiana Institute on Disability and Community. (2000). *Pathways to home and community: Promising practices for Indiana citizens with disabilities*. Bloomington, IN: Indiana Institute on Disability and Community.

KYLD. (2002, June 4). Retrieved from http://www.wild949.com/dj_hank.html

Marsalis, W. (2001). *Reflections on minstrelsy*. Retrieved from http://www.pbs.org/jazz/exchange/exchange_minstrel.htm.

Matsuda, M. J. (1989). Public response to racist speech: Considering the victim's story. *Michigan Law Review*, *87*(8), 2320–2381.

Minnesota Governor's Planning Council on Developmental Disabilities. (1992). *Shifting patterns*. St Paul, MN: Minnesota Governor's Planning Council on Developmental Disabilities.

O'Connor, T. (2002). Disability and David Lynch's 'disabled' body of work. *Disability Studies Quarterly*, *22*(1), 5–21.

Pollack, W. S. (1999). *Real boys: Rescuing our sons from the myths of boyhood*. New York: Henry Holt.

Rodley, C. (Ed.) (1997). *Lynch on lynch*. Boston, MA: Faber and Faber.

Rosenbaum, S. A. (1992). The alien cloak of confidentiality: Look who's wearing it now. *John F Kennedy Law Review*, *4*(1), 23–63.

Rosenbaum, S. A. (2001). When it's not apparent: Some modest advice to parent advocates for students with disabilities. *UC Davis Journal of Juvenile Law & Policy*, *5*(2), 159–198.

Rosenbaum, S. A. (2003). Hammerin' Hank: The right to be raunchy or FM freak show? *Disability Studies Quarterly*, *23*(3). Retrieved from http://www.dsq-sds.org/article/view/432/609

Rosenbaum, S. A. (2004). Aligning or maligning? Getting inside a new *IDEA*, getting behind *no child left behind* and getting outside of it all. *Hastings Women's Law Journal*, *15*, 1–37.

San Francisco Chronicle. (1997a). Editorial—Airwaves pollution. *San Francisco Chronicle*, Retrieved from http://www.sfgate.com

San Francisco Chronicle. (1997b). Editorial—Radio on the 'Edge'. *San Francisco Chronicle*, November 23. Retrieved from http://www.sfgate.com/cgi-bin/article.cgi?file=/chronicle/archive/1997/11/23/ED7963.DTL

Schleien, S. J., Rynders, J. E., & Green, F. P. (1994). Facilitating integration in recreation environments. In M. F. Hayden & B. H. Abery (Eds.), *Community living for persons with mental retardation and related conditions* (pp. 121–146). Baltimore, MD: Paul H Brookes Publishing Company.

Sherry, M. (2002, November 20). *Don't ask, tell or respond: Silent acceptance of disability hate crimes*. Paper presented at the Greater Bay Area Interuniversity Disability Studies Consortium, Berkeley, CA.

Shoultz, B. (Ed.) (1991). *Annotated bibliography on supported employment*. Research and Training Center on Community Integration: Center on Human Policy, Syracuse University.

Shuttleworth, R. P. (2006). Disability and sexuality: Toward a constructionist focus on access and the inclusion of disabled people in the sexual rights movement. In N. Teunis & G. Herdt (Eds.), *Sexual inequalities and social justice* (pp. 174–208). Berkeley, CA: University of California Press.

Smull, M. W. (1998). Some thoughts from the field: Invited response to articles on self-determination. *Journal of the Association for Persons with Severe Handicaps*, *23*(1), 53–56.

Sullivan, J. (1998). Wild dogs: Really raunchy antics that outrage listeners are part of the winning formula cooked up every morning by KYLD's Doghouse Team. *San Francisco Chronicle*, May 15.

Wehmeyer, M. (1992). Self-determination: Critical skills for outcome-oriented transition services. *Journal for Vocational Special Needs Education*, *15*(1), 3–7.

Wehmeyer, M. L. (1998). Self-determination and individuals with significant disabilities: Examining meanings and misinterpretations. *Journal of the Association for Persons with Severe Handicaps*, *23*(1), 5–16.

Whillock, R. K. (1995). The use of hate as a stratagem for achieving political and social goals. In R. K. Whillock & D. Slayden (Eds.), *Hate speech* (pp. 28–54). Thousand Oaks, CA: SAGE.

Wild949.com. (2002, September 16). *Gay Pride S.F. 2002*. Retrieved from http://www.wild949.com/jacor-common/globalphotos.html

Wilgoren, J. (2002). Arab and Muslim comics turn fear into funny. *New York Times*, September 1.

14 Hate speech as an expression of disablism

An examination of reported hate speech experiences and consequences

*Terje Olsen, Janikke Solstad Vedeler, and John Eriksen**

In this chapter, we discuss the results from the first national survey in Norway on disability hate speech, based on a questionnaire to members of disabled people's organisations (N = 947). We concentrate the discussion on the reported reactions and responses, e.g., follow-up and non-follow-up to hate speech incidents from the persons themselves and their family, friends, workplace, school, and police. Special attention is paid to the combinations of reported activity restrictions and subjective undermining of personal well-being, as together these two dimensions can be understood as the outcome of being exposed to disablism. Our findings are discussed with reference to Carol Thomas's (Thomas, 1999, 2012) theory of disablism.

Introduction

In 2013, a ban on hate speech against disabled people was introduced in the Norwegian Penal Code. However, little was known from empirical studies about the phenomenon of hate speech in Norway, and thus in 2016 the Directorate for Children, Youth and Family Affairs commissioned us to conduct a study on hate speech and disability. We decided to take a broad perspective, examining the extent and scope of hate speech against disabled people as reported by disabled people themselves in our nation-wide survey (Olsen, Vedeler, Eriksen, & Elvegård, 2016). What we found was that a substantial portion of those who responded had been exposed to hate speech (Vedeler, Olsen, & Eriksen, 2019). More than one-third reported that they had been exposed to hate speech in the previous 12 months.

In this chapter, we examine what the consequences of hate speech are and discuss whether these consequences can be interpreted within the framework of *disablism*. This concept "refers to the *social* imposition of *avoidable restrictions* on the life activities, aspirations and psycho-emotional well-being of people categorised as 'impaired' by those deemed 'normal'" (Thomas, 2012, p. 211, italics in the original); just like sexism and racism, disablism is an expression of social oppression. In our analysis, we apply the two dimensions of disablism as outlined by Carol Thomas: barriers to doing and barriers to being. We investigate the reactions of those targeted of hate speech (Thomas, 1999).

Our study was not restricted to utterances that might fall within the legal understanding of hate speech. As elaborated on in the introduction to this book, hate speech is embedded in cultural contexts. As such, we are aware that definitions and operationalisations may vary between countries. In the Norwegian language, the word "hate" represents a strong expression to most people, with connotations of hostility and animosity. This implies that the threshold for using the concept "hate speech" is high. We use a social science approach to the phenomenon of hate speech as outlined by the Norwegian Equality and Anti-Discrimination Commission. Like others (Parekh, 2012), the Commission emphasises that hate speech includes the use of "degrading, threatening, harassing or stigmatizing speech which affects an individual's or a group's dignity, reputation and status in society" (LDO, 2015).

The consequences of hate speech are manifold and harm people and society in several ways. Firstly, disability hate speech directly affects people's self-esteem and identity. This sometimes has very serious consequences for those persons who are targeted, their families and relatives. Secondly, disability hate speech sends a message of fear and anger that has consequences for disabled people in general. This message affects the group's dignity, reputation and status in society. Thirdly, disability hate speech has negative effects for wider society as it scares people with disabilities from involving themselves in society, including in public debates.

We start this chapter by contextualising the phenomenon of disability and hate speech in Norwegian society by outlining the development of disability policy before we move on to examine and discuss the reported consequences of hate speech.

Disability and social policy in Norway

Norway represents a Nordic welfare state model (Pedersen & Kuhnle, 2017) that provides, comparatively speaking, generous welfare benefits and services to all its citizens. Since the 1960s, the principles of normalisation and social inclusion have been important ideals for the development of welfare policy, social services, and legal rights. Normalisation implies that people with disabilities should be provided with services within their local communities on par with other citizens in order to secure full societal participation and inclusion (Nirje, 1969; NOU, 2001; Tøssebro, 2013). One concrete translation of this principle was the deinstitutionalisation of institutions for people with intellectual disabilities that started in the late 1980s (Tøssebro, 2016). Until the early 2000s, the focus continued to be on supply of welfare services (money transfers and in kind), but it then shifted towards a stronger emphasis on statutory rights.

Increasing awareness developed among politicians and disabled people's organisations that the welfare services were not raising living conditions for people with disabilities. Despite integrated services, political objectives of equal participation and a growing recognition of disability as a relational phenomenon, statistics and research continued to show great disparities between people with and without disabilities. These disparities applied to most significant parameters, including levels of education and employment participation (Tøssebro, 2013). Inspired by anti-discrimination legislation introduced in the US in 1990 and the EU directive of 2000 on equal treatment in employment (CEU, 2000), a need for better protection against discrimination and unfair treatment in the labour market was recognised as important to increase social inclusion and reduce discrimination. Strategies to increase accessibility to the physical environment also received attention.

In order to strengthen the commitment towards breaking down disabling barriers, discrimination and inaccessibility, new legislation was introduced in 2009, namely the Discrimination and Accessibility Act.[1] Norway's ratification of the UN Convention on the Rights of Persons with Disabilities (UNCRPD) in 2013 further reinforced the legal rights of people with disabilities. As part of the ratification, a ban on hate speech against disabled people was introduced in the Norwegian Penal Code in 2013, which up until then had only included ethnicity, religion, and sexual orientation. The increased awareness, internationally and nationally, that people with disabilities may be targets of hate speech paved the way for our study. Until 2016 there was little knowledge about this phenomenon in Norway, apart from research on violence that showed that more disabled people report worries about exposure to violence and threats than non-disabled people do (Ramm & Otnes, 2013).

Data and sample

This chapter draws on data from our nation-wide electronic survey distributed via e-mail to all members of 13 disabled people's organisations. The organisations were selected to secure a variation of impairments in the total sample. We made personal contact with each organisation's secretary general to make sure they had adequate membership records, including email addresses of members. Each member was informed in an email from their organisation that the questionnaire was available to them at a given internet link, alongside a brief presentation of the research project. An adapted version of the questionnaire was distributed to members of organisations for people with visual impairments, readable by braille display and screen reader.

The questionnaire was pretested and subsequently some modifications were implemented. The survey was conducted during Spring 2016. A total of 947 respondents answered the questions. Data was recorded and analysed in the Statistical Package for the Social Sciences (SPSS) package.

The questionnaire included questions about:

- Respondent's background;
- Experiences of different types of hate speech; and
- Respondent's own reaction to hate speech, including whether respondent told other people.

As noted above, the word "hate" has rather strong connotations in the Norwegian language. Furthermore, "hate speech" is not a concept that forms part of daily language, even though it is gaining some foothold and may be more frequently used by younger people. It is not always clear what individuals exactly mean by these words, neither is it clear how such speech is different from other types of negative reactions that disabled people may experience in social interactions. Therefore, the survey included a total of 18 items covering different negative experiences, ranging from derogatory language to physical violence.

These 18 items were partly adapted from the one used in the British research project, Living in Fear, (Beadle-Brown et al., 2014) and partly based on categories of hate speech outlined by the Norwegian Equality and Anti-Discrimination Commission. Professor Julie Beadle-Brown graciously made the British study Living in Fear available to us, which greatly assisted the development of our own measures of disability hate speech.

Of the 18 items, five represented actions other than speech: actual violence (two items), unwelcome touching ("Someone touched my body without my consent") and theft ("Someone stole from me or damaged my things"*)*. One item ("Other unpleasant things happened to me") is residual and unspecific. These items were excluded from our analysis. The item "Someone stared or laughed at me" was deleted since it refers more to body language than to speech (use of words), although this distinction might not always be clear.

Thus, we ended up with a list of 12 items that we classified as hate speech in the study, some distinct and some overlapping. These ranged from "saying bad things" to threats of violence or statements such as "you should not have been born" or "you have no right to live" (see Table 14.1 below for a full list).

Table 14.1 Experiences of hate speech in the previous 12 months by educational level and main activity*

	Hate speech experience	
Educational level	**Per cent**	**N**
Primary education	47	76
Secondary education	38	323
Tertiary education	35	413
Total hate speech experiences 319/851	37	
Main activity		
Ordinary employment	32	217
In education	41	56
Combination of work, education and welfare benefits	47	110
Sick leave/disability allowance	50	195
Day centre/labour market measures	58	33
Unemployed	55	22
Old-age pensioner	17	203
Total 319/857	37	

* Missing values (32/28) were excluded from the analysis.

Our focus is on *verbal utterances* as experienced by the respondents, irrespective of whether they were a legal offence. We classified some of the 12 items as hate speech, but some may not have been subject to legal prosecution if taken to court, which they seldom are. In Norway, as in most other countries in the Global North, free speech is highly valued and usually the police do not register hate speech against disabled people as such. Likewise, victims do not report most instances of disability hate speech. For instance, only two cases were reported to the police in 2017 (The Norwegian Police Directorate, 2017).

Altogether the questionnaire included 33 questions that were organised with fixed response alternatives, and with some room for supplementary comments.

Recruiting respondents electronically via disabled people's organisations is cost- and time-effective. However, it offers few opportunities to judge how representative the sample is. Having said that, when compared to recent studies based on data from Statistics Norway (Molden, Wendelborg, & Tøssebro 2009; Ramm & Otnes, 2013), our sample shows almost identical distributions for gender and age. But our sample differs from that of Statistics Norway in two respects. We had significantly more respondents with tertiary education (48% as against 23%) and fewer respondents in ordinary work (25% as against 44%).

In addition to the survey, we conducted interviews with seven people involved in work against hate speech and disability. These people either worked in disabled people's organisations (four persons) or for the Equality and Anti-Discrimination Ombudsman (three persons). The objectives of these interviews were to provide insight into the phenomenon of hate speech towards disabled people, as well as to provide insight into what measures could be implemented to prevent hate speech taking place. We draw on the interview data when trying to understand the relationship between hate speech and disablism.

For ethical and legal reasons, respondents were informed that the study was restricted to persons above 18 years of age. The study has been approved by the Norwegian Social Science Data Service, which supervises the implementation of ethical issues in research.

To what extent are disabled people exposed to hate speech?

In the questionnaire, respondents were presented with our list of 12 statements/utterances that we here term disability hate speech, and asked to mark those statements they had experienced the last 12 months. From a total of 947 respondents, 361 – or 38% – reported at least one such experience.

We see from Table 14.1 that being exposed to hate speech is associated with the educational level of the respondent and employment status. Almost half (47%) of our respondents with primary education reported at least one hate speech experience, around 10% more than for respondents with higher education. Moreover, about a third in ordinary employment reported hate speech, as opposed to more than a half of the respondents who were not in ordinary employment (unemployed, on sick leave/disability pension, or under different labour market measures). We should also notice that being in education is associated with increased exposure to hate speech compared to being in regular employment (41% vs. 32%). When education is combined with work or welfare benefits, hate speech is reported even more frequently (47%).

In terms of exposure to hate speech, one may say that being in ordinary work is best and better than being in education. However, being better educated is clearly an advantage. It is clear that being on a form of welfare support is also associated with increased exposure to hate speech. The one clear exception is being on old age pension. Old age pensioners report the lowest proportion of hate speech experience of all groups (17%).

Table 14.2 shows how often our 12 expressions of hate speech were reported in our survey. Some expressions, such as "Someone wrote or said bad things about you" were experienced quite frequently (reported by 68% of the 361), while "Threats of violence" was reported by 11%. In our data, hate speech on the internet or social media was reported rather infrequently (from 3% to 17%, depending on the type of media). One reason for these low figures may be that our sample only included respondents above 18 years of age.

Experiences of different forms of hate speech were common (not seen from Table 14.2): 62% of our respondents reported between two and five different hate speech types. Hate speech was experienced in different locations – most often in public places such as shops, pubs, parks (52%), but also on public transport (28%) and even at home (24%).

Table 14.2 Different forms of hate speech experienced in the previous 12 months. Multiple responses

	Frequency	*Per cent*
Someone wrote or said bad things to you or about you	245	68
Intimidating statements about you or your disability	184	51
Statements about you as helpless or weak	148	41
Statements about you as being an economic burden or welfare recipient	123	34
Statements about you as being unpleasant to hear or look at	65	18
Someone wrote bad things about you or offended you on social media or internet	61	17
Someone wrote bad things to you or about you in (SMS) or email	58	16
Someone threatened to do bad things to you	58	16
Statements that you should not have been born or do not have a right to live	40	11
Have received threats of violence	40	11
Someone wrote bad things to you or about you in newspapers, internet media or debate forums	32	9
Someone wrote bad things to you or about you on Instagram or Snapchat	11	3

Does hate speech pose barriers to being and barriers to doing?

As demonstrated above, hate speech takes on different forms. The British disability and gender researcher Carol Thomas sees disablism as a form of social oppression involving two components: (1) social imposition of restrictions of activities on people with impairments, and (2) socially engendered undermining of their psycho-emotional well-being (Thomas, 2012). These two components are also respectively referred to as barriers to doing and barriers to being (Thomas, 1999, p. 60). Our survey data included 11 forms of restrictions on social activities as consequences of hate speech, and eight forms of effects on psycho-emotional well-being.

The restrictions on everyday life ("barriers to doing") that were reported were:

- Avoid certain places or situations (63%)
- Stay at home (48%)
- Avoiding raising my opinion or getting involved in public debates (38%)
- Stop doing activities I used to do before (34%)
- Avoid going out in the evening and night (30%)
- Don't see friends (19%)
- Avoid public transport (16%)
- Had to move house (12%)
- Don't go to school (9%)
- Don't go to work/day centre (9%)

The psycho-emotional undermining of well-being ("barriers to being") that were reported, were:

- Affects self-confidence (66%)
- Worry about certain situations (65%)
- Become depressed and sad (62%)
- Feel more uncertain in everyday life (58%)
- Reduced life quality (58%)
- Become more introverted (54%)
- Reduced self-realisation (46%)
- Afraid of going certain places alone (42%)

A total of 316 respondents had given a valid response. As we can see from the list above, typically reported restrictions in everyday life include stopping from going to certain places and staying at home more. Of those who have experienced hate speech, 63% and 48% respectively report this. Avoiding raising one's voice in public debates and stopping doing certain activities are other commonly reported effects of hate speech (38% and 34%). Respondents report that hate speech affects self-confidence; they worry about certain situations and become depressed and sad (respectively 66%, 65%, and 62%). These are the

Table 14.3 Reported consequences and disablism components: barriers to being and barriers to doing

	Barriers to being					
Barriers to doing	No conseq.	1–3 conseq.	4–6 conseq.	7–8 conseq.	Sum, per cent	Sum, N
No consequences	84	34	13	3	27	94
1–3 consequences	14	51	65	23	42	143
4–6 consequences	2	15	21	51	25	84
7–11 consequences	0	0	1	23	6	22
Sum, per cent	**100**	**100**	**100**	**100**	**100**	
N	**50**	**105**	**96**	**92**		**343**
Per cent	**16**	**31**	**21**	**27**	**100**	

Gamma 0.765

most typically reported reactions in terms of the undermining of psycho-emotional well-being.

According to our data, these two components of disablism are clearly related. As is seen from Table 14.3, most respondents who reported that hate speech undermined their psycho-emotional well-being had also experienced that hate speech reduced their level of activity. In addition, most (84%) respondents who did not report that hate speech undermined their psycho-emotional well-being reported no experience of activity restrictions. Generally, the more barriers of one kind that our respondents reported (barriers to being), the more they also reported of the other kind (barriers to doing) (Gamma = 0.765). Our data thus support Thomas's view that barriers to being are linked to barriers to doing (Thomas, 1999, p. 60).

Do people tell others about their hate speech experiences?

According to the experts we interviewed, a ready alternative for disabled people when "bad" things are written or said about them is to overlook the incident(s) and not hear or see the utterance as an expression of hate. Disabled peoples' organisations have also been reluctant to address the issue of hate speech. It is just too unpleasant, or the utterance confirms one's role as a victim. In other words, some degree of awareness seems to be required for a person to realise or recognise that he or she is in fact the target of hate speech.

How did our survey respondents react when they were exposed to hate speech? Did they keep the incident(s) to themselves or did they choose to tell other people? Our data contrast with the expert interviews: a majority reported that they told others. Twenty-one per cent of all the 361 respondents who had experienced hate speech reported that they had told no one about their hate speech experiences. More than half of the respondents had told someone in their family (54%), and half had told their friends (50%). Considerably less had told people at their workplace (bosses, union representatives or colleagues, 22%) or at school (officials or fellow students, 16%). More than one in four had told people working within the social support system (27%). Nine per cent of the respondents answered that they had reported the incident(s) to the police. Very few of these are recorded in police statistics (The Norwegian Police Directorate, 2017), as previously noted. We also notice that social media is not an important source for communicating hate speech experiences.

Respondents had the option of multiple responses to this question. We found that our respondents very often told both family and friends (84%) and that very few informed "outside" actors without also telling family and friends, possibly with a hope that someone would do something to stop hate speech. Thus, it is clear from this data that communicating to other people is a very common way to tackle hate speech. Not only did they tell other people, whether they were close or more distant (at work, school, in the support system etc.) but they usually told more than one person.

Does this openness about hate speech experiences hold in all cases? What is the effect of multiple exposures to hate speech? Does more hate speech lead to increased withdrawal or a greater need to tell others?

In Table 14.4, we have related type of reactions to the number of hate speech exposures. First, we see that keeping to oneself and not telling others shows only moderate variation and did not systematically increase with the number of hate speech exposures. In other words, there is no clear tendency demonstrating that our respondents tend to withdraw to a greater degree with more frequent exposure to hate speech.

In Table 14.4, we have separated those who have told others into two groups: those who just told someone else without any action being taken, and those who told others with action being taken. Interestingly, we see that with more frequent exposure to hate speech, the more often the incidents are reported to others with some action taken. It seems, then, that among the majority who report hate speech to others, a more active strategy is adopted when hate speech is experienced more frequently.

Table 14.4 Hate speech experiences and types of reactions

	Number of hate speech experiences reported				
Types of reactions	*1–3 experiences (per cent)*	*4–6 experiences (per cent)*	*7–12 experiences (per cent)*	*Sum, per cent*	*Sum, N*
Keeping to oneself	22	27	19	23	75
Telling others, but no action taken	41	33	31	37	120
Telling other, with some action taken	37	40	50	39	127
Sum, per cent	**100**	**100**	**100**	**100**	
N	**191**	**96**	**36**		**322**

Gamma 0.054

How does disablism affect respondents' reactions to hate speech?

Table 14.4 demonstrates the simple effect of the frequency of hate speech experiences as reported by our respondents. More specifically, how do barriers to doing and barriers to being (i.e., what we interpret as disablism) and their respective intensity (more barriers of each kind) affect our respondents' reactions to hate speech?

We illustrate this relationship in Table 14.5. Reactions to hate speech are also here "Keeping to oneself" or "Telling others," either with no action or some action being taken. Intensity of disablism is represented by the number of barriers (*both* barriers to being *and* barriers to doing) on two levels, at least one and at least five.

We notice that the effect of reporting at least one barrier of each kind does not differ much from the simple effect of 1–3 hate speech experiences, as shown in Table 14.4. The proportions of those keeping the experience to themselves or telling others (with or without some action being taken) are very similar. However, when we look at what we might term "very strong disablism" (at least five reported barriers), a somewhat different pattern from that of simple disablism emerges (Table 14.5). With strong disablism, more respondents kept the hate experience to themselves (an increase from 23% to 31%), while there is a lesser tendency for respondents to report the hate speech experience with the prospect of some action being taken (a moderate drop from 40% to 36%).

Thus, we are able to notice one effect of disablism: we demonstrated in Table 14.4 that the *number* of hate speech experiences had no clear effect on our respondents' reaction (keeping to oneself/telling others), but when combining the two aspects of disablism, barriers to being and barriers to doing, we see that disablism is associated with a greater degree of withdrawal. This finding supports Thomas's claim that disability is associated with psycho-emotional effects as well as restrictions on activities, and that the corresponding barriers to being and barriers to doing are interactive and compounded (Thomas, 1999).

Table 14.5 Disablism and hate speech reactions

	Degree of disablism	
Reactions to hate speech	*At least one reported consequence of each type (per cent)*	*At least five reported consequences of each type (per cent)*
Keeping to oneself	23	31
Telling others, but no action taken	37	33
Telling other, with some action taken	40	36
Sum, per cent	**100**	**100**
Total number	**322**	**64**

We should notice, however, that this effect of disablism it not very strong in our data. Additionally, Hanisch (2014) has questioned Thomas's claim based on an extensive analysis of Norwegian data, concluding that "to the extent that disabling processes are ontologically intertwined, they are no more so than any other social process" (Hanisch, 2014, p. 225).

Who are the people who chose to tell others about their hate speech experiences? Table 14.6 shows that young respondents (below 30 years of age) most often told others, and clearly more so than those over 30 years of age. We also notice that they seem to (moderately) change their "response strategy." When they report more barriers to doing and barriers to being (disablism), they turn from

Table 14.6 Disablism and reactions to hate speech, by age and education

		Disablism	
Age	*Reactions*	*At least one reported consequence of each type (per cent)*	*At least five reported consequences of each type (per cent)*
18–29 years	Keeping to oneself	17	15
	Tell others, no action taken	33	23
	Tell others, action was taken	50	62
	Sum per cent/N	**100/48**	**100/13**
30 +	Keeping to oneself	24	35
	Tell others, no action taken	28	35
	Tell others, action was taken	38	70
	Sum per cent/N	**100/183**	**100/51**
Education			
Primary	Keeping to oneself	32	42
	Tell others, no action taken	28	16
	Tell others, action was taken	40	42
	Sum per cent/N	**100/25**	**100/12**
Secondary	Keeping to oneself	18	30
	Tell others, no action taken	42	43
	Tell others, action was taken	40	27
	Sum per cent/N	**100/25**	**100/12**
Tertiary	Keeping to oneself	24	35
	Tell others, no action taken	28	35
	Tell others, action was taken	38	30
	Sum per cent/N	**100/183**	**100/51**

passively telling others to telling others who try to do something about it. This is seen in a moderate increase from 56% to 62%. Respondents above 30 years of age behave differently. More keep the hate speech experience to themselves (up from 24% to 35%) and fewer respondents report that they tell others with a prospect of some action (down from 38% to 30%).

In terms of the respondents' education, we see from Table 14.6 that telling others with some action being taken is a ready option at all educational levels (40%). With exposure to strong disablism, respondents with primary education tend to withdraw (an increase from 32% to 42%), while more respondents with tertiary education choose to tell someone with some possible action taken.

We can conclude, then, from Tables 14.5 and 14.6 that when our respondents were being exposed to strong disablism, many chose to withdraw and not to tell others about their experience. Those who still chose a more active strategy of telling others with a prospect of some action being taken were either young or had higher education.

Conclusion

We have demonstrated that more than one in three of the respondents to our nation-wide survey reported at least one kind of hate speech experience (as we defined the term) during the past year. This finding contrasts with what emerges from the interviews we did with professionals who specialised in the issue of hate speech and disability.

In these expert interviews, the following common understanding emerged: hate speech in public discourse is a well-known phenomenon when it concerns sexual or ethnic minorities. All experts recognised that the social phenomenon of hate speech towards disabled people is not at all new, but that regulating and reporting hate speech is a rather new concept within the field of disability. Disabled people very often encounter hate speech in their daily life and in public discourse, but the conceptualisation of this phenomenon as a large-scale social issue requiring additional protections and responses is new. They related this partly to the fact that it may be existentially difficult to fathom that one is the target of hate, and partly to the fact that disabled people's organisations have been slow to place the concept and its harsh realities on their agenda.

These apparently contrasting findings from the survey and the expert interviews give rise to some reflections. First, while hate speech puts the target in an uncomfortable position that might trigger withdrawal, responding to a list of negative utterances in an anonymous questionnaire might be less stressful. We also notice that our questionnaire data demonstrated clear tendencies to withdraw as a response to hate speech, but also that some respondents demonstrated a willingness to meet such experiences in a more active way. Second, it could well be that times have changed and that disabled people now meet negative reactions from other people in a more open way. And third, it is quite likely that disabled people with hate speech experience are over-represented in our sample, since disabled people with no such experience (or conscious experience of hate speech) may have found the questionnaire of little relevance to them and thus did not respond.

Our data demonstrates the potential of using the concept of disablism as a theoretical perspective to study the effects of hate speech as opposed to simply counting and summarising the number of hate speech experiences. We find not only withdrawal but also active initiatives to counter hate speech. In general, we may find in policy papers and among disabled peoples' organisations an increasing awareness of discrimination and of social and cultural structures that oppress disabled people, and our survey shows that this may be particularly so among young people and people with higher education. Several factors contribute to increased attention and counter-strategies to hate speech. Norway's ratification of the CRPD, the government's national strategy against hate speech, and a growing interest in disabled peoples' organisations all seem to be having the effect of raising awareness while taking steps to prevent hate speech and to protect people against it. However, with more than one-third of our respondents reporting clearly negative utterances from other people, there is still a long way to go.

Notes

* Terje, John and Janikke would like to thank the Norwegian Fritt Ord Foundation for support in the final stages of this book project.

1 This act was merged into one general act, Equality and Discrimination Act, in 2018, covering gender, sexual orientation, ethnicity, and disability.

References

Beadle-Brown, J., Richardson, L., Guest, C., Malovic, A., Bradshaw, J., & Himmerich, J. (2014). *Living in fear: Better outcomes for people with learning disabilities and autism (Main report)*. Canterbury: Tizard Centre, University of Kent.

CEU. (2000). Council Directive 2000/78/EC of 27 November 2000 establishing a general framework for equal treatment in employment and occupation. Official Journal L.

Hanisch, H. (2014). Psycho-emotional disablism: A differentiated process. *Scandinavian Journal of Disability Research, 16*, 211–228.

LDO. (2015). *Hatytringer og hatkriminalitet [Hate speech and hate crime.]*. Oslo: Likestillings- og diskrimineringsombudet.

Molden, T. H., Wendelborg, C., & Tøssebro , J. (2009). *Levekår blant personer med nedsatt funksjonsevne [The Living Conditions of People with Impairments]*. Trondheim: NTNU Samfunnsforskning

Nirje, B. (1969). The normalization principle and its human management implications. In R. Kugel & Wolfensberger, W. (Eds.), *Changing patterns of residential services for mentally retarded*. Washington DC: President's committee on mental retardation.

NOU. (2001). *Fra Bruker til borger [From user to citizen]*. Oslo: Statens forvaltningstjeneste, Informasjonsforvaltning.

Olsen, T., Vedeler, J. S., Eriksen, J., & Elvegård, K. (2016). *Hatytringer. Resultater fra en studie av funksjonshemmedes erfaringer. [Hate speech. Results from a study of disabled people's experiences.]* (Vol. 6/2016). Bodø: Nordland Research Institute.

Parekh, B. (2012). Is there a case for banning hate speech? In M. Herz & P. Molnar (Eds.), *The content and context of hate speech: Rethinking regulation and responses* (pp. 37–56). Cambridge, MA: Cambridge University Press.

Pedersen, A. W., & Kuhnle, S. (2017). The Nordic welfare state model. In O. P. Knutsen (Ed.), *The Nordic models in political science: Challenged, but still viable?* (pp. 249–272). Bergen: Fagbokforlaget.

Ramm, J., & Otnes, B. (2013). *Personer med nedsatt funksjonsevne: Indikatorer for levekår og likestilling. [Persons with disabilities: indicator on living conditions and equality.].* Oslo: Statistisk sentralbyrå.

The Norwegian Police Directorate. (2017). *Hatkriminalitet. Anmeldelser 2017. [Hate crime reportings 2017.].* Oslo: The Norwegian Police Directorate.

Thomas, C. (1999). *Female forms: Experiencing and understanding disability.* Buckingham: Open University Press.

Thomas, C. (2012). Theorising disability and chronic illness: Where next for perspectives in medical sociology? *Social Theory & Health, 10*(3), 209–228.

Tøssebro, J. (2013). Two decades of disability research in Norway – 1990–2010. *Scandinavian Journal of Disability Research, 15*(Suppl. 1), 71–89.

Tøssebro, J. (2016). Scandinavian disability policy: From deinstitutionalisation to non-discrimination and beyond. *Alter – European Journal of Disability Research, 10*(2), 111–123.

Vedeler, J. S., Olsen, T., & Eriksen, J. (2019). Hate speech harms: a social justice discussion of disabled Norwegians' experiences. *Disability & Society, 34*(3), 368–383.

Index

For Product Safety Concerns and Information please contact our EU representative GPSR@taylorandfrancis.com
Taylor & Francis Verlag GmbH, Kaufingerstraße 24, 80331 München, Germany

www.ingramcontent.com/pod-product-compliance
Lightning Source LLC
LaVergne TN
LVHW011122300926
849160LV00008B/478

9781032086057